Dewey's Empirical Theory of Knowledge AND Reality

THE VANDERBILT LIBRARY OF AMERICAN PHILOSOPHY offers interpretive perspectives on the historical roots of American philosophy and on present innovative developments in American thought, including studies of values, naturalism, social philosophy, cultural criticism, and applied ethics.

SERIES EDITOR

Herman J. Saatkamp, Jr.
Indiana University & Purdue University at Indianapolis

EDITORIAL ADVISORY BOARD

Kwame Anthony Appiah (Harvard University)
Larry A. Hickman (Southern Illinois University)
John Lachs (Vanderbilt University)
John J. McDermott (Texas A&M)
Joel Porte (Cornell University)

Hilary Putnam (Harvard University)
Ruth Anna Putnam (Wellesley College)
Andrew J. Reck (Tulane University)
Beth J. Singer (Brooklyn College)
John J. Stuhr (Pennsylvania State University)

Other titles in the series include

The Philosophy of Loyalty
new paperback edition
Josiah Royce

Genuine Individuals and Genuine Communities:
A Roycean Public Philosophy
Jacquelyn Ann K. Kegley

The Loyal Physician:
Roycean Ethics and the Practice of Medicine
Griffin Trotter

The Thought and Character of William James
new paperback edition
Ralph Barton Perry

Dewey's Empirical Theory of Knowledge AND Reality

JOHN R. SHOOK

Vanderbilt University Press
Nashville

© 2000 Vanderbilt University Press
All rights reserved

First Edition

04 03 02 01 00   5 4 3 2 1

Library of Congress Cataloging-in-Publication Data

Shook, John R.
  Dewey's empirical theory of knowledge and reality / John R. Shook. — 1st ed.
    p. cm. — (The Vanderbilt library of American philosophy)
  Includes bibliographical references and index.
  ISBN 0-8265-1355-7 (alk. paper)
  ISBN 0-8265-1362-X (pbk. : alk. paper)
  1. Dewey, John, 1859-1952. 2. Empiricism—History. 3. Knowledge, Theory of—History. 4. Metaphysics—History. I. Title. II. Series.
  B945.D44 S56   2000
  191—dc21   99-6698

Published by Vanderbilt University Press
Printed in the United States of America

Contents

Preface	vii
Abbreviations	ix

INTRODUCTION   1

    Genetic Explanation of Dewey's Philosophy

CHAPTER ONE. THE OPPORTUNITY OF DEWEY'S EARLY PHILOSOPHY   7

    Dewey's Epistemology vs. His Metaphysics • The Traditional Account of Dewey's Development • The "Problem" of Dewey's Early Philosophy

CHAPTER TWO. ABSOLUTE IDEALISM   21

    Idealism and Sensationalistic Empiricism • Knowledge and the Psychological Standpoint • Psychology as Philosophical Method • Classifying Dewey's Idealism

CHAPTER THREE. WUNDTIAN VOLUNTARISM   71

    Organic Voluntarism and Teleological Psychology • Knowledge and Will • The ReflexArc • The Foundations of Functionalism

CHAPTER FOUR. THE ABSOLUTE OF ACTIVE EXPERIENCE   121

    Absolute vs. Functional Truth • The Self and Experience • Moral Judgment and the Functionally Social Self

CONTENTS

CHAPTER FIVE. THE LOGIC OF CONDUCT   163

    Reasoning and Experience • Intelligence and Knowledge • Experimental Science

CHAPTER SIX. THE RECONSTRUCTION OF EPISTEMOLOGY   217

    An Empirical Theory of Meaning • An Empirical Theory of Knowledge • An Empirical Process of Verification • Instrumentalist Naturalism

APPENDIX. CHRONOLOGY OF SELECTED DEWEY WRITINGS   270

Notes   278
Bibliography   296
Index   308

Preface

Both instrumentalism and empiricism have fallen into widespread disrepute in post–World War II Anglo-American philosophy. This book, primarily aimed at the exposition and defense of John Dewey's instrumentalist epistemology and empiricist metaphysics, is a contribution to the general rehabilitation of these philosophical positions. Empiricism became largely synonymous with nominalistic subjective positivism, obscuring Dewey's efforts to avoid positivism by transforming valuable Kantian and Hegelian insights into a nonrationalistic metaphysics. Instrumentalism, tied to empiricism's fortunes, has likewise fallen on very hard times. When current philosophers even recognize it, they typically treat only straw-man versions that receive brief summary and even briefer summary judgment. But that has largely been the fate of pragmatism as a tradition of thought, along with idealism and empiricism, after their eclipse by the successive marching forces of logical positivism, language-analysis philosophy, and physicalist naturalism. Most of these forces have regrettably perceived instrumentalism and empiricism in the light or, more accurately, the lack of light, resulting from this eclipse of their own making. Reading such sophomoric "refutations" of a "pragmatism" perfunctorily erected for quickly gratifying victories should arouse the question of which philosophers actually prefer what is pleasant to what is true.

Dewey's thought directly grapples with, and perhaps occasionally rivals, the most central issues and theories that Plato and Aristotle, Locke and Hume, Kant and Hegel, and Galileo and Darwin have to offer. When present-day mainstream philosophy shakes off its dogmatic slumbers to find that these thinkers are indeed relevant and helpful to its concerns, and there are small signs of such awakenings, then it will also discover how Dewey's philosophy offers an outstretched hand of assistance. There is exceedingly little of significant current philosophy that Dewey did not see embodied to some degree in rival philosophies alive in his own day, but unfortunately his valuable transactions with them are nearly forgotten resources now. This book, by uncovering some of these resources, can function as a map displaying how Dewey tried to advance upon the philosophies of the past and also how Dewey's philosophy can relate to the advancement of philosophy into the future.

PREFACE

Many people deserve my heartfelt thanks for their assistance with my own philosophical progress. First and foremost my gratitude goes to Peter H. Hare, who directed my dissertation at the State University of New York at Buffalo. Much of the originality of this work stems from the intellectual freedom and wise counsel that I received from him. Another important stimulus was Frank Ryan's work on Dewey and our wonderful conversations. Other Dewey scholars to whose writings I am gratefully indebted include Greg Pappas, Tom Alexander, Jennifer Welchman, Raymond Boisvert, John Stuhr, and Larry Hickman. Larry and his staff provided warm hospitality and assistance during my very productive visit to the Dewey Center at Southern Illinois University. For several years the good wishes and support of Herman Saatkamp, Jr., the general editor of the Vanderbilt Library of American Philosophy, gave me encouragement to complete this book. The managing editor of Vanderbilt University Press, Bill Adams, and the anonymous referees for the Press have made helpful comments that are much appreciated. Meg Nyberg and Jeff O'Connell have given very helpful research assistance.

This book draws on material read at conferences or already published. Portions of chapter 1 and chapter 5 were presented as a paper, "Dewey and Pragmatism," read at the Second Annual New York City History of Philosophy Conference, Hunter College, New York City, in May 1998. Portions of chapter 3 were first published as "Wilhelm Wundt's Contribution to John Dewey's Functional Psychology," *Journal of the History of the Behavioral Sciences* 31 (October 1995), pp. 347–369. Portions of chapter 5 are from a paper, "Peirce and Dewey on Scientific Contingency," read at the Annual Meeting of the Society for the Advancement of American Philosophy, Toronto, in March 1996. Portions of chapter 6 are from a paper, "Dewey's Reconstruction of the Logic of Realism," read at the Society for Realist/Antirealist Discussion meeting with the American Philosophical Association in December 1998. Other portions of chapter 6 were first published as "John Dewey's Struggle with American Realism, 1904–1910," *Transactions of the Charles S. Peirce Society* v.31 (Summer 1995), pp. 542–566. I thank the editors of the above journals for permission to reprint material from these articles. I am also grateful to Larry Hickman and the Dewey Center at Southern Illinois University for their permission to quote from *The Works of John Dewey*. Without any exaggeration I can say that the research for this book simply would not have been possible without the existence of this definitive critical edition of Dewey's collected works.

Abbreviations

Standard references to John Dewey's work are to the critical edition, *The Collected Works of John Dewey, 1882–1953*, edited by Jo Ann Boydston (Carbondale: Southern Illinois University Press, 1969–1991), and published as *The Early Works: 1881–1898* (*EW*), *The Middle Works, 1899–1924* (*MW*), and *The Later Works, 1925–1953* (*LW*). These designations are followed by volume and page number. Quotations are made from *The Collected Works of John Dewey, 1882–1953: The Electronic Edition,* edited by Larry A. Hickman (Charlottesville, Va.: InteLex Corporation, 1996).

Standard references to Charles S. Peirce's work are to the *Collected Papers of Charles Sanders Peirce*, ed. C. Hartshorne, P. Weiss, and A. Burks, 8 vols. (Cambridge: Harvard University Press, 1935–1958). References are cited by *CP* followed by volume and paragraph number. References are also made to the *Writings of Charles S. Peirce: A Chronological Edition*, ed. Edward C. Moore (Bloomington: Indiana University Press, 1982–1993), cited by *Writings*, volume, and page number.

Introduction

This investigation of Dewey's empirical theory of knowledge and reality has three interrelated goals. First, it attempts a comprehensive account of the reasons for the emergence of Dewey's empiricist pragmatism from his early idealistic philosophy. This account corrects many prevalent misunderstandings, by revealing the central roles played by idealistic tenets in his mature philosophy. Second, this book examines Dewey's epistemological principles, his defenses of these principles, and his critiques of major rival epistemologies. Third, the relationships between Dewey's epistemology and metaphysics are explored in order to reveal their essential dependence on each other. This book defends a view of Dewey's philosophy first and foremost as an empiricism, which grounds his specific theories of mind, inquiry, and knowledge.

The first chapter explains why a satisfactory account of the progress of Dewey's thought has been lacking and why such an account is essential to a full understanding of his mature philosophy. The second chapter explores Dewey's early contributions to neo-Hegelian idealism, displaying both an allegiance to idealistic fundamentals and an original outlook on the nature of mind. The third chapter centers on Dewey's idealistic philosophy of mind and experience in the light of his inspiration from the doctrines of the world's foremost experimental psychologist, Wilhelm Wundt. The unique synthesis of these elements resulted in Dewey's functional psychology, which in turn required the reconstruction of his views on the nature of truth, the self, the absolute of experience, and religious and moral ideals, as described in chapter 4. This reconstruction permitted Dewey to offer a thoroughly empirical metaphysics to replace the other idealists' metaphysically transcendent absolute, which was also liberating for his theory of intelligence. Chapters 5 and 6 describe Dewey's mature philosophical views. Chapter 5 details how Dewey transformed the Hegelian dialectic of reasoning into an empirical theory of inquiry as problem solving, which in turn grounded his instrumentalist view of science. The answer to the oft-asked question of when Dewey left idealism for pragmatism is answered at the conclusion of chapter 5. Chapter 6 contrasts Dewey's empiricist understanding of meaning, knowledge, and truth with its transcendentalist competition, whether in the form of absolute idealism or dualistic realism. It concludes with a recapitulation and defense of Dewey's fundamentally empirical philosophy, explaining how his naturalistic theory of intelligence is set in the context of an empiricist metaphysics.

A Genetic Explanation of Dewey's Philosophy

The publication in 1939 of the first volume of the Library of Living Philosophers, *The Philosophy of John Dewey*, was widely met with enthusiasm and congratulations. The book's high goals apparently were met, as the contributing philosophers raised central issues and questions and received Dewey's careful replies. Reviewers nearly unanimously declared it a success. Whatever the eventual value of vigorous debate with a living philosopher, *The Philosophy of John Dewey* well exceeded the minimum expectation of "stopping certain of the grosser and more general kinds of misinterpretations."[1] Not all reviewers shared this optimistic assessment, however. Sterling Lamprecht expressed his dismay at the widespread difficulty commentators had with Dewey's theory of knowledge.[2] He selected Arthur Murphy's "Dewey's Epistemology and Metaphysics" as typical of such difficulty. Murphy interpreted Dewey's statement that "the true object of knowledge resides in the consequences of directed action" as a denial of the possibility of knowledge of things as they exist before inquiry.

This difficulty is even more curious, Lamprecht points out, because Dewey's reply to Murphy states that he does not hold that antecedent things cannot be known, yet only three pages before this reply he also states, "It is a truism that, while one is engaged in knowing, the things to be known are still future."[3] Lamprecht can reconcile these seemingly contradictory views only in the likelihood that Dewey has a very peculiar meaning for "the things to be known." A great many difficulties could likewise be accounted for—his "strangely subjectivistic and misleading terminology" must be a lingering symptom of his early non-naturalistic philosophy. Instead of protesting Murphy's interpretation, Lamprecht suggests, Dewey should be more helpful by "analyzing his own historical development" to supply a genetic account of his logic. If the development of Dewey's own theory of knowledge were genetically explained, then his present philosophical position could be better grasped as the emergent result of a long transformative growth. The advantages of such an explanation, Lamprecht appears to be suggesting, would be two-fold. First, Dewey's terminology would be better grasped by his readers, and second, such a genetic history would itself illustrate the methodology and worth of a genetic study. "Physician, heal thyself" is thus the moral of Lamprecht's admonishment.

Introduction

We can agree with Lamprecht that, for a philosopher who finds the finest knowledge of a thing in the genetic study of how it came to be, it is quite ironic that Dewey had not tried to help his critics by executing a complete genetic inquiry into his own philosophical theories. On occasion he gave some detailed insight into early influences and initial transitions towards pragmatism and naturalism, but he notoriously refused to provide details about any developments after his drifting away from idealism.[4] The very brief and fast-paced summary of important persons and events after 1905 which concludes Dewey's "Biography" raises more questions than answers and does virtually nothing along the lines of Lamprecht's recommended inquiry into Dewey's theory of knowledge. Perhaps, as Lamprecht mentions, someone else could perform this important task, or perhaps, in the nearly sixty years since his review, scholarship on Dewey's philosophy has supplied the required exegesis. My study of this scholarship has persuaded me that this possibility has not yet been fully realized. While important pieces of this puzzle are scattered across many articles and books, to which I am most indebted, many pieces still need to be brought to light so that a coherent and plausible story of the emergence of Dewey's epistemology can be told. This book is my attempt to reveal those pieces and tell as complete a story as possible. Its focus on the historical development of Dewey's epistemology should not be construed as an assertion that such understanding is *necessary* for grasping his epistemology. Dewey himself protests that view. (*LW* 14: 7) One hopes that the understanding offered here is near to being *sufficient;* and in any case his mature instrumentalism is directly discussed in chapters 5 and 6.

Dewey's philosophy defends the genetic method of understanding, claiming that discontinuous slices of observations miss the organic growth and that the exclusive study of the mature product prevents an adequate understanding. This book's exposition tries to be faithful to this genetic method, which I believe improves on historical or topical approaches to his thought. Some books on Dewey's philosophy are historical surveys, summarizing his philosophy in a chronological fashion. Recording his thought on many philosophical issues at stages in his career poses difficulties portraying the evolution of his views on any particular topic, for example, on ethics or knowledge. Other books have a topical focus, on one or a few of Dewey's mature philosophical positions. They ably present his established views, but it can be hard to explain why he held these views, since they are the flowering of a long and continuous intellectual growth. Both the historical and topical approaches to Dewey therefore tend to induce the reader to believe that only Dewey's mature thought is relevant to philosophy today and worthy of serious study and that Dewey's earlier thought (especially his earliest Hegelian period) is irrelevant, or even harmful, to the illuminating study of his mature thought. Many works on Dewey's philosophy openly affirm both theses; they are an essential part of the "traditional" story of the progress of his thought. This tradition and those few studies that oppose this tradition with greater respect for his early thought are described in detail below.

This book gives a genetic account of Dewey's philosophical development. Its chapters are organized around those fundamental principles concerning knowledge and reality which Dewey accepted early in his career and retained in adapted form for his mature thought. The exposition will follow the birth, growth, and maturation of these principles. The selected principles, concerning experience, meaning, judgment, value, knowledge, and truth, are most of the underpinnings for Dewey's philosophy. The historical approach will not be abandoned, however. What clearly distinguishes this book's organic exposition from the typical historical survey is the way that the fundamental principles of each stage are discussed. For each principle, an explanation for its adoption is followed by a look at its role for his mature philosophy. For example, from very early on Dewey held that perceptions were not instances of knowledge, and he wielded this principle against idealists and realists throughout the rest of his career. The exposition will allow the reader to see that this principle is indeed quite fundamental and also how Dewey's mature thought developed out of earlier views. The final chapter, describing Dewey's naturalist stage as the culmination of the preceding stages, will argue that his naturalism and instrumentalism are neither contradictory nor merely complementary, but integral to each other. This argument will combat prevalent notions that his instrumentalist epistemology amounts to a type of positivism, irrealism, or idealism, sharply conflicting with his quite realistic naturalism. This book, although not attempting a thorough exposition of the major works of his later philosophy, is therefore a preparatory guide to his most important books, *Experience and Nature* (1925) and *Logic: The Theory of Inquiry* (1938).

It may be objected by some at the outset that "epistemology" is in this context a misnomer, since Dewey so often used it as a term of abuse. The most appropriate reply is to point out that because he was unable to persuade his contemporaries to drop the term "epistemology" and because he does indeed offer a theory of knowledge himself, the invention of another label for "theory of knowledge" seems profitless. In brief, knowledge for Dewey arises when things are reconstructed by reflective thinking with new meaning and then verified as capable of directing us to our goals. Epistemology is thus the empirical study of this knowing process, as he says in "The Experimental Theory of Knowledge" (1906).

> Literally of course, "epistemology" means only theory of knowledge; the term *might* therefore have been employed simply as a synonym for a descriptive logic; for a theory that takes knowledge

as it finds it and attempts to give the same kind of an account of it that could be given of any other natural function or occurrence. But the mere mention of what *might* have been only accentuates what is. The things that pass for epistemology all assume that knowledge is not a natural function or event, but a mystery. (*MW* 3: 119)

This book focuses on Dewey's theories of experience, mind, judgment, intelligence, knowledge, truth, and reality. His ethical, aesthetic, and religious views will necessarily be discussed as well, since they are organically connected with his psychological, logical, and metaphysical positions. Dewey's educational, social, and political thought is only treated in a peripheral and subsidiary manner as the backdrop for his epistemology, not for the purpose of derogating these philosophically ultimate topics, but only to restrain this book's exposition from attempting to cover the entire of Dewey's philosophy.

The particular theses defended by this book which run counter to, or give novel additions to, the traditional understanding of Dewey's philosophy are the following:

1. Dewey's naturalistic empiricism is the organic maturation of his efforts to elaborate a consistent theory of idealistic philosophy.

2. Dewey's functionalist psychology was an essential component of this maturation, and was primarily inspired by George Morris and Wilhelm Wundt, not by William James or Darwinian evolution.

3. Dewey's instrumentalist epistemology, as a variety of voluntarism, maintained a teleologically behavioristic psychologism in the face of the strong anti-psychological logicist trends in philosophy.

4. Dewey's rejections of the "spectator" theory of knowledge and the notion of absolute mind were not a consequence of his attainment of pragmatism, but rather one of the stimuli towards it, as he reconstructed idealism to ensure the centrality of human social experience.

5. Dewey's principles of instrumentalism were developed in the course of formulating a functionalist account of moral deliberation and practical conduct.

6. Dewey's instrumentalist logic and theory of truth was the consequence of his arrival at functionalism and empiricism, and was not nearly so indebted to Peirce's and James's pragmatisms as is commonly assumed.

7. Dewey's theory of knowledge should be recognized as a serious contribution to empiricist epistemology.

8. Dewey's instrumentalism is not a positivistic verificationism incompatible with his behaviorism, naturalism, or emphasis on science.

9. Dewey's empiricist epistemology demands a reconstruction of the realism/antirealism debate.

10. Dewey's metaphysics must be understood as the result of this reconstruction, and hence as coherently organic with his epistemology.

CHAPTER ONE

The Opportunity of Dewey's Early Philosophy

> *The fixed structure, the separate form, the isolated element, is henceforth at best a mere stepping-stone to knowledge of process, and when not at its best, marks the end of comprehension, and betokens failure to grasp the problem.*
> John Dewey, "'Consciousness' and Experience," 1899

Dewey's Epistemology vs. His Metaphysics

Throughout Dewey's entire philosophical career he held that objects of knowledge are created by the process of knowing. This primary epistemological thesis should not be confused with any metaphysical stand, despite the obvious temptations. For instance, if one assumes (as many realists do, but Dewey did not) that knowing is solely a subjectively mental affair, then one could infer that Dewey thought that objects of knowledge were also mental. Alternatively, if one assumes (as many realists and idealists do, but again Dewey did not) that reality consists of nothing but objects of knowledge, then one could infer that Dewey believed that reality is created by human knowing. Going even further, if one assumes contra Dewey that knowledge is the only relationship we can have with reality (as some relativists and idealists hold), then his epistemology appears to imply, as no two people come to knowledge in identical ways, that we each live in a different known world. Leaving mistaken presumptions aside, his mature philosophy does offer a metaphysics. In fact, when it comes to metaphysics, his philosophy yields an embarrassment of riches. His early career was marked by an allegiance to absolute idealism, the first two decades of this century saw his philosophy defend a "naive" realism, and his later, post-1925 thought elaborated a thoroughgoing naturalism. Briefly outlined, Dewey's idealism located the meaning of all reality within a universal consciousness; his naive realism stated that things are what they are experienced to be; and his naturalism described experience as the product of environment-organism transactions. Furthermore his epistemology and metaphysics has an explicit connection in a secondary epistemological thesis also held by Dewey for nearly his entire career: the process of knowing essentially requires the purposive manipulation of natural things in the environment.

Understanding Dewey's epistemology and metaphysics is quite difficult, to say the least. Indeed many philosophers have found their understanding to be completely obstructed by Dewey's own pronouncements, since they could not reconcile his statements. Notable among them are his contemporaries Frederick J. E. Woodbridge, Evander B. McGilvary, George Santayana, Arthur O. Lovejoy, Sidney Hook, Bertrand Russell, and Arthur Murphy. Murphy's diagnosis of the problem is both typical and instructive. In Murphy's view, Dewey must use the term "experience" in two incompatible ways. Sometimes experience is the joint linking humans to a world which antedates the existence of humans, and sometimes experience is the immediate terminus and resolution of all inquiry, including inquiry into the relations between humans and the world.

Their incompatibility can be seen, Murphy argues, in the conflicting roles played by "the world." On the first, the world is used to provide the setting for experience, helping us to grasp the proper relationship between the world and human beings. On the second, experience is used to provide the setting for the natural world, offering a way to see how the world is related to us within experience. Put another way, the first conception of experience portrays inquiry as a process taking place within the natural world containing objects and humans, while the second portrays the world as a cognitive product of inquiry taking place within experience. To express Murphy's difficulty in terms of the two epistemological theses outlined above, the first conception, of "naturalistic" experience, allows us to understand Dewey's secondary epistemological thesis in this way: the process of knowing, taking place through experience, is a transaction between humans and the world in which humans manipulate natural things. The second conception, of "immediate" experience, allows us to grasp Dewey's primary epistemological thesis: natural things can only be known as serving the cognitive needs raised within problematic experience. Unable to reconcile these two conceptions, Murphy prefers to emphasize the secondary thesis at the expense of the importance of the first. He concludes that Dewey's metaphysics tries to serve two masters and fails both, since it requires "an unhappy discrepancy between experience as it ought to be if its place in the natural world is to be made intelligible, and experience as it must be if Dewey's epistemology is correct."[1] Murphy's suggested resolution is to avoid a "hopelessly anthropocentric view of things" by treating the results of inquiry not as merely instrumental to direct experience, but as "information about the causes and conditions of human experience."[2] Inquiry, for Murphy, must not be subservient to immediate experience but must be responsible for describing the conditions under which experience occurs. In sum, experience must be dependent on the natural world; the natural world cannot be dependent on experience.

Murphy therefore rejects Dewey's metaphysics of "naive" realism insofar as it attempts to portray immediate experience, instead of natural reality, as metaphysically ultimate. Natural reality, containing things such as humans, their experiences, and physical objects, should be metaphysically ultimate. Dewey's metaphysics must be fundamentally about natural existences and only secondarily about experiences and knowings occurring within existence. The proper relationship, Murphy claims, between metaphysics and epistemology on which Dewey's readers should focus is the one in which a sound metaphysics grounds the enterprise of epistemology, not one in which epistemology is permitted to set the tasks and limits of metaphysics.

Murphy is, as already mentioned, hardly alone in perceiving an incompatibility between some of Dewey's metaphysical and epistemological views. Neither is Murphy alone for recommending an interpretation of Dewey defending the metaphysics of existence over the metaphysics of experience. Sidney Hook also asserts that an undue emphasis on metaphysics as the independent inquiry into experience's traits undermines Dewey's attempt to offer a truly naturalistic account of experience's place in nature.[3] Hook accordingly dismisses not only efforts on Dewey's part to describe immediate experience per se, but also any effort generally to read him as using experience in anything but a naturalistic sense. Hook and Murphy thus agree that naturalistic metaphysics must prevail over any experiential metaphysics: human inquiry lies in a natural setting, not just a setting of immediate experience. Naive realism, on their readings of Dewey, thus must be only a manifestation of his preoccupation during those two decades with the refutation of other epistemologies. Hook says as much when he briefly describes Dewey's efforts to replace dualistic epistemology, referring to them as largely negative and dialectical.[4] Only naturalistic metaphysics can be consistently maintained as Dewey's fullest and finest expression of his philosophy. Ralph Sleeper agrees too; Dewey could not really have a "metaphysics of experience" because then Santayana would be right to accuse Dewey of having a "half-hearted naturalism."[5] Santayana, like Murphy, believed that a metaphysics of experience would improperly reduce the meaning of all terms ostensibly referring to natural things to mere ideational phases of inquiry created within experience. The dangerous implications of a metaphysics of experience beholden to epistemology, and hence incompatible with a fully naturalistic philosophy, have been drawn by many more scholars. For example, from the perspective of philosophy of science, Hans Reichenbach argues that Dewey's epistemology amounts to nominalistic verificationism and denies "independent reality to scientific objects."[6] Another example comes from aesthetics, as Stephen Pepper was dismayed to find in Dewey's *Art as Experience* (1934) many metaphysical statements about experience which in his view cannot fit a naturalistic account of aesthetic experience.[7]

Further cataloguing of the long history of this sort of criticism is amply supplied by Thomas Alexander.[8] Lest the impression be given that the numerous critics of experiential metaphysics should drown out its few defenders, other philosophers should receive mention who have been unwilling to submerge

Dewey's metaphysics of experience and instrumental epistemology beneath a purified naturalism. John Herman Randall, Jr., had a profound respect for the role of immediate experience in Dewey's philosophy and saw no inherent conflict between Dewey's metaphysics of experience and his naturalism. Metaphysics is empirical for Dewey and hence must be a "disinterested pointing to the ultimate traits of experienced Nature."[9] Richard Bernstein and John J. McDermott also found experience to be the focus of Dewey's metaphysics.[10] John Stuhr, identifying metaphysics with Dewey's pronouncement of naive realism (things are what they are experienced as being), infers that no meaning could be attributed to anything apart from its experienced function. "To say, then, that something is physical, psychological, or mental—is to say that it is (a feature of) a certain sort of transaction which is experienced as being, among other things, in a certain relationship and involvement with social and meaningful human experience."[11] Raymond Boisvert was, so far as I am aware, the first to explicitly call for the repudiation of the "metaphysics of existence" tradition in Dewey scholarship. Hook and Richard Rorty stand accused of trivializing Dewey's experiential metaphysics so that it can be conveniently discarded.[12] Boisvert's revitalization proposal focuses on the central role of form for Dewey's entire philosophical career. Thomas Alexander lauds such efforts and similarly proposes to rehabilitate the role of potentiality for Dewey's aesthetic-oriented metaphysics.[13] My own study of Dewey's epistemology resurrects the role of purposive action in his metaphysics of experience. The reader should not infer that any of these defenses of experiential metaphysics could not recognize the value of other approaches to Dewey's metaphysics. Rather, we agree that a metaphysics of existence is to some degree misguided and harmful to the full understanding of his philosophy's complexity and diversity. Our common claim is that Dewey's metaphysical inquiry into existence could not possibly be other than an inquiry into *experienced* existence and that he never intended to produce two metaphysics, one for existence as experienced and another for existence itself.

Another feature common to the defenders of experiential metaphysics is their unabashed eagerness to undertake serious study of Dewey's early philosophy. They find many central principles there which Dewey retained, perhaps in modified form, for the remainder of his career. These principles provide the underlying continuity beneath the surface changes of philosophical labels. Absolute idealism, instrumentalist empiricism, pragmatic naturalism—the reader might supply even more combinations and permutations of various terms to categorize Dewey's philosophy at any particular stage of his long career. Such labels are rarely enlightening, however. What must be discovered behind them are the actual philosophical tenets that Dewey held. When they are examined together, Dewey's efforts to do metaphysics by directly examining experience itself cannot be meaningfully isolated from his pragmatism or naturalism. This common ability to find deep and lasting connections between Dewey's early idealism and late naturalism might just be coincidence, save for the fact that the opposition, supporting the metaphysics of existence, nearly uniformly ignores or denigrates any feature of his philosophy which savors of idealism. This traditional opposition typically reacts with repulsion at any hint of idealistic leanings in Dewey's later writings, and experiential metaphysics is accordingly tarred with a wide brush as a lingering malaise upon his naturalism. Many commentators explicitly blame Dewey's early period for leaving unfortunate aftereffects which distorted his terminology or caused lapses into dialectical argumentation or occasionally dragged his pathbreaking thought back to old hopeless ruts. The evidence, it seems, points to idealism as the primary locus of contention causing the disagreement between the defenders of experiential metaphysics and the tradition of metaphysics of existence. Another sign that idealism is the source of controversy is the fact that the obvious method of resolution, coalescing the two metaphysics by arguing that Dewey's philosophy took existence and experience to be identical, is explicitly rejected by the tradition of metaphysics of existence.

Those who see a conflict between Dewey's instrumentalist epistemology and his metaphysical naturalism are, not surprisingly, those who affirm the primary value of his metaphysics of existence and regret that his instrumentalism was never completely liberated from his early idealistic allegiance. Their opponents, who believe that Dewey's theory of experience supporting his instrumentalism should not be set aside, accordingly seek a resolution of the apparent conflict. The ultimate goal is an understanding of the mutual support between his epistemology and his unified metaphysics. The exact locus of the problem of Dewey's early philosophy can therefore be expressed as follows: does an accurate, consistent grasp of his mature philosophy require the repudiation of all idealistic tenets of his epistemology? This book argues in the negative: Dewey's instrumentalist epistemology is idealistic in so far as it asserts that the known object is created by the process of knowing. Along the way it will be shown how the two metaphysics, of experience and existence, are really not separable. His epistemology is an organic whole, and, contrary to the traditional account, continuity with his metaphysics does prevail over the entire course of its emergence.

The Traditional Account of Dewey's Development

It has long been a commonplace of pragmatism scholarship that Dewey's contributions to the pragmatic school of thought were made possible largely through the influence of William James and, to a lesser extent, of Charles S. Peirce. To emphasize the force of this intellectual impact, the typical story of Dewey's early period describes a high degree of reliance on leading absolute idealists. This reliance begins with his graduate education at Johns Hopkins University and pervades his years at the University of Michigan (1884–1894; the 1888–1889 year was spent at the University of Minnesota). His philosophy during this decade is portrayed as completely within the orbit of absolute idealism, conforming closely with the views of George Morris, T. H. Green, F. H. Bradley, and John Caird. The story then recounts a conversion episode happening sometime between 1892 and 1896. In this episode the central failures of idealism are made manifest to Dewey, and, luckily stimulated by his study of James, he converts to the standpoint of evolutionary naturalism. Rescued from idealism's clutches, Dewey's psychology can now be termed "functionalism," which he develops at the University of Chicago (1894–1904). His 1896 "Reflex Arc Concept" essay is taken to show how much Dewey had imbibed from his pragmatic predecessor's fount. His 1903 *Studies in Logical Theory* (and especially its dedication to James) is held up as the sign of his complete repudiation of idealism and the acceptance of his now "mature" thought into the welcoming pragmatic fold. Finally, upon James's death in 1910, Dewey is recognized as the next generation's heir to the throne as pragmatism's champion.

Elizabeth Flower's story of Dewey's development in *A History of Philosophy in America* is quite representative of the traditional account. All the features outlined above are present: Dewey's early conformity with absolute idealists; James's decisive influence; the 1894 *The Study of Ethics: A Syllabus* as proof of conversion, since it "displays a shift in commitment now to empirical psychology and it is unmistakably aligned with ethical naturalism";[14] and the 1903 *Studies in Logical Theory* as the sign of complete conversion. The tension within this story is palpable. Flower herself says that "the reversal seems sharp and inexplicable, or explicable at best in terms of external influences."[15] Unable to find sufficient reason in Dewey's own work for the drastic about-face she has described, Flower sets herself the task of situating his work in larger settings to see if these contexts can help. This experiment leads her to two theses. First, naturalistic themes can be found in Dewey's earlier work. Despite his idealism he respected scientific psychology and retained some of the commonsensism of his earliest Vermont experiences. Second, Dewey's mounting interest in pedagogy and social justice, while at Michigan and especially Chicago, can account for his social psychology, which in turn helped to produce naturalistic functionalism. Armed with some sense of continuity between the early and mature periods of his career, Flower proceeds with an account of Dewey's safely naturalistic psychology, theory of inquiry, and social philosophy. The subtitle of her essay, "Battling against Dualisms," is therefore only relevant to his mature philosophy. Unable to make use of Dewey's own work to determine the causes of his conversion to naturalism, Flower has nothing to say about the possibility that the progress of his earlier thought had something to do with his repudiation of dualisms. The reader is left to conclude, falsely, that his philosophy had something to say against dualism only after 1903. Flower's essay is an excellent example of

The Opportunity of Dewey's Early Philosophy

the artificial difficulties that the traditional story can create. Locked into the schema of "conformity to idealism—James's stimulus—evolutionary naturalist," the tradition is bereft of any possibility that an account of Dewey's philosophical development could truly possess organic continuity. That is not to say that the tradition does not pay lip service to the notion of continuity. Flower's use of the term rises in frequency as she struggles more and more to locate any continuity in his thought. However, continuity is not the priority for the traditional story. There is another motive of even greater weight, which involves the magic words "naturalism" and "realism."

The attractive charms and conveniences of the traditional tale must be admitted before any critique could proceed, and they are numerous and weighty. The most significant advantages are threefold. First, the development of pragmatism is drawn in a simple linear manner. Second, pragmatism's relationship with idealism can be portrayed as thoroughly antagonistic. Third, the relevance of Dewey's later philosophy to current philosophy can be advertised without any shame for his "immature" intellectual recklessness. These advantages have outweighed the disadvantages of the tradition for many decades since pragmatism's eclipse by logical empiricism and analytic linguistic philosophy in the 1940s and 1950s. Pragmatism's few friends could do little more than ensure that classical American pragmatism would not fade completely out of sight. This long campaign was difficult enough; the arousal of the dominant sects' suspicion of idealistic notions, thereby risking outright dismissal at first glance, was understandably avoided as much as possible. From today's perspective this campaign's success is incontrovertible. Perhaps that time saw pragmatism discussed more frequently than not as just an interesting but flawed verificationism. Perhaps pragmatism was usually reduced to a straw man for an easy victory by the correspondence theory of truth. Echoes of these discussions are heard yet in the classification of pragmatism as a subjectivist or nonepistemic theory of knowledge or as an example of religious or moral apologetics. Still, pragmatism avoided idealism's fate. If the victors over idealism "approached idealism's castle only to find it deserted," as Russell once quipped, those who encountered pragmatism often stole a few bricks for their own philosophy's fortress. The defeat of idealism owed a great deal to pragmatism's initial attacks, and many philosophers then and since have found wisdom in some pragmatic viewpoint. Nowadays pragmatism's positions on belief, learning, knowledge, and truth (and, to a lesser extent, on reality, the self, and religious, moral, and aesthetic experience) are widely considered worthy of serious study and debate.

However, our present-day perspective also allows us to see that these successes have rendered those three essential advantages to the traditional story of Dewey's development to be advantages no longer. No sophisticated study can now afford to simplify pragmatism to a few theses originating with Peirce and passed on through James to Dewey. Diversity and pluralism, watchwords of pragmatism, truly apply to the philosophies of the pragmatists. It is easier to find in their writings disagreement over specific formulations of pragmatic tenets than to perceive their common overarching vision of philosophical method and results. Emphasis on disagreement does not by itself doom attempts to show linear development or to display common traits of mind, but careful examinations reveal that the most cherished tenets of one pragmatist were more often than not ignored, denied, borrowed but heavily reinterpreted, or confirmed through independent investigation by another pragmatist. For example, Dewey did not take up a serious examination of Peirce's writings until at least 1916 or thereabouts and never agreed with Peirce's understanding of the purpose of logic or his definition of reality. Furthermore Dewey himself declares that James's later pragmatism was not a formative factor, but rather his early psychology. The many difficulties an exasperated Dewey had with James's specific formulations of pragmatism even led him in 1908 to suggest that the "school" of pragmatism be dissolved.[16]

The second advantage, from emphasizing pragmatism's critiques of idealism, has similarly become more of a burden than a help. It is much clearer now that Peirce developed a peculiar variety of realism that could arguably be better classified as an idealism. James is no paradigm of realist conformity either. His radical empiricism and pragmatism is too close for comfort to subjectivism or positivism for many. The third advantage, accruing from Dewey's supposed repudiation of idealism, is now also unimpressive to today's better informed audience. Recent studies of Dewey's development have helped to show that his relationship with absolute idealism was quite complex and far-reaching. The present work belongs to this new genre of Dewey studies, since it argues that his theory of knowledge was in large measure the result of his completion of a consistent idealism, not created as a replacement for it. Renewed interest in Dewey, and to a large degree pragmatism in general, was first stimulated by Richard Rorty, who placed Dewey among a small pantheon of edifying philosophers who dismissed "truthfulness to reality in the sense postulated by philosophical realism."[17] Rorty's understanding of the goals and methods of Dewey's philosophy rightly has been questioned, but this dispute has only broadened interest. Concerning his philosophy of science, Dewey's exemplary devotion to naturalism and modern science cannot hide the potential antirealism in instrumentalism.[18] Furthermore idealism's enduring significance for his pragmatic ethics has been persuasively established.[19] Contrary to expectations, then, Dewey's important relevance to current issues has been heightened not by his safe status as a realist, but by his controversial status as a critic of fundamental realist tenets.

Dewey's Own Account of His Influences

The traditional account of Dewey's development, by stressing an abrupt break with idealism and a heavy reliance on James, tends to ignore Dewey's own rare but penetrating observations concerning the primary stimulants and positive influences on the course of his thought. The three most valuable essays on this subject are "The Development of American Pragmatism" (1922), "From Absolutism to Experimentalism" (1930), and "Biography of John Dewey" (1939).[20] Taken together, these essays offer many insights into the influences on Dewey's theory of knowledge. The following lists these influences roughly in chronological order, not necessarily in any order of significance.

1. Thomas Huxley's physiology text used in a junior course taken at the University of Vermont in 1877–1878. Dewey reports in "From Absolutism to Experimentalism" that he found there "a sense of interdependence and interrelated unity that gave form to intellectual stirrings. . . . Subconsciously, at least, I was led to a desire a world and a life that would have the same properties as had the human organism in the picture of it derived from study of Huxley's treatment" (LW 5: 147–148).[21]

2. George S. Morris's lectures at Johns Hopkins University from 1882 to 1883 on the failings of British empiricism and Kant and on the advantages of Hegelian absolute idealism. Dewey says that "acquaintance with Hegel has left a permanent deposit in my thinking" in "From Absolutism to Experimentalism." He adds that while Morris was hardly the only idealist Dewey read during his graduate study, Morris's objective idealism was more critical of Kant than the rest, having come to Kant through Hegel and not the reverse. Dewey says that one of the two most important historical antecedents of instrumentalism was "a critique of the theory of knowledge and of logic which has resulted from the theory proposed by neo-Kantian idealism and expounded in the logical writings of such philosophers as Lotze, Bosanquet, and F. H. Bradley. . . . I myself, and those who have collaborated with me in the exposition of instrumentalism, began by being neo-Kantians . . ." (LW 2: 14). Morris's influence continued after Johns Hopkins, as they were philosophy colleagues at the University of Michigan from 1884 to 1888. "The years of Dewey's association with Morris in Ann Arbor were those in which his philosophical position was closest to German objective idealism" ("Biography of John Dewey," p. 21).

2. A. Hegelianism replaced the oppressive "separations" of New England culture with a theory of social unity that found objective mind in the cultural environment and made social psychology the only possible psychology ("Biography of John Dewey," pp. 17–18).

When combined with James's "objective biological approach," philosophy, Dewey became convinced, must attend to the social sciences and arts, so that the importance of social categories such as communication and participation may be recognized (*LW* 2: 159).

2. B. Hegelianism offered the possibility of replacing formal logic and offered the notion that reason only dealt with "truths about the structure of the universe" with a logic of learning in which thought was the "means or instrumentality of *attaining* knowledge . . ." ("Biography of John Dewey," p. 18).

3. The new biological conceptions of psychology, in G. Stanley Hall's lectures at Johns Hopkins on Wilhelm Wundt's experimental and theoretical psychology and in William James's 1890 *Principles of Psychology*. Organic evolution established the notion that the purpose of the nervous system (and hence of intelligence) is to use sense stimuli to make adequate responses to the environment for the organism's needs. The new psychology therefore aimed to replace rationalist and introspectionist psychologies (*LW* 2: 14–16).

3. A. Dewey discerned that "the relation between psychology and philosophy was an intimate one, but one which must be worked out on the basis of the new experimental psychology" ("Biography of John Dewey," p. 22). Chapter 3 explains why Wundt was the greatest influence on Dewey's understanding of experimental psychology and its relevance to philosophy.

3. B. Dewey is careful to say that James's influence came not from his 1907 *Pragmatism* or later writings which affected Dewey, but his earlier psychology. "James's influence on Dewey's theory of knowledge was exercised not by the *Pragmatism*, which appeared after Dewey's theory had been formed, but by chapters in the *Principles of Psychology* dealing with conception, discrimination and comparison, and reasoning" ("Biography of John Dewey," p. 23).

3. C. Dewey credits Darwin's scientific methodology with more than just replacing a static notion of "species" with an evolutionary one. Darwin's attack on final causes was more important for philosophy, which now "forswears inquiry after absolute origins and absolute finalities in order to explore specific values and the specific conditions

that generate them." Evolutionary naturalism thus transforms the philosophical understanding of intelligence itself ("The Influence of Darwinism on Philosophy," *MW* 4: 10).

4. George H. Mead's theories of scientific psychology. Dewey and Mead were philosophy colleagues at Michigan and Chicago from 1891 to 1904. Dewey states that Mead "started from the idea of the organism acting and reacting in an environment" and developed "an original theory of the *psychical* as the state occurring when previously established relations of organism and environment break down and new relations have not yet been built up; and, through inclusion of relations of human beings with one another, a theory of the origin and nature of selves." Dewey did not develop these ideas himself, but rather "took them over from Mead and made them a part of his subsequent philosophy, so that, from the nineties on, the influence of Mead ranked with that of James" ("Biography of John Dewey," p. 26).

5. The practice and theory of education. Dewey participated in the study of grade school education while at Michigan was involved with two textbooks for teachers. At Chicago he was the chair of pedagogy along with philosophy and psychology; ran the "Laboratory School," an experimental elementary school; and wrote two books on education. Of special influence in this area was Ella Flagg Young, a district superintendent of the Chicago city schools; his wife, Alice Chipman Dewey, who served as principal of the consolidated elementary schools in 1903–1904; and Jane Addams at Hull House, who sharpened Dewey's "faith in democracy as a guiding force in education" ("Biography of John Dewey," p. 29–30). Dewey opined that philosophers should focus on education "as the supreme human interest in which, moreover, other problems, cosmological, moral, logical, come to a head" (*LW* 5: 156).

6. The scandalous logical separation between science and morals. "[T]he construction of a logic, that is, a method of effective inquiry, which would apply without abrupt breach of continuity to the fields designated by both of these words, is at once our needed theoretical solvent and the supply of our greatest practical want." Dewey declared that his search for such a logic was more significant for instrumentalism's development than most other reasons (*LW* 5: 156–157). From his earliest writings on ethics, Dewey struggled with the logical notions of self, will, realization, goals, value,

and action. Ethics, he decided, could not possess a method of problem solving distinct from the method of scientific inquiry, which in turn demanded a reconstruction of the "is-ought" and "fact-value" distinctions.

The "Problem" of Dewey's Early Philosophy

Lest the accusation stick that an artificial and exaggerated tradition has been constructed in preceding pages, additional illustrations of some proposed solutions to the "problem" of Dewey's early philosophy are found in a representative sample of explorations into his early philosophy: works by Morton White, Joseph Ratner, Lewis Hahn, Neil Coughlan, Bruce Kuklick, and H. O. Mounce.[22] This group stands for the many studies which do not seem particularly beholden to the "metaphysics of existence" faction but nevertheless belong to the tradition because they all set the terms of solving the "problem" by asking "when exactly did Dewey abandon idealism?" White's is the most thorough, because of the wealth of detail and quotations on many of Dewey's writings. Such attention to detail, concerning not only his psychological and logical theories, but also his ethical, educational, and social thought, permits White's account to be the least objectionable of the lot. James's role is very muted, Dewey's break with idealism was not rapid but extended across both his Michigan and Chicago years, and the full conversion does not take place until 1900–1903. The present work will contradict White's account in only two major areas. First, White credits Darwin with drawing Dewey out of Hegelianism, by explicitly contradicting the Hegelian notion of universal mind. This author finds no such contradiction; Dewey's transmutation of universal mind into universal active experience was a far, far more complex process. Second, while White rightly points out that Dewey's rejection of Lotze should not be mistaken for a wholesale rejection of idealistic epistemology, White does not directly grapple with Dewey's continued allegiance to the fundamental idealistic tenet: known objects are created by the process of knowledge. The reader is left with the false impression that Dewey is no longer an idealist in any meaningful sense. The same impression is deliberately created by Ratner, whose essay is throughout marked by a strong motivation to disassociate Dewey's unfortunate early Hegelianism from his later functionalism and naturalism. The effect of Hegelianism was one of "unquestioning discipleship" that required Dewey's emancipation by James's *Principles of Psychology*. Despite giving lip service to Dewey's statement that Hegel left a "permanent deposit," Ratner declares that Dewey's efforts to reconcile Hegel with his own ideas "proved to be impossible" and he was thus fortunate to be "completely on his own."

Hahn's essay is quite similar to White's and Flower's, because Darwin receives the credit for eliminating Dewey's idealism. Naturalism is thus free to reconstruct the rest of Dewey's philosophy thoroughly: "The Universal Consciousness or Mind was replaced by nature, and the central continuity came to be a biological and cultural one between man and his environment rather than a continuity within Universal Consciousness."[23] Dewey's metaphysics of experience is relegated to a brief notice that Dewey was interested also in aesthetic experience. The present book reverses Hahn's account by showing that Universal Mind was replaced in Dewey's philosophy not by nature, but by *experienced* nature. Furthermore it will be argued that aesthetics was not peripheral but rather integral to Dewey's metaphysics and epistemology. Coughlan, like White, provides excellent detail on many facets of Dewey's early thought and has no role for James's psychology either. Mead's significance receives its due; Dewey's transition to pragmatism is held by Coughlan to be the result of their collaboration at Chicago on the functionalist revision of the reflex arc concept in 1896. On the whole Coughlan avoids much of the traditionalist schema but nevertheless pays the price of laying a tremendous burden on a single work. As will be explained, Dewey's psychology contains no abrupt breaks, since his functionalism is greatly indebted to older idealistic themes. Kuklick's exposition is the least traditional of the group because here Dewey's instrumentalism is more the result of gradual terminology alteration than a quick revolution of ideas. Even as late as 1903, Kuklick points out, Dewey considered himself a neo-Hegelian, having "replaced religion with a politically concerned sociology." Able to project a scientific posture, Dewey carried on with his anti-dualistic theology by attacking any dichotomy between human experience and any absolute, whether a material world, a theistic god, or an absolute mind. Kuklick does not fall prey to the *deus-ex-machina* use of Darwin's influence either. Far from divorcing Dewey from idealism, "Darwin allowed Dewey to articulate the neo-Hegelian program he wanted to work out in 1890 in contrast to Green's abstractions."[24]

With Mounce's description of Dewey's philosophical growth we find ourselves back in very familiar territory. The occasional mention of a variety of influences is swept aside by the triumvirate of Hegel, Darwin, and James. While Mounce cannot decide if James's greatest influence lay in his pragmatic radical empiricism or his biological psychology, it appears to be beyond question that Dewey discovered the breakdown of the theory-practice distinction in the work of Peirce and James, attracting him to pragmatism. Mounce drives to a surprising conclusion, however: Dewey's empiricist philosophy, while avoiding idealism, was too positivistic to prove compatible with naturalism or science. The explanation for Dewey's positivism, however, is not bound up with the other pragmatists, who rejected positivism. Instead Mounce submits that Dewey's thought was just part of a widespread weltanschauung trying to replace religion.

I submit that the traditional account of Dewey's development, originally established at a time when his realism and naturalism were overemphasized, has almost thoroughly pervaded scholarship on pragmatism. The abandonment of the traditional account arrives when two things are accomplished. One, the many strands of his philosophy must be properly related, both to each other at a particular point in his career and to their replacements/supplements as his career progressed. Two, the rightful responsibility for the strands, whether from an influential thinker or from Dewey's own creative genius, must be justifiably identified. If these goals can be attained, as is attempted herein for Dewey's epistemology and metaphysics, then the "problem" of his philosophy has been solved. Really this problem is but an opportunity: to replace the traditional account, to understand fully the emergence of Dewey's epistemology, and to reveal this epistemology's harmony with his metaphysics.

By accomplishing these tasks, one finds that Dewey gradually abandoned absolute idealism from 1887 to 1891, gradually developed functionalist psychology from 1884 to 1896, and established instrumentalism from 1891 to 1903. All three of these events were based on some idealist and voluntarist principles accepted in the earliest years of his career, from 1883 to 1886. Dewey never rejected two central principles of idealism: experience is philosophically absolute, and knowledge transforms experience to creates its objects. From the start of his career he also accepted two central principles of pragmatism: thought is inextricably involved with the desires and volitions making up purposive conduct, and thought thereby serves the needs of successful activity by an individual in the natural environment. Dewey always held that there are natural things independent of inquiry and its logical elements such as ideas, judgments, knowings, knowledge's objects, etc. By integrating these principles, Dewey created an empirical theory of knowledge and reality.

CHAPTER TWO

Absolute Idealism

> *The title "Hegelian" is rather wildly thrown about nowadays, and has naturally fallen into some disrepute. No one who by trial has become aware of the difficulty of mastering, and still more of appreciating, Hegel's system, would be in a hurry either to accept the title for himself or to bestow it upon another.*
> T. H. Green, Review of Caird, *A Critical Account of the Philosophy of Kant,* 1877

Before turning to Dewey's own writings, some preparation must be made for the plunge into that philosophical school called "absolute idealism." As Green himself tells us, this school cannot be neatly pinned down and categorized. Indeed even its membership is not easily identifiable, perhaps least of all by those who admit an indebtedness to Hegel. Because appreciation for any portion of Hegel's thought, much less for his entire system, is even rarer in the present philosophical environment, efforts to define carefully Dewey's own debts cannot be too strenuous. Dewey could never have been a typical absolute idealist, since that creature is mythical. Making our task even more difficult is the fact that Dewey's idealism was never even a close duplicate of any other absolute idealism.

Idealism and Sensationalistic Empiricism

Dewey's philosophical growth into absolutism was marked by three gradual stages. First, Dewey learned how German idealism from Kant to Hegel exposed every fatal weakness in British empiricism. Second, he learned how Hegel exposed the central flaws of Kant's system. Third, Dewey fastened on what he viewed as Hegel's unstinting allegiance to the true meaning of the "psychological standpoint": that for philosophy, experience is the only absolute. Dewey's own allegiance to this principle carried him to some surprising consequences, which are typically ignored in the traditional story of his development in its rush to proclaim his disentanglement from absolutism. It cannot be emphasized too strongly that, from the start of his career, Dewey considered himself an empiricist because of his philosophical commitment to experience alone. His argumentative rejections of other empiricisms typically appealed to a direct examination of experience. If the failures of alternative empiricisms, together with his own examinations of experience, brought him to idealistic conclusions, then in Dewey's view empiricism has been philosophically *completed,* not replaced.

British Empiricism's Failures

Even before pragmatism's eclipse, efforts to distance Dewey's philosophy from idealism were undertaken. A primary example is the strident response by F. C. S. Schiller, the self-proclaimed humanist and British ally to pragmatism, to an article by Sterling Lamprecht titled "An Idealistic Source of Instrumentalist Logic."[1] Lamprecht was probably surprised by the controversy. More familiar than most with Dewey's entire career, he saw his essay about T. H. Green's influence on Dewey as a piece of unproblematic intellectual history, as the calm and reasonable tone of his essay indicates. Schiller, enjoying the long-awaited demise of the archrival school of idealism, leapt to the defense of Dewey's reputation. Scolding Lamprecht for committing a fallacious historical inference by deducing an intellectual debt from what Schiller saw as just a coincidence of a few fundamental theses, he decried any involvement of idealism with pragmatism. Granted, both pragmatism and idealism proceed from a similar critique of sensationalistic empiricism. Lamprecht nevertheless overlooked the possibility that their critiques were independently inspired, and he ignored the fact that the totally opposed spirits of these philosophies precludes any significant overlap.

The evaluation of this debate must start with the specific critiques of British empiricism that Lamprecht found both in both idealism and pragmatism. (1) Meaning cannot reside in a sense-impression or in accumulations of sensations, but only in the idea, which is a mentally active inference or suggestion relating one experience to others. (2) Perceptions are not the simplest and surest type of knowledge, representing external things and grounding all derived knowledge, but rather the meaningful result of attentive analysis for the purpose of discovering new relations between things. (3) Thought does not passively conform to a natural reality in order to attain knowledge and truth, but instead must creatively reorganize experience to produce knowledge and truth. Lamprecht was not eager to overemphasize Dewey's reliance on idealism, as he pointed out their many divergent theses. No idealist met with Dewey's full approval, and, specifically, many tenets of T. H. Green's system were rejected. Most important, experience prior to thought cannot for Dewey consist of totally relationless entities, and human knowledge does not have for its aim the understanding of eternally existing relations held fast by the absolute mind. Rather thought deals with experiences of things which already possess many natural relations, and the relations of any additional understanding have no existence anywhere prior to thought's creative work.

To be fair to Schiller, it is true that Lamprecht nowhere recognizes the profoundly opposed spirits of these philosophies.[2] On the other hand, Lamprecht makes out a very good case, which this chapter will confirm. He correctly concludes that Dewey's mature theory of knowledge, while quite original, would not have been possible without his thorough study and absorption of many idealistic themes. While no longer idealistic in the full sense of the word, metaphysically as well as epistemologically, the growth of his philosophy did not receive inspiration from British empiricism but rather from Continental idealism's critiques. The three principles above are together sufficient to distinguish Dewey's instrumentalism from most rival systems of his time. These rivals (for example, new and critical realism, logical positivism, and British empiricism) all receive Dewey's condemnation for misunderstanding the nature of meaning, the purpose of thought, and the origin of knowledge and truth. For all of Lamprecht's insights, however, we must remember that his account does not pretend to be the full story, as the reasons for Dewey's rejections of rival idealistic systems are not explored. These reasons arose in the course of developing his own understanding of the essence of idealism while at Johns Hopkins University and the University of Michigan.

Influences from Morris and Trendelenburg

John Dewey was one of the very few recipients in his day of an American Ph.D. in philosophy who did not undertake some study in Germany. This fact in itself may not seem unusual, considering that in 1884 Dewey was one of only a dozen or so recipients of that recently established degree. However, nearly all of Dewey's professors had done what he did not, as would most of his own generation's philosophy students. It was considered customary during the latter half of the nineteenth century for advanced students of philosophy (and many other fields, especially medicine) to spend one or more years at Leipzig, Göttingen, Jena, or Berlin. Why was John Dewey an exception to this rule? The simple explanation lies in the fact that in an era when American philosophy was looking to Germany for its inspiration and education, Dewey did not have to go there. Germany came to John Dewey at Johns Hopkins University, in the persons of George Sylvester Morris and Granville Stanley Hall.

During the two years when Dewey pursued his doctorate at Johns Hopkins University, the philosophy department consisted of three instructors: George Sylvester Morris, George Stanley Hall, and Charles Sanders Peirce. Peirce had little effect on the young Dewey,[3] but Morris and Hall were a profound, if often contradictory, influence. Their teachings were extremely novel in their native country. Morris was one of only a handful of American academics who taught neo-Kantian and neo-Hegelian doctrines. Hall's experimental psychology was an even greater rarity, as only William James of Harvard and George T. Ladd of Yale were extensively familiar with the new psychology. The presence of these two philosophies at John Hopkins is quite remarkable in itself, and it also proved to be very fortunate, as they collided with great force in the absorbing mind of one graduate student who found both philosophies powerful and impressive. Dewey was first converted to Morris's version of neo-Hegelian idealism. George S. Morris taught at John Hopkins during the fall semesters from 1878 to 1884. He left a semester before Dewey did, both taking permanent positions at the University of Michigan. From 1882 to Dewey's departure from Michigan for Minnesota and Morris's death in 1888, Dewey and Morris were a team, sharing an idealistic outlook on philosophy. Morris's idealism was partly shaped by T. H. Green's neo-Kantian criticisms of older British and Kantian systems, which argued that these philosophies had unsatisfactory descriptions of experience and poor psychological theories of the origin and extent of knowledge. The notions of the bare sensation prior to knowledge and the thing-in-itself beyond any knowledge were rejected as impossible existences. Accordingly all of reality must be contained within knowing experiences, which together constitute a mental self. This all-encompassing mind, the Hegelian absolute, contains as parts all of the finite human minds. Morris's idealism was also shaped by the concept of the organic, which dictated that the real nature of anything must be conceived only through an explication of the function it serves as a part of a greater whole. Dewey described his favorable encounter with this concept in Huxley's physiology textbook at the University of Vermont. Morris reinforced it with a vision of knowledge as the comprehension of the complete interdependence of all portions of reality, by way of Trendelenburg's organic Aristotelianism.

Trendelenburg was professor of philosophy at Berlin University from 1833 to 1872.[4] He was nearly single-handedly responsible for three epoch-making philosophical movements in Germany: revitalizing the study of Aristotle, stimulating a neo-Kantian revival, and inaugurating the post-Hegelian, but still recognizably romantic, field of epistemology. The guiding vision linking these endeavors was Schelling's teleologically organistic naturalism. Trendelenburg taught that the process of the universe, guided by its final cause, brought together all its parts in working unity. Any part can only be understood by a logic which discovers its proper function in the evolution of the whole. And there can only be one organon, one logic, one theory of knowledge, for all fields of inquiry. Philosophy's task is the elaboration of this logic. In direct opposition to the Hegelian system, there is no separation between metaphysics, logic, and the several sciences, since they fundamentally use the same scientific method.

Morris's studies in Germany from 1866 to 1868 included three semesters of Trendelenburg's lectures. The essential doctrines which Morris found in Trendelenburg, aside from the abiding respect for the history of philosophy, are enumerated by Dewey in "The Late Professor Morris."

> Although Trendelenburg had incorporated within his own teaching the substantial achievements of that great philosophical movement which began with Kant and closed with Hegel—the ideas, for example,

of the correlation of thought and being, the idea of man as a self-realizing personality, the notion of organized society as the objective reality of man—he had taken a hostile attitude to these positions as stated by Hegel and to the method by which they were taught. While Professor Morris was never simply an adherent of Trendelenburg, he probably followed him also in this respect. At least, he used sometimes in later years to point out pages in his copy of Hegel which were marked "nonsense," etc., remarks made while he was a student in Germany. It thus was not any discipleship which finally led Mr. Morris to find in Hegel (in his own words) "the most profound and comprehensive of modern thinkers." He found in a better and fuller statement of what he had already accepted as true, a more ample and far-reaching method, a goal of his studies in the history of thought. (*EW* 3: 7)

Trendelenburg had convincingly proven to Morris that the Hegelian logical dialectic of thesis, antithesis, and synthesis as constitutive of absolute reality was a hopelessly confused effort. As a replacement Morris later found persuasive the idea that the individual mind is an organ with its own teleology, actively functioning within the absolute organism. This would obviate any need for a dualistic system of physical and mental reality and could provide for a monism without determinism.

Rosenstock has thoroughly explored Morris's debts to Trendelenburg and has suggested many ways in which fundamental philosophical views were likely to have passed on to Dewey. For our purposes three principles must be highlighted. First, the highest level of understanding is teleological: to know completely a thing is to situate it in its context of growth to find its origin. This "genetic" mode of knowledge, applied to the psychological problem of explaining an individual's knowledge, provides Dewey with his primary epistemological thesis. Knowledge itself must be teleologically understood, in its own proper context, as a growth out of materials that it has actively and intentionally made its own. Second, the proper context for human knowledge is mind's environment: the human mind develops in concert with nature, by interacting with nature in intelligent ways. Mind and nature, for Trendelenburg, Morris, and Dewey, are harmoniously fitted together. Nature is never inscrutable and impenetrable to mind, and mind is not passively aloof and distant from nature. Organically one, the human mind and the natural world seem designed to grow together. Third, as organic growth demands developmental change, mind and nature must manifest such change. The timelessness of the absolute held attractions for other idealists but not for these philosophers. Dewey from the start could not countenance anything real—mental or physical—that is insusceptible to time, motion, change, growth, and decay. Since all three philosophers rejected dualism, preferring an all-encompassing reality holding all parts in its organic unity, all three therefore believed that time, motion, change, growth, and decay were categories truly applying to ultimate reality. As Dewey developed his own independent philosophy, it never strayed from these fundamental philosophical standpoints.

Dewey acquired two theories of the mind as a graduate student. In addition to the idealism of Morris, Dewey learned the new experimental psychology of Wundt from G. Stanley Hall. Hall was the first recipient of the Harvard Ph.D. in philosophy, in 1873. As his philosophy doctorate was awarded (by William James) in the area of psychology, he received the first American Ph.D. in psychology as well. He began teaching at Johns Hopkins in the spring semester of 1883, and Dewey took classes with Hall for two semesters. Dewey was the first of Hall's students to graduate, and, as his dissertation was nominally in the area of psychology ("The Psychology of Kant"), Dewey was the second recipient of an American Ph.D. in psychology.[5] Hall regarded Morris's philosophy with antipathy, seeing in idealism everything against which the new psychology was fighting.

Knowledge and the Psychological Standpoint

When Dewey, at the age of 22, came to Johns Hopkins University in the fall of 1882, he already had two publications to his credit.[6] Dewey could read philosophical German, had a close understanding of both Scottish intuitionalism and Kant, and may already have been acquainted with Hegel. His next publications were written after Dewey had begun to study Morris, Green, and other neo-idealists, and accordingly the tenor and methods alter considerably to reflect their influence. Dewey spoke to the Johns Hopkins Metaphysical Club on "Knowledge and the Relativity of Feeling,"[7] which was subsequently published in January 1883. In this article Dewey attacks the epistemological side of agnosticism, which was the nineteenth century's version of nominalistic and sensationalistic empiricism. It encompasses positivism, some varieties of neo-Kantianism, associationalism, and some evolutionism. They have in common a way to resolve the dispute between religion and science, by arguing that we cannot have knowledge of ultimate being, of reality, since by nature our knowledge is limited to phenomena, appearance, and the relative. Dewey understands it as amounting to the epistemological theory that all of our knowledge originates from, and is relative to, our senses. As he uses the terms, sensations and feelings are synonymous, and thus he sets himself to showing that it is impossible to prove that all of our knowledge consists of relative feelings. He selected as his principal opponent the major figure of agnosticism, Herbert Spencer. Spencer's philosophy of the unknowable attempts to delineate responsibilities for religion and science in a manner prevalent since Kant: science deals with the knowable phenomena, while religion deals with faith in the unknowable realm safe beyond the reach of science.

Knowledge of the Absolute

Dewey starts by asking how it is, on the premise of sensationalist empiricism, that we could know that *all* our knowledge is relative. His own view is that sensational experience clearly is relative, but he does not hold that all our knowledge consists ultimately of sensations. He argues using a *reductio* that in order for us to know that any of our knowledge is relative, we must know of the existence of that to which knowledge is relative: the nonrelative, or the absolute. The absolute is the one ultimate reality; it is that which is not relative to, or dependent on, anything else. Those philosophers who have denied that we could know anything about the absolute are thus forced to claim that the absolute exists. Dewey points out that Spencer claims exactly this. But it is one thing to argue that the relative cannot exist without the existence of the absolute and another to hold that we can only have knowledge of the relative. As the agnostic holds the latter as well as the former thesis, Dewey feels entitled to ask how, on the agnostic's sensationalistic grounds, can we know of the existence of the absolute, since that knowledge is required in order to know of the existence of the relative. The agnostic cannot answer this question, since he holds that all of our knowledge is of the relative only. Dewey's argument is an attempt to trap the agnostic by showing that the two positions are contradictory, since the agnostic's only argument for the conclusion has the feature that the conclusion contradicts one of the needed premises. Hence the sensationalist's position is a failure, and Dewey concludes that we cannot hold that all of our knowledge is relative. If we agree that sensational knowledge is relative, as both Dewey and the agnostic believe, then we must admit that sensational knowledge cannot exhaust all of our knowledge, and thus some of our knowledge does not consist of just sensations. Alternatively, even if a philosopher believes that sensational knowledge exhausts all of our knowledge, then he is forced to hold that such knowledge is thoroughly objective (as Hume seems to often admit). Either way, we must have some access to objective knowledge, or knowledge of the absolute.

Dewey provides another objection to the existence of an absolute beyond the reach of knowledge (*EW* 1: 26). The bare assertion by Spencer and other sensationalists that the absolute exists and that nothing further could be known about the Absolute is totally barren and meaningless. Dewey argues that any statement of the form "X is" lacks meaning because it fails to predicate anything of the subject. Existence cannot be a predicate, because "when it is said that something *is*, it is meant that *something* is." A concept must have some positive qualification in order to have any meaning, but the notion of the unknowable is a purely negative one; it is supposedly what is forever beyond the reach of consciousness. Furthermore the assertion of the existence of the unknowable is self-contradictory. "To say that something beyond consciousness is known to exist, is merely to say that the same thing is and is not in consciousness." Therefore the contents of consciousness must exhaust reality.

Dewey's idealism departs here from the subjective idealism lurking in sensationalism and is instead a preliminary expression of absolute or objective idealism. To see this, remember that the notion of subjective idealism depends on the existence of the subjective, which in turn relies on the relativity of consciousness, which in turn relies on the objective. The notion of a sole *individual* mind exhausting reality is impossible and self-contradictory, while a collection of separate individual minds would likewise each be solipsistically trapped inside their own perspectives. Absolute idealism holds that while individual minds exist, they are but a portion of the ultimately real consciousness comprising total reality. This absolute consciousness cannot be viewed as fundamentally individual or subjective. Objective, or absolute, idealism is the only appropriate term for this philosophical position. This too brief account of absolute idealism cannot do justice to its many issues and problems, but further elaborations and qualifications will be presented as Dewey's philosophy encounters them.

Dewey's next criticism of the unknowable states that in order to know that something is relative, it must be demonstrated that it exists in some relation to something else. This relation is typically one of dependence or of cause and effect, but, whatever the relation, it must be asserted to exist for the argument to proceed. The agnostic must admit that this relation must then exist between the unknowable and the knowable: "As long as its sole characteristic is unrelatedness to consciousness, it and the content of consciousness have nothing to do with each other; and to make one the ground of asserting anything regarding the real nature of the other is absurd" (*EW* 1: 27). Besides, even if there is some such relation, sensationalism must assert that it is unknowable too since it cannot be a sensation or the product of sensations (*EW* 1: 27, 31–32). With this Dewey can put together a summary of the argument proving the complete relativity of feeling. The argument requires four known premises: there must be an absolute object, the object must be in consciousness, it must be related somehow to consciousness, and these relations cannot be feelings. Dewey agrees with all four elements, but the agnostic cannot since knowledge of the last three is impossible according to the sensationalist theory.

Dewey pursues the point that there must exist a relation between the absolute and the relative by revealing how specific arguments for relativity rely on them both. He uses the terms "subjective" and "objective" to restate the argument, replacing the "relative" and "absolute," respectively. Dewey states that a feeling, a sensation, can be subjective, just as science tells us: sensory knowledge is relative because it is conditioned by and dependent on the character of light, the body's sensory organs, etc. If it is then concluded that knowledge of the objective, of unconditioned real existence, becomes problematic, then we are only contradicting

Absolute Idealism

the premises: our knowledge of the objective real existence of the light, the body's senses, etc. These objects—"the waves of ether, the structure of the retina, etc.—are not themselves feelings, and never have been" (*EW* 1:28). Dewey then considers the phenomenalist view that these objective things are actually the possibilities of sensations and hence still relative. However, this only leads to an infinite regress, because we must still require of this theory that it explain how it could be known that these things are subjective as well. Such an explanation must refer to other objective things, Dewey argues, because merely to refer to another subjective feeling would not prove subjectivity: "the mere fact that one feeling is the antecedent of another could never give any reason for asserting that feeling was relative in comparison with an unknown object." Therefore, Dewey concludes "that to prove the relativity of feeling is impossible without assuming that there are objects which are known not through feeling" (*EW* 1: 29). In other words we can know that something is subjective only if we also know that something else is objective. The doctrine that all of our knowledge is relative or subjective requires an appeal to absolute or objective knowledge. Doubtless *some* of our knowledge is relative, but to know this is to confess that we do have some nonrelative knowledge, or knowledge of the absolute.

Dewey then attacks a common argument for the relativity of all sensational knowledge. This is the argument which says that since *under the same conditions* different people have different sensations, these sensations must be subjective. They cannot be objective, the argument goes, because the objective is precisely that which remains the same while any or all other things change. Dewey simply points out that this argument depends on a statement of "the same conditions." The argument works only if it is supposed that it can be known that the conditions are the same. Thus it is assumed that there is knowledge of that which can be independent of the observers, or in other words, the argument assumes that there can be objective knowledge. To give an example, suppose it is pointed out that two people looking at an object can see two different colors. We can conclude that their sensations of color are relative/subjective only if other possibilities are eliminated. Two important ones are (a) they are not looking at the same object, and, if there is but one object, then (b) it is multicolored. Therefore we can know the desired conclusion only if (a) and (b), at least, are assumed to be false. If the arguer does so, he is claiming to know that they are false. But such knowledge cannot be given in the observers' sensations, be they of color or of any other type. The knowledge claims must be of the objective sort, and thus the argument (to show that color sensations are relative) is convincing only if appeals to objective knowledge are made. Dewey believes that colors (and other sensations) can be relative knowledge, since he has no trouble accepting the existence of objective knowledge. However, the sensational empiricist, the one who wants to argue that *all* knowledge is sensational and relative, does have such trouble. The proof that all knowledge is relative must always fail, doomed to commit what can be termed the "agnostic" fallacy since its logical force relies on the presumption of nonrelative knowledge.

However artificially dialectical Dewey's arguments might appear, they retain their force against simplistic agnostic and sensationalistic positions. He kept them in his arsenal and occasionally brought them to bear on philosophers in later decades. For example, the sense-data epistemology of Bertrand Russell questions whether we can "know that objects of sense ... exist at times when we are not perceiving them"[8] and thus calls into question the existence of the external world. Russell's attempt to show that the external world cannot be known—because our only knowledge consist of sense-data existing relative to the individual—commits the agnostic fallacy. Dewey's response questions Russell's ability to establish a category of internal mental states without necessarily assuming a category of external things. See chapter 6 for further discussions of Dewey's objections to the thing-in-itself and sensationalism.

Dewey is now prepared to give a positive account of the nature of feeling: "a feeling is a specific determinate relation or reaction given in consciousness between two bodies, one a sensitive, the other a non-sensitive object" (*EW* 1: 31). We can make some important observations at this point. First, Dewey accepts the common psychological view that sensations are caused for an organism by objects existing beyond the body. Second, the sensations, the objects, and the relations between them must be known and hence in consciousness according to the above arguments. Dewey consistently equates the condition of being known with being in consciousness, and this sort of terminology is shared by Morris and the other idealists of that era. Third, Dewey must embark upon an examination of the nature of relations since he depends on them in his account. He is quite sensitive to this obligation and next gives us a glimpse into the role that relations play in his theory of knowledge. Dewey states that while others have denigrated subjective knowledge, there is really no reason to consider knowledge concerning the relations holding between a sensitive organism and objects as inferior to other sorts of knowledge. After all, there is no fundamental difference between this and knowledge of the relations between two objects, such as gold and acid, and furthermore there cannot be any knowledge where there are no relations. "Except upon the theory that the real nature of things is their nature out of relation to everything, knowledge of the mode of relation between an object and an organism is just as much genuine knowledge as knowledge of its physical and chemical properties, which in turn are only its relations." (*EW* 1: 31) With this statement Dewey shows that he holds that the "real nature of things" is provided *only* through their relations with other things, and since Dewey equates relations with reactions, things' real natures and properties are just the results of their interactions with other things.

Dewey concludes with a statement of his absolute idealism. Since our knowledge of the objective and its objective relations (which indeed must constitute it) cannot be themselves subjective sensations, then they must be provided by the relations of consciousness. Dewey here relies on a principle declaring that knowledge is constituted by the relations supplied by consciousness. "Since a feeling can be known as relative only when referred to an object, this object cannot be a feeling, nor constituted by a feeling. The object must, then, be relative to a thinking consciousness." A feeling's "relativity consists in a specific ratio between a sensitive and a non-sensitive object, which are constituted by relations to self-consciousness" (*EW* 1: 33). And this self-consciousness "is the ground and source of relations" which means that it cannot itself be related to anything else, so it is properly called the absolute. Self-consciousness both exhausts reality and is the absolute, sustaining everything within it. A large number of presuppositions must be supplied in order to make Dewey's rushed conclusions fully comprehensible. Suffice it to say that he is relying on an elaborate portrait of the nature of self-consciousness and its role in knowledge. We can look to Morris to see this portrait, locating Dewey's arguments in Morris's works.

The term "relativity of knowledge" is found in Morris's *British Thought and Thinkers* where he discusses Sir William Hamilton and Herbert Spencer. Throughout this work he attacks the notion that our knowledge is limited to sensations and completely inadequate to reality. Morris uses the term in question first while discussing Hamilton's acceptance of Kantian doctrine of the unknowability of the unconditioned real.[9] Morris says that the notion of the unknowable "would never occur to the human mind, and be made a theme of inquiry, if the whole nature of mind were absorbed in sensible, static consciousness." Morris's antipathy towards the "thing-in-itself" consistently arises throughout his career. Such antipathy is a necessary component of neo-Kantian and neo-Hegelian philosophies, and he acquired it during his German studies. Dewey also heard it from Green, Caird, et al. "But, as we cannot apply to it any one of the categories, the conception of it is for us empty and meaningless," argued Caird in his 1877 *A Critical Account of the Philosophy of Kant.*[10] Morris was convinced of this position, prior to his acquaintance with the neo-idealists, since he inherited from Trendelenburg a critique of Hegelian logic. On this critique Hegelian logic requires the conceptions of pure thought and pure being. As Morris reports, since neither of these can have any significance for us, the dialectical process cannot start unless some positive content is smuggled in.[11]

Those philosophers who equate the unconditioned, or absolute, with the unknowable are doing so under the influence of a sensationalistic epistemology, which holds that sensations are both permanently conditioned and the source of all knowledge. Morris argues that since the notion of the unconditioned, or absolute, does exist, we should conclude that a person is more than "simply a bundle of perceptions or impressions, or a complex series of mere conscious *states,* but that there is a dynamic element in him, an ideal real nature, a spell of potent reason, a spirit, for whose activity sense is but the occasion and subsidiary instrument."[12] When discussing Spencer, Morris says that if a person's knowledge is constrained to the realm of the sensible, then

> It were psychologically impossible that the conception of the sensibly unknowable should enter his mind. The fact that it does thus enter is immediate proof that man is more than a physically sensitive organism, and that knowledge is something more than merely mechanical, analytical dissection and registry of passively felt experiences, or of "phenomena." It indicates that his is an actively living, rational nature, capable of organic insight, of rational conceptions.... [13]

Here Morris is not reversing his position on whether we can conceive of the unknowable, since here he qualifies it and speaks only of the *sensibly* unknowable, which is different from the contradictory notion of the consciously or conceivably unknowable. On this standpoint, since the senses do not provide by themselves complete consciousness or knowledge, there must be many things (indeed, everything) which are unknowable to the senses. Put another way, Morris accepts the complete relativity of sensations or feelings; the real problem begins only when a philosopher (usually a British philosopher, in Morris's view) declares sensations to be the sole source of human knowledge. Morris has no quarrel with any attempt to "recognize the phenomena as given matters-of-sensible-fact, and to demonstrate the 'law' or rule of order which is observed to hold good concerning their varied coexistences and sequences."[14] Such a mental science is "a thoroughly legitimate work," but danger and error awaits if it "takes its own peculiar explanations to be, in the one case, final, or, in the other, exhaustive."[15] This mental science is no different in method than any other science for Morris. But there is another and far better way to investigate the mind, called mental philosophy or rational psychology, which is concerned with mental functions. "The names of these functions are many, as, consciousness, memory, intelligence, reason, will. All these, and others, are *active functions* of mind."[16] This view of the mind replaces sensationalism, which holds that these are instead merely mental *states* and which upholds the proper role of an active mind supplying relations. "It is true, the 'relational element,' as such, is not given in sensible, static consciousness, but in rational, dynamic self-consciousness, for it is a characteristically ideal *function;* it is intelligible, and not sensible."[17]

Morris held that knowledge lies in the relations which self-consciousness provides, that "process" accurately characterizes the mental, and that self-consciousness distinguishes itself into functions as it organically evolves and grows. As we saw, there was no mention of the latter two notions in Dewey's article, but they begin to appear in Dewey's next publication and imbedded themselves in his philosophy permanently. In Morris's idealism the question as to the proper relation between consciousness and object is answered by a conception of the two united in one "organic" unity. Because of this unity, the only way a distinction between thought and thing can arise is through a process which takes place *within* conscious experience. Dewey makes his first mention of the organic and the functional in his next publication.

The Origins of Experience

Dewey's April 1884 article "Kant and Philosophic Method" presents an exposition of Kant's philosophy, together with some Hegelian criticisms of the sort Morris and other neo-idealists have made. The primary inspirations lie in Caird's *A Critical Account of the Philosophy of Kant*, published in 1877; Morris's *Kant's Critique of Pure Reason: A Critical Exposition*, published in 1882; and Green's 1883 *Prolegomena to Ethics*.

Dewey alerts us at the outset that the philosophic method is the criterion of truth. This criterion amounts to "having some principle which, true on its account, may also serve to judge the truth of all besides" (*EW* 1: 34). The main question is whether Kant accomplished this goal. Kant held the categories, and hence all knowledge, to be subjective, because he accepted the notion of the relativity of knowledge in the form of sensational empiricism. Following British thought, Kant conceived of a mechanical or external relation between reality, the senses, and the categories. Objects mechanically related have a distinct existence, are foreign to the others, and are able to act on each other. "The material, the manifold, the particulars, are furnished by Sense in perception; the conceptions, the synthetic functions from Reason itself, and the union of these two elements are required, as well for the formation of the object known, as for its knowing" (*EW* 1: 37). "Though the categories make experience, they make it out of a foreign material to which they bear a purely mechanical relation" (*EW* 1: 39). Dewey claims that the dependence on mechanical relations doomed Kant's search for the criterion of truth.

This sort of criticism was ubiquitous among the neo-idealists. Caird, summarizing Kant's transcendental deduction, says that "in a way, the identical self, the categories, time and space, and the manifold of sense, appear as independent things, and Kant seems to construct experience, as a watchmaker constructs a watch, out of pre-existing parts."[18] Morris says that Kant has a "purely mechanistic point of view. . . . Kant persists in considering the process of knowledge, or, more particularly, the relation between subject and object, in its superficial, mechanical aspect."[19] The analogy of the watch illustrates this Hegelian attack on Kant's philosophy. The watch is experience, and the parts are sensory materials and the understanding's categories. Only through the cooperation of both can the watch run, but the two sorts of parts have nothing else in common. Analogously the categories per se are purely formal thought, purely a priori; the sensations are bare content, completely contingent. Somehow they work together to produce experience, but aside from this work they have nothing else in common.

As Dewey puts it, Kant argues that "while thought *in itself* is analytic, it is synthetic when applied to a material given it, and that from this material, by its functions, it forms the objects which it knows" (*EW* 1: 37). Since all of the synthetic functions of the understanding are still producing results which are separate at this point, to ensure that our experience is together in a coherent unity there is another operating synthesizer, which "Kant calls the synthetic *unity* of Apperception, or, in brief, self-consciousness" (*EW* 1: 38). The term "apperception" refers to the process by which the existing mental order alters and assimilates incoming perceptions so that they can contribute to the mental unity. The term "self-consciousness" gains its meaning when it is contrasted with mere "consciousness." The latter term refers to the realm of the mind consisting of bare sensations. In Morris's words,

> "Consciousness," as distinguished from "self-consciousness," is what we have termed "sensible consciousness." It is consciousness as considered in empirical psychology—a fixed and finished product, a complex series of "states" or "feelings," a sum of "mental phenomena" which we find already existing, and which, prior to exact investigation, are roughly imagined to be the purely mechanical result of the action, upon one indefinable mental "subject," of "objects" whose nature is wholly foreign to the subject.[20]

Morris is here describing what he considers to be Locke's, and well as Kant's, account of phenomenal mind, or "consciousness." His difficulty basically concerns the distinction Kant makes between the aesthetic and the analytic, or the sense and the understanding. Sense is the material supplied from without, and the understanding is the set of categories supplied from within. While Kant in the "Transcendental Aesthetic" says that space and time are introduced a priori first into sense, the understanding still has yet to perform its work, and so true experience has yet to be realized. Aside from this difference between Locke's and Kant's accounts of sense, the only other difference Morris sees is that Kant recognized that such sensory consciousness barely deserves the name and fails to be our experience because it cannot provide its characteristic unity and wholeness. What can accomplish the latter is "self-consciousness," which unifies the work of the understanding's categories. With this explanation Kant tries to provide what Hume could not: "experience as an intelligibly connected system" (*EW* 1: 38). Pure sensationalism could never be an accurate description of our experience of synthetic a priori truths, or of our experience a as unified whole, since a series of isolated and externally related perceptions could never give rise to the truths of physical science nor the unity of self-consciousness (the nineteenth-century version of Descartes's dictum that the mind has no parts). All of the British neo-idealists agreed on this point with Kant, following Green in his decisive attacks on British empiricism. They also agreed that the ultimate criterion for success for Kant is whether our experience is completely accounted for. That is to say, the truths presented in experience itself require no justification. Much of Kant's *Critique of Pure Reason* revolves around them. Dewey states that when Kant "inquires what is the criterion of truth for the latter [actual experience], . . . the answer he finds to be 'possible experience' itself" (*EW* 1: 37). Hence, for Kant, the method by which we can verify and know all truths consists in looking to experience itself to see them. Dewey notes that

> On the one hand, the criterion of the categories is possible experience, and on the other, that the criterion of possible experience is the categories and their supreme condition [self-consciousness]. This is evidently a circle, yet a circle which, Kant would say, exists in the case itself, which expresses the very nature of knowledge. It but states that in knowledge there is naught but knowledge which knows or is known—the only judge of knowledge, of experience, is experience itself. (*EW* 1: 38)

Dewey has here begun his long relationship with the term "experience." In this article experience is just self-consciousness, which is also knowledge. The equation of experience with knowing is a defining mark of his early idealism and drives many of its arguments. As we have seen, it provided the way to eliminate the thing-in-itself. Since it impossible, according to Dewey, for there to be anything beyond the realm of self-consciousness (since we could not conceive of, or have knowledge of, such a thing), we must conclude that nothing can exist which is not in experience. Kant violated this Hegelian principle at least three times by affirming the thing-in-itself, the phenomena of sensible consciousness, and the categories of the synthetic unity of apperception. The easiest way to move from this disastrous position is to see what is left after getting rid of these three offending notions. If the (impossible) thing-in-itself is eliminated, along with the sensationalism, then the remainder is an experience in which the categories are imminent in, and not external to, experience: "the categories, in and through self-consciousness, constitute experience . . ." (*EW* 1: 38–39). Dewey thus goes back to the notion of experience which originally motivated Kant: experience as we find it is an intelligibly connected systematic whole. There can be no criterion of truth which relies on the existence of something which is not part of this experience, and no part of experience can be set up as the test for the rest, so Dewey is constrained to say that the criterion of truth is simply the whole of experience.

This vague answer is a rudimentary statement of a coherence theory of truth. Nothing beyond experience can determine what is true, and one portion of experience cannot be used to pass judgment on the rest. Dewey does not expand on the latter point, but we can supply an explanation by observing that for Kant, and also for Hegel, one result of accepting the systematicity of the categories comprising experience is that nothing within this whole receives sufficient priority so that it may ground the rest. As Caird quotes from Kant,

> Reason so constitutes a sphere so completely separated from all others, and so thoroughly united within itself, that we cannot intermeddle with any part without touching all the others, or settle a single point without determining for everything its place and relation to everything else. *Outside* of this sphere, there lies nothing that could better our judgment in regard to what lies within it; and *within* it, every element is dependent for its value and use in its relation to all the rest. And as in the structure of an organized body, the meaning and purpose of each member can only be deduced from the idea of the whole, so it may be said of such a criticism that it is not to be depended on, unless it has been brought to Absolute and exhaustive completeness, and that it has done nothing unless it has done everything.[21]

The "criticism" to which Kant refers is the complete account of the operations and bounds of reason. It is Dewey's goal as well, and it receives that name of "philosophic method," or the discovery of the criterion of truth. Kant here provides the key metaphor: the organism. It is hardly original with Kant, as Dewey points out in his 1888 *Leibniz's New Essays Concerning the Human Understanding*. However, it is in some regions of post-Kantian idealism that this metaphor develops from a mere analogy, used to help the reader understand an important viewpoint, into the guiding vision which carries an entire philosophy and without which the reader will never gain entrance. Morris appealed to this guiding vision, and it did not take Dewey long to be comfortable using it as well: "the relation of categories to experience is the relation of members of an organism to a whole" (*EW* 1: 38). The categories constitute the entirety of experience, and "method will consist in making out a complete table of these categories in all their mutual relations, giving each its proper placing" (*EW* 1: 39). So long as each category coheres with the rest, it is capable of carrying its share of the truth. It cannot provide absolute truth in itself; with the antinomies Kant proved, to the satisfaction of most idealists, including Morris and Dewey, that all the categories break down and are untrue if they are isolated and singly applied to absolute reality.[22]

Dewey does not elaborate on the connection between the notion of experience as organism and the relative adequacy of each of the categories to attain truth. He instead proceeds to tackle what must be the next question after having asserted that the categories exhaust experience: if Kant's aesthetic must be rejected as leftover sensationalism and if the categories are to be synthetic, just what are the categories supposed to be synthesizing? Dewey poses this question and supplies an answer.

> Previous methods failed because they made no allowance for synthesis—Kant's because the synthesis can occur only upon matter

foreign to it. Thought in the previous theories was *purely* analytic; in Kant's it is *purely* synthetic, in that it is synthesis of foreign material. Were thought at once synthetic *and* analytic, differentiating and integrating in its own nature, both affirmative and negative, relating to self at the same time that it related to other—indeed, through this relation to other—the difficulty would not have arisen. (*EW* 1: 40)

Dewey provides an example. When Kant believed that a human being's knowledge is conditioned by external things (objects) acting upon bodies (subjects) he was not mistaken. The Hegelian realization is that on this account (and indeed on all of the accounts provided by empirical psychologists), both the subject and object mentioned are *known* things, quite far from being unknown. For example, psychologists tell us that vision is dependent on physical light. Now, is this light a completely unknown entity? On the contrary there is a great deal of knowledge about it. We can recall here Dewey's similar argument in the preceding article. Remembering that, for the idealists, knowledge implies presence for self-consciousness and that this self-consciousness operates through the categories, Dewey concluded that the known object exists thanks to the work of the categories. Since the same argument can be made for the subject, Dewey says: "Yet this individual and these things are but known objects already constituted by the categories, and existing only for the synthetic unity of apperception or self-consciousness" (*EW* 1: 41). *Both* the subject and object of the psychologist are really known objects in the true sense of the term, and knowing self-consciousness remains the true subject.

This is hardly a helpful example of how reason can analyze experience into elements which can then be synthesized into knowledge. But this is not Dewey's goal, because he has equated experience with knowledge. This means that he must abandon the view that all knowledge is the result of synthesis. Knowledge cannot be the result of anything, because any attempt to find something prior to knowledge, prior to self-consciousness, must end in failure. This is indeed Dewey's position: everything in our experience is a known object. The known objects are constituted by (not created by) the categories. The categories are universals, and the objects are particulars which are composed of the cooperative work of categories. The categories can cooperate in such a way (analytically) so as to distinguish particulars (such as sunlight and human visual organs). These things then emerge (for the word "enter" would be incorrect, as it connotes that they existed prior to the categories' work) in our experience. Once distinguished (or differentiated, as the result of negation) they are materials for synthesis. Dewey is careful to point out that they are *known* materials prior to synthesis. This is the purpose of his great stress on the known character of the object conditioning the known subject in the above example.

The Organic Dialectic of Relations

Dewey often speaks of "relations" in this article, and a clarifying word must be said about this terminology. The distinction between external and internal relations has already been drawn when the Kantian viewpoint of the mechanical and reciprocal relations between the thing-in-itself, the phenomena, and the categories was criticized by the neo-idealists. These relations are also referred to as external relations because the effects they have on each other and the resulting product of their cooperation do not alter their own preexisting essential natures in any way. Just the opposite is true for internal relations, for on the neo-idealist view, things which have internal relations do not have essential preexisting essences prior to their cooperation in creating a product. The whole, which is composed of (and not created by) its constituent members, determines the nature of those members. We have returned to the metaphor of the organism, for while it is true that the whole organism is composed of member organs, these organs would lose their status *as organs* if they were considered apart from the whole organism. Thus the internal relation can also be referred to as the organic relation.

Both Morris and Caird believe that content and form, sense and concept, phenomena and category, can only exist where they are elements and members of the higher unities which we have in knowing experience. They agree that this is the true lesson, taught by Hegel, of Kant's efforts in the *Critique of Pure Reason*. When they are disposed to treat Kant charitably, they tell us that Kant should have realized that no part can exist separately after being torn out of the whole. His predisposition to empirical psychology led him to the notion that sensation and category have a nature independent of the other and that they interact mechanically in order to form our experience. However, post-Kantian criticisms, and especially Hegel's commentaries, have shown that both have an existence and a character only as members of a larger whole. Without this larger whole, they cannot exist. Accordingly Caird and Morris use the organic metaphor to indicate that when we speak of the elements of knowledge we must realize that we can understand what they are only through reference to a larger whole. These wholes are everywhere: they are the objects of our knowledge, they are the things in our experience, and even all of our experience in its entirety can be considered as a whole. When Dewey proceeds to describe further the relations holding between the subject and the object, he uses this language:

> Whether we consider the relations of subject and object, or the nature of the categories, we find ourselves forced into the presence of the notion of organic relation. The relation between subject and object is not an external one; it is one in a higher unity which is itself constituted by this relation. The only conception adequate to experience as a whole is organism. (*EW* 1: 42)

Does this help explain how Reason can be both analytic and synthetic, as Dewey immediately asserts after the above statement? It seems as if knowledge of members is required (resulting from analysis) before knowledge of a whole can be attained (resulting from synthesis). Yet Dewey has said that true knowledge of the members requires reference to the whole. Which came first, knowledge of the part or of the whole? Dewey does not say. He only repeats his contention that the correct philosophic method consists of finding the entire system of categories and determining the role each plays within it. "The method takes the totality of experience to pieces, and brings before us its conditions in their entirety. The relations of its content, through which alone this content has character and meaning, whereby it becomes an intelligible, connected whole, must be made to appear" (*EW* 1: 43). The method then seems to be that of first reducing experience to its components through analysis and then rebuilding it to discover all of the relations between the pieces through synthesis.

Dewey proceeds to discuss some features of post-Kantian idealism bearing on these issues, "found chiefly in Hegel and his 'Logic'" (*EW* 1: 43). He begins with Hegel's accusation that Kant assumed that the categories, while objective in the sense that they are uniform and permanent for all human beings (since, as Morris puts it, not even Kant would go so far as admit that his *Critique of Pure Reason* was only about his own reason),[23] these categories are still subjective in so far as they are in the realm of the mind-dependent and not the mind-independent. Kant had no right to assume the latter, by the following argument. As the purely mind-independent is impossible, so therefore the notion of the purely mind-dependent is also impossible, as the two notions gain their entire meaning only by opposition to one another. Put another way, there cannot be any purely objective or subjective existences, and thus it is impossible to consider thought and thing as residing in two separate realms. The notion of the individual mind is constituted by the cooperation of the categories and nothing else, as is the notion of the material object. In this way all of reality is constituted by the categories. As these are mental, reality consists of the operations of a mind whose operations can be traced through the dialectic of reason. This compressed argument provides the cornerstone of Hegelianism and neo-idealism: being and thought are not *ultimately* two different entities, though very often we take them to be so. Doing so can be justified only if we realize that reason distinguishes them within our self-consciousness. The categories are the medium for doing so, and hence they themselves cannot be either objective or subjective; they "belong to a sphere where the antithesis between subject and object is still potential" (*EW* 1: 44). The next section explains the notion of the negative in Hegel, making reference to the analytical abilities of Reason. Hegel stressed that the process of making distinctions, separating out objects, requires determinations; for example, red cannot be green. The extreme result of negation would be Hume's portrait of sensory experience, where each impression is unique and among them nothing in common can be found. Spinoza is Dewey's example of the opposite extreme, where every difference is illusory and must be absorbed into ultimate reality, which is but one pure substance. The advantage of Hegel's position lies in its permission for Reason to create both difference and unity.

Dewey gives the name "Dialectic" to the process of Reason by differentiating and unifying. Greater detail is provided as he briefly outlines the Hegelian scheme.

> Dialectic is the construction by Reason, through its successive differentiations and resumptions of the differences into higher unities, of just this system [of the categories in their organic entirety]. If we take any single category of Reason. . . . Reason itself is immanent in this category; but, since Reason is also differentiating or analytic, Reason must reveal itself as such in this category, which accordingly passes, or is reflected, or develops into its opposite, while the two conceptions are then resumed into the higher unity of a more concrete conception. (*EW* 1: 45–46)

Hegel's description of dialectic can be found in his *Logic*.[24] Hegel reserves the term "speculation" for the creation of the higher unity,[25] but Dewey compresses Hegel's account of the operations of Reason. Hegel's *Logic* cannot be discussed here. For our purposes, we need to see that Dewey has adopted the schema (but not the content) of the Hegelian dialectic as the means to attain the criterion of truth. According to Dewey, the dialectic allows us to see how all of the categories relate to each other organically, and will permit us to find the Absolute truth when the complete system is exposed. (*EW* 1: 46) While he does not use the term "Absolute" here, the entire system is the Absolute, and can be characterized also by the "Idea," which is the name for the last category produced by the final synthesis. Since the categories are properly termed "mental" (so long as no connotation of the subjective is retained) the Absolute is seen to be an Absolute mind or spirit. This conclusion, while expressed by Dewey, is exactly the essence of Morris's philosophy, announced and defended in every one of his articles and books. However, Morris rarely uses the term "dialectic" except as a term of derision, and nowhere incorporates it into his own philosophy. He adopted the view that all of the categories can be placed into organic relations in order to reveal the systematic whole, without inquiring into any details. Dewey adopts this view as well, but also in this article showed some interest in pursuing Hegel's dialectical method of finding this Absolute whole. However, like Morris, Dewey does not attempt to follow out such a dialectic, or comment on Hegel's attempt, in this published article or in any other. Nor will Dewey even mention dialectic in reference to his own philosophy ever again. However, the vision he presents of an organically developed system of categories will not fade quickly from his philosophy.

Absolute Idealism

The most important aspect of this article lies in Dewey's conception of a Reason which both analyses and synthesizes, demarcating both the objective and the subjective. It will also be used extensively in future articles, but it marks the first sign that Dewey is by no means shackled to the philosophical system expounded by his teacher and colleague G. S. Morris, because this conception of Reason is almost entirely absent from Morris's philosophy. Nowhere in Morris's writings can there be found any mention of the possibility that mind, Reason, or the understanding is responsible for creating the parts of experience which can then be synthesized. Morris tells us continually that all knowledge is the result of synthesis.[26] He tells us that the notion that there could exist on its own a realm where only disconnected phenomena reside is a notion proven completely false.[27] Morris even tells us that the objects of our knowledge can later be broken down into simple phenomena or impressions by a process of analysis: "the simple impression and its unity are, in the order of our knowledge or conception, late products of analytical abstraction."[28] But beyond these positions Morris never advanced.

Dewey was vitally interested in the question, if knowledge is only the result of synthesis, just what is being synthesized? Morris could not provide an answer, and it led Dewey to the pursuit of issues that Morris avoided. Dewey found in Kant the glimmerings of an answer: perhaps the mind was responsible for creating the elements so that they could enter self-consciousness before being synthesized. They must enter self-consciousness, lest they be unknown things-in-themselves and subject to philosophical expulsion by Dewey's own arguments. The place where he found the inspiration for this possibility is in Kant, who after having defended the position that for human beings the understanding can only operate on what the senses provide, remarks that perhaps for a divine being no senses are necessary. Both Caird and Morris repeat this remark. "Now, suppose that the conceiving understanding were to some being also a faculty of perception. Such a being would possess the power of 'intellectual intuition' or of perception through the understanding."[29] But Morris does not pursue this notion. Caird declares that "if indeed we had an understanding which generated as well as connected the manifold, which was a source of differentiation as well as integration—which, in other words, created its own object, then by such an understanding, self-consciousness could be realized without any matter being presented to it from without for synthesis."[30] Caird does follow up on the suggestion, and later says:

> In a sense, analysis and abstraction constitute an important and even a necessary step toward the truth. It is only when we sever the elements of knowledge from each other by analysis, that we can distinctly see the link of connection that binds them together. It is only when we isolate and fix in abstraction the correlated parts of the

organic whole of truth, that we become clearly conscious that they *are* correlated. Synthesis in the highest sense is possible, only when analysis has done its perfect work.[31]

Caird here has provided a way to understand Hegel's use of negation. It is mentioned by Hegel during a discussion of "Finite cognition" but for Hegel the Analytical and Synthetical methods are but "reason in the shape of understanding" and hence limited in value.[32] Caird elevates them to a higher status, and Dewey uses them for participation in dialectic. While negation is essential, as Dewey observes, its role can be better understood as being that of analysis. He adopts this view and incorporates it into his exposition of the dialectic, following Caird.[33] Caird takes the "organic whole of truth" as existing prior to our knowledge of its components' interrelatedness. Indeed, he must do so, since he believes both that all of consciousness consists of knowledge, and that all of our conscious experience consists of wholes, not parts. Thus we can only experience known wholes, and our knowledge of the parts only proceeds by keeping the whole in mind while we create abstractions, which will in turn be "smaller" wholes as well, linked with other "sub-wholes" in internal, organic relations to form the original whole. We can spot the links through the understanding's synthesizing function. Caird gives a glimpse at an alternative process.

> We begin in knowledge with a part, though this involves a false conception of the part as if it were a whole: but the effort to combine this part with other parts gives rise to a contradiction, which cannot cease till the abstraction of our first conception is corrected, or, in other words, till the parts are deprived of their false independence, and defined anew as elements of a greater whole.[34]

Here the influence of Hegel's logic is evident as Caird is describing a recognizable interpretation of the dialectic process. Our experience begins with a wide assortment of provided wholes. We realize that some "contradict" each other, and the effort to resolve the problem ensues with our understanding's synthetic efforts. Success comes when some of the wholes are gathered together, their independent natures are stripped from them, and they are combined by giving them new characteristics proceeding from the internal relations that they will have as members of a new organic whole. They might retain some of their features in the process, but no longer will it be possible to think that they could exist independent and unaltered apart from their new whole. This process of reducing conflict and contradiction is also recognizable as the effort to attain truth through coherence. At each stage along the way the new wholes are seen as being "more true" than the previous wholes which formed them. When we realize that Absolute truth will be reached only when all contradictions are eliminated, then we will consider our present conceptions of the world as only "relatively" true. Neo-idealism is marked by this common portrait of the efforts of the human mind, whether or not an idealist followed Hegel's own dialectical scheme (which few did) or agreed with Hegel that the process will terminate with only one final conception or "Idea" of the Absolute (which was also very controversial among idealists). Thus we can try to follow Dewey when he says near the conclusion of his article that

> Reason must be everywhere, and in all its forms, propose itself as what it is, viz., Absolute or adequate to the entire truth of experience; but, since at first its *form* is still inadequate, it must show what is Absolutely implicit in it, viz., the entire system. That at first it does, by doing what it is in the nature of the Reason which it manifests to do, by differencing itself, or passing into its opposite, its other; but, since Reason is also synthetic, grasping together, these differences must resolve themselves into a higher unity. (*EW* 1: 46)

The understanding of the world must be coherently whole, but it isn't now, because our understanding's conceptions, which together constitute all the things in our experience, contradict each other in all sorts of differences and opposites. There is awaiting us a systematic exposition of all of the content of our experience, but our understanding can't get at it yet. So the understanding or Reason goes about trying to unify the parts for which it is responsible, by synthesizing inadequately true parts into more adequately true wholes. The end of this process is a final conception which allows the understanding to conceive of all of the content of self-conscious experience at once. This conception is both absolutely true, and since self-consciousness exhausts all of reality, the conception captures all of reality.

We can now grasp the essence of Dewey's earliest absolute idealism. Hegelianism is characterized, among other things, by a refusal to consider being and thought as two ultimately different realms. Dewey agreed with this position, as we have seen. Therefore, the understanding, or Reason, which "captures all of reality" must therefore be nothing other than all of reality itself. This conclusion permits Morris to say that the entire organically related system of the activities of the understanding are nothing other than Absolute reality itself. Morris used the term "spirit" to denote the active understanding, and thus expressed his philosophy often by saying that Absolute reality is Spirit. Dewey does not use the term "spirit" in this article, preferring "Reason." He is not here concerned to equate this Reason with God, as is Morris, although he will do so later. However, they agree that Reason is Absolute reality.

The Psychological Standpoint

In 1885, while teaching at the University of Michigan with Morris, Dewey worked on two main enterprises. The first was a textbook on psychology, which had been in his plans since his freshman year at Johns Hopkins.[35] The second was an attempt to clear a philosophical space for his psychological views against rivals, which simultaneously could provide the grounds for a *rapprochement* between the traditional British philosophy and the new Germany-inspired neo-idealist philosophy. Here we will discuss the second enterprise first, as it has chronological as well as logical priority. Dewey's *Psychology* will be discussed in the next chapter. Dewey published two articles in *Mind*, receiving the "post of honor" to lead off two consecutive numbers; these were the January 1886 "The Psychological Standpoint," and the April 1886 "Psychology as Philosophic Method."

In "The Psychological Standpoint" Dewey attempts two tasks. First, he is trying to convert the dualist and the solipsist over to absolute idealism, using their own premises. Second, he wants to establish that for psychology to be a proper science, it cannot be limited to the study of individual consciousness alone, but must take into account knowledge of the Absolute consciousness. The article takes its name, not from Morris, Green, or Wundt, but from the neo-idealist James Seth and the British psychologist James Ward. These two philosophers each used the term "the psychological standpoint" prominently in the first significant work of their careers, in the same year: 1883. This coincidence probably struck the observant Dewey as really no mere coincidence, and besides providing him with an essay title, it gave a spark of light to the issues he was struggling with.

We find Dewey first using the term "psychological standpoint" in a letter he wrote in November 1883 to his former teacher, H. A. P. Torrey.[36] There Dewey describes his thoughts on the nature of the unconscious activities which must play an enormous role in determining our conscious experience. Such a role is given to the unconscious by not only neo-idealism but also by Wundtian psychology, which powerfully influenced Dewey's philosophy, as the next chapter reveals. Each employ a psychology in which mental processes operate upon materials to create conscious experience, but neither the processes nor the materials are consciously observable by us. Dewey's rejection of the possibility that they are permanently unknowable and beyond any and all consciousness leads him to the alternative view, that they are the content of a self-consciousness which transcends our own conscious experience and constitutes ultimate reality. He declares that his reasonings on this matter started from the "psychological standpoint" but concluded with the transcendentalist Absolute self-consciousness. This consciousness is permanent (eternal, without origin or decay), identical (a complete unity), and supportive of all the states of consciousness we experience. The details of such support need elaboration, but Dewey believes that the best approach is to consider unconscious psychical activities as functions through which the mind apperceives. He has worked out the outline of a plan which could hopefully preserve both the theories of psychology and the demands of absolute idealism. The foundation would be the "psychological standpoint."

Absolute Idealism

Seth's work was his "Philosophy as Criticism of Categories," a contribution to a collection of neo-idealist thought published in 1883 called *Essays in Philosophical Criticism*. There Seth criticized Kant, as did Green, for failing to completely renounce the "psychological standpoint" inherent in British philosophy. For the British, this standpoint treated human experience as the result of an external physical world mechanically acting upon an individual mind. Kant failed to complete his *Critique*, Seth argued, by failing to examine this most basic assumption about the origin of experience. This failure's fruit was the retention of paradoxical and contradictory notions: the thing-in-itself, the chasm between the *a priori* and the *a posteriori*, and the mechanistic theory of the origin of experience. Hence Kantianism requires a purification and reconstruction in which the origin, purpose, and interrelationships of the categories of experience can be fully understood. Seth did not use Hegelian themes to accomplish this reconstruction. He, like Green, had as many complaints against Hegel as he did against Kant, and so this essay remains on a critical and negative plane. Dewey, however, would have been very sympathetic to Seth's critique of British empiricism and Kant, as it confirmed Morris's own criticisms. Seth later created a furor over the independent existence of the individual self, defending it against what he viewed as a complete annihilation by Hegelian absolutism. Dewey took great interest in this scandalous development; we will encounter Seth again in chapter four.

Ward's 1883 article in *Mind*, "Psychological Principles I: The Standpoint of Psychology," along with its second part and their inclusion in his 1886 *Encyclopaedia Brittanica* article "Psychology," was quickly and widely influential. His work in the 1880s has been credited with nothing less than the destruction of the foundations of associationalistic empiricism and faculty-psychology.[37] Ward rejected the existence of discontinuous elements of experience requiring a mental uniting process, in favor of an experience characterized by continuity and unity through a process of gradual and flux-like change. He owed these views to influences from German psychology and philosophy: Kant, Herbart, Lotze, Wundt, and Brentano.[38] With them Ward effected a quick revolution in British and American psychology nearly single-handedly. Two philosophers in particular appreciated Ward's work on this topic, as they were making very similar efforts: William James and Shadworth Hodgson. James himself was much indebted both to Ward and to Hodgson.[39] All three espoused what was called the "stream of consciousness" perspective on experience, which Hodgson was the first to mention and use in a philosophical publication in 1878.[40]

To British philosophy Ward owed his principle that psychology dealt with *individual* experience, that is, with experience as it for individual lives. He called this principle "the standpoint of psychology." Other standpoints include that of the "concrete" sciences, like mineralogy and botany, or the "abstract" sciences, like metaphysics. Psychology, argued Ward, takes a unique standpoint on experience, the psychological standpoint, when it undertakes its responsibility to investigate the whole of experience individualistically.[41] A universalistic standpoint would consider the objects and events of experience insofar as they are for all, or as they are objectively. Psychology does not deal with experience in such a manner, as it is instead concerned with experience as it is subjectively, for the individual.

> Of all the facts with which he [the psychologist] deals, the psychologist may truly say that their *esse* is *percipi;* inasmuch as all his facts are facts of presentation, are ideas in Locke's sense, or objects which imply a subject.... Psychology, then, never transcends the limits of the individual: even the knowledge that there is a real world, as common-sense assumes, is, when psychologically regarded, an individual's knowledge, which had a beginning and a growth, and can have an end.[42]

In this manner Ward decides that the standpoint of the psychologist on experience should be that of the subjective idealist. He does not mean that the psychologist must assume this metaphysical viewpoint personally—rather, the psychologist is studying experience as it is without any ontological commitments, and thus as it is for a subjective idealist. In this standpoint, everything exists solely for the subject. It is the psychologist's task to study the genesis of human experience in all its forms and modes, as traditional British philosophy asserts. However, the results of such study have no bearing on epistemology, according to Ward, and he thus rejects the attempt to use psychology to give an account of the origin, process, or limit to knowledge. Epistemology is concerned with questions about what we *ought* to believe or hold to be true, but psychology can only explain how we in fact come to our beliefs. Psychology cannot have a bearing on epistemology because psychology's own principles rely on a theory of knowledge; as a science it must, and does, take for granted some epistemological tenets. To ask that it attempt to justify a theory of knowledge would send it on a viciously circular track.[43] For Ward then, psychology must assume an ontology, including the existence of the subject for whom experience occurs, and a theory of knowledge which permits it to make truth claims.

Dewey begins "The Psychological Standpoint" article by noting that, thanks to Green's writings, the essential disagreement between German transcendentalism and British empiricism has been laid bare. He does not enter into a discussion of Green's efforts, but he is drawing his readers' attention to Green's attacks in his introductions to the *Works* of Hume, where empiricist sensationalism is assailed for destroying the possibility of self-consciousness. Dewey's deep appreciation for Green's efforts and their incorporation into his own philosophy is expressed: "It is the *psychological* standpoint which is the root of all the differences, as Professor Green has shown with such admirable lucidity and force" (*EW* 1:

Absolute Idealism

122–123). After praising Green, Dewey immediately abandons him and proposes to recast the whole issue. Instead of seeing in Green's criticisms the demonstration of a fundamental impasse on the basic nature of experience between the two traditions, Dewey offers a way of seeing a fundamental agreement. We should not find in empiricism an incorrect psychological standpoint, as Green did, but rather fault empiricism for a failure to hold consistently to the psychological standpoint for which it was originally responsible. Dewey offers the uniting principle, the psychological standpoint, which British philosophers have championed as the true philosophic starting point and method:

> We are not to determine the nature of reality or of any object of philosophical inquiry by examining it as it is in itself, but only as it is an element in our knowledge, in our experience, only as it is related to our mind, or is an "idea".... Or, in the ordinary way of putting it, the nature of all objects of philosophical inquiry is to be fixed by finding out what experience says about them. (*EW* 1: 123)

Dewey also makes reference to this principle elsewhere in the article by stating that all knowledge is relative: it is always relative to, or dependent on, consciousness. His attraction to this principle is apparent if we recall how he stressed in previous publications that experience itself must be the sole arbiter of reality and truth. Nothing beyond the realm of conscious experience can be appealed to when doing philosophy; the existence of vast dangers and contradictions involved there have been amply demonstrated by the neo-idealists. This principle was also of utmost importance to British philosophers, who understandably claimed it as their characteristic guiding light and method. To accuse another philosopher of abandoning experience in favor of some assumption, formula, presupposition, a priori tenet, or the like was the dismissal of choice in philosophical debate of that era.

After requiring that philosophy consistently look to experience, Dewey says that psychology is "the scientific and systematic account of that experience." Without providing any elaboration or justification for this abrupt pronouncement, he asks that the reader not assume that psychology should make "any assumption regarding its 'individual' or 'introspective' character" (*EW* 1: 123–124). Having stated his version of the psychological standpoint, the need for clarification on the purpose and domain of psychology stands out in sharp relief. But Dewey is content at this stage to move on to a discussion of how British philosophers, having affirmed the psychological standpoint, went on in their philosophies to forget and violate it. The long and short of the poor history of British philosophy goes like this: Locke explained experience using unknowable substances, Berkeley used a transcendent God, and Hume used unknowable sensations. Dewey does take the trouble to reiterate the neo-idealist attack on sensations since he anticipates the objection that Hume did not appeal to any unknowables but rather simply analyzed experience into its components to reveal that experience is ultimately composed of grouped and organized sensations. Dewey states his agreement with this method and the existence of sensations but points out that, as the results of analysis, they are known entities. On this interpretation, Hume then decided that they must also be capable of existing prior to conscious, knowing experience. Dewey finds this move to be fallacious:

> The dependence of our knowledge upon sensations—or rather that knowledge is nothing but sensations as related to each other—is not denied. What is denied is the correctness of the procedure which, discovering a certain element *in* knowledge to be necessary for knowledge, therefore concludes that this element has an existence prior to or apart from knowledge. (*EW* 1: 125)

Such a conclusion does not worry a philosopher who is untroubled by the assertion of entities beyond the realm of knowledge, but this philosopher has obviously forgotten the psychological standpoint and has gone over to ontology or metaphysics (*EW* 1: 126–127). Dewey has consolidated his central philosophical vision by wrapping up the value he found in the neo-idealists' critiques of empiricism and Kant. It would not be too much to say that with this principle—that elements found within knowledge should not be taken to have an independent existence beyond or before knowledge—Dewey cleared the start of a revolutionary path for his career. The specific application here, to the question of the prior existence of sensations, is found throughout the rest of his career. He never lost an opportunity to chastise philosophers, be they self-proclaimed empiricists, realists, or idealists, for assuming that the knowledge process starts from prior given sensations.

In regard to Ward's statement of the nature of psychological inquiry, Dewey has charged Ward with a fundamental error of procedure. By taking a person's experience really to be only what the psychologist finds it to be, the psychologist is only substituting existences of his own creation for whatever truly occurs in that person's experience. However, it is not only experimental psychologists who can make this error. Anyone who introspectively analyzes their experience can isolate various elements and mistakenly believe that these elements must have existed prior to their isolation. Irrespective of whether sensations are "discovered" by one's own introspective efforts, or by the psychologist's scientific inquiries, the true origin of such "original" sensations lies in nothing other than the discoverer's own intellectual processes. Sensations exist *only for knowledge;* Dewey from the very beginning of his career rejected any empiricist or neo-Kantian claim to the contrary. The seeds of his discontent with fellow idealists were sown here, and with this thrown gauntlet of challenge Dewey has done nothing less than effectively to proclaim himself, and himself alone, to be the true idealist. The full details of this internecine quarrel will be discussed shortly, but first it must be made clear that Dewey on this issue has anticipated in print his fellow pragmatist, William James, by four years. James's 1890 *Principles of Psychology* also exposed the unfortunate prevalence of what he called the "psychologist's fallacy," in which the psychologist confuses "his own standpoint with that of the mental fact about which he is making his report."[44] Dewey adopted the term "psychologist's fallacy" soon after. This adoption has caused many commentators to infer that he learned that sensations could not be independent of knowledge from James. For example, J. E. Tiles asserts that until reading James, Dewey was an ordinary neo-Kantian who held that sensations are originally unrelated and meaningless until synthesized by the mind's categories to create experience.[45] But this is, as shown above, precisely the idealistic doctrine that Dewey initially *rejected*. Dewey *never* was a neo-Kantian, unlike T. H. Green, but rather a neo-Hegelian, and a rather unique one at that.

The "psychological standpoint" gradually evolved in later years into the "postulate of immediate empiricism." The key difference is that the latter principle clearly exposes the standpoint's main implication: knowledge exists and grows only within a larger context of other kinds of experiences. The germ of this realization already exists, however, in Dewey's limited grasp of the Hegelian cycles of intellectual analysis and synthesis, acting on more and more thoroughly known experience. Even by 1905 the main obstacle for most other philosophers has survived unchanged; they still assume that some elements within an experience as known must have existed prior to that knowledge. Armed with this assumption, they create innumerable puzzles, looking for the cause of the contrast between the selected stimulus as first experienced and as later known. The cause, the consensus seems to be, is that the original sensation was *subjectively* experienced, distorting its "real" nature, while the sensation as known is *objective*, revealing its real nature. The first only really existed in one's mind; the second is a revelation of reality as it really is. The utter pointlessness of this entire chain of reasoning always frustrated Dewey. Realist and idealist alike get trapped in that miserable debate called epistemology only because of a fallacious first step, which only immediate empiricism (as Dewey elaborated in the first decade of the twentieth century) can avoid.

> I start and am flustered by a noise heard. Empirically, that noise is fearsome; it really is, not merely phenomenally or subjectively so. That is what it is experienced as being. But, when I experience the noise as a known thing, I find it to be innocent of harm. It is the tapping of a shade against the window, owing to movements of the wind. The experience has changed; that is, the thing experienced has changed—not that an unreality has given place to a reality, nor that

some transcendental (unexperienced) Reality has changed, not that truth has changed, but just and only the concrete reality experienced has changed. (*MW* 3: 160)

The evident contrast between the initial and later experience is, if one assumes that "the tapping of the shade" is the "real" sensation revealed by knowledge, a matter of concern requiring explanation. On that assumption, since the first experience does not contain "shade tapping" but only a fearful noise, the fear must be the result of subjective emotional superimposition. Immediate empiricism rejects this logic: the shade tapping, as created by knowledge, must not be read back into the original experience as the "real" stimulus to the fearful experience. In his 1915 "The Logic of Judgments of Practice" Dewey again identifies this fallacious move as the root cause of all epistemological pseudo-problems.

> As matter of fact every proposition regarding what is "given" to sensation or perception is dependent upon the assumption of a vast amount of scientific knowledge which is the result of a multitude of prior analyses, verifications, and inferences. What a combination of Tantalus and Sisyphus we get when we fancy that we have cleared the slate of all these material implications, fancy that we have really started with simple and independent givens, and then try to show how from these original givens we can arrive at the very knowledge which we have all the time employed in the discovery and fixation of the simple sense data! (*MW* 8: 64)

The "psychological standpoint" is therefore central to the development of Dewey's philosophy. But at this early stage of his career he also believed what he would later deny, that knowing experience and conscious experience were identical. This principle and the psychological standpoint are nevertheless compatible, and they shaped Dewey's approach to the question of how experience originates.

Individual and Universal Consciousness

Dewey realized that psychologists and philosophers often picture to themselves the origin of experience by considering an infant who must be receiving pure, unadulterated sensations. They are able to conceive how the environment stimulates and causes the sensations for the baby. These sensations can be referred to as the "relation" between the organic body and the stimulating environment (*EW* 1: 128–129), and experimenters can try to understand the relations that hold between the outer stimulus and the inner response. Dewey claims that he has no objection to this attempt to understand such an origin of knowledge, since it is the sort of psychology of which he approves. He avoids contradicting himself by distinguishing between two kinds of consciousness: the individual and the universal. He has no problem with any attempt to understand scientifically the origins of *individual* consciousness. But since consciousness is not exhausted by the sum of all the individual consciousnesses, the comprehension of their origin in no way provides an explanation of the origin of *all* of consciousness. Dewey points out that, during a psychologist's explanation of the baby's consciousness, the psychologist uses known entities: the environment, the baby, the sensation. All of these exist in consciousness and not beyond it: "Surely it is not a baby thing-in-itself which is affected, nor a world thing-in-itself which calls forth the sensation" (*EW* 1: 128). How could we make reference to them or experiment on them, otherwise? And if all along the psychologist only used known entities in the explanation,

> Consequently he is not accounting for the origin of consciousness or knowledge at all. He is simply accounting for the origin of an individual consciousness, or a specific group of known facts, by reference to the larger group of known facts or universal consciousness. . . . in short, that the *becoming* of consciousness exists for consciousness only, and hence that consciousness can never have become at all. That for which all origin and change exists, can never have originated or changed. (*EW* 1: 129)

The dizzying use of the term "consciousness" with quite different meanings obscures Dewey's intentions. He often forgets to specify which kind of consciousness he means when he simply uses the term "consciousness" alone. We must determine whether he means the individual subjective consciousness, the universal objective consciousness, or simply consciousness in the unprejudiced denotative sense which he asked his readers to adopt at the outset for the purposes of the article. Dewey uses the third meaning while arguing for his major points, as he needs common ground between himself and his readers. When for other purposes he takes for granted the established existence of individual and universal consciousness, he sometimes simply uses "consciousness" for one or the other. We shall have to understand his intentions through the context. And when he has shown that the individual and universal consciousnesses arise from consciousness proper, he will refer to it as absolute consciousness. In the above quotation the lone term "consciousness" is used denotatively. It has at least the following characteristics: it had no origin, it cannot change, it encompasses all known facts, and individual consciousnesses somehow share and grow in it without encompassing all of it. A reasonable question is whether consciousness and universal consciousness are exactly identical in meaning for Dewey. The answer is that they cannot be identified. His position on consciousness is an echo of Green.

> Should the question be asked, If this self-consciousness is not derived from nature, what then is its origin? the answer is that it has no origin. It never began, because it never was not. It is the condition of there being such a thing as beginning or end. Whatever begins or ends does so for it or in relation to it.[46]

Dewey characterizes the relationship between the individual and the universal consciousness and the role of the psychologist at this point by saying that the psychologist studies how consciousness differentiates and develops itself into different forms, or sets of relations, which constitute the individual consciousnesses, using elements of universal consciousness, for example, the known baby (*EW* 1: 129–130). This genetic account will discover the relations which hold between all of the elements of consciousness, thus discovering the "relations of subject and object, and the relations of Universal and Individual, or Absolute and Finite" (*EW* 1: 131). The first task is taken up in part 2 of the article, and the second task in part 3. This list of tasks for psychology indicates that Dewey regards the individual and the universal consciousnesses as elements *within* consciousness itself. He accordingly finds that when a psychologist assumes at the outset of inquiry that consciousness is subjective or individual solely, a violation of the psychological standpoint has taken place since the issue of whether consciousness is individual or not must be settled by looking to consciousness with an unprejudiced eye. Unfortunately psychology has been afflicted with the assumption that consciousness is subjective only. Two schools of philosophy result: reasoned, or transfigured, realism and subjective idealism. For Dewey the former is the dualistic position of Locke's representationalism and Kant's transcendental idealism, while the latter is the typical British approach best represented by the phenomenalism of John Stuart Mill and Alexander Bain.

These philosophies share a goal with each other and with Dewey: to try to find a way to reconcile two undoubted theses, *first*, that all knowledge must be relative to consciousness, and *second*, that consciousness is relative and dependent upon something beyond it (*EW* 1: 132). Dewey accepts both theses. The problem is one of correct interpretation and explanation so that both can be consistently accepted as true. Reasoned realism makes its attempt using the "unknowable" or the "thing-in-itself" to account for the second thesis but thereby violates the first thesis. Subjective idealism distinguishes within consciousness the subjective and objective consciousness. It declares that the objective consciousness is the external and material universe ordered by space and time, while the subjective consciousness is the internal realm (the ego or mind proper) characterized by feelings, emotions, and ideas (*EW* 1: 134).

Subjective idealism, Dewey claims, confuses consciousness in the broad sense (as including both subject and object) with subjective consciousness. This claim by itself is not supportable on the evidence Dewey has produced and thus appears very weak. He interprets subjective idealism as holding that the subjective consciousness is all that truly exists and that this consciousness is capable of producing the objective world, which is still part of itself after all. "The essence of Subjective Idealism is that the subject consciousness or mind, which remains after the 'object world has been subtracted,' is that for which after all this object world exists. . . . to Subjective Idealism, the consciousness for which all exists is the consciousness which is called mind, Ego, 'my being'" (*EW* 1: 135). This interpretation is self-contradictory, as Dewey explains, but it is far from clear that Bain, or any other philosopher of that time, believes that the subjective ego is all that exists, as evidenced by the quotations from Bain which Dewey uses. Ward himself makes this point.[47] Bain's position lies far from Berkeley's idealism and should be classified instead with phenomenalism. This seems to escape Dewey, and thus he fails to see that phenomenalism is far closer to his own position than the perceived subjective idealism.

There is something disturbing Dewey which prevents him from fully understanding phenomenalism, and it lies in the mentioned assertion by Bain and others that psychology, or mental science, has to deal with the ego, or mind proper, only, leaving the objective realm to natural science (*EW* 1: 134). Interestingly Ward rejects this position, claiming that, by the psychological standpoint, psychology must analyze the distinction between subjective and objective consciousness and show how it arises from the presentations. The term "presentations" is Ward's denotative term for experience, analogous to Dewey's "consciousness," and is used for the same reason, as Ward finds the predominant "phenomena" too connotatively stained.[48] Hence with this pronouncement Ward has duplicated Dewey's position. However, Ward has still retained his own distinct version of the psychological standpoint: "the facts of psychology and the facts of physics are, as known *to somebody,* both facts alike facts of psychology, whatever else they may be." Again: "the removal of the subject removes . . . all presentation or possibility of presentation whatever." And again: "the natural outcome of speculation from the psychological standpoint is [subjective] idealism."[49]

Ward thus tries to do two contradictory things, which attracts Dewey's close attention. Ward first says that psychology can and should be responsible for seeing how the subject-object distinction arises from presentations (Dewey's "consciousness"), but then tells the psychologist that such an endeavor is possible only by assuming that this distinction arises *in a subject's* presentations (Dewey's "individual consciousness"). This contradiction provoked Dewey's criticisms, and his proposed resolution. What if

> it were admitted that this subject, mind, and the object, matter, are both but *elements within,* and both exist only *for,* consciousness—we should be in the sphere of an eternal Absolute consciousness, whose

partial realization both the individual "subject" and the "external world" are. . . . The only possible hypothesis upon which to reconcile the two statements that mind is consciousness with the object world subtracted, and that it is the whole of our conscious experience, including both subject and object world, is that the term "Mind" is used in two entirely different senses in the two cases. In the first it must be individual mind, or consciousness, and in the second it must be Absolute mind or consciousness, for and in which alone the individual or subject consciousness and the external world or object consciousness exist and get their reality. (*EW* 1: 135, 136)

Put another way, the subjective and objective find a common origin and unity in the absolute consciousness. Here it must be remembered that when Dewey uses the term "unity" he does not mean identity. He is referring to the organic unity, in which elements possess their essential natures and functions only because of their relationships inside an encompassing whole that unites them together. Thus Dewey's position is that the individual and the universal arise from, gain their nature from, and have a unity within the larger whole of absolute consciousness. To understand this position better, ask this question: is the absolute consciousness something beyond an individual consciousness? For Dewey this question must be answered in the negative, as the better way of expressing their relationship is to say that the individual consciousness is but a way of viewing the absolute consciousness and that this way of viewing places a limitation on consciousness, creating the element of individual consciousness. Another question would be that if the absolute consciousness is not beyond individual consciousness, does this imply that my individual consciousness exhausts all of consciousness and hence all reality? Dewey's answer is no because individual consciousness is by nature limited. For an organic whole neither the elements nor the functions can be understood, known, except by reference to other elements and functions of the whole and the whole itself. Morris's curious attempt at a dialogue with a human hand tries to make this same point and by analogy attempts to demonstrate how the individual self-consciousness must, in light of its ability to universalize and know objective reality, find itself to be a functioning member of the absolute spiritual realm.[50] Dewey has undertaken a proof of the same point. He agrees with Ward that psychology must take all of conscious experience for its material and only requests that this principle be maintained consistently as the true and valid psychological standpoint. The presupposition that experience, *all* consciousness, is necessarily subjective and individual takes an ontological or metaphysical standpoint instead, as it requires an assumed understanding of the distinction between the objective and the subjective realms of reality. An echo of the logic driving Dewey's earlier attacks on the "agnostic fallacy" is heard here. The natural objection, which he raises himself, asks how it is possible that the

Absolute Idealism

individual consciousness can know the universal consciousness, since it is his own admission that the individual can be distinguished from the universal. If it cannot, then the universal consciousness is an unknowable thing-in-itself. If it can, then it is just within the individual consciousness anyway, and so only the individual consciousness exists from the start (*EW* 1: 138–139).

Dewey's answer starts by making the point that this objection assumes that he holds that individual consciousness and universal consciousness are mutually exclusive and jointly exhaustive for all of consciousness from the start. But this is not Dewey's position. Since the subjective and the objective find their origin and unity in absolute consciousness, what one typically calls "my consciousness" really is, at bottom, no such thing. Consciousness taken in a certain manner, that is, as the feelings, emotions, ideas, etc., of consciousness, forms our understanding of "my consciousness." But consciousness, experience, is not limited to such experiences as these. Here Dewey parts with Bain, Ward, and all others who believe that experience (consciousness) is by nature limited and individualized. He agrees with those who find great significance in the discoveries of physiology, biology, and evolution. They point to the dependence of individual consciousness on biological and physical processes, which extend continuously from the far past to the present and are hence mostly prior to personal minds. But Dewey then points out that our knowledge about these events implies that an individual consciousness can transcend itself and know how it arose. British psychology has long been doing this; the universal standpoint is taken whenever an attempt is made (for example, by the "plain historical method" of Locke) to explain how experience, beliefs, or knowledge arise in individual minds (*EW* 1: 140–142). It is sheer perversity to have accomplished so much in this science only then to ask the question which typically commences the frustrating epistemological enterprise: if I am limited to my individual experience, how can I ever have knowledge about that which must be beyond it? Dewey is trying to show that the only way you could ever know yourself to be a limited consciousness requires you to first know a larger whole, of which your individual consciousness will be then but a portion. In brief the only way for this epistemological question to start is already to know the answers and then forget them. Dewey's final conclusion is that individual consciousness cannot exhaust all of consciousness.

In his summary Dewey manages completely to confuse the issues with loose terminology. He abruptly drops the term "Absolute consciousness" and uses "universal consciousness" in its place, departing from Bain's and Ward's usage of "universal."

> Consciousness has shown that it involves *within* itself a process of becoming, and that this process becomes conscious of itself. This process is the individual consciousness; but, since it is conscious of

> itself, it is consciousness of the universal consciousness. All consciousness, in short, is self-consciousness, and the self is the universal consciousness, for which all process is and which, therefore, always is. The individual consciousness is but the process of realization of the universal consciousness through itself. Looked at as process, as realizing, it is individual consciousness; looked at as produced or realized, as consciousness of the process, that is, of itself, it is universal consciousness. (*EW* 1: 142)

It is unfortunate that Dewey changed his terminology, since it confuses the reader and makes a large difference to the theory. We can see the change best with three selections from three consecutive pages. "Since consciousness does show the origin of individual and universal consciousness *within itself,* consciousness is therefore both universal and individual" (*EW* 1: 140). "The psychological standpoint is necessarily a universal standpoint..." (*EW* 1: 141). "It [individual consciousness] knows that it has its origin in processes which exist for the universal self, and that therefore the universal self has never become" (*EW* 1: 142). We can see that initially both universal (objective) and individual (subjective) consciousness are manifestations of absolute consciousness, and universal consciousness has an origin. Then abruptly Dewey forgets his dictum that the psychological standpoint must be neither individual nor universal. At the end of the article there are only two kinds of consciousness, the universal and the individual, and the universal consciousness can never have an origin. We must explain this significant alteration, as well as account for his first mention of two things: self-consciousness and a "process of realization."

The use of the term "self" connects Dewey with Morris, who through great stress on the term was able to preserve personality at every level of spirit. Dewey here expresses his agreement that all consciousness is self-consciousness, that is, consciousness is necessarily a continuously organic whole without divisions or separations. Accordingly both the individual and the universal consciousnesses are self-consciousnesses, but there are not really two completely distinct selves—there can be ultimately only one, the universal. The individual self is an aspect, an element within the universal, but it nonetheless possesses a wholeness, a self. The thesis that the universal consciousness realizes itself through a process involving the "becoming" or growth of the individual also connects Dewey with T. H. Green. The essence of Green's metaphysics is that all of reality, since it must depend on concrete universal relations lest it fall apart into an impossible chaos, is composed of objective phenomena resting in a synthesized, organic, and absolute whole. Since relations are essentially mental, the universal absolute is mental or self-consciousness. This argument and its conclusion is precisely Morris's in his post-1880 writings. He never tired of emphasizing the doctrine that everything requires the relational synthesizing activity of intelligence for its

Absolute Idealism

existence. As for the question of the relationship between the whole and human knowledge, Green states that

> the system of related facts, which forms the objective world, reproduces itself, partially and gradually, in the soul of the individual who in part knows it.... [O]ur knowledge of any part of the system implies a like union of the manifold in relation ... [and] is only possible through the action upon feelings of a subject distinguishing itself from them. This being so, it would seem that the attainment of the knowledge is only explicable as a reproduction of itself, in the human soul, by the consciousness for which the cosmos of related facts exists—a reproduction of itself, in which it uses the sentient life of the soul as its organ.[51]

Dewey's first theory, call it the "emergence" theory, is that both the objective and the subjective together arise out of a logically prior absolute consciousness and thereby entertain mutual relations between them. But at the conclusion we find instead hints of the "reproduction" theory: Green's vision of the objective, absolute consciousness recreating itself in a subjective and individual self by way of the sensory experience, thereby engendering superior/subordinate relations. On Green's theory there are only two modes of consciousness. On Dewey's emergence theory there are three modes of consciousness. Their disagreement is serious and is not merely an apparent one caused by terminological problems.

The emergence theory finds in universal consciousness only partiality and abstractness, while the latter finds universal consciousness self-sufficient and complete. The idea that the objective world, constituting the entire absolute consciousness, must reproduce itself and recreate its systematic relations inside the individual so that it may be known to the individual is completely foreign to the emergence theory. On the emergence theory absolute consciousness is to be left completely uncharacterized as neither universal nor individual. Also there is no need at all for the individual to undergo limited and partial experience, taking the contribution of universal consciousness to gain knowledge of the whole. The universal and individual are already united by something more fundamental: the absolute consciousness. On the reproduction theory, if it were not for sensory experience, the individual presumably would be forever cut off by that dualism between it and the absolute consciousness.

The best explanation for Dewey's confusion seems to be that while he is trying to convert his British opponents over to absolute idealism and to show to them and his fellow idealists that psychology cannot be limited to the study of individual consciousness, he wants to use the term "consciousness" in an unprejudiced, uncommitted, and fundamental manner. Here both the individual and the universal consciousnesses require each other and the absolute consciousness for their unity. But at the conclusion of the article, as Dewey enjoys the fruits of his labors, the real fundamental reality announces itself as the universal consciousness, and the individual consciousness becomes solely dependent on it instead. The "aspect" tactic, where consciousness can appear now individual, now universal, depending on the viewpoint taken toward consciousness, is replaced by the "realization" tactic, in which universal consciousness fundamentally exists and gains knowledge of itself only by reproducing itself into an individualized and partial consciousness.

Dewey, although forcing a substantial agreement between his results and Green's at the end of the article, should not on these grounds be classified as an obedient disciple. His follow-up article, "Psychology as Philosophic Method," announces Dewey's disagreements with Green and other neo-idealists.

Psychology as Philosophic Method

Dewey's search for the philosophic method, begun with the "Kant and Philosophic Method" article, continues with the April 1886 "Psychology as Philosophic Method." In the former article he found in Hegelian dialectic the means to determine how all of the categories of experience organically relate. In this article Dewey announces that psychology, since it must examine both the universal and individual consciousnesses and all the relations between them (as shown in "The Psychological Standpoint"), must be the ultimate science of reality, contra both the British empirical tradition and the neo-idealists. Dewey argues that there is nothing more fundamental for philosophy to do. Side issues, such as the philosophy of nature or the science of logic, can remain with philosophy proper (*EW* 1: 148). But if the aim is to account for, and give meaning to, all the elements of experience, psychology is in the best position to accomplish every explanation required, and hence it can no longer be considered as merely one of the specific sciences.

The Primacy of Psychology

Dewey's article argues that the fundamental character of neo-idealism, resting on its insistence that all reality is self-consciousness, is at odds with the notion, shared by both T. H. Green and Edward Caird, that humanity can be regarded in two opposed manners. People can be regarded as limited and individual objects within objective reality so that the objective relations of action and reaction between the environment and the organism's mental phenomena can be studied. They can also be the unlimited, universal self-consciousness which encompasses all relations and experiences. According to these leading neo-idealists, psychology is that objective, concrete science which deals with humanity in the former manner, while philosophy is the universal science dealing with humanity in the latter manner. Psychology for the idealists thus studies how the limited consciousness of humanity develops out of the absolute consciousness (*EW* 1:

145–147). Hence there is a sizeable agreement among many British psychologists and neo-idealists on the task of psychology. The only significant difference is that the latter group finds the objective realm to be a manifestation of absolute consciousness, instead of unknowable matter (Locke, Spencer), or the objective portion of an individual mind (Bain). Dewey accordingly attacks the neo-idealists much in the same manner as he attacked British philosophy: he points out that if psychology is to study how the objective realm manifests itself in an individual consciousness, psychology must already be in a position to study the entire realm of reality of both the individual and the universal consciousness. Psychology cannot allow consciousness to be pre-divided into two modes or kinds. It cannot be asked to limit its study to the effects of the one upon the other, and then told to consider itself as merely one of the abstract, partial sciences, studying only an aspect of humanity.

> Psychology, as science of the realization through the individual of the universe, answers the question as to the significance of the whole, and at the same time gives the meaning of the parts and of their connection by showing just their place within this whole. . . . Self-consciousness means simply an individualized universe; and if this universe has *not* been realized in man, if man be not self-consciousness, then no philosophy whatsoever is possible. If it *has* been realized, it is in and through psychological experience that this realization has occurred. Psychology is the scientific account of this realization, of this individualized universe, of this self-consciousness. What other account can be given? (*EW* 1: 148, 149)

The conclusion is that if psychology is to study just individual consciousness, it cannot do so without knowledge of, and reference to, the universal consciousness. Hence it must study all the relations between the individual and the universal consciousness. But when it does that, all pretense that psychology is a limited, abstract science must be dropped. The idea that philosophy is more fundamental than psychology must also be abandoned. Hence they must merge as one science, and there is really no distinction between humanity as a limited consciousness and as the absolute consciousness. Dewey does not question this distinction's *relative* validity, as it makes the science of psychology possible, but as the distinction arises within conscious experience itself (as it must—otherwise how else could we know the distinction?) then it comes within psychology's purview.

> Man in his experience, at different *stages* of it, finds it necessary to regard himself in two lights,—in one of which he is a particular space- and time-conditioned being . . . and in the other the unconditioned eternal synthesis of all. At most the distinction is only one

of various stages in one and the same experience, both of which, as stages of experience—one, indeed, of experience in its partiality and the other of experience in its totality—fall within the science of experience, viz., psychology. (*EW* 1: 150)

Here we have the first mention of the stages of psychological experience. We must take note of Dewey's assertion that "not only does self-consciousness appear as one of the stages of psychological experience, but the explanation of the simplest psychological fact—say one of perception, or feeling, or impulse—involves necessary reference to self-consciousness" (*EW* 1: 151). This sounds paradoxical—Dewey is saying that all psychological facts, even those of the development of self-consciousness, involve reference to self-consciousness. How could the explanation of its own origin require reference to itself, if it does not yet exist? The answer is that there can be a confusion between self-consciousness, as it is taken two different ways: as it is in experience and as it is in "psychological experience." Self-consciousness is concurrent with every experience, as he repeats throughout the article. Psychological experience is experience taken in the limited, individual sense. Thus it is impossible for us to experience without also experiencing self-consciousness, but it is quite possible to experience psychologically the origins of an individual self-consciousness as it arises out of materials that are not yet self-consciousness and are the results of the universal consciousness reproducing itself in the individual from the level of perception up through the stages needed to create self-consciousness. The entire story of this process is for Dewey's *Psychology* to tell; this article only describes how such a psychology is possible and why it must take over the central function of philosophy itself.

The thesis that psychology is just philosophic method can be contrasted with two other philosophic methods: the philosophy of nature and the philosophy of logic. The philosophy of nature applies the results of objective science to questions concerning the origins and validity of human knowledge. This is the typically British methodology and results in a preoccupation with perception alone, as can be seen in its principle that the criterion of truth for an idea lies in its perceptual origins. In an effort to counteract this sensationalism, German methodology starts from the British results and then stresses on the necessary intelligibility of experience. Such intelligibility requires relations, which in turn require a logic somehow to systematize and prioritize them, resulting in Kant's synthetic unity of apperception or Hegel's dialectical logic. Dewey finds in both of these methodologies a fatal willingness to abstract an admittedly necessary *portion* of experience and make it the criterion of knowledge.

> Both of these proceedings go in abstraction from its real being and cannot give the real method of philosophy. In short, the real *esse* of

things is neither their *percipi*, nor their *intelligi* alone; it is their *experiri*. Logic may give us the science of the *intelligi*, the philosophy of nature of the *percipi*, but only psychology can give us the systematic connected account of the *experiri*, which is also in its wholeness just the *experior*—self-consciousness itself. (*EW* 1: 151–152)

Dewey organizes his criticisms of both philosophical traditions into this tidy framework. British philosophy has elevated contingent perception to the detriment of necessary intelligence, while German philosophy has responded with the reverse movement. For Dewey, both are required parts of the greater whole: self-conscious experience. But this position is not that of Kant, who denied that the operations of self-consciousness are matters of experienced fact, nor that of Green, who in a similar manner declared that the operations of the larger, absolute consciousness are forever beyond the reach of human consciousness. Psychology/philosophy must have a special relationship with the other sciences. These special sciences abstract away a portion of experience to give an explanation of it on their own terms and categories. Each science's conclusions have a relative validity, but absolute validity can reside only with the final conclusions of psychology, because it studies all of experience. "Mathematics, physics, biology exist, because conscious experience reveals itself to be of such a nature, that one may make virtual abstraction from the whole, and consider a part by itself, without damage, so long as . . . the attempt is not made to present this partial science as a metaphysic, or as an explanation of the whole, as is the usual fashion of our uncritical so-called 'scientific philosophies'" (*EW* 1: 159).

While each of the special sciences can acquire its materials from selected and analyzed portions of experience, psychology cannot, and so it must confront the question of how it gains a hold on its all-encompassing subject matter and whether it too is responsible for providing explanations. Dewey's answer agrees with that of Caird, Green, and Lotze: of the whole of experience there can be no explanation (because only parts of the whole can explain other parts) and thus it is sheer fact (*EW* 1: 162–163). This answer doubtless does not get at the real issue confronting Dewey's theory, for if psychology is somehow to provide "the organic living unity and bond" for the sciences, what is the criterion of success for a psychology which proposes to do so? To this question he has no detailed answer, for this article's purpose is only to outline a programmatic scheme. Green demonstrated that reality is a unified, absolute self-consciousness, but he fell victim to the prevalent notion that human consciousness is limited and individual *only* and can never reach an identity with the absolute. For Dewey such a dualism is completely unwarranted and creates an unknowable thing-in-itself. While he expresses his gratitude to Green's work (oft-quoted in traditional accounts, needless to say) he completely rejects Green's final metaphysical views, describing them as tantamount to making philosophy impossible (*EW* 1: 153–154). Many commentators have pointed out Green's unfortunate results, the first of whom was Green's neo-idealist compatriot Edward Caird.[52] Dewey's pattern of criticism, as well as the quotations from Green which Dewey uses (with the exception of one sentence), is identical with Caird's at the conclusion of his 1883 article "Professor Green's Last Work"[53] (*EW* 1: 560–561). Dewey thus has one fundamental agreement with Green and two fundamental disagreements. They agree on reality as an absolute self-consciousness although Dewey reaches this conclusion in a different manner than Green. Green's methodology relied far more on Kant than Hegel, and it has been rightly observed that he, least of all of the neo-idealists, should be called a Hegelian.[54] Dewey disagrees with Green's adoption of the individualistic standpoint, preferring the psychological standpoint. He also disagrees with Green's insistence that intelligible relations completely constitute ultimate reality, finding instead that experience is the wholeness out of which comes the abstraction of relations.

Dewey's relationship with Hegel can now be summarized. In Dewey's eyes, Hegel's helpful corrections to Kant were the rejection of the thing-in-itself and the adoption of the notion of the organic whole, the *Begriff* (*EW* 1: 153), but his other central doctrine, the dialectic, cannot achieve its goal to account for all of spiritual reality alone. Hegel's dialectic cannot be equated with any actually existing reality since it merely sets up a purely hypothetical entity. And the process of the dialectic itself presupposes experience in order to give content to the concepts in the categories. Once this is seen, we should understand Hegel's dialectic as being a movement *from* spiritual nature *to* logic, and not the reverse (*EW* 1: 164–165). This critique of Hegel's dialectic is identical to that of Trendelenburg and, subsequently, of Morris. Hegel's oft-noted inability to deal with particular contingency in his system is symptomatic of his attempt to give absolute explanations of experience using only logic. "Logic cannot reach, however much it may point to, an actual individual" (*EW* 1: 166). Neither Dewey nor many other critics have been impressed with Hegel's assertion that the absolute *Idee,* as reached by the dialectic, must exist since it could not help but include the category of being as it is the "poorest of the categories." Even if the *Idee* is allowed to stand, it looses all content as it has swallowed up into itself all of the distinctions which gave it life (*EW* 1: 166). Dewey concludes the article by suggesting that the reasonable alternative to the other philosophies discussed is to see that logical entities have their nature as essential members of experience and not as constitutive creators of experience (Hegel, Green), nor as completely apart from experience (Kant, empiricists, intuitionalists). To this end experience itself must never allow ultimate dualisms, but only relative ones, and the relations these share in making the whole of experience should be the proper subject matter for psychology, "the complete systematic account of man" (*EW* 1: 167).

Illusory Psychology

Dewey was no doubt hoping for an answer to his path-breaking articles from any of his intended audience, either from the subjective idealist or the absolute idealist camps. Perhaps even Alexander Bain, the elder spokesman for the British associationalists, or Edward Caird, the senior defender of British neo-idealism, would take a pen in response. The editor of *Mind*, G. Croom Robertson, recognized the novelty of Dewey's approach and rewarded the two articles with the lead-off position in his journal, probably figuring, and hoping, that it would provoke the two opposed camps into another confrontation. Both Dewey and Robertson were to be disappointed. A response to Dewey came, but from an entirely unexpected quarter: the private scholar, founder, and president of the Aristotelian Society, Shadworth Hodgson. An independent and original thinker, his philosophy is difficult to classify. His insistence that experience was reality, and was always experience of an individual self, aligned his philosophy with subjective idealism and represents a forerunner to personal idealism and to William James's radical empiricism. Hodgson evidently enjoyed his work, taking up another refutation with a prejudiced eye towards stamping out a fresh spark of unfortunate Hegelianism. Dewey must have been very frustrated by this poor model of philosophical disputation and by his failure to gain the attention of any major British philosophers.

Hodgson's primary aim was to expose Dewey he viewed as a Hegelian transcendentalist pretending to appeal to experience while clandestinely importing presuppositions of a most illegitimate sort. That it should be Hodgson who would take the trouble to respond quickly is somewhat understandable, as four aspects of Dewey's articles were especially relevant to Hodgson's own philosophical theories and attitudes. First, of the British-tradition philosophers then active, Hodgson had written most extensively on the question of the proper dividing line between philosophy and psychology. Second, Hodgson had staked his entire philosophy on appeals to experience. He even called his position "experientialism" so that his philosophy would not be taken for an empiricist's, who in his view had a poor account of the nature of experience. Third, Hodgson attempted to rehabilitate metaphysics from the low status it had acquired in Britain, by relinking it with Aristotle's original conception of the study of being qua being, which was eminently possible using only experience. Dewey's rejection of metaphysics as contrary to the psychological standpoint threatened this endeavor. Fourth, his contempt for German critical and transcendental philosophy, save for the minor figure of Maimon, was boundless. The chief error they made was to assume that the ego, the subject, possessed a causal agency aiding the creation of experience, "whereupon all Germany went mad."[55]

Hodgson's recommendation is to abandon postulates purporting to explain experience and instead to "have recourse in the first instance to experience itself, and see what its content is, apart from any hypothesis of its cause or mode of production."[56] The greater portion of Hodgson's article consists of derisive commentary on quotations from Dewey which make mention of a "postulate" or a "presupposition," taken out of context so that they can become obvious evidence of Dewey's forgetful yet inevitable betrayal of pure experience. Dewey objects to this procedure in his response: "Mr. Hodgson's aversion to some expressions is so acute that he seems hardly to have asked himself in what connection these phrases are used. . . . It thus appears to me that the mass of Mr. Hodgson's direct specific criticism is so beside the mark that it is needless to undertake a detailed review of it" (*EW* 1: 169).

The remainder of Hodgson's article consists largely of an exposition of his own "stream of consciousness" approach to experience and his theory of the proper relationship between philosophy and psychology. Hodgson takes no notice of Dewey's arguments in either article at all, simply accusing Dewey of falling victim to the typically transcendentalist "fallacy of first generalizing his own consciousness and making an *ens logicum* of it, and then reconverting it into a really existent consciousness with the attribute of omniscience" (*EW* 1: xliii). This accusation is good evidence that Hodgson either did not read or ignored Dewey's rejection of Hegel's, and Green's, attempts to make absolute consciousness into a purely logical entity. Hodgson also did not bother to take seriously the psychological standpoint.

> Now there are many assumptions which we have to use care, often anxious care, and take much trouble and acquire painful instruction in order to avoid. But our own individuality is not one of them. . . . When a Germanising enthusiast tells you, as a primary and self-evident truth, that the whole being of the phenomenal world depends on consciousness, instead of arguing the point, ask simply—on *whose*. (*EW* 1: xlvi, xlix)

Apparently Hodgson's dislike for assumptions did not extend to his own, and an opportunity for serious philosophical debate was squandered. Dewey must have been disappointed at such a quick dismissal. Echoes of Hodgson haunted Dewey for a long time. His 1925 *Experience and Nature* was still doing battle with this ghost.

> When the notion of experiences is introduced, who is not familiar with the query, uttered with a crushingly triumphant tone, "Whose experience?" The implication is that experience is not only always somebody's, but that the peculiar nature of "somebody" infects

experience so pervasively that experience is merely somebody's and hence of nobody and nothing else. (*LW* 1: 367)

The Stream of Consciousness

Dewey's reply criticized Hodgson's "individualized stream of consciousness," using a repetition of his arguments from earlier articles. Dewey agreed that on the level of perceptual feelings consciousness is individual since such psychological entities exist as a result of the provisional distinction between the universal and the individual consciousness. But experience itself possesses no such duality. Hodgson has taken a psychologically constructed (abstracted from experience) entity, the perceptual feeling, and placed it as the immediately given of experience. Then Hodgson has assumed a philosophical interpretation of experience, that of individuality, and configured immediate experience into the pure stream of consciousness (*EW* 1: 171). Dewey saw in Hodgson merely a revival of Humean psychology with only made a small but misused improvement: a flowing stream has replaced a compartmentalized train. Either way, this sort of consciousness lacks the necessary conceptual contribution.

> I speak, not as a Germanizing transcendentalist, but according to my humble lights as a psychologist, when I say that I know nothing of a perceptual order apart from a conceptual, and nothing of an agent or bearer apart from the content which it bears. As a psychologist, I see the possibility of abstractly analyzing each from the other, and, if I were as fond of erecting the results of an analysis into real entities as Mr. Hodgson believes me to be, I should suppose that they were actually distinct as concrete existences. (*EW* 1: 171–172)

Neither Dewey's articles nor the exchange with Hodgson had any discernible effect, as further numbers of *Mind* are devoid of any other commentary. I am aware of only two references to Dewey's articles, published decades later.[57] In fact, if it were not for a preserved letter, there would be no evidence that it was attentively read by anyone at the time. In a letter to Hodgson, William James makes mention of the Dewey-Hodgson exchange: "I have read . . . also your paper on poor Dewey, which I approve in the main."[58] This mention of Dewey by James is often quoted to give the impression that he found little value in Dewey's articles. James's dislike for Hegelianism would naturally place him closer to Hodgson's side, but perhaps we should also listen to James in another letter: "Hodgson is constitutionally incapable of understanding any thoughts but those that grow up in his own mind,—with all the desire in the world to do justice to them, he simply can't reproduce them in himself."[59] We should be content to leave the final word concerning the Dewey-Hodgson debate with James. Dewey's rejection of

Hodgson's notion of the "stream" of consciousness raises the natural question of his reaction to James's own version, which is taken up in chapter 3.

Classifying Dewey's Idealism

We are now in a position to situate Dewey's initial idealistic philosophy in relation to other neo-idealisms of his time. There is close agreement on the proper methods of attacking British empiricists, whose central failure is an inability to account for self-consciousness and hence any knowledge worthy of the name. Knowledge cannot consist of isolated sensations or any accumulation or series of them because knowledge requires meaning and meaning requires relations between experiences. Thus only mental activity can supply the relating meaning. The more general point is that knowledge cannot be completely relative to something unknown, be it meaningless sensations or a "unknowable" external reality. Locke's material world, Kant's "thing-in-itself," and even the Hegelian absolute (should it be postulated to exist beyond possible human experience) all stand condemned in Dewey's idealism. Neo-idealists agreed that to exist and to stand in intelligible relations within the whole absolute were, philosophically speaking, synonymous. Yet, within neo-idealism, divergent modes of thought must be distinguished, and Dewey's own philosophy must be carefully classified.

The Cairdian School of Idealism

Dewey's thorough repulsion of anything that could not possibly be an object of human experience forced him to undertake a complete reconstruction of idealism first. This reconstruction, aided by his inheritance of the organic metaphor as a model of understanding and reality, quickly set him at odds, on some issue or another, with the rest of the British neo-idealists. Even those neo-idealists to whom Dewey is the closest in outlook and principle receive his disapproval fairly early on. Nevertheless sufficient agreements with a few locate his early idealism within the larger realm of neo-idealism. Dewey's early philosophy should be categorized as belonging to the Cairdian phase of idealism. The more superficial evidence for this claim should start from Dewey's lavish praise for Edward Caird's 1889 *The Critical Philosophy of Immanuel Kant* (*EW* 3: 180–184). This may be balanced by his criticisms of Caird's approach to psychology, mentioned above. Deeper examination of the thought of Edward, and his brother John, reveals the close similarities indicative of a significant and lasting intellectual influence. These similarities are matched by their disagreements with other schools of neo-idealism, principally those led by T. H. Green, Andrew Seth, and F. H. Bradley.

Edward and John Caird, a philosopher and a theologian, together started a school of Hegelian idealism in the late 1860s and led the idealist movement after

Green's death in 1882.[60] While marked by a firm religious commitment to the spiritual awareness of God's infinitude, their philosophies went beyond apologetics to an effort to ground metaphysics and epistemology on sound Hegelian principles. Those principles started from a conviction that the world must be an intelligible system and must be intelligible to us. On this last point a difference arose between the Cairds and T. H. Green, who did not try to describe the features of the absolute. Edward Caird took this reluctance as an unfortunate sign of Green's separation of the world into two distinct realms, the absolute and the human. The absolute in Green's hands was given a role dangerously close to the Kantian thing-in-itself. Thus Caird never agreed that knowledge could be described simply as the "reproduction" of the eternal system into human consciousness. Knowledge, according to Hegel, must lie in the unity of nature and spirit. For him it was necessary to show that the kingdoms of nature and spirit are one, in spite

> of all their antagonisms; nay it was necessary for him to show that this antagonism itself is the manifestation of their unity. . . . What had been regarded as Absolute opposites or contradictories, mind and matter, spirit and nature, self-determination and determination by the not-self, must be united and reconciled, and that not by an eternal harmony, but by bringing out in distinct consciousness the unity that lies beyond their difference, and gives it its meaning.[61]

Such a ringing declaration of the essence of philosophy resounded in Dewey's ears. It brought Hegel in line with the organic idealism from Morris,[62] and it outlined a program of further work to be done. How could philosophy establish the meaningful and harmonious unity of all reality, not merely in the negative manner of attacking dualistic empiricisms, but in a positive manner of philosophical demonstrations starting from experience itself? The prize was truly worthy of the effort, as this demonstrated unity would be nothing less than the proof of humanity's essential relationship with God the Absolute. Dewey described the impact of this vision upon him as a graduate student:

> [I]t supplied a demand for unification that was doubtless an intense emotional craving, and yet was a hunger that only an intellectualized subject-matter could satisfy. It is more than difficult, it is impossible, to recover that early mood. But the sense of divisions and separations that were, I suppose, borne in upon me as a consequence of a heritage of New England culture, divisions by way of isolation of self from the world, of soul from body, of nature from God, brought a painful oppression—or, rather, they were an inward laceration. My earlier philosophic study had been an intellectual gymnastic. Hegel's synthesis of subject and object, matter and spirit, the divine

and the human, was, however, no mere intellectual formula; it operated as an immense release, a liberation. (*LW* 5: 153)

Steven Rockefeller points out how Dewey's early views on the moral and religious will follow those of John Caird.[63] Dewey also received inspiration from Caird's criticisms of Kant's moral philosophy of the second *Critique*.[64] As he gradually moved away from the theistic absolutism of Morris and Caird, their vision of the incorporation of religious experience into all other phases of experience remained with him.

Edward Caird's particularly organic portrayal of the nature of knowledge also fell in line with Morris's, as each criticized Kant's failure to locate both sensations and the synthesizing categories in human experience. Caird, with Morris and Dewey, argued that the court of final appeal for any philosophical explanation of knowledge must ultimately be human experience—not individual sensations and not abstract concepts—and hence neither inductive nor deductive logic can fully capture knowledge's growth. This accounts for Dewey's lasting contempt for any philosophy that makes either logic the paradigm of reasoning.[65] Concerning reasoning, as we have seen above, Caird supplied an interpretation of Hegel's dialectic as a new transcendental logic, revealing the analytic/synthetic movement of thought within experience. Scientific method, as a primary example of reasoning, can be properly comprehended only by this transcendental logic, according to Caird. Science must receive its completion in philosophy, however, as the reciprocal scientific categories (cause-effect, accident-substance, etc.) are reconciled by an understanding of their fundamental unity in knowledge. Dewey accepts in full this promise of Hegelian logic and explores its potential in articles through the 1890s. Caird's retention of the empiricist notion of psychology as the study of specifically individual experience, as opposed to the metaphysical study of the eternal self-consciousness, did come under fire from Dewey. On this point the neo-idealists had nothing to say in reply. Perhaps it was perceived as merely a terminological dispute of Dewey's own creation or as just a tempest in a teapot stirred by his exaggerated notions of what an idealistic psychology could accomplish. In any case his pleas for psychology as philosophy were ignored.

Dewey's membership in the Cairdian school of idealism is additionally supported by the fact that he consistently sided with the Cairds in their critiques of other leading versions of neo-idealism. The Cairdian rejection of T. H. Green's notion of the absolute, echoed by Dewey, has been mentioned. The Cairds also repudiated Andrew Seth's "lapse" into personal idealism, as did Dewey.[66] The Cairdian response to F. H. Bradley's notion of the absolute was again dismissive since its evidently nontheistic and nonrational character clashed with Cairdian theism. Dewey paid little attention in print to Bradley's metaphysics before 1906. Bradley's only influences, and they were significant, lay in ethics and logic.

Absolute Idealism

There is yet another revealing connection between Dewey and the Cairdian school. Caird's most distinguished disciple, John Watson of Queen's University in Ontario, Canada, received Dewey's explicit recognition on three occasions. First, Dewey describes Morris's standpoint by comparing him with Watson. "Like his contemporary, Professor John Watson, of Kingston, he combined a logical and idealistic metaphysics with a realistic epistemology" (*LW* 5: 152–154). Second, Dewey praised Watson's critique of hedonism as a definitive refutation and used it for his own criticisms.[67] Third, the Note to the 3d edition of *Psychology* (1891) credits Watson, along with William James and James Ward, for contributing to its improved theory of sensations.

An Empirically Idealistic Epistemology

Let us summarize the primary principles of Dewey's early epistemology. These principles form much of the backbone of the rest of his philosophical career; together with principles concerning the activities of mind engaged in learning experience (discussed later on), the foundations of Dewey's instrumentalism are fairly complete. These epistemological principles, it must be remembered, are closely linked with his metaphysical views concerning the teleologically organic nature of absolute reality and all its members.

1. A meaningful experience relates a present mental state to temporally distinct mental state. It is an experience of a thing which refers to another thing.

2. Meaning cannot reside in a sense impression or in accumulations of sensations, but only in the idea, which is a mentally active inference or suggestion relating one experience to others.

3. Meaning cannot be explained by referring to meaningless experiences or mind-independent objects.

4. Knowledge is an increase in meaningful experience through the correlative intellectual processes of analysis and synthesis.

5. Knowledge cannot consist of isolated sensations or any accumulation or series of them. Knowledge requires meaning, and meaning requires relations between experiences; only mental activity can supply the relating meaning.

6. Sensation or perceptions are not the simplest and surest type of knowledge. They do not represent external things and ground all derived knowledge. They are instead the meaningful result of

analyzing attention for the purpose of discovering new relations between things.

7. Knowledge cannot be completely relative to, or explained by, meaningless entities, such as meaningless mental states, the conceptually empty "thing-in-itself," or the conceptually empty "synthetic category."

8. Thought does not passively conform to a natural reality in order to attain knowledge and truth, but instead must creatively reorganize experience to produce knowledge and truth.

9. All philosophically genuine entities must be meaningfully experienceable, including intellectual processes, their starting materials, and their results.

11. Any subjective and objective distinctions must be grasped within the larger context of experience. The self and the object, as entities existing within the knowledge relation, exist only as correlative intellectual distinctions made within experience.

12. Ontological dualism must be rejected since it is not philosophically explanatory.

13. The self is not ontologically prior, and experience is not intrinsically subjective.

14. The experienced world is philosophically fundamental and absolute.

Dewey's allegiance to these principles throughout his career justifies the classification of his epistemology as "empirically idealistic." It is empirical because he appealed to experience alone as the ultimate arbiter of any science, philosophy and epistemology included. No transempirical forms, categories, or things-in-themselves are permitted. His epistemology is idealistic because Dewey held that knowledge's proper object is established by the knowing process. Human knowledge is created in the process of synthesizing mental activities. In sum, there exists nothing which could be known, or actually is known, without the involvement of the mind's own creative activities.

CHAPTER THREE

Wundtian Voluntarism

> *Of all the books on psychology this work [Wundt's Physiologischen Psychologie] is undoubtedly the most indispensable to the student who seeks to become familiar with the science in its present phase.*
> James Ward, "Notice of *Physiologischen Psychologie*," 1881

The considerable impact of Wilhelm Wundt's philosophical and psychological theories on Dewey's thought has been recognized only to a limited degree. If an account of his intellectual influences includes Wundt, a rare occasion in itself, it is deemed sufficient to mention that during Dewey's graduate education at Johns Hopkins University from 1882 to 1884, he received instruction in experimental and physiological psychology under a former student of Wundt, G. Stanley Hall. A very few accounts additionally claim that Dewey struggled in a couple of early papers to find common ground between Hegelian idealism and some experimental results from this emerging field of psychology. However, these accounts find no other connections between Wundt's thought and the progress of Dewey's thought toward instrumentalism.[1] Only a handful of writers discover in Wundt's philosophical outlook a fundamental connection, the notion of organism, with the version of idealism dominating the earliest years of Dewey's career.[2] The inspiration from Wundt's principles not only guided Dewey toward organicism (with its accompanying teleological orientation to functionalism and voluntarism), but also toward the principle of continuity (with its rejection of dualistic chasms). These principles, conjoined with the idealistic tenets discussed earlier, laid the foundations for the emergence of Dewey's functional psychology and his instrumentalist version of pragmatism.

His 1896 paper "The Reflex Arc Concept in Psychology," is rightly identified as one of the founding documents for these two developments.[3] The manifesto of the Chicago functionalists, "The Reflex Arc Concept" remains one of the most significant and influential works in the history of psychology. For Dewey, it served as the springboard to his functional and pragmatic analyses of human conduct, inquiry, learning, logic, morality, and knowledge. This article should be viewed not as a starting point, but as the outcome of Dewey's own progress toward psychological functionalism. While the views of "The Reflex Arc Concept" were never so well expressed previously, they existed long before its writing. Dewey had adhered to them closely ever since he became acquainted with both idealism and experimental psychology at Johns Hopkins in 1883. Researchers who have looked into this matter have typically found James's 1890 *Principles of Psychology* to be the primary source of inspiration for Dewey's work on the reflex arc.[4] This matter deserves a closer examination. James indeed reinforced Dewey's own views, as the many schemas and examples drawn from James easily reveal, and James aided Dewey's progress in the direction of a naturalistic and biological psychology. Nevertheless James does not deserve the amount of credit typically granted for the inspiration behind the "Reflex Arc Concept" and hence for Dewey's functionalism itself. The basic ideas in this paper can be dated back to much earlier articles written from 1884 to 1886 which Dewey conceived largely through a contribution of Wundtian principles.

Organic Voluntarism and Teleological Psychology

The story of Wundt's influence on Dewey begins with the observation that Dewey, having attained a thorough understanding of German idealism during his graduate studies under the tutelage of George Morris, was in an excellent position to appreciate and find persuasive Wundt's philosophical framework and psychological methodology. Such understanding and appreciation eluded most of Dewey's contemporaries,[5] and this ignorance unfortunately persisted for a long time thereafter. Recent investigations into Wundt's thought convincingly argue that Anglo-American philosophers, psychologists, and historians of psychology have promulgated an interpretation of Wundt which profoundly differs from his actual principles and doctrines.[6] This difference is attributed to Wundt's membership in the German idealist tradition, which was not properly understood or was ignored by those sympathetic to the English psychology of associationism. Specifically it is now widely claimed that both E. B. Titchener and G. Stanley Hall selectively read into and/or distorted portions of Wundt's texts to find support for their quite different theories of the mind. Wundt became known to most American scholars largely through Titchener and his translations of portions of Wundt's works. Subsequent writers followed Titchener's eminence; his version of Wundt has prevailed, reaching its apogee in Boring's account of Wundt in a highly influential history of psychology.[7]

If Dewey's mature thought is compared with the older interpretation of Wundt as paradigmatically represented in Boring's essay, there is little resemblance, but a comparison with the new revised interpretation of Wundt reveals many similarities. Dewey's and Wundt's psychologies viewed the mental as process instead of substance, emphasized that purposive, voluntary activity is integral to intelligence, dramatized the mind accordingly as constructive activities and functions, regarded feeling and aesthetic sense as central to the formation of judgment, and saw in lived experience not atomic sensations but rather a continuous and organic whole. They held some basic philosophical tenets in common. Experience is the common starting point for all of the sciences, from physics to psychology, and each science must be permitted to use those explanatory principles which permit the best understanding of the phenomena pertaining to that field. Psychology as a science should use teleological concepts and causality in its methodology and cannot be forced to conform mental processes to physiological mechanistic causality in order to understand them. Philosophy should neither attempt to legislate a priori to the sciences, nor should it permit the abandonment of its problems over to the sciences. Philosophy can only aid the attempt to gain internal coherence within each science, and search for a unified worldview providing coherence among not only the sciences but the other realms of human thought as well. Furthermore ontology should be the result of successful methodology and not the reverse. Any commitment to existences (other than the granted existence of our conscious experience) should only proceed from successful theoretical explanation.

Of course, Dewey and Wundt were not alone in espousing such principles. Some of them are central to one or another of the prominent psychologists and philosophers of the late nineteenth and early twentieth centuries. Also Dewey and Wundt disagreed concerning many other issues. To determine the extent of their relationship we will make a further examination of Dewey's studies with George S. Morris and G. Stanley Hall and of his publications in psychology from 1884 to 1886.

Voluntaristic Idealism

Morris, like many other thinkers of his day desiring to retain free will and morality in the face of a scientific materialism, wanted a compromise. Some, such as the British philosophers whom Morris closely studied, took refuge in idealism. Morris was attracted to Hegel's views, but he was worried about an implication of the Hegelian view of God and the world in which the absolute process of the dialectic took away all personal responsibility. Morris was wary of an Absolute Spirit whose dialectical process could kill the free will and hence the life of the person as easily as materialism. Even on an Aristotelian interpretation which Morris attempted in the manner of Trendelenburg, the teleology of the organic living absolute could suppress or completely erase the teleology of the individual. How could a human being sustain its personal inner-directed activities while also having some firm relationship with the greater whole which must encompass everything? Morris attempted a compromise. He drew inspiration from the fact that an organ of the body can retain its own proper function and purpose, exercising it through the development of its potential into actual activity, while being at the same time part of a larger organism without which it could not exist. The organism has distinct purposes of its own, yet in turn cannot achieve them without the complete cooperation of all of its organs. Applying this to humanity,

Morris declares that "by his self-conscious personality . . . man finds himself, not cut off from, but indissolubly bound up with, all the rest of existence, including the Absolute (God) itself. It is thus precisely by his personality that man finds himself taking hold upon the infinite, joined to it, and capable of becoming organically one with it. . . ."[8] This position might allow the complete absorption of human initiative and free-will into the Absolute, but Morris continually stressed that the notion of personality must be irrevocably linked with our conception of ourselves and of God. Since Morris's notion of "personality" includes the permanence of individual potential, the individual retains that potential despite any relationship with the larger whole of the Absolute. Insofar as the individual actively and willingly develops that potential, one can also participate in the development of the Absolute. This sort of idealism has received the label "voluntarism" since it focuses on the human exercise of the will. The will actualizes human potential towards the proper participation in reality's ongoing processes.

For Dewey, the idealistic orientation received from Morris first played a heavy role in his own idealism, and then in later years manifested itself in Dewey's attacks on all dualisms. Throughout his career he regarded any philosophical dualism as defective and requiring repair. Dewey's theory that the mind is inherently functional is essential to that repair. This theory stems ultimately from the organic portrait of mind drawn by Morris: the essence of any portion of consciousness is determined by the purpose it serves for a larger whole. This philosophical standpoint, for lack of a better term, can be best described as an organic absolute idealism. While most attractive for the young Dewey, its central drawbacks revolved around its complete lack of specificity. Morris all too glibly used the terms "activity," "will," "function," "organ," and the like, without any clear definitions or a comprehensive psychological theory. Fixated on the development of a Christian apologetics, and never persuaded fully that psychology was essential to this task, Morris exploited the rhetorical power of the "organic" terminology without much care for details.

Morris was not alone is espousing an voluntaristic portrait of humanity. T. H. Green also placed the voluntary will at the center of human nature. More importantly, he elaborated a highly influential theory of the interrelationships between will, thought, and desire. For Green, the act of will is the primary essence of humanity, and thought and desire are but distinguishable aspects of that act. The will is not one faculty among others, and could not act independently of desire or thought.

> The will is simply the man. Any act of will is the expression of the man as he at the time is. The motive issuing in his act, the object of his will, the idea which for the time he sets himself to realize, are but the same thing in different words. Each is the reflex of what for the time, as at once feeling, desiring, and thinking, the man is. In willing

he carries with him, so to speak, the whole self to the realization of
the given idea.⁹

Green did not have any proof for these claims, and, like Morris, held psychology in utter disdain. They were insensible to the exciting new psychological research emerging from Germany, but Dewey was not. He was extremely receptive to a detailed theory of the mind which could supplement, while remaining compatible with, the organic and voluntaristic idealism of his inheritance. This theory was Wundt's experimental psychology, acquired by way of G. Stanley Hall.

Hall was brought to Johns Hopkins University for one purpose: to promote the new psychology and its practical applications. This psychology was largely the creation of one man, Wilhelm Wundt, and was principally taught from one text: the second (1880) edition of his *Principles of Physiological Psychology*. In Hall's words, "the psychology I taught was almost entirely experimental and covered for the most part the material that Wundt had set forth in the later and larger edition of his *Physiological Psychology*."[10] Wilhelm Wundt (1832–1920) was professor of philosophy at Leipzig University, where he founded the world's first experimental laboratory for psychology. This citadel of experimental psychology produced most of the experimental psychologists holding philosophical chairs in German universities. Two generations of American college students also flocked to his lectures, including William James and G. Stanley Hall and many other American psychologists. Wundt's protégés founded psychological laboratories based on his model at their own universities. G. Stanley Hall studied experimental psychology with William James at Harvard and then directed the laboratory research with many students, including Dewey, at Johns Hopkins. While Hall never closely agreed with Wundt's psychological orientation and theories, his own independent psychology was still slowly developing out of many influences during his stay at Johns Hopkins. Only Wundt's views were the content of Hall's teaching when Dewey took his courses.[11] After Wundt's *Principles*, Dewey read his *Logik* (1880–1883), *Ethik* (1886), and *System der Philosophie* (1889). Dewey's attitude toward Wundt is revealed in the three articles written during the years 1884–1886 that deal directly with the new experimental psychology.

"The New Psychology," written during Dewey's second year of graduate study, expounds the methods, discoveries, and principles belonging to what Wundt called "physiological psychology," and it is to him that Dewey credits the psychological information presented in this article.[12] It begins by drawing a sharp distinction between the British and Scottish psychology on the one hand and the German new psychology on the other. The former was responsible for reducing "that rich and colored experience, never the same" to a completely finished analyzed and schematized display of mental phenomena. The latter refuses to treat a human life as an individualized machine, and it cannot be individualized because "we know that his life is bound up with the life of society, of the nation in the *ethos* and *nomos;* we know that he is closely connected with all the past by the lines of education, tradition, and heredity." It is far from mechanical because "our mental life is not a syllogistic *sorites,* but an enthymeme most of whose members are suppressed," and "psychical life is a continuance, having no breaks into 'distinct ideas which are separate existences'" (*EW* 1: 49).

As Dewey lists these and many more differences between the two psychologies, we can see how this new psychology would have been instantly appealing to someone with an appreciation for the German idealist heritage. Each of the new psychology's virtues which Dewey identifies corresponds to central ideas in neo-Hegelian idealism: the notion that the human mind is primarily a social entity and only secondarily an individual entity; that the individual mind and conscious experience cannot be equated since there are in addition mental operations responsible for creating that experience; that the old faculty and associationalistic psychologies used arbitrary distinctions to create unwarranted breaks into the continuity of the process which is mental life. The virtues that Dewey identifies can be classified according to their inspirational origins. There were two fundamental kinds of psychology involved with the new psychology, proceeding from the distinction between *Naturwissenschaften* and *Geisteswissenschaften:* the physiological and experimental psychology and the social or ethnopsychology. With respect to the latter, Wundt believed that as a result of to the extreme complexity involved in the higher sociohistorical nature of humanity, which includes morality, language, and in general any portion of human life which essentially requires participation in the larger social sphere, experimentation is quite impossible. The social sciences here have their proper domain. However, experimentation has its place when the lower functions of the mind are to be investigated, making experimental and physiological psychology possible.[13]

Dewey goes on to say that while its results are coming to be recognized, there is one serious misconception regarding the new psychology. Despite widespread opinion to the contrary, the new psychology does *not* mean to assert that its methodology and discoveries permit the explanation of the psychical life through the physical life. While reference to physical and physiological conditions is used in experiments, that does not imply that the mental realm can be completely known in terms of, or can be reduced to, the neurological events which undoubtedly accompany them. Dewey asserts that there can be no grounds for such an implication: "Physiology can no more, of itself, give us the what, why, and how of psychical life, than the physical geography of a country can enable us to construct or explain the history of the nation that has dwelt within that country"[14] (*EW* 1: 52). Dewey tries further to justify this position by arguing that since the realms of the physical and psychical are distinct, explanations of psychical events can only be made in similarly psychical terms.

Of course, this sort of justification relies on the very division between the mental and the physical, which is precisely what can, and often did, come under attack by many psychologists and philosophers, as the extensive dependencies and correlations between them were revealed by the new psychology. Dewey postpones any mention of further argument on this topic to the end of the article, when he introduces teleological considerations. He instead discusses some of the experimental results provided by the new psychology. With regard to sensation, it has been discovered that there is nothing in our experience which should rightfully be termed "immediate," but it is all instead a product of mediating processes. Even the simplest states of consciousness appreciable by introspection, for example, colors or tones, are really complex since they are decomposable through the new experimental method. Thus all experiences are the result of unexperienced sensations. Dewey explains that

> [T]he most complex landscape which we can have before our eyes, is, psychologically speaking, not a simple ultimate fact, nor an impression stamped upon us from without, but is built up from color and muscular sensations, with, perhaps, unlocalized feelings of extension, by means of the psychological laws of interest, attention, and interpretation. It is, in short, a complex judgment involving within itself emotional, volitional, and intellectual elements. (*EW* 1: 54–55)

Dewey here has stated an all-important theoretical standpoint. To declare that our experience is the product of the emotional, volitional, and intellectual elements is to leave behind the entrenched notion that these three activities are separately functioning and merely mechanically interacting mental processes. This theory marks a tremendous leap for psychology, and throughout Dewey's career it will play a central role; the key idea behind his later "Reflex Arc Concept" article has been already adopted here. It also marks Dewey's first intellectual intersection with the world's premier psychologist who helped to establish this theory of psychology. Wundt had arrived at this stage after a long and difficult struggle, first, to establish the new experimental psychology, and second, to create a theory which could explain the experimental findings.

Wundt's Psychology

In the introductory statement to his *Physiological Psychology*, second edition, on "The Task of Physiological Psychology"[15] Wundt uses a distinction between the starting points of the natural sciences and psychology. While all of the sciences start from observations of experience, the natural sciences (such as physiology) begin from observing the external world and psychology starts from observing the internal mental processes in experience. "Physiological psychology" can be the science which attempts to discover the relations holding between them.

Ideally it could attempt to understand life by merging the results of external and internal perception[16] into one theory of the mind. This attempt would rely on the discovery that the stimuli and movements of the subject can be controllably measured, which, if a parallel correspondence is postulated, could permit the indirect control and measurement of psychical events and processes.[17] Wundt's own primary research interests concerned the unification of sensation and volitional movement, grounding his theory of the mind. His first book bore Leibniz's motto, *nihil est in intellectu quod non fuerit in sensu, excipi nisi ipse intellectus*, which indicated his early allegiance to the view of the mind as active and creative and his typically German rejection of British empiricism. His use of the concept of apperception throughout his career is the result. In Wundt's psychology experience is the result of apperception, an internal constructive *and* attentive volitional process, providing a mental life different in quality from whatever hypothetical sensations originated from external stimuli. This emergence in actual experience of new qualities prevents us from ever being able to experience any of the supposed original sensations.[18] Dewey agreed with Wundt's estimation of Leibniz as the first philosopher to apply the biological concept of organism to the study of the mind. It was Leibniz's distinction between mere perception and apperception which broke with the Cartesian notion of self-consciousness and was destined to influence Kant. Dewey also located in Leibniz's philosophy the first effort to carry out a metaphysical plan inspired by the concept of organism, which Dewey effusively praised in his 1888 *Leibniz's New Essays Concerning the Human Understanding*.

Wundt rejected as contrary to scientific psychology the notion of a Cartesian mental substance, instead preferring to speak of the mind as an activity or process. Most important, Wundt goes beyond this familiar Leibnitzian and Kantian theme by including muscular sensations of the body's activities in the apperceptive process, producing directed and controlled movements. The activity of the mind is a unified whole, coordinating sensory input and bodily movements into structures for dynamic purposive responses.[19] Any mechanical theory of the activity of mind is rejected since it would require distinct mental entities interacting in some realm of mind and hence would lack an appreciation for the mind's creative and purposive powers. The processes which are mind do not permit a hard and fast distinction between representation, feeling, and willing; accordingly the "faculty psychology" should be discarded. The mind may seem to resolve itself into discrete portions, each having different responsibilities, but Wundt regarded such a separation as artificial. For Wundt the mind was an interrelated whole, performing many connected functions at once, each recognizable only in an advanced stage of psychological development. However, although we can so distinguish them, that does not imply that they have thereby achieved a new state of relative independence. By taking them too independently, other psychologies have fallen into grave errors. Erecting them into separate entities or functions creates the need to postulate even more elaborate mental activities to explain how they can cooperate.[20]

The crucial role of volition in the mind's processes for Wundt's psychology aligns him with those philosophers who give the will a central importance for human experience. Wundt accordingly took the label of voluntarism for his psychology, and he acknowledged his debts to Leibniz, Fichte, and Schopenhauer regularly in his works.[21] This voluntarism proceeds from the conviction that volitional action, broadly construed, is the paradigmatic mental event.[22] On a metaphysical level Wundt's idealism elevated volitional action to the status of the sole reality. The essence of a human being is its will, and all wills are interconnected through one all-encompassing will, the supreme will of God. The unfolding of the world's progress was a demonstration of the actualization of God's will. Wundt combined this psychological/ontological voluntarism with the traditional German notion of apperception to form a hybrid which distinguished his psychology. The fundamental volitional activity was characterized by Wundt as a drive or impulse, *Trieb,* which was the central apperceptive whole having among its components the ability to synthesize sensational content and motor control. This apperceptive whole was capable of growth, as the assimilation of experience, broadly construed, created newer and higher abilities and functions.

Wundt's theories thoroughly inform Dewey's understanding of the new psychology's firmest discoveries. After the discussion of the example of visual perception, Dewey explains the results of other kinds of work in empirical psychology. They are possible because of the increasingly detailed understanding of the components of the nervous system, their functions, and their interrelations. Inferences are then made from an existing physiological process to a perhaps hitherto unknown mental process. The required principle making such inferences possible is that "... if a certain nervous arrangement can be made out to exist, there always is a strong presumption that there is a psychical process corresponding to it ..." (*EW* 1: 55). In this way physiology can lead to psychical discoveries. Dewey offers some examples. After the discovery that nervous impulses take an appreciable time for travel, researchers (principally Wundt himself, though Dewey does not mention any by name) investigated whether the same was true for various mental activities and found this to be so. An even more significant example involves the discovery that

> The brain cells which form the physical basis of memory do not in any way store up past impressions or their traces, but have, by these impressions, their structure so modified as to give rise to a certain functional mode of activity. (*EW* 1: 56)

This discovery radically transformed older metaphysical views on the nature and purpose of the memory. More important, generalizations from this work on memory will proceed to pervade the entire mental realm quickly. Dewey gives little sign he is even aware of these possibilities, though they will soon contribute to his views on mind. He goes on to identify his choice for the fundamental concept underlying the new psychology: organism. The entrance of this explanatory conception into psychology has affected the understanding of mind at both the individual and the social level. At the individual level Dewey views it as responsible for leading to

> the recognition of mental life as an organic unitary process developing according to the laws of all life, and not a theatre for the exhibition of independent autonomous faculties, or a *rendezvous* in which isolated, atomic sensations and ideas may gather, hold external converse, and then forever part. (*EW* 1: 56)

Dewey has his focus on the use of the metaphor of organism to characterize the mind, which allows stress to be placed on the essential unity of the mind. Such stress will not permit the faculty or the associationist theory to gain a foothold in the new psychology. We can note here that neither Wundt nor his commentators use the organic metaphor in this manner.[23] The "laws of all life" reference draws attention to the independent methodology of the new psychology. It has freed itself from the strictures of older metaphysical views, allied itself with biology, developed proper investigating procedures, and in so doing has become truly scientific. Also, by making regular use of the term "process" to indicate that activity is basic to the mental, Dewey has joined in with a major point of agreement between Wundt and Morris. These two usually disparate thinkers display their common German idealist heritage, well expressed by Morris when speaking of the self-consciousness: "Here we have an *ideal activity* which (paradoxical as this may sound) constitutes the *agent:* the agent *is* only through its *activity.*" For Morris this was true for anything: "Existence, *as such,* or absolutely and truly considered, is in no sense whatever *passive,* but is absolutely and only *active.*"[24]

At the social level Dewey uses the organic metaphor to place the individual mind as a part of the greater social realm forming the whole. From biology we learn that the idea of the organism requires the idea of environment. The same also is true for mind. The concept of the individual mind requires the concept of the organized social life. As a result we must recognize the "impossibility of considering psychical life as an individual, isolated thing developing in a vacuum" (*EW* 1: 56). Now, Dewey would have to admit that few philosophers disagree with this statement. Even Locke's empiricism stipulated that the mind grows in an environment providing sensory inputs. Dewey is here revealing his bias toward the view that the truly mental life can only flourish in an environment which includes other developed minds, which together permit growth and achievement. The correct understanding of the mind requires the "idea of the organic relation of the individual to the organized social life into which he is born, from which he draws his mental and spiritual sustenance, and in which he must perform his proper function or become a mental and moral wreck" (*EW* 1: 56). Dewey would later explore the ramifications of this position with George H. Mead at the University of Chicago in the 1890s.

Organism and Voluntarism

The organic relation holding between part and whole is the only way to conceptualize mind for Dewey. He has read into Wundt what he is capable of associating with his idealistic outlook, producing a novel commentary. The use of the metaphor, however, does not result in a caricature of Wundt's theory. As Dewey understands the metaphor, Wundt's stress on the unity of a interrelated whole encompassing all of the mind's activities is quite amenable to this sort of characterization. The use of the term "development" points to another aspect of Dewey's use of the organic metaphor. Life is fundamentally characterized by both growth and purpose; the truly organic must display purposive growth. Dewey says that the new psychology "emphasizes the teleological element, not in any mechanical or external sense, but regarding life as an organism in which immanent ideas or purposes are realizing themselves through the development of experience" (*EW* 1: 60). For Dewey the concepts "mechanical" and "external" are opposed to the organic and the internal, though this may not have been clear to his readers. The term "immanent" is used to convey the notion of potentiality, where the potential of an organism exists, in some manner, in the actual organism. These notions reflect the Aristotelian framework inherited indirectly from Trendelenburg. What fails to cohere with this otherwise recognizable portrait is Dewey's statement that experience is the medium of expression for the realization of the organism's purposes. Aristotle held that the organism is the medium of expression, not the organism's experience. The way to see Dewey's intent here is to recall that from the Hegelian viewpoint the organism has lost its biological orientation: the organism is the mind, not the body. The body is but a portion of experience, and experience is the whole of the organic mind. Life and organism are here being treated as primarily mental and only secondarily biological. Dewey has in effect reversed the order of concept-metaphor. At first the concept was the biological organism, and the metaphor was the organic mind; now the organic mind is the concept. Since for Dewey experience and mind are interchangeable terms, we get the result that the organic mind has as immanent within it a teleological element, which in the course of life expresses that potentiality in the actual developing organic experience. Dewey is not departing from Wundt's voluntaristic psychology, which also depends on a distinction between the physically mechanical and the mentally teleological. Wundt never thought that the discovery of a physiological structure to which a mental process can be correlated thereby served as an *explanation* of that mental process. That position relies on the principle that the mental realm operates only according to "mental" or "psychical" or "psychological" causality.[25] The psychological concepts of purpose and volition are too essential to the understanding of mental events to be replaced with physical causality, which discards purpose in favor of mechanical causes.

Dewey's use of the organic metaphor and his voluntaristic approach to mind have a profound impact on the way knowledge and action are to be related. For Dewey the modern view of the origin of knowledge has found no role for the will in the process of acquiring knowledge, instead assuming the passivity of the mind during the acquisition of knowledge. Locke's and Hume's empiricism is the paradigm here, but even Kant is guilty of holding to such passivity, for while the synthesizing process is active, there is no direct engagement of the human will. In some early writings on religion Dewey elevates the demand for the will's role in the exercise of knowledge to a divine command. His first book, an edition of *Selections from the Writings of George MacDonald, or, Helps for Weary Souls*, offers a glimpse of Dewey's own views.

> Truth is a very different thing from fact; it is the loving contact of the soul with spiritual fact, vital and potent. It does its work in the soul, independently of all faculty or qualification therefor, setting it forth or defending it. Truth in the inward parts is a power, not an opinion.[26]

Dewey similarly offers two ways in his 1884 "The Obligation to Knowledge of God" to express the close relationship between knowledge and will. "We have forgotten that every fact known demands something of us; we have forgotten that there is no knowledge except as our desires, our interests, our purposes, in short, the whole bent of our moral nature is concerned" (*EW* 1: 61). First, knowledge demands something of us: "knowledge does not become real knowledge until the commands which it lays upon the will have been executed" (*EW* 1: 61). True knowledge is portrayed as something which directs and orders human action in the social and moral spheres. Failure to act on known facts, even those of science, results in excessive intellectualism and leads to their decay into worthlessness. Any knowledge about the world, and even the world itself, is nothing for human beings "save where it is brought into relation with man's nature and activities" (*EW* 1: 62). This view is a sign of Dewey's refusal to grant any existence or meaning to a nonparticipator in the human realm. He applies this general point by adding that since all human activity strives for God, then all knowledge must ultimately aid in our "approach to God" (*EW* 1: 62). Second, knowledge will not even come into existence except through the participation of human desires: "there is no knowledge of anything except as our interests are alive to the matter, and our will actively directed toward the end desired" (*EW* 1: 62). The acquisition of knowledge requires a goal and a desire to attain that goal, which permits an active seeking for knowledge. Dewey is here expressing a *teleological* conception of knowledge to replace a mechanical conception in which knowledge is the result of processes needing little or no volitional activity. We can recall how the ideas of Locke, the impressions of Hume, and the phenomena of Kant come into existence with little more effort required of the us than the uncovering and orienting of our sense organs. Dewey wants to require much greater effort and activity than that and is searching for an improved psychology to detail the workings of the acquisition of knowledge. He is at this early stage sure of only two necessary components of such a psychology. Knowledge will only result from the organism's activity, and this activity must take place within a larger social and religious realm.

Explanatory Principles

In Dewey's April 1886 article "Soul and Body" he continues to use Wundt's principle that any sufficient explanation of mental processes must be teleological. Dewey explains this in great detail, relying primarily on Wundt's work, and in so doing expands on the subjects broached in "The New Psychology." Dewey is less concerned with the general principles of physiological psychology here than he is with Wundt's principle that mind must be understood as possessing purposes. Research in physiological psychology, especially on animals, seems to support the existence of such purposes in the organism by finding series of reactions to stimuli which could not be explained by purely mechanical means. Dewey uses these findings principally to defend the new psychology against the religious fear of any mechanistic explanation of life by arguing that if psychological research is properly done, its resulting findings will not be susceptible to materialistic interpretations.

Dewey finds in the required psychological category of purpose evidence that spirit is at work in the live organism, not as a separate Cartesian substance, but as "immanent in the body." This immanence is the expression typically used by Morris and Dewey to refer to Aristotelian teleological potentials invested in the organism. Dewey wants to preserve a distinction between soul and body, but it could not result in a substance dualism; as we have stated, this position accorded exactly with Wundt's own intentions. Therefore it would be a severe error to see in Dewey's use of the term "soul" an unfortunate Cartesian reversal of Wundt's psychology. If by "soul" one intends the older psychological notion, then Dewey rejected the soul. But Dewey has adopted the word to stand for his conception of mind most likely because he wanted to preserve its religious overtones for his intended audience, the readers of *Bibliotheca Sacra*.

This is the significance of Dewey's warning at the outset of the essay against any attempt to understand the relation between mind and body by trying to see "into the bowels of the molecules constituting the brain, and behold from their mutual attractions and repulsions, a sensation and a thought engendered" or by being able to "contemplate the soul, seated as on a throne in the body, thence sending forth her messengers to lay hold of the nerves and cause them to bring her reports of what is going on in the outlying regions of her domain, or to execute her orders among refractory subjects" (*EW* 1: 93). Dewey is repeating Wundt's own Leibnizian objection that a mechanistic model is poorly suited to the adequate comprehension of the soul's activities.[27] Instead of trying to imagine visually the relation between a metaphysically manufactured substantial soul and body, we ought to depend upon our ability to explain scientifically the facts: "The sole question is: what principles, conceptions, shall we use in order to explain these facts, i.e., in order to render a consistent, intelligible account of them?" (*EW* 1: 94). Dewey is telling the reader that the envisioning of a mechanical model to understand something, which may work in the purely physical sciences, will not function in psychology. The paradigm must change to one congenial to understanding life; it will therefore operate on different principles. Not surprisingly, the paradigm offered by Dewey will be that of the organism.

Dewey proceeds to gives interpretations to the discoveries of physiology and experimental psychology, reasoning from the physiology of the nervous system. Since it is homogenous in activity (it is composed entirely, from the brain to the sense organ, of nerve cells and fibers, which both transmit the nervous energy), therefore spirit/soul/mind cannot be limited to activity in only some portions of the nervous system. The soul must then be somehow vitally connected with the entire material nervous system, or not at all. The search for that part of the brain called the "the seat of the soul," occupying many prominent psychologists of the time, must be in vain. Dewey explains the reason for this:

> Either there is absolutely no connection between the body and soul at any point whatever, or else the soul is, through the nerves, present to all the body. This means that the psychical is immanent in the physical. To deny this is to go back to the Cartesian position, and make a miracle of the whole matter—to call in some utterly foreign power to make the transition which is actually found. This may cater to our love of pictures, but it is out of the line which we have laid down for ourselves. The nineteenth century substitute of a double-faced substance is only another excursion into the land of fancy sketches. (*EW* 1: 96)

If neither dualism nor a revived Spinozism is the answer, then Dewey has but one alternative to offer: the principle of immanence. With the bare mention of this term he sets to defending it, requiring the reader to proceed through the defense in order to learn just what he means. Dewey explains that the nervous system is not merely reactive to a stimulus, but alters and impedes the transmission of nervous energy towards a response. The energy released by an initial stimulus flows through a nerve into and through the nerve's cell, altering the amount of energy transmitted. There is resistance, just as there is resistance to electricity through a wire, and there can be complete impedance by the cell. The cell can supplement the stimulus energy by using a continually replenished store or even by taking some of the energy from stimuli (*EW* 1: 95, 97–98). This state of affairs prevents an uncontrollable chain reaction of completely released energy.

> Every nervous action is, therefore, a reciprocal function of stimulation, excitation, and inhibition; control through repression. Every nervous activity is essentially an adjustment. It is called forth through the stimulus, but the stimulus is not the sole factor; it does not wander at its own sweet will, but is checked and directed by the reacting activity, the inhibiting. (*EW* 1: 98)

Dewey then makes an enormous assumption in order to bring his discussion in line with a leading concept in psychology, the reflex action. He takes it that the nervous system as a whole is analogous "in a general way" to an individual part. "Since the fibres correspond, in a general way, to the peripheral nerve system and the cells to the central, it may be truly said that the stimulating or exciting is the peripheral, and the reacting and controlling is the central or ganglionic" (*EW* 1: 98). But it seems that Dewey has forgotten his allegiance to the homogenous character of the nervous system. The reflex action or arc had been widely accepted by this time as the basic unit of nervous activity. Dewey himself would have been acquainted with the theory early in his education; one of the most influential accounts of the reflex action is contained in T. H. Huxley's *Lessons in Elementary Physiology*. There Huxley offers the theory that while many stimuli from the senses automatically go to the spine and then out to the motor nerves, perhaps the same occurs with the brain involved as intermediary as well. With the interaction of a complex and flexible brain, there could arise innumerable acquired reflex actions.[28] The reflex action could then be conceived as a series; senses transmit stimuli to a controlling and directing central nervous center which in turn sends out a motor response.

Dewey is recommending that the brain, since it corresponds to the cell's adjusting activity, is analogously responsible for the adjusting activity for the nervous system. He sees in this the result of the soul's work since such adjustment is teleological: "there is a fundamental mode of nervous activity; in this the psychical is immanent. This mode of activity is the adjusting activity; therefore the psychical is immanent in the physical as directing it to a given end" (*EW* 1: 98). Dewey seems to be lending credence to the notion that it is the brain alone which displays the soul's activity. This is entirely contrary to the intent of his first argument that the psychical activity must be distributed (though perhaps not evenly) throughout the nervous system. Perhaps Dewey is bending to the pressure of common opinion on this matter. However, it is far more likely that he found attractive the theory that the undoubted complexity of the brain provides it with the ability to coordinate an unlimited number of reflex actions.

Dewey next takes on the task of showing how the reflex action requires a teleological understanding. Here the experimental evidence revolves around the study of the stimulation of decapitated frogs. Such a frog will succeed in touching a stimulated spot on its body with a leg despite a series of obstacles involving the loss of the use of one or another leg. Dewey quotes Wundt's conclusions: "These observations . . . show that the animal can adapt its movements to its changed conditions" (*EW* 1: 100). The ability to adapt under diverse conditions is the crucial finding to support the existence of goal-directed behaviors. A frog's nervous system is capable of altering the response to a stimulus until the goal is attained. This implies, so goes the argument, the insufficiency of materialistic mechanism since it seems impossible to understand how such a mechanism could be able to adapt to altered conditions. The final conclusion is that the entire nervous system is permeated with goal-directed activity, or the activity of the soul.

Dewey sums up by stating that "the psychical is immanent in the physical; immanent as directing it toward an end, and for the sake of this end selecting some activities, and adjusting and co-ordinating the complex whole, so as, in the simplest and least wasteful way, to reach the chosen end" (*EW* 1: 100). Physical causality cannot explain the experimental results, but final causality can. The materialist accordingly cannot help but admit the existence of irreducibly teleological behavior, and such behavior cannot be reasonably attributed to matter without admitting into matter an immanent psychical element. The same goes for the Darwinian-inspired "attempts to make the teleological an accidental product of the mechanical" which use notions such as "selection" and "survival of the fittest" and so on. But the terminology used here simply takes teleology from the organism and places it in nature instead (*EW* 1: 100–103). And there can be no "cause and effect" interaction between body and soul for Dewey since the soul is "transcendent," although the soul is "awakened" by the physical body (*EW* 1: 106). The two are so constituted as to present a unified whole: the organism. For Dewey a complete understanding of the organism must in addition to mechanistic physiology also use teleological concepts. In the study of the soul or mind, teleological concepts alone are necessary.

Of great importance is Dewey's final argument for the more sophisticated view that there is a differentiation within the soul, corresponding to differences between nervous structures, and that the soul performs its direction of nervous activity by creating changes and developments in these nerve structures over time. Dewey notes that physiological psychology supports the principle that "the lower the function, the more perfectly and narrowly it is localized" (*EW* 1: 109). This would indicate that a simple reflex is specific to an area of the spine, for example, while the complex thought or idea would have a broader location. Here Dewey uses the then-controversial physiological theory that it is the connections between the cells, and not the cells themselves, which are responsible for nervous structures. He easily draws an analogy, arguing that the more complex the spiritual purpose, the more sizable, complicated, and interconnected the nervous tissue dedicated to that purpose. "If the idea be very complex, it may possibly have relations to all the cells in the brain" (*EW* 1: 110). Dewey then states with approval two of Wundt's principles regarding these matters. The first says that each purpose or function has a developed structure of the nervous system from which to manifest itself. The second says that the development of such a structure will proceed toward greater effectiveness as the organism has the need to use it (*EW* 1: 111). He then sums them up by referring to the entire process of development as the formation of habit and distinguishes between those most necessary for an organism's survival and those which may be needed only as circumstances warrant. The former can take shape in unconscious reflexes and instincts, passed on by heredity. The latter cannot because higher activities must be flexible: "There must be a constant growth, adjustment to new relations, intellectual and moral, and this requires plasticity, variability" (*EW* 1: 111). Dewey concludes the article by recalling Aristotle's dictum that "the body is the organ of the soul" and declares, "organ presupposes function, and soul and body are related indeed as function and organ, activity and instrument" (*EW* 1: 112).

This final statement of "The Soul and Body" must be regarded as singularly important. Written around the same time when Dewey was exploring and defending the territory of absolute idealism in his "The Psychological Standpoint," "Psychology and Philosophic Method," and the textbook *Psychology,* it stands as a much-needed corrective to the traditional view that in 1886 Dewey was just another orthodox Hegelian idealist. He was in fact, as we have seen, a highly unusual idealist who had a very difficult problem: given that the retention of a metaphysical dualism is highly undesirable, how should psychologists and physiologists attempt to understand human life? Could there not be a different metaphysical approach to unify explanatory principles? Attempted resolutions have typically tried to simply reduce one realm to the other, starting the idealist versus materialist debate.[29] Dewey is trying to help the situation by eliminating not one system of ontology in favor of another, but rather the notion that only one can be correct and true. Methodology comes first, and ontology is to be a secondary result. The nature of psychology as a field of science should no longer be predetermined by metaphysics: "The sole question is, what principles, conceptions, shall we use in order to explain these facts, i.e., in order to render a consistent, intelligible account of them?" (*EW* 1: 94). The facts are not to be prejudged: only the results of inquiry have the right to tell us what exists. And the results of psychology and physiological inquiry support the theory that the organism displays both teleological *and* mechanistic activity, although in Dewey's opinion the teleological view provides the better explanation of the overall behavior of an organism.

These considerations supply the meaning of the term "immanence." We are not to suppose that we must somehow imagine two disparate substances, the physical and the psychical, distributed and encased together to create an organism. Rather, since what requires explanation is the organism's activity, the two theoretical standpoints which turn out to be needed each give rise to talk of a "body" and a "mind." Do both of them exist? Yes, according to Dewey, since they are just ways of expressing the mechanistic and the teleological aspects of the organism's existence. The common objection to this attempt, which declares that the soul must be the metaphysically suspect addition to an obviously existing physical body, presupposes that we know the physical (the mechanical) in some prior and fundamental way and that a heavy burden of proof should be placed upon any theorist who wants to add anything to this body. Dewey believes that the burden of proof should be upon both and that to the degree that these or other theories prove satisfactory then they should be admitted. Since teleology provides an explanation, then "souls" exist, in the original Aristotelian sense. Souls are not ontologically immanent, but *methodologically* immanent. Dewey's position is that the organism's existence and activity is to be somehow pretheoretical for psychology, and the physiological analysis of the nervous system and the psychical analysis of mental activity can provide two separate theories.

The fundamental concept for teleological physiology is the "function." Performing a double duty in Dewey's psychology, it refers to a component of the nervous system and to a component of the mental processes. To phrase the meaning of "function" like this is to risk a great deal of confusion since it is defined using terms impregnated with the old dualistic thinking: the nervous system is of the physical realm, and the mental process is of the spirit realm. But its potential to overcome dualism led Dewey to explore its possibilities. One of these possibilities included its ability to overcome the dualism inherent in the current conception of the reflex action, and the "Reflex Arc Concept" was the result.

Knowledge and Will

The most significant feature of the *Psychology*[30] in comparison to other psychology texts of that time, aside from its absolute idealism, was the use of the threefold scheme of knowledge, feeling, and will. This scheme uses alternative terms. Knowledge is cognition, intellect, understanding, or thinking; feeling is emotion, affection, sensibility, or interest; will is volition, conation, or desire. Dewey uses most of these alternates throughout the text. The many different terms are indicative of the scheme's long, varied, and controversial history.[31] Kant gave it a powerful defense in his theory of pure reason, practical reason, and judgment. In general, their advocates have construed them variously as mental powers, faculties, activities, processes, or functions. These philosophers (along with Wundt and Dewey) together aim to correct the unfortunate tendency to devote excessive attention to the mind's intellectual aspect.

Psychological Methodology

In an early section of the *Psychology* Dewey summarizes his vision for the methodology guiding psychological investigation.

> The object of the science of psychology is to take the concrete manifestations of mind, to analyze them and to explain them by connecting them with each other. We shall regard the existing states as the result of the action of certain processes upon a certain raw material. We shall consider, first, the raw material; second, the processes by which this raw material is worked up or elaborated; and third, the concrete forms of consciousness, the actual ideas, emotions, and volitions which result from this elaboration. The first two accordingly correspond to nothing which has separate independent existence, but are the result of scientific analysis. The actual existence is, in all cases, the third element only, that of result. (*EW* 2: 26)

Dewey is anxious to forestall metaphysical interpretations of his methodology. He is not offering a metaphysical dualism in which physical events possess an ontological independence from mental events. No cause-and-effect explanation of the origin of sensations is possible: such an explanation is possible only when there is a "quantitative identity" between the proposed cause and effect, but a state of consciousness cannot be quantitatively measured. Furthermore any material object is known only through mind and cannot be used in turn to explain mind. Dewey is repeating the argument of his first publication, "The Metaphysics of Materialism," in which mind is shown to be at least as fundamental as matter, and hence matter cannot swallow up or account for the mental (*EW* 1: 3–8). For psychology, however, it is perfectly legitimate to appeal to explanatory principles, be they about mechanical matter or teleological mind, so long as it is understood that they are all a theoretical product of intelligence.

Dewey's philosophical methodology is purely theoretical and must not be converted over to a metaphysical thesis. Neither nervous affectations nor sensations in themselves really exist, and they cannot be experienced as such outside of the context of knowledge; these notions are only theoretical. While theoretically explanatory in psychology (Dewey relies on them himself, after all) they have no real existence independent from knowledge. The infant never really perceives nervous affectations or isolated, discriminated sensations, while the adult may experience something like such sensations only if his discriminatory abilities are trained properly. The adult, however, is not perceiving experience as it really is; to suppose so is to commit the psychologist's fallacy. The psychologist is compelled to postulate "a psychical unit beyond further analysis, and forming the basis and material out of which the concrete forms of knowledge are built up by means of certain processes and laws to be hereafter studied. This elementary unit he calls a sensation" (*EW* 2: lxii).

As this statement is replaced in the third edition (1891), it might be supposed that Dewey has abandoned his belief in the usefulness of theoretical sensations. But this would be to ignore completely his reliance on them throughout chapters 3 and 4 concerning knowledge and the entire section on feeling, none of which was altered in any essential way regarding sensation in subsequent editions. Sensations are also an integral part of his 1896 "Reflex Arc Concept" essay. The real reason for his substitution is to forestall any misunderstanding on the reader's part that Dewey believes that "original" experience, such as that of an infant's, consists of individualized sensations. The replacement passage offers a vision of the original experience which borrows heavily from William James. James quotes from Dewey's first edition passage in his 1890 *Principles of Psychology* in order to classify Dewey as one of those idealistic philosophers "who are least inclined to make much of its (sensation's) importance, or to pay respect to the knowledge which it brings." James's classification is quite unjust, however. Dewey does believe that objectified feelings (blue this, cold that, etc.) are a minimal grade of knowledge. He should hardly be lumped together with James's idealistic straw men who allegedly believe that all knowledge consists solely of relations. Dewey (with Morris and Caird) always held that relations without terms are just as meaningless as sensations without any relations to anything else. To hold that completely unrelated sensations are impossible to experience is hardly the same position as holding that knowledge subsists entirely in relations alone. James throughout his *Psychology* conflates the two in order to score points against idealists such as Green, Caird, and Bradley. In his own defense Dewey amends the offending passage for later editions, not to admit that it was wrong, but to insert a clearer warning to those who would misread his intentions. Dewey continued to believe that psychology had every right to postulate sensations in the course of investigating the mind's sensitivity to its environment just as he continued to believe that a grave philosophical error is committed by converting those sensations into original experiences. Even the original experience had by an infant is, philosophically speaking, but a theoretical creation of the psychologist, which James would admit. It of course plays no role for the infant's own knowledge, for it has none; its existence qua known is for psychologists.

The revised passages inserting an acceptance of James's notion of the original sensations of infancy are therefore no replacement, but a supplement to Dewey's use of sensation in his psychological theory. Since Dewey believed that the most basic apperceptive processes are awakened by sensation to create the infant's experience, that experience would possess a minimal continuity and organization and not at all display a discrete cacophony of completely unrelated sensations, just as James also argued. Sensations must play three very different roles in order to answer three very different questions. First, what are the primary sensory stimuli apperceived by any mind? Second, what are the first experiences like for an infant? Third, what are basic or novel experiences like for an adult? These questions have quite different answers. James attacks idealists for their disregard for the knowledge that basic experiences bring: this knowledge "by acquaintance" cannot be replaced by the more sophisticated relational "knowledge-about." But even James would pause at the question of whether a newborn could possess *knowledge* of a blue object, unable as it is to perform such a discrimination. In the end James does want to credit a newborn with such knowledge because he is trapped in the either-or fallacy of relational knowledge or no experience existing at all. Whatever the obscurities of other idealists, Dewey certainly grounded his philosophy on the third possibility that experience presents a continuum of gradation, from bare consciousness having only the minimal amount of relatedness that basic apperception provides, to the more thoroughly interrelated experiences that provide sophisticated knowledge such as scientific understanding. However, he does insist that a sensational feeling must at least attach to any object in order to be called knowledge. Blue things may be perceptually known, but blueness as a detached and isolated feeling does not qualify as knowledge because it possesses no significance, no objectivity, no universalization. Feelings are the individual, unsharable aspects of experiences and hence cannot by themselves constitute any kind of knowledge (*EW* 2: 215–216). If "knowledge by acquaintance" means for James such a particularized and uniquely unsharable feeling, then Dewey cannot agree that such acquaintance qualifies as knowledge. Sense-data, however necessary for psychological theory, cannot be knowledge but only a component of knowledge. Throughout his later battles with sense-data empiricists and realists he never capitulated on this issue. Sensations are highly useful, indeed necessary, for the knowledge process, but their utility does not rest on an ability to convey knowledge. It is the very knowledge process itself which engenders their utility as selected perceptions. Whatever the purity of original sensations, such purity only renders them for Dewey completely useless for knowledge. Only as discriminated, categorized, and objectified perceptions could experience begin to constitute knowledge.

Confusion between the three questions concerning sensations and experience causes J. E. Tiles to infer from Dewey's alterations a rejection of the idealistic position on the mind's integration of sensations.[32] Tiles finds in Dewey's agreement with James—that the infant's experience would be a "homogenous continuum"—an agreement that there is no need for any intellectual machinery to convert sensations into experience. However, as argued above, Dewey and James do not always mean by "sensation" the same thing. Tiles assumes that by sensation Dewey must mean the first experience of life or the discriminated particulars of perception—but neither is the case. Those discriminated particulars are a minimal grade of knowledge for Dewey, not original sensations, which cannot be, by his definition, experienced at all. By original sensation James means the first simple experience of infancy, but already this is *experience*, which is the product of intelligence acting on sensations, according to Dewey's psychology. By confusing these issues, Tiles supports the notion that, thanks to James, Dewey need no longer hold that any mental activity is needed to provide for a minimal grade of experience and hence perceptions can be taken to be pure knowing presentations of real objects and their qualities. But if that were the case, then Dewey would join the new realists, who would declare that, in perception, perfectly adequate knowledge of real objects could be taken as given to us. Dewey fought against new realism precisely over this tenet. There is never any given knowledge, he countered, relying on arguments dating back to his Johns Hopkins years. Furthermore thinking in the narrow sense never applied for Dewey to the mind's basic apperceptive functions anyway. There is a reason why "Thinking" is Dewey's label in the *Psychology* for the fourth stage of knowledge, not the collective label for all of the mind's activities. Thinking involves conceptual analysis and judgmental synthesis. It acts upon experience, not sensations.

It is quite wrong to assert, as Tiles does, that only after reading James was Dewey free to explore the functions of thought working with an already somewhat organized experience. The impression is imparted to the reader that Dewey is indebted to James for abandoning the notion that the mind must synthesize experience to gain knowledge. If that notion had indeed been lost, then the rest of Dewey's instrumentalism is complete folly, and he might as well have been just another positivist. As a last point Tiles's quotation on p. 30 from a much later article of Dewey's concerning neo-Kantianism is simply a non sequitur. Dewey was never a full-fledged neo-Kantian to begin with, but here Dewey is praising the lesson he had learned from the start: that sensations are but postulated theoretical entities with no real existence. To assert that sensations cannot really exist is hardly the same as claiming that psychology is forbidden from postulating them. James would agree since he too uses sensations in his own psychological theories. James could not possibly have helped to convert Dewey from neo-Kantianism since Dewey had long since advanced far beyond it. Dewey also goes beyond James in the treatment of sensation in a very significant respect. There is an important lesson to be learned from the fact that one or more of the five senses must be engaged in activity for proper sensation to result.

> No special organ can be purely passive, even physically speaking, in sensation. It must adjust itself to the stimulus. . . . We must sniff with our nostrils. The tympanum of the ear must be stretched; the eye-lenses must be accommodated, and the two eyes converged, and each must have muscular connections. . . . Thus the activities of our

own body and those of external bodies are indissolubly associated from the first. (*EW* 2: 47)

This psychological principle supports Dewey's contention that volitional activities are ever-present in experiences, even of the most rudimentary sort. Only two different volitional processes need to be theoretically postulated, apperception and retention, in order to account for all knowledge. "Apperception may be defined, at the outset, as the reaction of mind by means of its organized structure upon the sensuous material presented to it. Retention is the reaction of the apperceived content upon the organized structure of the mind" (*EW* 2: 78, italics deleted). There are three stages of apperception. Association is the mind connecting sensations into larger wholes (*EW* 2: 83). Dissociation occurs when the mind, while associating, emphasizes some sensuous elements and neglects others (*EW* 2: 105). Attention is relatively active association, where because of some interest or goal the mind exerts greater control over the association process so that sensations are united "into one whole, with reference to their ideal significance; that is, with reference to the relation which they bear to some intellectual end" (*EW* 2: 118). These kinds of thought processes all have one thing in common: as thought activities, their ultimate purpose is to economize mental force by synthesizing experiences into unities.

> The tendency to shun isolated elements and to force connections wherever possible is perhaps the fundamental law of mental action. This law economizes mental force. Ten elements united into one idea are grasped and carried almost as easily as any one of the ten separately. Moreover, through this tendency to connect the mind realizes for itself the maximum of significance; it gets the fullest possible experience; or, if we use the word sensation in its broadest sense, gets the completest and richest sensation. The mind's instinct for a full unity often leads it astray, but it is the secret also of all its successes. The discovery of laws, the classification of facts, the formation of a unified mental world, are all outgrowths of the mind's hunger for the fullest experience possible at the least cost. (*EW* 2: 84–85)

The organic growth of experience is thus the final end of mental activity. Here we have in 1886 the psychological doctrine grounding Dewey's view of the connection between mind and experience: mind is that purposefully active aspect of experience that organizes other portions of experience in ways serving to increase further its significance. Because mind is but the intellectual aspect of experience, as Dewey reminds us, it too grows in powers as experience develops. Mind is not a separate engine of knowledge production distinct from experience; if that were so, then there would be no intrinsic connection between the mind's abilities and accumulated experience. The lack of such an intrinsic connection in Kant's system was precisely the target of Dewey's attacks in earlier essays. If the increase in mental powers permitted by thoughtful experience be called "learning," then Dewey held that philosophy must respect the organic unity of learning and experience. Experience is absolute, not mind. If mental activities are to be distinguished in experience, there must be sufficient theoretical justification, and the essence of that justification must rest on the need to explain the evident growth of human experience. This psychological methodology lasted unchanged throughout Dewey's career, even as his specific theories of mental activities evolved over time, from the apperception theory of 1886, to the reflex arc concept of 1896, to his later psychology of the behavioral act.

Processes of Knowledge

We should first notice that Dewey distinguishes association and dissociation from attention. The first two, although activities of the will, are mechanically oriented to the past while attention is teleologically oriented to the future. After Kant the question of which mental processes were under the reign of the self's purposes was central. Many, following Kant, sharply separated the intellectual mental activities from the practical. However, Dewey did not relegate the practical intellect to only the ethical or religious realm. The voluntaristic standpoint, of which instrumentalism is but a refinement, finds in higher intellectual activity a teleologically selective aspect. Dewey clearly places himself in this camp, and hence his early philosophy has been rightly called "voluntaristic idealism." It differs from Morris's type of voluntaristic idealism in that Morris only remotely saw purposive action in intellectual processes and never elaborated on any details, preferring to stress the moral duties arising from the connections between the individual and God. Thanks to Wundtian voluntarism Dewey has access to such details, which he packs into the *Psychology*.

Association must fuse into one whole experience all concurrent sensations, regardless of their sensory origin. Two factors permit changing experience: the sensations themselves alter over time, and the self which is performing the association also alters. Dewey is relying on the principle of apperception that when a sensation is fused into the whole self, it alters the whole to some degree. Thus altered, the self will apperceive differently from then on. "The self, in its *specific* character, in short, is changed by every experience through which it passes" (*EW* 2: lxxv). Since it can happen that a degree of similarity can hold between a present apperceptive act and one in the past, successive association (also called re-presentation or redintegration) also happens, for "when any associating activity recurs, all elements which have been previously involved in it, recur also" (*EW* 2: lxxvi). This stage permits the next, which is the formation of habits. Habits are "all that is mechanical in the life of the soul. . . . a connection of ideas or acts that, if one be presented, the rest of the series follow[s] without the intervention of consciousness or the will" (*EW* 2: 100). Habit

> arises when the association has been so often performed that one act not only serves as a sign to consciousness that the next must be performed, but when the sign has become fused with the act signified. ... So in the formation of the act of walking, the various acts necessary for its performance no longer form separate successive members of a series, but the end of one is the beginning of another. (*EW* 2: 101)

The rejection of the serial for the continuous here is the key to understanding the progress Dewey has been making from the "Soul and Body" toward "The Reflex Arc Concept." Even in the most mechanical and unconscious arena of the mind Dewey sees wholes made from parts. The advantages of habit formation are easy to enumerate: they allow easy dealings with the more permanent features of the environment, both natural and social, and thus liberate higher mental activities for the "power of adaptation to new circumstance, the ability to grow" (*EW* 2: 103).

Dissociation prepares the mind for attention by allowing the mind to take control of the apperceptive processes by concentrating on some natural features of experience. The greater the intensity, duration, or frequency of sensations or the greater the pleasurable or displeasurable the feeling of the sensation, the more easily will the mind be spontaneously attracted to the emphasis of these over other more neutral sensations during the apperceptive processes (*EW* 2: 108–109). This attraction now permits the mind to take full advantage of the mobility of the sense organs. Eyes can be oriented toward sights; hands can be grasping for touches; things can be brought to the tongue for tastings. In addition sensations can have acquired features. These features result from redintegration so that sensations will relate to varying degrees with portions of previous experience. The mind thus acquires interest. Dewey explicitly connects a coherence theory with interests:

> The new experience will harmonize with some past experiences, and be incongruous with others. There will be on the one hand a feeling of fitness, of satisfaction, which will lead the mind to be content with the connection, and on the other hand a feeling of unrest which will lead the mind to investigate the relations of the two. (*EW* 2: 110)

This interest in later stages permits the intellectual comprehension of past experiences and allows future directed mental growth by means of attention. Dewey notes that "attention" can be used in a broad sense as synonymous with any mental activity, but he will use it in the more specific sense to distinguish it from the mechanical (and hence nonpurposive) mental processes. The notions of control and goal orientation operate at this level of attention, along with the more familiar meaning of "will." As we saw in its definition, attention involves two new elements: ideal meaning and significance, and intellectual goals. It is no accident that these two factors are involved in the same mental process. Interests aroused by the lower stages will serve as the goals while meaning exists where there is an integrated whole experience formed out of the sensation plus all of the reintegrated elements it provoked. Briefly put, attention uses meanings to select materials from experience in order to realize interests (EW 2: 118–119). The key for the transition from mere interest in harmony/disharmony to a goal which looks to the future is this: "attention always selects with reference to some end which the mind has in view, some difficulty to be cleared up, some problem to be solved, some idea to be gained, or plan to be formed" (EW 2: 119).

Dewey gives the notion of a mental goal its content by linking harmony/disharmony with problem solving. The self acquires its goals by noting coherence or incoherence and then aims to eliminate the incoherencies by somehow using the coherencies. Put another way, since the mind is continually striving to determine if a new experience will mesh with experience, the mind is goal-directed toward finding out how well a new experience can be idealized and given meaning. It will always gain some meaning, but there are degrees of meaningfulness. The mind acquires an interest in attentively attempting to figure out how to make an experience harmonize as much as possible. "Its aim is to see every fact as dependent upon every other fact, or all as members of one organic unity" (EW 2: 127). If a stage of mind cannot deal with an experience successfully, then it becomes a problem at the next level. Dewey is quick to point out that actually there are some similarities and differences among minds as to which sorts of experiences will be harmonized. All minds seek knowledge, but there are different kinds of knowledge. The minds of an artist, a botanist, and a farmer will pay attention to different elements of the experience of a plant because they have different intellectual goals (differing kinds of attention to meaningfulness). As we shall see, the philosopher is the one who is interested in the highest level of knowledge, the harmonious unification of all fields of knowledge.

The concept of adjustment plays an important role here (EW 2: 122–123). The attentive interests of the mind try to adjust to unexpected and poorly harmonized experiences. If such an experience occurs but once, the mind takes little interest at first, but it will anticipate for a while a repeat occurrence using the most similar past experiences to give it some meaning, however little. Repeated occurrences will heighten interest and thus raise the attention level, which is to say nothing except that the mind will be better prepared for the attempt at a more complete integration. This attempt will be performed with two activities of attentive comparison: one for unification and the other for discrimination. They are like fusion except they are at the intellectual level instead of the sensual experience level. The mind can simultaneously consider two mental contents to find their similar and dissimilar elements. Similarity will produce a relation of meaning for the two, while a dissimilarity will permit the two to remain separate in consciousness. Dewey's theory of the unifying and discriminating abilities of mind is thus the fruit of his Hegelian notion of the synthetic and analytic functions considered in the last chapter.

Retention is but the corollary to apperception. If the self can affect sensations, this apperception of sensations can affect the self. An infant is born with a few inherent instincts to organize experience from the start, and then apperception takes over to remold the self as well as the sensations (*EW* 2: 131). Where are our past experiences?

> Our past experiences have no more *actual* existence. They are gone with the time in which they occurred. They have, however, *ideal* existence, existence as wrought into the character of the self, and as fixing its definite nature, and this is what we mean by retention. . . . Retention organizes the mind in certain directions; that is, it gives it organs for certain kinds of activity. (*EW* 2: 132, 133)

Just as the cooperation of the body's organs permit all bodily activities, the mind's mental organs (functions, powers, abilities, *etc.*) must cooperate and develop for the various stages of knowledge to occur. Dewey's reliance on teleological biology reaches a crescendo in this discussion of the mind and its organs:

> The only illustrations of its nature can be drawn from vital phenomena. It corresponds to the reception, digestion, and elaboration of food by the living organism. As the tree is not merely passively affected by the elements of its environment—the substances of the earth, the surrounding moisture and gases—as it does not receive and keep them unaltered in itself, but reacts upon them and works them over into its living tissue—its wood, leaves, etc.—and thus grows, so the mind deals with its experiences. And as the substances thus organized into the living structure of the tree then act in the reception and elaboration of new material, thus insuring constant growth, so the factors taken into the mind constitute the ways by which the mind grows in apperceiving power. But even this analogy is defective as concerns the higher activities of the mind. To make it complete we should have to suppose that the tree knew what it was thus assimilating, and why it did so, and that it selected and manipulated its nutriment with special reference to its own development along certain lines. The mind in retention not only forms its own structure, but is conscious of, and can direct, the processes by which it does so. (*EW* 2: 132–133)

Retention is thus required to emphasize firmly how the mind's learning development takes place in concert with growing experience. The essential nature of mind's "organs" lies in conceptual judgment. It would be very misleading to portray conceptual judgment as the sole vehicle of all knowledge instead of as only the vehicle of thinking, as Dewey holds. Thinking has a definite but limited role to play as one of mind's activities in the larger context of experience, which has emotive and volitional aspects as well. To believe that judgment, and hence thinking, is just the sum and substance of knowing experience, much less of all experience, is already far too intellectualistic for Dewey. With this reminder we can see how the idealized experiences acquired by apperception and retention are put to use in the service of expanding future experience.

Elements of Will

Ideas/concepts are universal meanings. When attributed to a particular object, an idea and its object are the predicate and subject of a judgment. While the systematic growth of judgments constitutes the increase in scientific knowledge, the quest for systematization is often blocked by contradictory judgments. When a person recognizes such contradictory judgments, the mind is thrown into a state of doubt. Dewey has very little to say about the process of reconciliation in the *Psychology*, but he does add that only express contradiction can create doubt and its counterpart, disbelief. Disbelief occurs only when a judgment has been rejected for failure to cohere with the system of knowledge. Hence universal doubt or disbelief is impossible: "Denial must be because of some affirmation" (*EW* 2: 191). The affirmative knowledge we possess is our basis for proceeding further, but progress requires the acquisition of more experience. This acquisition is a risk as well as an opportunity; no judgment is so entrenched that it might not be set aside in the name of the overall increase in coherence.

The acquisition of novel experiences in order to form new judgments requires the attentively purposive selection of perceptions using our senses. The role of volition does not cease with this contribution. Even reasoning, the most sophisticated level of conceptual judgment, requires the attentive activity of analysis and synthesis upon experience. Such attentive activity of the perceptual or the reasoning sort receives the label of "experiment" in a handful of important passages. The following quotation is from the third edition.

> There has been a theory in psychology that individual objects are impressed upon the mind as wholes without any constructive activity of the mind, and that this process, perception, gives us knowledge of reality. The activity of mind from this point on was supposed to consist in combining and separating these wholes, so that the results are more or less artificial in nature, and constitute a departure from the simple realities made known to us in perception.

But this theory falls into a double error. In the first place, perception or knowledge of particular things is not a passive operation of impression, but involves the active integration of various experiences. It is a process of reaching out after the fullest and richest experience possible. In illustration, consider the process of scientific observation. The mind does not wait for sensations to be forced upon it, but goes out in search of them, supplying by experiment all possible conditions in order to get new sensations and to modify the old by them. Secondly, such processes as imagination and thinking are not mechanically working upon percepts, but are their transformation and enrichment in accordance with the same law of a demand for the unified maximum of meaning. (*EW* 2: 138)

To declare that knowledge is a matter of "reaching out" conveys its nature in a most blatantly physical way. Dewey is not speaking metaphorically here; it is the act, not the knowing, which is primary. Knowledge is but an element of the act, as clearly stated in his discussion of will. While all experience has intellectual, emotive, and volitional aspects, it is the responsibility of the will to link them all together. Indeed Dewey is prepared now to go even farther: only the will possesses concrete actuality, because knowledge and feeling are but theoretical distinctions to understand will. Furthermore the will is itself but a synonym for the organism's action.

> The performance of the action is the existence of the will. The will is the concrete unity of feeling and intellect; the feeling carries us to a certain result, the intellect takes cognizance of this result, the end, and of the means to it, and now places this as a conscious motive or end in the feelings, and controls them thereby. The whole process is will. The intellectual operation of representing the means and the end, and the feeling which impels us to the end, have no separate existence. (*EW* 2: 328)

The will is an actuality requiring three interrelated processes: impulses spur experimentation, intellect keeps track of the means/end results, and feelings provoke the motivated search for coherence among the results. The participation of the intellect is required for any action, no matter how simple. Put another way, theory to some degree must be involved in any practice—a central doctrine of Dewey's later instrumentalism.

Dewey's insistence on the purely theoretical character of mental components and activities, structures and functions, has come to fruition. Having no real existence, intellect, feeling, and volition are but ways of understanding the more fundamental unity of action. They are functionally, not ontologically, distinguishable. It is action, and only action, which really exists. This action, as he often reminds us, is active experience. It is not some action thing-in-itself to be understood, but action as experienced. While nominally interested in the psychology of the "soul," as he says at the start of the *Psychology*, by the book's end we discover that the soul is but functioning activity.

> The will (so far as physical control is concerned) is the body, so far as this is organized so as to be capable of performing certain specific and complex acts. . . . The will, therefore, gets concrete existence only so far as the soul, through its experimentation with the motor impulses, reaches an end, which is the intelligent, harmonious relation of these impulses. (*EW* 2: 328–329)

If it is forgotten what Dewey has already said about psychological methodology, and about the soul as purposive intelligence being but a theoretical aspect of activity, then it is possible to misread him. Such mention of the soul, as in the above passage, has spurred some to conclude that Dewey after all is the sort of idealist who still believes in the ontological reality of some spiritual substance. For example, Gordon Allport finds that Dewey did not repudiate "soul psychology" until around 1894, under James's influence. Allport concludes that James is responsible for Dewey's move to functionalism.[33] Dewey's frequent use of the term "self" might also lead a reader astray, as evidence that his idealism rested on the metaphysical reality of the self. The correction to this error is found in Dewey's own words: "the essence of self is the self-determining activity of will; that this will is an objectifying activity . . ." (*EW* 2: 362). Self possesses no ontologically prior reality, no metaphysical existence; it is but a theoretical way of describing purposive activity. "Self is, as we have so often seen, *activity*. It is not something *which* acts; it is activity" (*EW* 2: 216, Dewey's emphasis).

Upon will rests the entire burden of Dewey's psychological theories, and their link with his metaphysical views. The will is the activity which is both subjective and objective and unites the individual (feeling) with the universal (knowledge). The active will is the supreme conscious experience that cannot itself be explained because all explanation consists only of distinguishing its various organic components. Those components can be categorized into two main kinds: those pertaining to the individualized aspect of active experience (feeling), and those pertaining to the universal aspect (knowledge). In this way Dewey portrays the individual and the universal as organically and essentially linked through absolute active experience. Neither the individual self nor the universal truths of nature have any independent existence from each other or from active experience. Both are created and used only in the processes of active experience.

> We find the unity of the psychical processes already studied, and therefore their ultimate explanation, in the fact that man is a self; that the essence of self is the self-determining activity of will; that

this will is an objectifying activity, and that, in objectifying itself, it renders itself universal. The result of this activity is knowledge. The objectified will is science; the objectifying activity is the intellect. This will or activity also renders an account to itself of its own doings. It is internal to itself. The objective universal result is at one and the same time existent in the medium of the individual's consciousness. This subjective aspect of the activity is feeling. As expressing the furtherance or hinderance of the activity, it is pleasure or pain; as an accompaniment of an actual realization, it possesses content and is qualitative. (*EW* 2: 362)

Dewey is claiming to have reached the intended goals for his psychology/philosophy: to show how universal knowledge is possible for an individual and how understanding of their unity is philosophically possible for human beings. The philosopher can grasp the organic unity of individual and nature by seeing them as phases of absolute active experience. Mind is not absolute, and feeling is not absolute; both are only functional aspects of the progress of activity. While Dewey later uses the terms "organism" and "environment" to denote the individual and universal aspects, his fundamental standpoint never altered. Compare the passage quoted above in which Dewey uses the analogy of the living tree with this passage from *Reconstruction in Philosophy* (1920):

Let us begin with the technical side—the change in psychology. We are only just now commencing to appreciate how completely exploded is the psychology that dominated philosophy throughout the eighteenth and nineteenth centuries. According to this theory, mental life originated in sensations which are separately and passively received, and which are formed, through laws of retention and association, into a mosaic of images, perceptions, and conceptions. ... The effect of the development of biology has been to reverse the picture. Wherever there is life, there is behavior, activity. In order that life may persist, this activity has to be both continuous and adapted to the environment. This adaptive adjustment, moreover, is not wholly passive; is not a mere matter of the moulding of the organism by the environment. ... In the interests of the maintenance of life there is transformation of some elements in the surrounding medium. The higher the form of life, the more important is the active reconstruction of the medium. (*MW* 12: 127–128)

Voluntaristic psychology claims that it is the will, not the intellect, which is central to understanding life. Some voluntarists converted the will into a supreme metaphysical principle, following Fichte and Schopenhauer, but Dewey was never tempted in that direction. Voluntarism for Dewey from the start meant the study of the objective, active experience of human beings. This view coincided with his early idealism, which held that experience is not essentially subjective, but objective. The traditional account of his development, by stressing discontinuities between his early idealism and later behavioral functionalism, encourages the false notion that Dewey first fell into some sort of subjectivism and only later discovered (thanks to James and Darwinian evolution) how to permit objective behavior to ground his psychology. Nothing could be further from the case. The notion of individual subjective experience as a metaphysical reality was never acceptable to Dewey. Even its usefulness as a psychologically explanatory theory was suspect because he argued that the study of individual experience apart from its proper environing context could only result in confusion.

Revisions to the Psychology

The traditional account's story of James's influence on Dewey, through his 1890 *Principles of Psychology*, must be radically revised. What portions of the *Principles* could have influenced the second or third editions of *Psychology*? The Note to the second, 1891 edition tells us that "the only change involving an alteration of standpoint is in the general treatment of sensation" and credits James among others for the better theory of sensation (*EW* 2: 5). We have seen that Dewey never believed that psychology must postulate atomistic sensations in the original consciousness, already largely agreeing with James's stream of consciousness theory. "There is a certain original continuous substratum of sensation out of which the various apparently distinct sensations have been slowly differentiated" (*EW* 2: 35). Dewey had no trouble accepting the "stream" (so long as organic continuity, not disconnectedness, prevailed) on the level of ordinary experience, but he had not initially postulated a version of it at the level of infantile experience.

Despite Dewey's claim to the contrary, some other important changes were made for the third edition, as outlined by Reck in his "The Influence of William James on John Dewey."[34] The most significant is the overhaul which the section on conception receives (*EW* 2: 179–180). Conceptions become explicitly functional, and this clears up the matter as to how concepts can be universal. At first Dewey had been content to say only that a concept is the meaningful universality which captures relations. For the third edition, "the concept is the power, capacity, or function of the image or train of images to stand for some mode of mental action, and it is *the mode of action which is general*" (*EW* 2: 179). How should we interpret this alteration? Reck assumes that these revisions are consequences of James's influence. James says that "concept" as a term "properly denotes neither the mental state nor the mental state which it signifies, but the relation between the two, namely, the function of the mental state in signifying just the particular thing."[35] However, this functional notion of the concept is not a radically new element in Dewey's thinking and involves no fundamental "alteration in standpoint." We can recognize in the first edition how concepts are but a universalizing mode of mental activity. Dewey later referred explicitly to concepts as *functionally* universal modes of mental activity. But from our study of Dewey writings prior to 1886, it is evident that he understood all aspects of mental activity as functionally distinct modes of thought. If, as commentators eager to find a functionalist debt to James argue, the functionality of concepts is sufficient to yoke Dewey to James, then it is sufficient to yoke James to many idealists. As least as late as 1892 and probably even later, Dewey was an idealist, metaphysically and epistemologically. Dewey was stimulated to define more carefully concepts as he read his own theory in James's *Principles of Psychology*. Let us look at what Dewey says about the influence of the *Principles*.

> The psychological tendencies which have exerted an influence on instrumentalism are of a biological rather than a physiological nature. . . . Briefly, the point of departure of this theory is the conception of the brain as an organ for the coordination of sense stimuli . . . for the purpose of effecting appropriate motor responses. (*LW* 2: 14–15)

This theory does not really look so revolutionary, for it uses the term "brain" where Dewey had earlier used "mind." However, it should be noted here that Dewey's *Psychology* differed in one central respect from all other psychologies of that time period because it rarely mentioned the nervous system. It was considered practically obligatory to follow the scheme inaugurated by Wundt by beginning one's psychology text with a chapter or two on the results of physiological explorations into the nervous system. Dewey found little place for that (save during the discussion of sensation) even while discussing the reflex arc, which was closely related to nervous tissues in his "Soul and Body." In that article Dewey was prepared to draw numerous conclusions from biology, but that field of study was largely suppressed for the *Psychology* until he read James's *Principles of Psychology*. James should also be credited with convincing Dewey that evolutionary theory can shed light on origin, purpose, and functions of the brain, as it has evolved in the way it has in order to best aid the survival of the organism. This view, when combined with physiological psychology, can lead to conclusions about the psychology of belief and knowledge. This introduction to the principles of evolutionary and naturalized epistemology was certainly very helpful for Dewey's psychology, liberating it from more Hegelian terminology.

But it cannot be stressed enough that such naturalistic influences were not revolutionary for, much less incompatible with, Dewey's metaphysical views. In a 1892 letter to John W. Cook, he rejects the notion that the *Psychology* is inimical to physiological psychology.

> I have never at any time had any antagonism to physiological psychology—but have conceived it as delivering important methods & material. If I may venture to characterize my own book it was an attempt to interpret a vast mass of floating material of this character from the standpoint of what seemed to me the true idea of mind—a genetic active unity. By this method, it seemed to me new life might be given philosophic ideas which were becoming exhausted, while unity and meaning would be conveyed to a lot of facts which were isolated and specialistic. Succeeding time, while revealing many defects in execution, has only strengthened my faith in the general idea. To say I should in some cases now adopt a different method of statement or treatment is only to say that I have learned something in the last five years & that the science has progressed.[36]

Dewey adds that he values James's *Principles of Psychology* very highly, saying that James to his mind is "infinitely more" than a mere physiological psychologist. In a letter written to James in 1891, Dewey comments on his suggestions concerning consciousness in the *Principles of Psychology* (pp. 290–291). The key section of James's discussion goes as follows:

> Instead, then, of the stream of thought being one of *con*-sciousness, . . . it might be better called a stream of *Scious*ness pure and simple, thinking objects of some of which it makes what it calls a "Me," and only aware of its "pure" Self in an abstract, hypothetic or conceptual way. . . . The sciousness in question would be the *Thinker*, and the existence of this thinker would be given to us rather as a logical postulate than as that direct inner perception of spiritual activity which we naturally believe ourselves to have. "Matter," as something behind physical phenomena, is a postulate of this sort. Between the postulated Matter and the postulated Thinker, the sheet of phenomena would then swing, some of them (the "realities") pertaining more to the matter, others (the fictions, opinions and errors) pertaining more to the Thinker.[37]

Dewey expresses his admiration for this passage and tells James that it is an exemplary summary of the core of Hegel. As Dewey sees it, both the matter and the thinker are the result of growing organizations (at different levels) of the content of "sciousness." The above passage tantalized Dewey with its close brush with his own work.

> If I understand at all what Hegel is driving at that is a much better statement of the real core of Hegel than what you criticize later on as

Hegelianism. Take out your "postulated" 'matter' & 'thinker,' let 'matter' (i.e. the physical world) be the organization of the content of sciousness up to a certain point, & the thinker be a still further unified organization [not a unify-ing organ as per Green] and that is good enough Hegel for me. And if this point of view had been worked out, would you have needed any 'special' activity of attention, or any 'special' act of will? The fundamental fact would then be the tendency towards a maximum content of sciousness, and within this growing organization of sciousness efforts could find their place. At the risk, after all, of burdening you, it seems to me that on page 369 (I) you virtually fall into the meshes of the "psychological fallacy" (Let me say that I think the discovery & express formulation of this alone would have marked any book as 'epoch-making') I surrender Green to your tender mercies, but the unity of Hegel's self (& what Caird is driving it) is not a unity in the stream as such, but of the function of this stream—the unity of the world (content) which it bears on reports—It may seem strange to call this unity Self, but while Kant undoubtedly tried to make an agent out of this (and Green follows him) Hegel's agent (or Self) is simply the universe doing business on its own account.[38]

Interestingly Dewey then throws a barb at the neo-Hegelians in general for turning Hegel into a premodern scholastic. However, the self is really not an agent as Kant and Green suppose.[39]

The self is rather the unity of the function of sciousness. This last remark must have been disappointingly opaque for James, but it does indicate two things. First, Dewey was a committed idealist at this time, and, second, he was already quite prepared to agree with the eventual product of James's speculations on consciousness which were published in the late 1890s and early 1900s. James's neutral monism (the ultimate reality is the stream of sciousness), which is closely related to immediate empiricism (everything really is what it is experienced as), was never foreign to Dewey's own philosophical views. Dewey's letter also complains about James's need for a "special" attentive or willful act as completely unnecessary in light of James's own declarations concerning the postulated thinker. This complaint reaches publication in Dewey's 1894 "The Ego as Cause" (*EW* 4: 93–95).

It is especially ironic that, for all the claims made by the traditional story of Dewey's debt to James, Dewey did not alter his account of the reflex arc for the later editions of the *Psychology*. While this account is quite simplistic and plays no significant role in Dewey's primary engagements with knowledge and will, its unaltered presence belies the traditional story's heavy emphasis on his intellectual debt to James's theory of reflex arc for a functionally naturalistic standpoint.

Furthermore, when Dewey did publish the much more sophisticated "Reflex Arc Concept" paper, discussed below, he corrected James's account, which defined the start of reflex arc as a sensation. Dewey replaced the sensation with the act of seeing, which involves the coordination of the eyes in a particular direction. This replacement is required by his philosophical orientation toward the centrality of action; sensations, ideas, and the like are but functional distinctions made in the course of inquiry into action.

To summarize, despite the changes Dewey made to his *Psychology*, he did not radically or abruptly alter his fundamental standpoint on the nature of ultimate reality, experience, or mind by 1892. The several deletions of the "reproduction" of universal knowledge for individual knowledge might indicate so,[40] as many have noticed, but here too we must question whether this is a sign of changing metaphysical views. The alternative, and preferable, explanation relies on the tension in Dewey's philosophy between the emergence and reproduction theories of universal knowledge. He grew more uncomfortable with the term "reproduction," recognizing it as a useless holdover from Green's terminology. Dewey soon dropped all language intimating that knowing simply "reads off" the universal relations of nature. He never believed that to be the case, but he was only slowly developing the terminology to express its replacement. That terminology is recognizably functionalist by 1894, but his psychological standpoint is much older, predating his reading of James's *Psychology*.

The Reflex Arc

By 1892 Dewey had settled on the concept of reflex arc as the centerpiece for his voluntarist reconstruction of psychology and philosophy. The syllabus for his spring 1892 Introduction to Philosophy course describes the reflex arc as the self, and as an expression of the entire universe.

> The unit of nervous action is called the reflex-arc.... This term covers not simply the narrower "reflex" of physiology (the winking of an eye, for example) but every unified action, or completed portion of conduct. Illustrations: the movement of an amoeba, the impulse of a child for food, the perception of color, a word like "civilization," with its whole meaning, a virtuous act, a philosophic theory. Each is a unified action; and in this unity of action various conditions are brought to a head or focussed. Each is a co-ordination of certain experiences; each is an expression, more or less direct, more or less explicit, of the whole of life; it is the manifold circumstance of the Universe attaining a unity in action. Such an activity as finds

expression then in an entire reflex-arc is a whole, a concrete, an individual. It is the Self in more or less developed form. (*EW* 3: 212)

The distinguishable aspects of unified action in the reflex arc are now will and intelligence. That no mention of feeling occurs here or in the "Reflex Arc Concept" essay is probably not a coincidence, for the notion of the reproduction of universal knowledge into the individual knower does not appear either. Since feeling in the *Psychology* was supposed to be the individualized aspect of experience, providing meaning to the notion of the individual apart from the universal, Dewey is transferring the origin of the individual away from feeling to only will and intelligence. He soon held that the notion of experience *for me* arises as a factor in reflective thought, not in mere feeling. The emergence theory began to take hold in his philosophy in the early 1890s, and the roles of the universal and the individual were profoundly altered. So too was the function of feeling altered; the recognition of the resumption of harmonious knowing experience was registered by the intellect in the *Psychology*, but Dewey later shifted this function to feeling. The *Psychology* had already granted to feeling the ability to intuitively sense incipient intellectual harmony (*EW* 2: 264–265) so the final arrival of established harmony should be a matter of feeling too. This shift enabled Dewey firmly to link the aesthetics of feeling to the logic of intellect. The *Psychology* discusses aesthetics, but it has no important role to play in the functions of intellect and will; Dewey is barely able to surmise some relationship to ethics.

The novel addition to Dewey's theory of action is its social context. All action is now explicitly social action. The social nature of human conduct plays a large role in the 1891 *Outlines of a Critical Theory of Ethics*. In the 1892 syllabus the process of unifying action through unity, diversity, adjustment, harmonization, and return to unity can be read into social organization and evolution. The Hegelian promise, so attractive to Dewey when he first met idealism, of understanding the individual in terms of the social has finally been realized. This allows the portrayal of the development of human thought, including philosophy, in terms of these categories. Dewey's functionalism, by reconciling the two dominant modes of understanding, the psychological and the physical, offers a genuine third alternative to idealism and materialism. Here Dewey makes his first use of the term "instrumental" in explaining his views.

> Modern times present not a passive parallelism, but an opposition of materialism and idealism. . . . Parallel with the development of physical science was a development of psychological science. While physical science went to make the "external" primary and the "internal" a derivative from it, psychological science reversed the process. . . . Both start from the standpoint of knowledge, and attempt to read

> the world in terms of knowledge, that is, of contemplation or intellectual formulation. Just because both sides occupy the same fundamental standpoint the quarrel between them cannot be reconciled. The key to the reconciliation consists in shifting the point of view. Reality is not to be read in terms of knowledge as such, but in terms of action. So read, the opposition between the internal and the external, the physical and the psychical, ceases to be ultimate and becomes instrumental. We have in this distinction a means to the end of action. The physical and the psychical are recognized as the primary distributions of power requisite to the highest (freest) action. (*EW* 3: 228–229)

If philosophy must understand all realities in terms of activity and its functionally distinguished aspects, and if all activity is social behavior, then Dewey's philosophy is by 1892 a very strange sort of idealism at best. Indeed, by his own declaration above, he could not consider himself an idealist in the traditionally psychological sense. Of course, Dewey never did, rejecting from the start subjectivist psychology and philosophy. Neither the mental nor the psychical are philosophically ultimate; they are but functionally distinguishable aspects of social activity which have only *instrumental* existence. Although he does not refer to his philosophy as "instrumentalism" until 1904 (*MW* 3: 317), there is no reason to deny that he is recognizably an instrumentalist by 1892. Indeed, if instrumentalism is at bottom the recognition that all mental states must be understood functionally as conducive to action, including the intellectual states and processes, then Dewey was a full-blown instrumentalist by 1886. Since he was also an absolute idealist during this period (and probably beyond), then we may conclude that his allegiance to instrumentalism and absolute idealism had considerable overlap. From Dewey's own perspective, of course, they were organically integrated in his philosophy.

Those who rebel at the notion of their cooperation must be imposing some additional requirement on the notion of instrumentalism, a requirement which Dewey himself did not accept. If one argues, for example, that the additional requirement is the adherence to naturalism/realism, then the above reasoning would be quite unconvincing. This objection will be resolved later. For now, suffice it to say, the 1896 "The Reflex Arc Concept in Psychology" is often taken to be an admirably naturalistic perspective on psychology, with no idealistic notions. However, Dewey does not involve any metaphysical perspective with that discussion, which only develops further the functionalist reconstruction of the reflex arc offered in the 1892 syllabus. If the 1896 article has enough evidence of naturalism in its description of the reflex arc, then the 1892 syllabus does too. In 1894 Dewey refers to his tenet that activity is the primary reality as "experimental idealism" (*EW* 4: 264). We will have to look at many of his writings to find conclusive evidence of Dewey's metaphysical views during the 1892–1896 period.

Purposive Activity

The "Reflex Arc Concept" essay presents a full reconstruction of psychology's traditional understanding of the nature of the fundamental unit of mental activity, the reflex arc. This understanding incorporates the older triad of mental activity, feeling, judging, and willing, into the three portions of the reflex arc: sensation, thought, and act. Dewey argues that such a transfer only serves to bring along all of the problems faced by the older scheme since it was formulated in the post-Cartesian period, when dualism dominated the metaphysical landscape. This resulted in a strict division between the nature of sensation and thought. Sensation was conceived nominalistically while thought was considered to be universal. Thought was given the responsibility to organize chaotic and atomic sensations according to associations, principles, or laws. In this way the two were separate entities able to interact without joining together. The relationship that the will, or volition, bore to human activity was similar, as the concern to preserve free will kept volition apart from its effects, the latter being subject only to laws of the physical realm. Hence a means of interaction, without providing unification, was typically desired, and such interactionism infected the psychological notion of the reflex arc. Dewey criticizes this theory: "As a result, the reflex arc is not a comprehensive, or organic unity, but a patchwork of disjointed parts, a mechanical conjunction of unallied processes." He argues that from the point of view of physiological psychology such absolute distinctions and divisions between psychological states or events are unwarranted and undesirable. "More specifically, what is wanted is that sensory stimulus, central connections and motor responses shall be viewed, not as separate and complete entities in themselves, but as divisions of labor, functioning factors, within a single concrete whole, now designated the reflex arc" (*EW* 5: 97).

This sort of criticism of the reflex arc concept repeats itself throughout the article, but by itself seems to lack strength. Dewey's predilection for the organic over the mechanical could on its own win few converts to his theory. A much more effective strategy also used by Dewey made this article so influential. He argued that the purpose of the reflex arc concept is to explain the twin phenomena of the biological organism's aiming and succeeding at goals and the organism's learning from experience. The favored example is the child-candle instance, taken from James's *Principles of Psychology*.[41] The child sees the bright light and, reaching for it, is burned. How can the reaching be successful? And how is it that after the experience, the child is less likely to reach immediately for such a light again on seeing it? The real failure of the reflex arc concept is that the mechanical relations within the reflex arc fail to explain the phenomena, and hence there is a need for a different conception of the relationships among perception, judgment, and willing. The article's enormous achievement was a result of the plausibility of Dewey's organically inspired reconstruction of the reflex arc into the coordinated circuit of activity. This plausibility was not based on the attractiveness of the organic model per se, but its greater degree of success in explaining the phenomena.

The mechanical model of the reflex arc fails to account for the phenomena basically because it is too simple. On its premises perception can be a contributing cause of an action, through judgment and willing, but the reverse cannot be true: action cannot be a contributing cause of a perception. Thus the cause of a perception must then be exclusively "sought outside the process of experience itself . . . in an external pressure of 'environment'" (*EW* 5: 99). Yet the specific qualities of the perception of the candle light would not exist without the contribution of the act of looking: the motion of the head, the focusing of the eyes, the continued attention fixed upon the light, and so forth. The character of any perception is, Dewey argues, at least in part a result of the organism's activity which brings it to the perception. Since action can contribute to perception, as well as the reverse, Dewey then conceives of a reciprocal movement of causes. This movement goes from action to perception and back again, which may account for the first phenomena mentioned above, the reaching for the bright object. Since the reaching out is to the bright object and not just to anywhere, we must suppose that in this reciprocal chain of causes there is the successful coordination of the process of reaching. There must be error control: the perception of the reaching hand and the perception of the bright light must together guide the hand to an intersection with the light. This guidance process, with perception and action causally working together toward the goal, is referred to as the sensori-motor circuit.

> If the sight did not inhibit as well as excite the reaching, the latter would be purely indeterminate, it would be for anything or nothing, not for the particular object seen. The reaching, in turn, must both stimulate and control the seeing. The eye must be kept upon the candle if the arm is to do its work; let it wander and the arm takes up another task. In other words, we now have an enlarged and transformed co-ordination; the act is seeing no less than before, but it is now seeing-for-reaching purposes. There is still a sensori-motor circuit, one with more content or value, not a substitution of a motor response for a sensory stimulus. (*EW* 5: 98)

The next event is the stimulus of the burn the child receives upon touching the candle's flame. In keeping with Dewey's analysis we must say that the quality of the burn sensation is partially caused by the previous activity of seeing and reaching. Here he brings out the explanation of the second phenomena, that of learning, although he just as naturally could have discussed the learning process inherent in reaching out to seen objects. At this point Dewey reveals the essential contribution the organic theory makes to the discussion.

> Only because the heat-pain quale enters into the same circuit of experience with the optical-ocular and muscular quales, does the child learn from the experience and get the ability to avoid the experience in the future. More technically stated, the so-called response is not merely *to* the stimulus; it is *into* it. The burn is the original seeing, the original optical-ocular experience enlarged and transformed in its value. It is no longer mere seeing; it is seeing-of a light-that-means-pain-when-contact-occurs. The ordinary reflex arc theory proceeds upon the more or less tacit assumption that the outcome of the response is a totally new experience; that it is, say, the substitution of a burn sensation for a light sensation through the intervention of motion. (*EW* 5: 98–99)

Only an organic theory of stimulus, idea, and response can account for the fact that after an activity is stimulated by a sensation, a similar sensation in the future will evoke that activity; it will suggest or mean the original activity. It may or may not actually trigger that activity again; it may not if the suggestion it raises is not of a pleasing nature. Such a displeasing suggestion, such as the meaning of a bright light as a painful contact, will stall the act of reaching for it and instead provoke a doubtful consideration of what to do next. Dewey mentions the recently published work of his partners in psychological experimentation, James Angell and Addison Moore, which illustrates how this revised reflex arc theory is fully capable of explaining this learning process.[42] Special attention is owed to Dewey's claim that stimulus and response should not be considered as the mechanically interacting segments of an action, but as complete actions in themselves which receive coordination in the course of learning from experience. It is the coordinated and completed purposive act that is the paradigm of human conduct, and every functionally distinguishable part of any completed act must itself be an act as well. There can be no aspect of human behavior, according to Dewey's functional psychology, which does not stand in some organic relation to willful activity.

Mental Continuity

Experience itself is organic: experience cannot be disconnected; it cannot have any complete discontinuities. Everything which is in experience is colored by some preceding experience, or, put differently, experiences come in wide complex stretches and long durations rather than in quick pulses of momentary and completely distinct atomic events. Learning can then be explained in a manner analogous to a strictly associationistic explanation. The needed principle is stated quite well by James himself. If cerebral processes have once been aroused together or in immediate succession, any subsequent arousal of any one of them will tend to arouse the others in the original order.[43] If "cerebral process" is replaced by "idea," the associationist theory is expressed. James himself rejected the older atomistic and mechanical view of experience in favor of one very like Dewey's. The change to "cerebral process" permits associationism to adapt itself nicely to a different view of experience, and James used it extensively in his account of learning. Dewey does not expressly state this principle, but he takes it for granted as he proceeds. So long as the processes are understood to be continuous together, this principle describes the preservation of experience required for learning. Dewey would have no difficulty referring to this preservation as memory so long as it is not regarded as a storehouse for ideas. Rather, the preservation is one of habit, ingrained into the functional organization of the nervous structure. "The Reflex Arc Concept" is Dewey's functional reconstruction of psychological associationism, using notions originating with Wundtian apperception. Apperception itself now seemed to Dewey to be too restrictive, an excessive abstraction from the real organic whole which is responsible for mental activity (*EW* 5: 99n-100n). In later writings he sometimes mentions apperception in the Kantian sense with disdain. However, when mentioning apperception in the Wundtian sense as integral to learning from experience, Dewey's tone is one of approval. He had simply lost interest in the psychological postulation of preconscious sensations and was far more interested in applying his understanding of mind's analytic and synthetic functions to the study of reflective thought's transformation of experience.

The knowledge that physiology provides about the activity of the nervous structure provides Dewey with another way of arguing for the thesis that continuity prevails over all mental activity. Physiological psychology accepts the legitimacy of drawing inferences from physiological discoveries about the nervous system to the nature of the mind's operations and abilities. Dewey agrees in this article, and he infers from the continuity exhibited by the material structure and chemical activity of the nervous system that continuity must also reign over the mental life (*EW* 5: 103). The brevity of this argument indicates that he did not intend to place great weight upon it. We can understand this by remembering that the nature of such an inference was (and still is) extremely controversial. Only materialists, parallelists, or monists could have much sympathy for it. Dewey seems to express the inference in a monistic way by describing the sensori-motor process from both a physical and psychical side; he explicitly rejects the notion of a soul substance throughout. Therefore when he refers to the psychical, he is not talking about something in a purely mental realm. Echoes of the immanence theory of the "Soul and Body" article are very loud here.

The significant conclusion Dewey draws from his theory has to do with the nature of mental entities as he answers the question how are we to understand the relationships between undoubtedly different mental events and activities? Because of the reciprocal nature of the sensori-motor process, neither the stimulus nor the whole activity can be considered as prior to the other. For every stimulus there was action conditioning it, and for every action there was sensation exciting it. Therefore in any given situation (such as the child-candle instance), the question of what the stimulus was must be determined only in reference to the goal involved in the situation. This led Dewey to say that there is no absolute classification of mental entities into stimulus, response, etc. Rather a mental event's label is relative to some situation and, more specifically, relative to the organism's purpose in that situation. Without some purpose to its activity an organism's mental activity cannot be distinguished into kinds; therefore such distinctions are purely *teleological*. "The fact is that stimulus and response are not distinctions of existence, but teleological distinctions, that is, distinctions of function, or part played, with reference to reaching or maintaining an end" (*EW* 5: 104).

The Foundations of Functionalism

In the "Reflex Arc Concept" all the promise portended by the insights of the "Soul and Body" has come to fruition: the antidualistic organicism, the continuity of the physiological with the psychical, the functional distinctions of the parts, and the teleology of the whole. When Dewey went even farther in later work to extend these functionalist principles beyond stimulus and response to the mediating control of judgment and ideas, he arrived at a full expression of instrumentalism. In that theory the intellectual elements of mental activity (the concepts, judgments, etc.) exist solely in reference to practical goals, and their adequacy will be determined solely upon whether they aid in the attainment of those goals.

Organic Metaphysics

By 1886 Dewey was already in possession of very complex philosophical views on fundamental issues. His early philosophy has been called functional idealism, voluntaristic idealism, and experimental idealism. They can together adequately classify Dewey's early philosophy so long as it is understood that such idealism is objective, not subjective. There are many idealistic alternatives to subjectivism, however. The precise nature of Dewey's philosophy is specified by the relationships that it finds between mind and ultimate reality.

Dewey never adopted the notion that ultimate reality consisted solely of logical or conceptual relations. That was T. H. Green's view, but Dewey believed from the start that the Hegelian absolute could not be mental in such a restrictive way. Consciousness consists of more than a priori categories since it is an organic unity of both universalizing categories and individuated experiences, of concepts and percepts. Both members can be attentively distinguished to some degree, but their essential interdependence is demonstrated by the inability to understand one without the contribution of the other. Geoffrey Thomas observes that it is with great peril that one affixes the label "Hegelian" to T. H. Green.[44] If anything, Green was a neo-Kantian first and foremost. Neo-Kantianism as a movement in both Germany and in England always incorporated three fundamental Hegelian corrections to Kant: the necessary elimination of the thing-in-itself, the required presence of the synthesizing categories in consciousness, and the identification of ultimate reality with the absolute eternal consciousness. After this basic agreement, which Dewey and Green shared with all the neo-idealists, they quickly diverged on the specific topics of the absolute and knowledge. There was some overlap concerning the origin of motives and ethical duties, though Dewey was always critical of Green's ethical theory. The heart of the matter lies in Dewey's use of the peculiarly Greenian term "reproduction" and in their understanding of the nature of real relations. Green found reality to be ultimately composed of real concrete universals. This metaphysical relational realism was for Green expressed in the dictum that "*esse* is *intelligi*." But as we saw, Dewey rejected both "*esse* is *percipi*" and "*esse* is *intelligi*" for "*esse* is *experiri*," where experience incorporates both perceptions and relations (and, in the *Psychology*, feelings and will). Green's absolute was purely cognitional, while Dewey, since he declared that consciousness was always composed of cognitional, emotive, and volitional elements, found Green's absolute to be a bare abstraction and hardly knowable. A purely cognitional understanding of consciousness is also excessively abstract.

Dewey was already well on the way to equating explicitly consciousness with experience. If consciousness contains knowledge as a constitutive member and experience is the same as consciousness, then knowledge does not exhaust experience. Such a logical inference had not yet impressed Dewey by 1887, however. In the *Psychology* he declares that every experience must be a case of knowledge. But at least Dewey already realized that every experience could not be knowledge simply but was inextricably bound up with feeling and volition too. This implies that even where he uses "reproduction" to describe the origin of human knowledge, he must already mean something quite different from Green's intent. The most significant sign of this difference lies in the fact that while "reproduction" is mentioned a couple of times early on, the rest of *Psychology* does not use this term nor its cognates. Dewey's 1889 "The Philosophy of Thomas Hill Green," often taken to be his fullest expression of early discipleship, discusses at length the role of reproduction in Green's epistemology. However clearly this article explains Green's views on knowledge (and morality and religion), his attempt to expound persuasively another's philosophy without making criticisms for a religious audience (the readers of the *Andover Review*) should not be used to infer Dewey's full agreement. If read carefully in the light of Dewey's subsequent explicit criticisms of Green's moral theory, his concerns over our inability to know our ideal self and our full duty on Green's theory stand out clearly (*EW* 3: 27–28).

Morris viewed the personal self as a growing entity within a larger whole. Dewey quickly adopted this view and never abandoned it. But there is a question that must be answered immediately. Is the larger whole fixed and permanent so that a person goes over predetermined ground in the quest for knowledge and self-realization? Green's portrait of the absolute demands an affirmative answer to this question. But Dewey, following Morris, could not accept that answer. Morris's evangelical orientation required that personal efforts make a creative and an original difference to the overall functioning of the whole (God). Dewey similarly believed that ultimate reality must be susceptible to human activities. This tenet would later be manifested in his instrumentalist tenet that knowing, like any other experience, changes reality. Why was a term such as "reproduction" used, one which so easily fits Green's theory of knowledge but not Dewey's?

The charitable way to answer this question would be to suggest that Dewey was struggling for a way to express the notion that there are natural relations independent of the individual mind and that this mind is learning how to create an adjustment of internal mental functions to these outer relations. This answer would cohere with his later understanding of knowledge, but the temptation to read it directly back into his 1886 writings should be resisted. Still, his organic portrait of the world demanded that the individual mind subsist in organic relations with nature. Green saw the ultimate aim of knowledge reproduction as the complete internalization of all of the absolute relations. Such a theoretical result, however, demands two separate minds—the absolute and the human. Dewey wanted to avoid this dualistic result, insisting that as we know, we are really *becoming* the absolute. This growth is not mere duplication, but the true originality of new creation. Our creative efforts are at the same time the creative efforts of the absolute. The organic metaphor helps to show the proper role of growth. No organ grows so that it can duplicate the substance or function of the body, but rather the new functions of a growing organ contribute to new functions of the whole organism. Metaphysically the individual mind must not simply bear a copying relation with the absolute; copying implies a mechanical, external relation and hence dualism. The successful avoidance of dualism, Dewey began to see in the late 1880s, lay not merely in the philosophical demand that conscious experience is the ultimate philosophical category, but also in the demand that growth, not replication, be the purpose of *both* the individual mind and the absolute. The implications of this stand demanded the reconstruction of absolute idealism, and Dewey would obligingly follow this course through the 1890s.

Voluntaristic Psychology

Dewey's doctrine that mind is inherently functional stems from the organic portrait of mind drawn by Morris and Caird, which holds that the nature of any portion of consciousness is determined by the purpose it serves for the entire whole. His view that mind is primarily volitional arrives from Morris, Wundt, and Green to varying degrees. It was principally Wundt who stressed the organic relationships holding among the senses, the mind proper, and the will. Morris believed that knowledge is the result of activity, while Green kept the two further apart, preferring to stress the role of the will in ethical behavior. Green's account of learning does make reference to the role of practical activity, but it is poorly developed, and the role of motor volitions is uncertain. Dewey was at first closer to Green, seeing the volitional processes primarily as mere mental activity, as in apperception. From his study of the new psychology, Dewey granted muscular activity a far more important role in learning.

The label of "experimental idealist" could be quite misleading. Morris preferred to be classified as an experimentalist. Yet this term, like his other preferred term, "experientialist," stressed his view that his idealism was grounded in ordinary experience. When Morris used the term "experimental" he meant to draw attention to the occurrences of ordinary experience, and it had no connection with actual experiment as science conceives it. As Dewey developed his voluntarism, the term "experimental" changed meaning to reflect the participation of practical activity in the knowledge processes. For Dewey even the baby who attempts to coordinate the senses with motor actions is performing experiments, though of a very simple kind. Other terms have been used to classify both Morris's and Dewey's philosophies. For example, "dynamic idealism" suits them both, denoting their opposition to a static or passive picture of the mind. A colleague of Dewey's at Michigan, A. H. Lloyd, entitled a book *Dynamic Idealism,* indicating his close relationship with Morris and Dewey. "Personal idealism" was applied to Morris first, as he was part of the rising opposition (which included Andrew Seth) to the tendency of Hegelianism to destroy any individual teleology or personality, for either humanity or God. Dewey quickly absorbed the principle that the purposes of the individual largely define the individual, and he never relinquished the doctrine that any understanding of the nature or duties of the individual revolved around the goals, broadly construed, of the individual. Because of his heavy reliance on the organic metaphor, Dewey is also part of the larger movement called "organicism."[45] Organicism is not necessarily linked with idealism, as the case of Trendelenburg shows. Dewey himself in later years repudiated any effort to find idealism in his organicism: ". . . I do not believe that any school of philosophy has a monopolistic hold upon the interpretation of such words as 'whole, complete, coherence, integration,' etc" (*LW* 14: 38).

The full story of Dewey's intellectual debts to Morris and Wundt has been obscured for various reasons. Marc Jones points out the distortions in Wenley's interpretation of Morris in *The Life and Work of George Sylvester Morris.* According to Jones, Wenley's depiction of Morris as a relatively orthodox Hegelian after 1878 is accurate only if Morris's debt to Trendelenburg and Aristotelian organicism is ignored. It is precisely this debt which animates Morris's, and hence Dewey's, functionalism, voluntarism, and experimentalism. Unfortunately Morton White relied heavily upon Wenley's account (Jones's book was published five years after White's) for information on Morris.[46] White's Morris is thus a philosopher heavily indebted to Green's critiques of British empiricism, has no independent theory of reality, and no significant psychology. The interpretation of Dewey's early philosophy thereby gets infected with the same misconception in White's account. Another example of misinterpretation is that Wenley finds in Morris a complete disregard for the sciences. When this supposed lack of respect is transferred to Dewey, it becomes mysterious that he could have been strongly attracted to experimental psychology and come to declare that psychology and philosophy are really the same enterprise. It is no surprise then that no one, least of all White, was interested in discovering the relationships between Dewey and Wundt.[47] As other commentators followed White's lead, it became traditional dogma that only a sudden conversion to Darwinian evolution, facilitated by James's *Psychology*, could account for Dewey's burgeoning interest in biological psychology. What made matters worse was that, mentioned above, for a long time Wundt was considered as a mere associationist, hardly compatible with German idealism. Furthermore, according to Titchener's influential definitions of the opposing psychological viewpoints of functionalism and structuralism, Wundt was a structuralist.[48] Why did Dewey never mention Wundt in later reminiscences about influences? It was probably far easier to give credit to James, a close friend and fellow pragmatist, than to dredge up recollections of a German philosopher whose psychology inspired only temporary attention and whose reputation in the United States went into a steep decline in the early twentieth century. As a final twist of irony, James himself had a large debt to Wundt.[49]

There are a large number of similarities between Dewey's psychology and Green's *Prolegomena to Ethics*. Primarily Green and Dewey agree concerning the rise of intellect out of sensations. Another of Green's aims in the *Prolegomena* is to refute the notion that desire, intellect, and will are three separate functions which can interact but do not require each other. To do so, he talks of how "instinctive impulses" are transformed into desires/motives which allow knowledge of impulse-fulfilling objects, and he uses the term "feeling" interchangeably with impulse.[50] Knowledge in turn requires desire.

> In all exercise of the understanding desire is at work. The result of any process of cognition is desired throughout it. No man learns to know anything without desiring to know it. The presentation of a fact which does not on the first view fit itself into any of our established theories of the world, awakens a desire for such adjustment, which may be either by further acquaintance with the fact, or by a modification of our previous theories, or by a combination of both processes. The learner of course knows not how he will assimilate the strange fact till he has done so, but the idea of its assimilation as possible evokes his effort.[51]

Green distinguishes between speculative and practical thought but is quick to assert that they need each other to attain their truly common goal: the realization of desires. The most practical activity requires intellect while even the most abstract cognitive pursuit at every turn requires the motivational desires involved at every step in learning. But at the fundamental level will encompasses desire and intellect.

> Will is then equally and indistinguishably desire and thought—not however *mere* desire or *mere* thought. . . . but desire and thought as they are involved in the direction of a self- distinguishing and self-seeking subject to the realization of an idea. . . . The will is simply the man. Any act of will is the expression of the man as he at the time is.[52]

Green does not equate will with the absolute consciousness, desire with the individual, or knowledge with the universal, in contrast to the primary theses of Dewey's *Psychology*. The major difference between Dewey and Green at the psychological level lies in Dewey's more elaborate and sophisticated understanding of mental processes, provided by experimental psychology. This understanding allowed him to cast the main supports for functionalism and instrumentalism while Green never advanced beyond the conclusions expressed above. At the metaphysical level, Dewey replaced Green's notion of the absolute as the fixed system of logical relations with a notion of the absolute as active experience.

It has long been a canonical part of the traditional account of Dewey's development that the criticisms which Dewey made of Green in several articles from 1890 to 1894 signaled his disenchantment and eventual disengagement from absolute idealism. As we have seen, the standpoint behind these criticisms was already largely in place when Dewey discussed Green in "Psychology as Philosophic Method" in 1886. Dewey never saw eye-to-eye with Green on important matters beyond a few basic neo-Kantian and psychological starting-points. The notion that Dewey's relationship with Green should be the key factor in determining his relationship with absolute idealism must be abandoned. The only way to discover his relationship with idealism is properly to grasp his initial notion of the absolute and trace its evolution.

Dewey and James

Because of the combination of Wundt's psychology and Morris's organicism, Dewey upheld the indissoluble integration of cognitive and volitional processes independently of James's and others' efforts in that direction. This runs directly counter to the traditional account, but this claim must not be misunderstood since it pertains only to one aspect of relationship between Dewey and James. The undeniable impact of James cannot be underestimated, as Dewey has repeatedly declared. This impact came mostly from James's *Principles of Psychology*, though Dewey was well aware of James's positions on the theory of local signs, the innervation theory, and associationism by 1886, referencing James frequently on these topics throughout the *Psychology.* Dewey was then also aware of one of James's more philosophical articles which presage his pragmatism (the 1879 "The Sentiment of Rationality"), referencing it in the notes to chapter 14 of the *Psychology.* James there states that concepts are "teleological instruments" which serve diverse ends. An inspiration for Dewey's thinking might be found in this passage, but caution should prevail. James himself provides good ground for caution, noting that the neo-idealist John Watson agrees.[53] Of course, Caird, Morris, and Dewey were all teleological psychologists as well, and so no conclusions can be drawn on this point. James was already by 1879 far along the road to pragmatism, but there is no evidence that Dewey found anything but corroboration in James's writings concerning the functionality of concepts and the essential role of volition for knowledge.

The juxtaposition of two essays, published in the same year (1984), detailing James's influences upon Dewey serves to illustrate how a dissenting perspective can diverge from the traditional account of Dewey's development. The tradition is represented by Andrew Reck while the dissenter is Michael Buxton.[54] Reck credits James with pulling Dewey away from idealism on many levels and particularly for supplying the notions of the active mind and of the essential interrelatedness of feeling, thought, and will. This notion permitted Dewey to arrive at his reconstruction of the reflex arc concept. Buxton, with whom there is much to agree to in the main, takes issue with the "magic bullet" theory of Dewey's "conversion," which locates in one philosopher and one book the decisive psychological turning point of Dewey's career. While calling Wundt an "empiricist," a hardly adequate label, Buxton correctly analyzes Dewey's 1884–1890 works to discern how Dewey already possessed a robust understanding of the organic relations holding within experience and of the teleological activities of the individual mind operating in its environment. The many other areas, from evolutionary biology to logic to ethics, where Dewey also independently arrived near to James's own positions, are so well covered by Buxton's article that I must forbear a retelling.

On the nature of sensations, the biological nature of mind, and the nature of conceptual reasoning, Dewey's debt to James is the most extensive. However, on these subjects James did not overthrow Dewey's cherished idealist views but instead assisted his reconstruction of idealism, which was already well under way before 1890. As Dewey says in the Note to the third edition, the only "alteration of standpoint" involved sensation. No great idealist principle was at stake for Dewey on this matter. He was already by 1890 suspicious of any psychology reliant on atomistic sensations, enthusiastic toward the idea that mind can only be understood in its relations to nature, and insistent on the functional nature of reason. Dewey would not have found James's views persuasive unless they were consistent with his basic metaphysical and psychological standpoints and if they were guides towards solutions of problems that he had already formulated.

James did not inspire a "rebellion" against absolute idealism, but he did help Dewey move towards a more coherent idealistic philosophy and psychology.

A Functionally Idealistic Epistemology

The tenets of Dewey's organically idealistic heritage from Morris and Caird permitted him to discern in Wundt a specific psychological theory to breath life into them. By 1886 he was in possession of all of the central doctrines of psychological functionalism, and by 1892 Dewey had a recognizably complete instrumentalism. The following list, together with the preceding chapter's list, enumerates its epistemological doctrines.

1. Human experience possesses emotional, volitional, and intellectual aspects.

2. The intellectual aspect requires the presence of feeling and will.

3. Meaning has an ineliminable dependence on voluntary activity.

4. No experience is purely passive in nature.

5. Voluntary activity is necessary to imbue experience with value/meaning.

6. Meaning/value are essentially the same thing and must be understood teleologically.

7. Cognition is surrounded by, and is dependent on, valuable voluntary activities.

8. Cognition serves to increase the amount of meaning/value in experience.

9. Knowledge, as the result of cognition, is the product of willfully controlled experience.

10. Knowledge is surrounded and stimulated by the experience of the environment.

These principles, together with those of the previous chapter, are the foundation of psychological functionalism. Dewey's idealistic functionalism holds that mind's function is to grow into the absolute mind of reality's relations. The nature of this growth (mere copying reproduction, or creative emergence) was an ongoing difficulty for Dewey, but the basic tenet remained that knowledge is responsible for creating its object.

CHAPTER FOUR

The Absolute of Active Experience

> With reference to experience as it now is, [objective] idealism is half opposed to empiricism and half committed to it,—antagonistic, so far as existing experience is regarded as tainted with a sensational character; favorable, so far as this experience is even now prophetic of some final, all-comprehensive, or absolute experience, which in truth is one with reality. That this combination of opposition to present experience with devotion to the cause of experience in the abstract leaves objective idealism in a position of unstable equilibrium from which it can find release only by euthanasia in a thorough-going empiricism seems evident.
>
> John Dewey, "Experience and Objective Idealism," 1906

The 1886 *Psychology* offers a metaphysical theory of the absolute self, showing its metaphysical power through the human self's efforts to unite with it. It also offers a psychological portrait of the growing self in the process of growing experience, which includes the self's growing intellectual powers to know truth. The 1891 *Outlines of a Theory of Ethics* presents Dewey's moral philosophy as initially liberated from the tyranny of the absolute self. This liberation, Dewey realized, required a transformation of the other primary terms of his philosophy, but it took several years for him to work this out. His 1894 *The Study of Ethics* presents his full reconstruction of the nature of ideals, the self, and growing experience. While this text is nominally centered on the moral life, its real focus is on the practically lived life, which is of course for Dewey the only life. All three books agree that the intellectual life is but a functional aspect of the practical life. Therefore, unless Dewey's theory of practical experience is grasped, the evolution of his theory of the role of inquiry and knowledge cannot be properly traced.

Dewey's philosophy held that human experience must be the ultimate philosophical ground of appeal. While hardly a novel starting point for a philosopher, his own look at experience found that it is irreducibly organic. Continuity and functionality pervades all aspects of experience, thus placing "activity" at center stage. Activity for Dewey means far more than mere motion, though motion is at the heart of his naturalistic inheritance from Trendelenburg. Activity is also structured and purposive; some measure of meaningful regularity and goal directedness is implied. This expansive sense of active experience includes for Dewey that connoted by "experiment," which is part of his inheritance from Morris, who stated that philosophy "is nothing but the examination of our whole and undivided experience with a view to ascertaining its whole nature, its range, and its content."¹ By experience Morris did not mean that collection of atomic sensations to which empiricists typically refer, but that experience of a true empiricism, "resting on the only true substantive *experience* (=etymologically, *trial, proving*) possible for man."² Dewey caught this sense of experience from Morris, and both proclaimed, as Morris put it, that philosophical method which is "simply founded in and dictated by the recognition of experience in its whole nature, is alone entitled to be fully and without qualification 'experimental.'"³

The permanent value for Dewey's philosophy of the tenet that any experience must have such an active aspect cannot be overemphasized. Time and time again he appeals to this understanding of experience in his debates with other philosophies. When activity is a fundamental philosophical category, the philosophical understanding of experience must correspondingly be transformed.

> Experience becomes an affair primarily of doing.... The living creature undergoes, suffers, the consequences of its own behavior. This close connection between doing and suffering or undergoing forms what we call experience. Disconnected doing and disconnected suffering are neither of them experiences. Suppose fire encroaches upon a man when he is asleep. Part of his body is burned away. The burn does not perceptibly result from what he has done. There is nothing which in any instructive way can be named experience.... But suppose a busy infant puts his finger in the fire; the doing is random, aimless, without intention or reflection. But something happens in consequence. The child undergoes heat, he suffers pain. The doing and undergoing, the reaching and the burn, are connected. One comes to suggest and mean the other. Then there is experience in a vital and significant sense. (*MW* 12: 129)

Dewey is always careful to explain that "activity" does not denote mere motion or change, but connotes organic, living change. His metaphysics was never one of mere flux, despite the accusations of many interpreters. However one looks at experience, Dewey claimed, one must find meaningful, purposive experience. As his 1916 *Democracy and Education* clarifies,

> The nature of experience can be understood only by noting that it includes an active and a passive element peculiarly combined. On the active hand, experience is trying—a meaning which is made explicit in the connected term experiment. On the passive, it is undergoing. When we experience something we act upon it, we do something with it; then we suffer or undergo the consequences. We do something to the thing and then it does something to us in return: such is the peculiar combination. The connection of these two

phases of experience measures the fruitfulness or value of the experience. . . . When an activity is continued into the undergoing of consequences, when the change made by action is reflected back into a change made in us, the mere flux is loaded with significance. We learn something. It is not experience when a child merely sticks his finger into a flame; it is experience when the movement is connected with the pain which he undergoes in consequence. Henceforth the sticking of the finger into flame means a burn. Being burned is a mere physical change, like the burning of a stick of wood, if it is not perceived as a consequence of some other action. (*MW* 9: 146)

While Dewey always held that activity is essential to experience, he used the concept of activity on two levels in his early philosophy. Activity first and foremost philosophically denoted the essence of mind, indicating its ability to absorb sensations according to synthesizing rules of its own. But activity also biologically denoted the essence of the individual organism in its environment. As Dewey studied active experience, these two quite distinct notions of activity charged his early psychological writings, especially the 1886 *Psychology*, with a tension that occasionally erupted into contradiction. This tension is no more evident than where the will is concerned, and, as the will is central to the self, knowledge, and truth, then his discussions of these also suffer.

The *Psychology* defines its subject matter as the science of the phenomena of self-consciousness. As the book proceeds, however, it becomes apparent that while "self-consciousness" is often used interchangeably with "consciousness," at other times Dewey's discussion relies on their possession of distinct meanings. For example, when he declares early on that consciousness cannot be defined since it cannot be meaningfully distinguished from something else, he has used consciousness synonymously with self-consciousness. On the other hand, because Dewey theorizes that an individual's activity does not begins until one's actions are willed for one's self (and not just mechanically imposed), the self does not emerge until attentive volition takes cognitive control. Recounting the infant's growing interest in particular features of its world, he describes the emergence of self-consciousness out of mere consciousness (*EW* 2: 116). Mere consciousness is the realm of mechanical activities of apperceptive association, responsible for the transformative processing of sensations into minimally meaningful organic experience. While technically qualifying as mental activity and sufficient to refute the passive portrayal of mind offered by other empiricisms, such consciousness is the lowest level of experience. Roughly corresponding to the Kantian aesthetic, Dewey's notion of consciousness qualifies it as a minimal grade of knowledge, and he declares it as such. But deeper in the text it turns out that even this minimal consciousness cannot qualify as knowledge.

"The child spends his early years in learning to know. Knowledge is an acquired product, due to the possibility of connecting present experiences with the past" (*EW* 2: 81).

Dewey is struggling with his double inheritance. Where experience itself is being described, it necessarily is self-conscious, knowing, fully formed, and completely sufficient. But where an individual's experience is concerned, it displays a growth development from mere sensation (not experienced) to minimal consciousness to self-consciousness, a process of transition from not-knowledge to bare knowledge to self-knowledge, and a thorough dependence on the external environment to stimulate first its apperceptive and later its attentive mental faculties. The Greenian resolution of this dual description of experience is to reserve "self-consciousness" as a term only fully applicable to the absolute mind and apply "growth" only to individual consciousness. While Dewey does speak of the absolute as self-consciousness, he rejects the terms of Green's solution, for Dewey is resolved to force philosophy to make every aspect of the absolute experienceable to the individual. He offers a replacement in the *Psychology*, but he does not conceive his absolute solely in terms of intellectual knowledge. In order to best approach his conception of the absolute, the distinction between universal knowledge and individual knowledge must be examined.

Absolute vs. Functional Truth

According to Dewey's early idealism, distinctions and divisions can only arise within consciousness. Psychology therefore can only study "the various *forms* of consciousness, showing the *conditions* under which they arise" (*EW* 2: 8). Psychology has among its subject matters knowledge and volition. Since both have a universal aspect—knowledge is available to all individual intelligences, and the content of every potential action is universal—self-consciousness must be able to transcend the individual to attain universality. Psychology is therefore the study of these two aspects of self-consciousness and their interaction.

Universal Knowledge and Absolute Truth

In the introductory portion of the *Psychology* Dewey provides his definition of psychology.

> Psychology is the science of the reproduction of some universal content or existence, whether of knowledge or of action, in the form of individual, unsharable consciousness. This individual consciousness, considered by itself, without relation to its content, always exists in the form of *feeling;* and hence it may be said that the reproduction always occurs in the medium of feeling. Our study of

The Absolute of Active Experience

the self will, therefore, fall under the three heads of Knowledge, Will, and Feeling. (*EW* 2: 11)

Knowledge relies on feeling since the apprehension of an object starts with the effect of the object upon the mind. This effect is the interest, and it draws the mind's attention, which is an act of volition. Such attention permits learning, which produces knowledge (*EW* 2: 20). These three aspects of consciousness fit nicely with the definition of psychology as the science of the reproduction of some universal content in the form of individual consciousness. The universal content is knowledge; its duplicate in the individual consciousness has feeling attached to it while the will is responsible for the creation of the individualized knowledge as well as the universal manifestation of an individual interest or desire. The poverty of British psychology is evident compared to this far richer plan, for the British version of the "psychological standpoint" declares that the contents of the mind are only individualized feelings (sensations). It is little wonder that this barren starting point arouses the dire need to rely illicitly on additional mental processes (regular associations, synthesizing categories, etc.), and the futile effort to prove the existence of anything external beyond feelings. Dewey would have philosophers realize from the start that consciousness will not fit into compartmentalized individualities containing only entities abstracted from the truly wider and richer conscious experience. He warns against "regarding consciousness as something purely subjective or individual, which in some way deals with and reports a world of objects outside of consciousness" (*EW* 2: 25).

Dewey elaborates on the three types of consciousness used in his *Mind* articles. The universal consciousness is the universal content of consciousness (knowledge), the individual consciousness is the particular effect of consciousness (feeling), while the absolute consciousness is the necessary activity underlying the other two types of consciousness (will). By Dewey's own premises, if the universal consciousness is just the objective content of consciousness and if this objective content is but an abstraction from concrete experience, then universal consciousness cannot have any fundamental existence. Its existence relies on the logically prior existence of self-consciousness/absolute consciousness. This profoundly affects the question of Dewey's fundamental position on consciousness: does he hold the emergence or the reproduction theory? The answer must be, given his reliance on reproduction in the *Psychology* and given the impossibility of universal consciousness existing independently from conscious experience, that he is clinging to a contradictory position. Green's theory of reproduction did not suffer from this contradiction, as it held that the universal consciousness is metaphysically absolute and hence exists independently of, and logically prior to, individual consciousness. Reproduction can at least take place, although that raises many other difficult questions that Dewey would pursue in later publications.

However, Dewey wanted to reject the dualistic tendencies of Green's theory and its elevation of the intellectual aspect of experience into supreme reality. He declared, first in the *Mind* articles and then in the introductory chapters of the *Psychology*, that both the universal and the individual are but two aspects of a more fundamental consciousness. However, what then of reproduction? The term seems entirely inappropriate, and on further reflection it even appears to be the marker for a theory of the origin of individual experience that Dewey never really held.

The individual can be seen as finite and growing while the universal is independent from the individual. But this independence is only a relative independence, as both the individual and the universal must be in consciousness lest the "agnostic" fallacy be committed. There must be a more fundamental consciousness out of which the other two may emerge, in, for example, a psychology. And this consciousness, by Dewey's own declaration, must be nothing other than the consciousness of a psychologist. If this consciousness were beyond the psychologist's consciousness, then it becomes a mere thing-in-itself and absolutely unknowable. It cannot be postulated as the consciousness of an all-seeing God or an all-pervasive nature, but only the everyday consciousness of normal adult experience. According to Dewey, therefore, every day we see ourselves as finite yet infinite: finite because we believe ourselves to be bounded by a physical reality surrounding us; infinite because we *know* this physical reality and in so doing we have it in our consciousness. We can sympathize with Dewey's attraction to the reproduction theory, as it would rescue him from that "personal pantheism" of being *the* self encompassing reality. But on his own principles it would seem that he avoids dualism only at the cost of being God.

The fundamental question must be whether the content of universal knowledge possess a prior existence, both existentially and logically, to the content of an individual consciousness. An individual consciousness undoubtedly exists in time and undergoes birth, growth, and maturation. The events of this existence takes place within the absolute consciousness. If the answer to our question is affirmative, we seem to be invited by Dewey to take the misguided ontological standpoint and to view human intelligence as merely copying knowledge which already exists for Absolute consciousness. However, if the answer should be negative, then "reproduction" is an entirely inappropriate term. If knowledge must be both individual and universal, then Dewey is instead inviting us to take a methodological, not ontological, approach to understanding knowledge. As the individual grows in knowledge, then universal knowledge grows too—there is but one knowledge, in the process of emergence, with individual and universal aspects. This methodological approach is far more consistent with Dewey's insistence that psychology must at once study all forms of knowledge and not merely the individual. It is also entirely consistent with his rejection of Green's understanding of the absolute as consisting of the universal relations of

The Absolute of Active Experience

knowledge. To prevent the contents of universal consciousness from possessing an ontological independence of human consciousness (becoming a thing-in-itself), we must view universal knowledge as an artificial product of our own creation.

Dewey, however, was not prepared to announce such results in the *Psychology*, because of his lingering metaphysical standpoint that truth has existential and logical priority over any human possession of truths. Early in the *Psychology*, Dewey explains that

> Volition, or action, also has these two sides. The content of every act that I can perform already exists, *i.e.*, is universal. But it has no existence for consciousness, does not come within the range of psychology, until I, or some self, perform the act, and thus give it an individual existence. It makes no difference whether the act be to write a sentence or tell the truth. In one case the pen, the ink, the paper, the hand with its muscles, and the laws of physical action which control writing already exist, and all I can do is to give to these separate universal existences an individual existence by reproducing them in my consciousness through an act of my own. In the other case the essence of the truth already exists, and all the self can do is to make it its own. It can give it individual form by reproducing this universal existence in consciousness or self. (*EW* 2: 10–11)

The essence of truth *already exists:* human knowledge can but share in the truth through mind's own efforts. Once again, though, Dewey's experimental psychology betrays this initial definition. He later says that as the mind grows in knowledge, the web of relations so far built up in the individual mind serves as the test of any potential new known truth.

> Truth, in short, from a psychological standpoint, is agreement of relations; falsity, disagreement of relations. . . . It follows from what has just been said that the mind always tests the truth of any supposed fact by comparing it to the acquired system of truth. (*EW* 2: 189–190)

Other idealists, to the extent that they were willing to follow Green's lead, matched these metaphysical and psychological standpoints by arguing that the internal coherence of a mind's knowledge corresponds, more or less, to the absolute coherence of permanent truth. But in this last quotation Dewey declares that the psychological standpoint must take the individual's own internal coherence to be the final criterion *and* definition of truth. Other idealists could use the absolute as the definition of truth while allowing internal coherence to be the criterion of truth. Dewey appears to have been sorely tempted in that direction. But keeping in mind his own pronouncement that the psychological standpoint must be absolute for philosophy, he was also pulled in the opposite direction. On the stand that nothing may be permitted in philosophy which cannot be had in human experience, he must look askance at a definition of truth which locates its reality independently beyond human experience. Other idealists might reply that the truth *is* had in human experience when it is replicated in individual minds. But this reply will not do since Dewey is suspicious of any reality which is both the ground of truth and philosophically independent of human experience. That, after all, was the problem of the Kantian *Ding-an-sich:* the reality which was to be known could not, after all, be really known since it never could be directly experienced. Any promise that human knowledge really was of reality was an illusion since on Kant's own terms no individual mind could compare reality with its knowledge. Knowledge, if it is to be ultimately a matter of agreement, can only be known when *both* terms of the things in agreement can be experienced. The psychological definition of truth above satisfies this methodological requirement since it is the mind's responsibility to grasp at once the coherent fit of a new truth with the new, larger coherent whole. Both, the new knowledge and the larger whole of knowledge, are experienced together, and hence their fit is at once apparent. Or, in the case of a falsity, the lack of coherence is at once grasped within human experience. What function could an independent ground of truth serve for us? The answer, psychologically speaking, is none. From the psychological standpoint, then, any definition of knowledge or truth that is philosophically independent from human experience is an unnecessary, harmful, and eliminable excrescence. If psychology and philosophy are to become one, as Dewey promises, his idealistic metaphysics must be thoroughly overhauled. Dewey was not prepared to undertake this task in 1886, and the *Psychology* accordingly suffered from severe inconsistencies. If we now turn exclusively to the functional epistemology offered in the *Psychology*, these inconsistencies fade from view. There is no mention of reproduction, and until the chapter on intuition, no mention is made of individual or universal consciousness. In their stead are a tight-knit web of organic relations among knowledge, feeling, and will.

Functional Knowledge and Ideal Truth

Dewey's psychological theories of knowledge and truth are far more complicated than those of any of his idealist contemporaries. He was forced to answer two questions. What exactly does intellectual harmony consist of, and how does this notion of harmony square with his demand that the philosophical conception of the absolute cannot be separate from human understanding? Dewey's answer in the *Psychology* was that philosophy must conceive human knowledge in such a way so that no truth could escape it.

> From a psychological standpoint a judgment is called true when it harmonizes with all other judgments; false when it is in some

contradiction to some other. Suppose, for example, an individual interprets a distant cloud as a mountain. The judgment is false, because it does not agree with other judgments which he would be forced to make about the presentation with growing knowledge of it. (*EW* 2: 190)

This quotation is remarkable because Dewey goes beyond mere individual psychological truth, in which one ascribes truth to a judgment because of presently standing harmonious relations within one's mind. This passage offers a vision of a judgment's "objective" truth and its relationship with individual truth claims. The transindividual truth of a judgment consists of its harmony with present *and all future* known judgments. The prefatory clause, "from a psychological standpoint," does not reduce this statement's significance because for Dewey the psychological standpoint is the only legitimate philosophical standpoint. His philosophical theory of truth is indeed a coherence theory but a most peculiar one. Objective truth is not philosophically distinguishable from objective knowledge because objective truth is defined in terms of the ultimate limit of objective knowledge. It is only because human knowledge grows that any particular knowledge claim could be false and thus become known to be false. This strong falsifiability thesis, stating that it is possible for a truth to be true and a falsity to be false only if human knowledge could know them to be so, coheres with Dewey's notion of objective truth that is organically related to human knowledge. If the notion of objective truth had nothing essential to do with human knowledge, then only a weak falsifiability thesis could be sustained, which would say that any knowledge claim could be false and *might* become known to be false. Weak falsifiability is the privilege of a dualistic philosophy, but it must be rejected by Dewey.

Dewey's tightly linked theories of truth and knowledge stand as a firm repudiation of Green's philosophical system and any dualistic system which would define the ground of truth beyond the possible reach of human experience. Dewey understood full well that idealism is not necessarily a haven from dualism. After all, Green's absolute was not defined in such a way as to guarantee that it really could be humanly experienced, and his theory of universal truth was accordingly distinct from the human processes of gaining truth. The best way to avoid this fate, Dewey decided early on, was to define truth so that three principles could be retained. (1) Any claim to knowledge could not only be false, but also known to be falsified. (2) Human knowledge, because it is learned by degrees, approaches objective truth. (3) It must be possible for any objective truth to be humanly learned, and humanly known as objectively true. Dewey's coherence theory of truth in full states that truth is that harmonious system of judgments which would be known when all knowledge about all things has grown to its fullest possible extent. This coherence theory has a corollary. (4) No human claim to knowledge could be known to be objectively true until total knowledge has been attained. Human beings can at present only ascertain that a judgment *so far* coheres with their system of harmonious judgments.

The notion of defining truth in terms of the results of completed inquiry is closely associated with Dewey's fellow pragmatist Charles S. Peirce. The close similarity between Dewey's theory of truth in the 1886 *Psychology* and Peirce's theory of truth has rarely been explored. Despite occasional claims made asserting various intellectual debts on Dewey's part to Peirce, little serious work has been done in this area.[4] Those who are eager to uphold the traditional story have a need for such claims, of course. The problem is that there is precious little evidence to go on. Dewey's own stories of the rise of pragmatism naturally include Peirce, but he gives no explicit credit to Peirce for inspiring any instrumentalist tenet. Nor should he have; in only a few respects do their epistemologies even agree, and what agreement can be found is insufficient to reveal any debt to Peirce. Their divergent accounts of necessity and scientific explanation are discussed in section five, and their disagreement on the nature of logic is treated in section six. With respect to truth, Dewey clearest statement comes in the 1938 *Logic: The Theory of Inquiry.*

> The best definition of truth from the logical standpoint which is known to me is that of Peirce: "The opinion which is fated to be ultimately agreed to by all who investigate is what we mean by the truth, and the object represented by this opinion is the real." (*LW* 12: 343)

This quotation of Peirce comes from his 1878 "How to Make Our Ideas Clear."[5] Dewey's statement comes in the context of a defense of scientific fallibilism and should not be interpreted as a sign that he agrees with Peirce's use of the definition of truth to shed light on the nature of ultimate reality. Dewey's mature thought already had its own independent notion of ultimate reality, based on the doctrine of immediate empiricism. Furthermore Dewey was far more interested in later work to replace "truth" with "warranted assertability." This agreement with Peirce therefore does not help to determine *when* Dewey came to agree with Peirce.

To my knowledge, Dewey nowhere expresses a specific debt to Peirce for any philosophical position. Despite formulating what appears to be Peirce's definition of truth in the *Psychology*, Dewey gives no credit to Peirce. More pointedly, in this textbook Dewey is especially careful to list every other philosopher and psychologist who has any relevance to the issues covered, but there is not even one reference to Peirce's thought in the book's extensive notes. Dewey makes a vague expression of indebtedness to Peirce in a footnote to his 1893 "The Superstition of Necessity," but nothing can be inferred from this courtesy. The next significant reference to Peirce comes in 1904:

The Absolute of Active Experience

> Mr. C. S. Peirce (if I interpret him aright) believes that one of the chief advantages of the mathematical, or symbolic statement is that logic may transcend thereby the limitations of mere formalism and become a potent instrumentality in developing a system which has inherent reference to the pursuit of truth and the validation of belief. (*MW* 3: 66)

Again, there is no ground here for inferring an intellectual debt. Even though more approving references to Peirce are made by Dewey throughout the rest of his career, Peirce's influence must have been subdued concerning this fundamental issue. Because the precise nature of Dewey's early idealism has not been well understood, the compulsion to credit Peirce with inspiration toward coherentism and fallibilism (as well as continuity, voluntarism, and the teleological nature of concepts) is forgivable. However, in light of the philosophical commitments that Dewey had already made before 1886, his coherentist fallibilism (and his other positions) should no longer seem mysterious, but inevitable. It is quite possible that Dewey heard Peirce's views concerning truth and reality during their semesters together at John Hopkins. Still, the notion that Dewey absorbed them or even saw a fit between them and his burgeoning idealism, is just doubtful conjecture. It more likely that Dewey became well acquainted with Peirce's epistemological and metaphysical theses during the mid-1890s and only then recognized some measure of agreement. By that time, however, no sizable influence would have occurred, as Dewey's own basic functionalist positions on knowledge and truth had already been firmly established.

Two further points elaborating Dewey's early theories of knowledge and truth must be emphasized. First, Dewey holds that only judgments could properly be said to be true or false (*EW* 2: 189). This implies that the ground of truth could not be reality because reality for Dewey (unlike Green) does not consist of true judgments. This also implies that the ground of truth could not be any presently living human being's system of harmoniously known judgments. Second, Dewey holds that knowledge only applies to individual existing things in experience. This implies that complete knowledge of objective truth must be of an individual, and indeed Dewey as expected defines the absolute as that perfectly knowable individual which consists of the organic unity of the real and ideal (*EW* 2: 211–212). More important for Dewey's future philosophical development is the idea that because judgments are always of individual things then human knowledge consists of individually known things, and the objective truth consists of truly known individual things. Judgment, knowledge, and truth are all collective nouns, standing for judgments, known things, and truly known things. Dewey's insistence that only individual things may be known and only particular truths may be found was echoed repeatedly whenever he struggled against epistemologists who search for the relation standing between truth and human knowledge. For example, "The Experimental Theory of Knowledge" (1906) expresses this view as fundamental to understanding instrumentalism.

> That truth denotes truths, that is, specific verifications, combinations of meanings and outcomes reflectively viewed, is, one may say, the central point of the experimental theory. Truth, in general or in the abstract, is a just name for an experienced relation among the things of experience.... (*MW* 3: 126)

The bifurcation between Dewey's metaphysical idealism and functionalist psychology thus breaks out in his discussions of truth in the *Psychology*. Metaphysically truth already possesses an absolute reality in the timeless realm of the absolute consciousness, and the human task is to duplicate this truth in human knowledge. Psychologically truth is but an adjective of humanly known judgments that rightly applies to them if they would survive all inquiry into their objects. However compatible Dewey at the time believed them to be, we can with hindsight see which perspective on truth would win out. The difficulty which he was not yet prepared to overcome was to formulate fully a theory of truth which would not succumb to the fatal problems of subjective relativism. The notion of an absolute reality whose intellectual aspect is the compulsory force guiding humans toward convergently coherent truth was extremely difficult to replace. Only a complete reconstruction of idealism would suffice.

The Self and Experience

As we have seen, Dewey identified the self with volitional attentive activity in the *Psychology*. This activity, while necessarily accompanying all experience for Dewey, could not be said to define completely experience because experience has other aspects. In other words, it is impossible to find any portion of experience with which the active self has had nothing to do, but this fact should not be taken to imply the self is identical with experience. However, the self spoken of here in this context is the individual growing self and not the Absolute Self, or God. The role of God and its relation to human selves in Dewey's early system is extremely problematic because he says so little about this issue directly. Because God, like any real entity for Dewey, must be both an individual and knowable to some extent by human beings, he must allow that even our modest knowledge is, from the philosophical perspective, capable of reaching an intuition of the supreme individual. God can be intuited by us as "perfectly realized intelligence" (*EW* 2: 212), but this is only an approach from the side of knowledge, which stops short at a notion of the universal truth. Superior to knowledge is the approach to God from the side of will, where God is found by religious faith to be the "perfect will." As such, God is "the only Reality, and the Source of all activity" (*EW* 2: 361).

The Absolute of Active Experience

Human activity is therefore but an organic component of God, and because the essence of human existence is its activity, the essence of humanity lies in God's activity.

Absolute Active Experience and the Self

Dewey was treading on very uncertain ground here. He had no intention of asserting pantheism, but his philosophy, like Morris's and Caird's, could be easily interpreted as such. Pantheism for Dewey meant that individuality possesses no real existence since all qualities were but modes of the supreme substance. Green more easily escaped the charge of pantheism since his absolute was remote from natural and human concerns. Other idealists (notably Bradley) abandoned God as a metaphysical reality altogether. Dewey inherited this problem from Morris, and despite Morris's confidence that an organic view of God and the self would not eradicate selfhood, the real problem for Dewey now lay not in the reality of the self, but the efficacy of the self's activity. We unreflectively believe that we are the sole sources of our volitional activity. Dewey's early philosophy replaces this illusion with a view of human activity as really and only God's activity. Dewey's insistence that God is the only active reality belies the notion that he should be classified as a nineteenth-century panentheist.[6] The idealistic alternatives were stark: either embrace atheism, confess to pantheism, offer a version of panentheism, attempt to work out a Leibnizian monadology in which God is the supreme harmonizing monad distinct from other monadic selves, or define God as the sum total of all individual selves. Each alternative held many attractions to various idealists of the day, including an important philosopher, Andrew Seth.

Dewey's 1890 "On Some Current Conceptions of the Term 'Self'" is an excellent opportunity to determine his metaphysical views, their standing in relation to those of other neo-idealists, and their development out of his previous thought. This article was Dewey's last effort to speak directly to British neo-idealists as one of them. He would not publish again in *Mind* until sixteen years later ("The Experimental Theory of Knowledge" in 1906), as a staunch opponent of idealism. Such reticence should not be surprising. Like his earlier contributions to *Mind*, "On Some Current Conceptions of the Term 'Self'" was completely ignored by other idealists. The occasion calling forth Dewey's article was the publication of Andrew Seth's 1887 *Hegelianism and Personality* and the subsequent furor among idealists. Seth, from the early 1880s an ardent neo-idealist, abruptly announced his repudiation of the school of British idealism and especially its revered patron, T. H. Green.[7] His book explained that of all those who have benefited from the instruction of the German idealists, only he was in possession of its soundest results. These results could not include a philosophically reasoned justification for the Hegelian absolute. Instead reality consists solely of individual self-consciousnesses, God included, guaranteeing the reality of free and independent selfhood and thus morality. "I have a centre of my own—a will of my own—which no one shares with me or can share—a centre which I maintain even in my dealings with God himself."[8]

Dewey does not address Seth's moral concerns about absolute idealism but delves directly into Seth's arguments that try to show that no Kantian or Hegelian principle can be used to justify the existence of the absolute. Seth starts from an agreement with Kant's demonstration of the necessary existence of the permanent self-consciousness which guarantees the ability to experience a known world. The notion of this self-consciousness is identical with the notion of the intelligible world because the *intelligible* aspect of the world is just the *self-consciousness*.[9] Dewey says that this notion of the self is "clear and self-consistent," yet refuses to say whether he accepts its truth (*EW* 3: 57). But Seth quickly shifts ground. Kant, purified by his own methodology, must conceive of the transcendental self as only "the formal unity of the universe" and the sum of "abstract conditions, not concrete facts or metaphysical realities" (*EW* 3: 27, 28). Dewey correctly points out that this second notion of the transcendental self is much thinner than the first notion since the first self is indeed real—as real as the organized experience which Seth claims in the only reality. The second notion of the self is a mere logical concept, useful for grasping the nature of knowledge but unable to have any existence even as an aspect of the experienced world. Seth concludes that idealism must adopt the second notion and accuses other neo-idealists, Green especially, of attempting to infer fallaciously a really existing thing from the logical analysis of concepts. Without a metaphysically absolute God, Seth's new philosophy announced a Leibnizean revival, asserting God's own individual but separate reality.[10] Seth thus aligned himself with another critic of neo-idealism, Shadworth Hodgson, whose own "Philosophy of Reflection" is according to Seth "the most clear-sighted and thoroughgoing application of the Kantian method."[11] They agree that while Kant correctly discovered the real self, this self is completely individualized.

From Dewey's perspective the reappearance of Hodgson's contention that experience is always individualized experience must have been the return of a bad dream. Neither Hodgson nor Seth ever offered a proof for the view that experience is always that of the limited, individualized human being, but both consistenly used this premise to attack absolute idealisms. Seth has again thrown down the challenge gauntlet: the dare to try to prove the existence of an absolute mind by starting from individualized human experience. Dewey's response is a renewed defense of the absolute, but he curiously does not use methods similar to those of his earlier reply to Hodgson. Dewey takes a longer and more arduous trail instead because Seth's philosophy is far more complicated and troublesome than Hodgson's.[12] The metaphysical problem presented by Seth's view asks how experience can be considered to be both human and absolute. Seth attempted to resolve the problem by establishing individualized human experience as the absolute reality for philosophy and by defining the absolute as only a regulative

The Absolute of Active Experience

category of thought *for us*. Dewey finds this resolution unacceptable because Seth is still trapped in a contradiction. When arguing against the "metaphysical" neo-idealists, Seth wants to treat the self as a mere logical concept which should not be applied to existence, but when constructing his own vision of all reality, Seth has to treat the self as a regulative principle, without which the world cannot be intelligently conceived at all. The second use of the notion of the self is clearly different from the first because the first is forbidden any application to reality while the second, we are told by Seth, must necessarily be used to understand reality.

Dewey complains that Seth cannot have it both ways. He cannot praise Kant to demolish other neo-idealists, only to turn around and praise Hegel to construct his own metaphysics. Because Kant and Hegel mean two very different things by the term "thought," Seth makes progress only by conflating their meaning (*EW* 3: 60). This confusion on Seth's part provides Dewey with an opportunity to differentiate clearly the meaning of the "self" for Kant and Hegel and along the way to argue for his own notion of the self. Dewey first explains why the elimination of the Kantian thing-in-itself must profoundly alter the conception of sense and of thought, and he then explains how these alterations demand a reconstruction of the conception of the self.

Kant's system relies on four primary components: the thing-in-itself, the sensations caused by the thing-in-itself impinging on us, the categories of thought which transform the sensations into knowably cohesive experience, and the self that guarantees the categories' cooperative ability to present experience as always "my" experience across the temporal flow of experiences. The Hegelian reconstruction that Dewey offers, consequent upon the removal of the thing-in-itself, follows the lines that he had worked out in previous articles from 1883 to 1886. In sum sensations cannot be thought of as really existing experiences because they would be utterly meaningless for us and as inconceivable as the dreaded thing-in-itself. In the same respect thought cannot be considered as consisting of mere logical abstractions since concepts/categories are really aspects of experienced meaningful things. It is true that they can be considered for their own sake as universals, but they are meaningless in themselves. Their meaning lies in their true source of known experiences. Because real experience must always be ultimately considered as meaningful, there is no need for a "behind-the-scenes" self to do anything. This Hegelian critique leaves two options. Either the self is philosophically *equivalent to* the entire world (solipsism), or the self is just the continuing synthesizing activity going on *within* experience. Seth's collection of individualized selves is not an option offered by the correct interpretation of Hegel, Dewey concludes, but an utterly foreign presupposition imported with disastrous results.

Dewey then explains his understanding of Hegel's own positive contribution, which lies in the *Logic* of the *Encyclopedia,* and its study of the origin and application of the synthesizing categories. Hegel had two major problems with Kant's twelve basic categories: they seemed quite arbitrary, and they resulted in a static view of experience itself. On the first problem Hegel's logic "would derive the conceptions from a common root and place them in some organic connection with one another" (*EW* 3: 70). Dewey does not explicitly say what this common root is, but he makes special mention of the ideas of organism and teleology, which of course are his own foundational concepts. On the second problem Hegel's portrayal of the categories presents them as a growing, evolving movement of thought. Kant's categories, while conceived as active synthesizers, cannot be observed doing their work since all we experience is the synthesized, placid product. Such docility is hardly capable of accounting for all of the intellectual growth (child to adult) and hard thinking (problem solving) that human beings obviously manage. What are the categories really for? The start of Dewey's answer is to reply that the categories are the self's way of actively expanding the human intellectual powers. Or, more properly speaking, the self is nothing other than the actively expanding intellectual powers of a human being. The more detailed account of the process of this expansion is the explanation of the nature of the self, and Dewey's *Psychology* is just such an account. "On Some Current Conceptions of the Term 'Self'" instead offers a justification for Dewey's understanding of the fundamental relationships between the self and the categories on the one hand and the self and experience on the other.

The categories, the concepts used to increase coherent meaning in experience, can be directly experienced. They are, as the next section explains more fully, the universal aspect of known objects. Because known objects are experienced, their meaning is also experienced. More important, the process of conceptual change, during which things lose old meanings and acquire new meanings with the creation on new concepts, is also directly experienced. As the self is for Dewey precisely this process of intellectual change, he can speak of the self as being not one of categories of experience, the categories taken together, or the experienced world.

> As long as sensation was regarded as given by a thing-in-itself, it was possible to form a conception of the self which did not identify it with the world. But when sense is regarded as having meaning only because it is "there" as determined by thought, just as thought is "there" only as determining sense, it would seem either that the self is just their synthetic unity (thus equaling the world) or that it must be thrust back of experience, and become a thing-in-itself. The activity of the self can hardly be a third something distinct from thought and from sense, and it cannot be their synthetic union. What, then, is it? This is, I take it, the problem which finally emerges, when Kant is made self-consistent by the elimination of

the thing-in-itself, and when the logical or thought-factor of his philosophy is developed in the Hegelian manner. (*EW* 3: 73–74)

Dewey's answer to this all-important question is not offered subsequent to its asking, but in the four preceding paragraphs. He reserves the conclusion of the article for a weak defense of Green's philosophy. Green clearly saw (as Seth did not) the significance of this problem of identifying the self, and Green's solution at least responded to this problem. Dewey does not explicitly say whether he agrees with Green, content to have established his main point that Green did not commit the hypostatization fallacy as Seth has charged. However, in the middle of the article Dewey tips his hand to tackle the central issue he has raised.

> Experience can never be complete enough to have a content equal to that of self-consciousness, for experience can never escape its limitation through space and time. Self-consciousness is real, and not merely logical; it is the ground of the reality of experience; it is wider than experience, and yet is unknown except so far as it is reflected through its own determinations in experience,—this is the result of our analysis of Kant, the Ding-an-sich being eliminated but the Kantian method and all presuppositions not involved in the notion of the Ding-an-sich being retained. (*EW* 3: 68)

Without mentioning Green, Dewey has specified Green's own stand on the absolute self-consciousness. When Dewey goes on to reconstruct the rest of the Kantian presuppositions in the light of Hegel's logic, it becomes apparent that Dewey cannot agree with Green. Not only is such a mysteriously remote absolute self-consciousness highly dubious in its own right, it is quite unnecessary when the nature of the self and thought is reconstructed. Since concepts must always apply to known objects which are in space and time, the perceptual forms of space and time therefore constrict the applicability of thought, or, alternatively put, the world as it is for experience can never equal the world as it for thought (*EW* 3: 72). This inequality has two very important consequences for understanding the relationship of the self to experience. First, because the self is just the activities of thought, the self may strive for a conceptual organization of experience which can never really be attained. Second, because experience is constantly infused with novel objects as human beings interact with the environment, the self is always forced to deal with novelties that must be harmoniously integrated into the system of knowledge.

When Dewey says that actual experience is always found to be incomplete, he realizes that such incompleteness could only be realized if it is contrasted with something more complete. At this point the special role of the category of self-consciousness is crucial. Seth used the term "self-consciousness" in two incompatible ways: to describe the individual self and to describe the ultimate principle for understanding the universe. To avoid this incompatibility, Dewey does not equate "self" with "self-consciousness." These terms have quite different meanings. The self is all the activities of thought while "self-consciousness" refers to one concept of thought. Self-consciousness for Dewey is not a metaphysically transcendent entity such as Green's, but a regulative principle guiding all the rest of thought's processes. It has already been said that the "organic" and the "teleological" are fundamental categories for Dewey. His vision of "self-consciousness" embodies these completely to capture the vision of an entity within which all parts are functionally harmonized to the fullest possible extent. It is this vision which for Dewey is the ultimate category of thought and to which all other concepts must be directed. Hegel cannot be credited with specifically providing this category, but his logic did suggest to Dewey the need for a systematic organization of all concepts based on the progressive development of just one primary idea. Self-consciousness for Dewey is that idea. It can be ascribed to the self as one of its concepts used to guide the entire process of harmoniously organizing experience, using other concepts, to ever higher and higher degrees. Because the self can use this supreme category, the double realization can occur that experience does not yet have the fullest possible organization and that experience is being gradually harmonized in that direction. Dewey thus agrees with Seth only to the extent that any attempt to take directly this Hegelian category of self-consciousness for an actually existing metaphysical entity would be a fallacious substantiation of a category (*EW* 3: 73).

The Religious Will and the Ideal Self

However, in the absence of a direct inference, Dewey held out hope for a reasoned justification for asserting the reality of the supreme absolute self-consciousness through a full analysis of experience itself. This justification was to be grounded in a study of the religious will to discover the ultimate ideal existence. Dewey's study was inspired and bolstered by his fellow idealists, especially G. S. Morris, Wilhelm Wundt, T. H. Green, Edward and John Caird, and F. H. Bradley, who each used the notion of the religious ideal to support their absolute idealism. Among these philosophers Bradley deserves priority because his *Ethical Studies,* published in 1876, was the first idealist statement of moral theory and was profoundly influential for subsequent British and American idealism. Reflection on the nature of morality, Bradley argued, results in the religious consciousness because only there can we account for the existence of the evil aspect to our character and our striving to dominate it with our good aspect. Only the religious consciousness, with its declaration that the self really is the perfect ideal, can provide the moral will with a real object. Without this guarantee that the ideal is real, moral striving is senseless because moral rules by themselves are completely arbitrary. Of the divine Bradley says, "its positive character is that it is real; and further, on examining what we find in the religious consciousness, we discover that it is the ideal self considered as realized and real. The ideal self, which in morality is to be, is here the real ideal which truly is."[13]

T. H. Green also argued that the only ideal capable of fully expressing the potential of human nature was that of God. Unlike Bradley, Green did not emphasize the abject failure of social life to achieve this goal since he believed that social life is the only medium for any development of human potential.[14] With the other idealists Green agreed that self-realization requires the ideal of absolute perfection. In addition, Green's theory of the nature of ideals assisted Dewey's formulation of the nature of morality and religion. They agreed that ideals must not be external to the self's volitions because external ideals would be merely coercive commands to obey, and such obedience could not properly be called moral behavior. Purposive behavior aims at a goal, but this goal must be conceived by the actor as his or her own self's goal, or, put another way, the self must identify itself with the end to be achieved.[15]

John and Edward Caird likewise emphasized the religious demand that reality be essentially spiritual and that the individual must recognize this spirituality in order to surmount the finitude of any human goodness. The true self must be the eternal divine spirit that conquers evil, not in some potential, far-off future only to be imagined, but in the very present. Hegel supplies the correct understanding of the Christian saying, "he that saveth his life shall lose it, and he that loseth his life shall save it."

> The true interpretation of the maxim is, that the individual must die to an isolated life—i.e., a life for and in himself, a life in which the immediate satisfaction of desire is an end in itself,—in order that he may live the spiritual life, the universal life which really belongs to him as a spiritual or self-conscious being.[16]

Morris expressed these principles of the religious will in his own organicist manner. He lauded Hegelian philosophy as the only way to prove the organic wholeness of spiritual reality and the functional roles of individual spirits within that whole. Even though human experiences and actions are partial, underdeveloped, and impermanent when considered by themselves, religious faith as inspired by true philosophy lets us know that they cannot really exist in such an imperfect manner. They exist only because they are portions of the whole, real, and active experience that is God. As organic parts they are active only because the whole is active, and their activity is guided by the teleological power of God as the universe's final cause. Morris, more clearly than any other idealist, described God as the absolute active spirit, the true Life.

> Life in all its absolute purity is pure and unqualified activity. . . . That is no true activity which does nothing, and there is no true doing in which no aim or end is realized. No, the true and perfect

> doing, in which consists the true and perfect living, is a conscious, purposeful, and willing activity, which (on man's part) accomplishes the will of God, the absolute law of being, and so effectually realizes its own being.[17]

Religious faith is the affirmation that God's activity is identical with one's own activity, uniting what only seems separate from the perspective of those unable to find their true selves. Only those who assume that they are self-sufficient and separate beings would view God as just a distant, external authority over morality and a forceful, mechanical power over nature. But an examination of human experience reveals that self-sufficiency and separateness cannot really be our nature.

> Human experience is dependent, partial, incomplete. At its best, it is only a fragment. . . . But the divine experience, if I may employ the phrase, is not thus limited. It is independent, complete, absolute. But it is not thus rendered wholly foreign and alien in its nature to human experience, so that no inference may legitimately be made from the latter to the former. On the contrary, just because our experience is a "fragment," and a fragment of the living, organic whole, we may read in it the law and the nature of the whole. What human experience, therefore, is dependently and incompletely, that the divine "experience" is independently, completely, and without limiting qualification.[18]

Morris's teleological organicism closely agrees with Wilhelm Wundt's metaphysical principles. Wundt matched a voluntaristic psychology with a voluntaristic metaphysics, claiming that reality can be adequately described only in terms of the volitional activity. The will, declared Wundt, is the ultimate category of reality. The undoubted relationships among human wills unites them in a larger, completed whole, which in turn is the reality denoted by God. Reality's developing process is the actualization of God's will.[19]

Of course, these neo-idealists were drawing on much older philosophical ideas which can be traced back to Kant. By turning away from deism and its resulting natural law approach to the grounding of morality, Kant instead formulated the demands of a rational morality first and then tried to show why only a theistic religion can practically support those demands. The role of the idea of a theistic god is only hypothetical and regulative. It is not knowledge that brings us to the acceptance of God's existence, but an act of will. Post-Kantian idealism inherited the notion that human progress toward moral perfection essentially requires the careful exercise and control of the will, which in turn requires that one identify one's will with the will of God. This identification is itself an act of the human will, and as we saw above, many idealists of the second half of the nineteenth century understood this act of faith to be the supreme task of humanity. Dewey's early reading of Kant and Kant's English disciple Samuel Taylor Coleridge was apparently very significant for his philosophical and religious development. Herbert Schneider relates that late in his life Dewey was shown a copy of Marsh's edition of Coleridge's *Aids to Reflection* and was asked to reflect on its significance. Dewey spoke of how Coleridge inspired a "spiritual emancipation" during his University of Vermont years and that Coleridge "represents pretty much my religious views still. . . ."[20]

From other idealists, then, Dewey received his understanding of the moral and religious problem to be solved, and he heard a common theme running through their solutions. Dewey picked up this theme and conjoined it with his psychological postulate that purposive activity was metaphysically absolute. In light of the analysis provided by the *Psychology*, the intellectual, emotional, and volitional aspects of experience each provide an opportunity to discover the required justification. Because feeling is supposed to be the individual side of experience, it cannot be a candidate although the ultimate goal of feeling is the aesthetic ideal of complete emotional harmony. Knowledge is a better candidate since self-consciousness is a category of thought. But we already know that Dewey holds absolute truth to be the ultimate goal of thought and that this truth is, psychologically speaking, only an intellectual ideal. Furthermore truth is still but the intellectualized aspect of reality; it cannot be the absolute entire.

The remaining aspect of experience is will. By this process of elimination, the will is revealed to be the key. The will supplies the organic connection between the individual and universal; will is the self; will is both the origin of ideals and their realization. Furthermore, as previously noted, Dewey holds the will, the activity of experience, to be the ultimate reality. Thus the ideal of volition is attaining moral perfection, the perfection of the supreme personality, or God. The ability of humans to possess the ideal of moral perfection, together with the realization that we are moving toward the realization of this ideal in our characters, is our ability to unite ourselves with God.

> As we have repeatedly noticed, the choice of the motive constitutes, for ethical purposes, the attainment of the end. The will to be good is the good. In moral will, therefore, the ideal will is recognized as the ground of the actual self. The obligation of the perfect upon the actual imperfect self is the conscious manifestation of this fact. Furthermore, the unity of the ideal will as the goal, with the will which reaches this goal, the unity involved in all volition, is explicitly developed. Moral will makes definite and clear the meaning of intellectual and æsthetic action. Were it not for what we find manifested in moral will, the action of the intellect in searching for truth,

and the creative activity of the æsthetic imagination, would remain ultimately incomprehensible. (*EW* 2: 359–360)

However, because we realize that our performance of our specific duties in this world must always fall short of perfection, our uniting with God falls short. There remains a dualism, a divide, between our moral experience and God. That divide may only be overcome by what Dewey calls the religious will.

> The will, as religious, declares that the perfect ideal will is the only reality; it declares that it is the only reality in the universe, and that it is the only reality in the individual life. It makes it a motive, once for all, of action; and not of this or that action, but of life, and of life generically and absolutely. Religious will declares that the perfect will is the only source of activity and of reality, and that it is in itself perfect activity and perfect reality. It is the completely self-determined. In it realization and the ideal are one. There is no longer any dualism between the will as it is and the will as it ought to be. (*EW* 2: 360)

The attainment of this religious will once and for all breaks down the barriers between the individual self and absolute reality. By completely identifying one's reality with that of the absolute will, the notion that one is really but a limited creature trapped in space and time drops away completely. The real, religious nature of the self is not the intelligence which struggles to harmonize knowledge. It is not the feeling which searches for aesthetic beauty. It is not the will that aims toward moral perfection. All of these narrow efforts are doomed to fall short of reaching their ideal goal since they are really but aspects of absolute active experience. The real absolute must organically bind them together as one supreme activity. Because we are able to attain a conception of the perfect absolute ideal which unites them, we can conceive God. The religious will is the declaration that God's perfection will be nothing other than that supreme will which unites our subideals of truth, beauty, and goodness. And because this religious will is an experienceable act, the attainment of union with God is the experience of faith. This supreme experience ensures that the absolute, as Dewey so often has proclaimed, must be experienceable in order for it to be real. The ability to have faith, to identify the self's supreme ideal with God, is the placing of self-consciousness as the fundamental category controlling all of the other activities of the self.

Dewey's use of the religious will accomplishes three important goals, all sought by absolute idealists. The religious will (1) overcomes the limitations of the moral will, (2) accounts for the religious demand that the individual surrender the self to God, and (3) brings God into active human experience in an organic way. However, the religious will's affirmation of God as the self's supreme ideal raises important questions concerning the nature of this God. If this philosophy of the absolute is still nominally psychology, as Dewey desires it to be, then the final results of the *Psychology* do not square with the initial definition of psychology. That definition is "psychology is the science of the reproduction of some universal content or existence, whether of knowledge or of action, in the form of individual, unsharable consciousness" (*EW* 2: 11). The term "reproduction" is, in light of his understanding of the religious will, highly inappropriate. Reproduction implies that the original possesses a reality prior to, and independent of, any derivative copy. Dewey nowhere asserts the prior, independent reality of God, and this is because his idealism was never theistic. It was always Green, not Dewey, who tried to preserve as many of the important features of theism as possible. For Dewey, God is not external to human nature, but immanent in human nature. As has already been said, when Dewey describes absolute reality as the supreme activity, he really does mean to say that all human activity is but an aspect of that supreme activity. "Reproduction" should be replaced by "identification" because the meaning of "identification" implies both a oneness and a realization of that oneness. Dewey unfortunately starts off the *Psychology* by sounding like he follows Green, but the course of the text and a consideration of other articles written at that time show that he had been moving in a quite different direction.

If "identification" were instead applied to Dewey's understanding of the relationship between the human and the absolute, then this would lend great support to my thesis that it had always been Dewey's goal to arrive at an emergence theory of the individual self, not a reproduction theory. The growth of the self's powers to harmonize objects into knowledge, feelings into beauty, and volition into goodness is the gradual emergence of the self. Since the self is nothing other than the activities of experience, the self's growth is its emergence out of active experience, or, briefly stated, active experience simply grows more and more. Psychology/philosophy is the study of that growth and of that absolute ideal toward which it grows. Because this ideal can be realized in the supreme experience of religious will, the attainment of this ideal is always the final end toward which all the self's activities have been guided.

Moral Judgment and the Functionally Social Self

As has been recounted, by 1892 Dewey's philosophy had acquired an orientation toward the social as the most fundamental trait of experience and activity. Indeed, because his writings of 1891–1892 and thereafter defined experience as activity and declared all activity to be social, it should not be surprising that Dewey adopted around 1891 the view that the absolute is social in nature. Social conduct is the foundation while all other philosophical entities are but functionally distinguished elements of this absolute. For Dewey, all thought arises in problematic situations, where "what is to be done?" occupies the attention. His terminology reflects this commitment, making "practical" and "moral" synonymous as modifiers of the term "conduct." This identification is not a new development, as the *Psychology* had in effect declared that all practical effort is moral. However, the essentially social nature of all human conduct required a novel reconstruction of many of his other views.

The Social Self and the Absolute

The *Psychology* does not extensively discuss the social self. The section on "Social Feelings" (*EW* 2: 282ff) is his most thorough statement of the essential sociality of the self. There Dewey declares that all feelings are social in nature. Even the moral and religious feelings are but sophisticated developments out of ordinary social feelings. If it is recalled that the *Psychology* defines feelings as that individual side of experience, then we have either caught Dewey in a contradiction or discovered his primary understanding of the nature of individuality. The contradiction lies in taking feelings to be both social and individual, which seems manifestly impossible. Are feelings of the individual, in so far as they are individual, just the very opposite of social feelings? Dewey never believed this, going so far as to say that even "selfish" feelings have their root in the socializing function of sympathy, which is the ability to take feelings to be those of another. He appears to be claiming that the ability to identify feelings as one's *own* is predicated on the ability to feel emotions *with* another. His notion of the individual is not a stand-alone concept, but a concept that has internal relations to the concept of the social. The individual is properly definable only in terms of social relations, and the person is but one term in a polyadic relation with other persons.

There are other intimations that prior to 1891 Dewey was deeply committed to the view that society is the medium necessary for the realization of individual personality. His education at the hands of other idealists included the important notion of the "social organism" giving life to its individual members. Morris, for example, taught that without the social life, the individual person is nothing. Dewey recounts that such Hegelianism was profoundly influential, even after he had come to reject the absolute.

> Hegel's idea of cultural institutions as an "objective mind" upon which individuals were dependent in the formation of their mental life fell in with the influence of Comte and of Condorcet and Bacon. The metaphysical idea that an absolute mind is manifested in social institutions dropped out; the idea, upon an empirical basis, of the power exercised by cultural environment in shaping the ideas, beliefs, and intellectual attitudes of individuals remained. It was a factor in producing my belief that that the not uncommon assumption in both psychology and philosophy of a ready-made mind over against a physical world as an object has no empirical support. It

was a factor in producing my belief that the only possible psychology, as distinct from a biological account of behavior, is a social psychology.[21]

"Ethics and Physical Science" (1887) states that the individual is but an "outgrowth of the social tissue" (*EW* 1: 211). In a description of the ethics courses taught at Michigan in 1889, Dewey recounts how he teaches that

> the realization of personality both demands and occasions society, or the community of those having common interests and purposes, regulating themselves by common laws (implicit, conventional, or reflective), and recognizing common rights. This society with its substratum of expectations, institutions, laws and rights is characterized as the objective ethical world, as real in its way as the "external world" is physically. (*EW* 3: 49)

Dewey's convictions that conduct is always social and that an individual's behavior cannot be properly understood in isolation from the environment were two of his philosophy's earliest foundations and rested unaltered at the base of his mature thought. Bowing to customary terminology, Dewey allowed that "psychology" can be said to study the individual agent's conduct, so long as it is remembered that such study is necessarily partial and incomplete without the study of social activities. "Ethical Principles Underlying Education" (1897) describes the social nature of conduct.

> [C]onduct is of such a nature as to require to be stated throughout from two points of view. How this distinction happens to exist may perhaps be guessed at by calling to mind that the individual and society are neither opposed to each other nor separated from each other. Society is a society of individuals and the individual is always a social individual. He has no existence by himself. He lives in, for, and by society, just as society has no existence excepting in and through the individuals who constitute it. But we can state one and the same process (as, for example, telling the truth) either from the standpoint of what it effects in society as a whole, or with reference to the particular individual concerned. The latter statement will be psychological; the former, social as to its purport and terms. (*EW* 5: 55)

All aspects of an individual's character are thoroughly social in nature. As Dewey's *Human Nature and Conduct: An Introduction to Social Psychology* (1922) says,

> Honesty, chastity, malice, peevishness, courage, triviality, industry, irresponsibility are not private possessions of a person. They are working adaptations of personal capacities with environing

> forces.... Some activity proceeds from a man; then it sets up reactions in the surroundings. Others approve, disapprove, protest, encourage, share and resist. Even letting a man alone is a definite response. Envy, admiration and imitation are complicities. Neutrality is non-existent. Conduct is always shared; this is the difference between it and a physiological process. It is not an ethical "ought" that conduct should be social. It is social, whether bad or good. (*MW* 14: 16)

His equation of conduct with experience, and social functioning with conduct, brought radical new meaning to the term "experience." Dewey's frustration with the inability of "experience" to carry his complete meaning mounted over the years. It remained tightly bound up with the psychological, in the sense of purely individualized and subjective. In 1951 Dewey decided that "culture" should replace "experience" for the revised title of *Experience and Nature*.

> It is a prime philosophical consideration that "culture" includes the material and the ideal in their reciprocal interrelationships and (in marked contrast with the prevailing use of "experience") "culture" designates, also in their reciprocal interconnections, that immense diversity of human affairs, interests, concerns, values which compartmentalists pigeonhole under "religion" "morals" "aesthetics" "politics" "economics" etc., etc. Instead of separating, isolating and insulating the many aspects of a common life, "culture" holds them together in their human and humanistic unity—a service which "experience" has ceased to render. What "experience" now fails to do and "culture" can successfully do for philosophy is of utmost importance if philosophy is to be comprehensive without becoming stagnant. (*LW* 1: 363)

Dewey's entire philosophy, it is hardly too much to say, is a replacement of every dualism with the continuity provided by the absolute reality of the social experience. His naturalistic outlook does not emphasize the natural over the social since he insisted on their thorough integration with each other. The hypothesis of continuity indeed functions in his philosophy as a reminder that the natural must be an organic part of the social, and not the other way around. "Upon the hypothesis of continuity ... the social ... furnishes philosophically the inclusive category" (*LW* 3: 45).

The primacy of social conduct/experience was accompanied in his writings after 1891 with several associated theses. First, conduct is always individualized, as conduct is just purposive behavior at a specific place and time. There is no such thing as "conduct in general." Second, following from the specificity of conduct, sociality is similarly particular: there is no "society at large" over and above the social conduct of human beings. Third, although we may speak of social rules to which behavior should conform, social rules possess no existence beyond their functional role as an aspect of intelligent social conduct. Fourth, while rules are incapable of specifying exactly what should be done in any situation, they still are thus utterly practical/moral, because they are a necessary aspect of any deliberate conduct whatsoever and have no reality independent of conduct. Fifth, rules not only help to modify situations, they can be modified by situations, as reflective thought can adjust rules in the course of problem solving.

These principles concerning social conduct and rules are the foundations for Dewey's social functionalism, underlying his philosophies of morality and science. Based as they are on Dewey's psychological analysis of reflective experience, their philosophical import amounts to the demonstration of continuity between the moral and scientific spheres of experience, and they unify moral and scientific reflective thought. This unification should not be understood as an effort on Dewey's part to prove that scientific methods should be exclusively used to resolve moral problems, because this falsely suggests some sort of primacy on the part of scientific inquiry. Nor should this unification be understood as an effort to show why scientific laws should be used as premises for moral conclusions, because Dewey repudiated that sort of simplistic naturalistic ethics. Rather the unification of scientific and moral thought lies in Dewey's empirical discovery that *both* scientific and moral principles are social rules guiding practical conduct in the sense outlined by the five theses above. Because both kinds of principles are social rules and hence subject to the same analysis of human conduct, their roles in reflective thought must conform to the same procedures of inquiry. Dewey has fulfilled Trendelenburg's demand for a single organon of knowledge. Human deliberation does not occur in completely different forms because deliberation is always ultimately at matter of "what is to be done?" Some situations call for practical moral deliberation and others practical scientific deliberation, but the absolute primacy of active social experience, and the nature of practical difficulties, grounds the uniqueness of deliberation's pattern. Gregory Fernando Pappas has argued for this viewpoint on the experiential relation between morality and science, to which I am indebted.[22] I agree that it is doubtful that Dewey's study of scientific inquiry informed his moral theory; actually, as I also argue below, the reverse seems more likely.

Dewey confirms the primacy of moral theory for his theory of scientific inquiry. In "Experience, Knowledge and Value: A Rejoinder," he assumes an objective stance on his philosophy, speaking as if he were a critic. "Were I anonymously to turn critic of my own philosophy, this is the place from which I should set out. I should indicate that after insisting upon the genuineness of affectional and other 'tertiary' qualities as 'doings of nature.' Dewey then proceeds to emphasize in his theory of knowing, as that is manifested in both science and common sense, the operations of transformation, reconstruction, control, and union of theory and practice in experimental activity which are analogous to those involved in moral activity" (*LW* 14: 63).

Such a heavy emphasis on the essentially social nature of human conduct pushed Dewey's reconstruction of idealism to an even more advanced stage. In previous chapters we have seen how his tenets that human experience must be absolute and that this experience has the inseparably linked aspects of feeling, thought, and will required his dissent from other idealisms of his time. What Dewey apparently did not realize before 1891 was that his use of the religious will's ideal of self-perfection for the guide to behavior is not compatible with the use of social institutions for the proper origin and continuing guide of moral behavior. Their incompatibility rests on two facts. First, social institutions are notoriously unable to supply rules of perfect moral conduct. Second, an ideal of self-perfection could never give any specific guidance in the performance of one's current social duties.

As to the first point, it should be recalled that other idealists, especially Bradley, formulated the religious will as the only way to overcome a human inability to attain moral perfection as a functioning member of any actually existing human society. Put another way, this religious ideal of self-perfection is by design profoundly antisocial, having a different origin and a different purpose. Dewey's adoption of the religious will in the *Psychology* was doubtless motivated as much by his own need to integrate religion into his philosophy as by his desire to complete the idealist quest to demonstrate the presence of the Godly Absolute in human experience. However, the terms of the required integration had to be set by Dewey's commitment to the primacy of the social, which in turn had been determined by his resolution that psychology is not individual, but social. If, as Dewey came to realize, complete moral perfection was incompatible with actual social conduct, so much the worse for moral perfection. Moral conduct is not moral because it conforms to, or strives to imitate, the absolute ideal but because it is appropriate in its actual social setting. As Dewey explained in the 1891 *Outlines of a Critical Theory of Ethics,* the individual's conduct must serve social ends in order to be *conduct* at all, and society's ends must gain the person's commitment to use her own special abilities to accomplish them in order to be *moral* at all. Moral experience displays this double aspect and cannot show that type of religious ideal postulated earlier by Dewey as necessary for true human self-realization. Self-realization is completely social, and if there was to be any remaining role for religious ideals, their function must too be thoroughly social.[23] Bradley saw no religion in society's arbitrary and relative norms. Dewey turned that view on its head, locating real religion in the context of society's changing norms. Dewey took Christianity no longer to be the guarantee of moral perfection resting beyond the social realm, but an exaltation of the struggle for social progress itself. His identification of Christianity with the ideals of democratic society, first expressed in the early 1890s, is the political fruit of his reconciliation of religion with social psychology. His later writings on religion, especially *A Common Faith* (1934), expound this view of religious entities as democratically social ideals permeating religious experience.[24]

Dewey's analysis of moral experience, by revealing the essentially social character of conduct, questioned the usefulness of an ideal of moral/religious perfection. Such questioning is the purpose of "Green's Theory of the Moral Motive" (November 1892). The remoteness of Green's absolute, felt so keenly in Dewey's metaphysical ruminations, now manifested itself in his ethical theorizing too (*EW* 3: 159). Metaphysics need not be a threat to ethical theory, Dewey argued, unless it portrays the conditions of moral conduct as entirely separate from actual human behavior. Just as Green's absolute of experience never manifested itself as absolute in actual human experience, so too has Green's absolute ideal of the self never manifested itself as a guide in actual human conduct. Actual conduct must always fall far short of the proper ideal. Actual conduct therefore stands in a contradictory position: as conduct, it is supposed to be the realization of the ideal, but as actual human conduct, it could never be the ideal's realization to any significant degree. In this manner Dewey not only harshly attacks Green, but indirectly Morris, Caird, Bradley, and Dewey's own use of the religious will in the *Psychology*.

> Instead of being a tool which can be brought into fruitful relations to special circumstances so as to help determine what should be done, it remains the bare thought of an ideal of perfection, having nothing in common with the special set of conditions or with the special desire of the moment. Indeed, instead of helping determine the right, the satisfactory, it stands off one side and says, "No matter what you do, you will be dissatisfied. I am complete; you are partial. I am a unity; you are a fragment, and a fragment of such a kind that no amount of you and such as you can ever afford satisfaction." In a word, the ideal not only does not lend itself to specification, but it negates specification in such way that its necessary outcome, were it ever seriously adopted as a controlling theory of morals, would be to paralyze action. (*EW* 3: 163)

Dewey's insistence that theory have a practical bearing on decision-making displays his growing insight into the role of thought in active experience. By 1891 he had developed an understanding of theory which permitted his psychological insights into meaning, judgment, and reasoning to contribute to his understanding of human conduct. Theory for Dewey denoted those special principles, called "rules," concerning some subject matter which should be used to analyze a problematic situation's features. This analysis is directed by the rule to select out particular features of a situation and ignore others. The next necessary step is synthesis, where a proposed reintegration of the selected features creates a provisional judgment of what is to be done. The final step is the performance of that act. Its success approves the judgment as correct. If unsuccessful, the judgment and possibly also the rule require adjustment.

The notion of the perfected absolute self cannot be a rule, for it equally condemns all aspects of any situation as fragmentary and pointless. Put another way, the notion of the absolute self could not be consistently applied to human experience. If it were applied, then human experience would lose its fragmentary and incomplete character. But without such flaws there is no need to do anything, much less any need to think about what to do. Recall that neo-idealists (including Dewey) held that human intellectual effort aims at increasing the harmonies within experience. If we really could apply the absolute idea of self to experience our experience as perfected, then what is the point of thought? Green argued that without some conception of perfection, the intellect could not improve experience's harmony. However, Green himself confessed that the moral standard of whether a person's efforts are directed toward perfection or not is hardly a practical standard for any actual circumstances since we cannot know with any degree of assurance another person's true motives and because fastidious moral reflection may not lead to virtue.[25] Since Green distinguishes the practical question of what one ought to do from the moral question of what should one be, he can only say that the moral ideal raises the self-questioning conscience necessary for the human advancement toward truly moral behavior. Because one must estimate the consequences of one's act to judge it good or bad in addition to ensuring that one's motive was only for the best outcome, a morally sensitive conscience striving to be perfect is insufficient for making any actual decision of conduct. Therefore, as Green concludes, no rule of conduct can be derived from the formal ideal of self-perfection.[26]

In contrast to Green's insistence that progress requires the ideal of perfection, Dewey came to see that if the conception of perfection were in place, no improvement would be required, and no action would be taken. Because experience evidently displays the growth of organization through an individual's activity, the idea of self-perfection could never really be an idea at all, but only an empty notion, akin to the Kantian thing-it-itself. The interesting parallels between Dewey's earlier rejection of the thing-in-itself and Dewey's rejection in 1891 of the absolute self cannot be overemphasized. Both stand condemned, not only because they are intrinsically nonexperienceable entities, but also because neither are capable of explaining the actual features of human experience.

The reader will recall how forcefully Dewey proclaimed in his earliest essays that experience is the one thing that cannot be philosophically explained. On that principle the only origin of the notion of improved harmonious experience must come from human experience itself. The perfect self is but an illegitimate abstraction from ordinary experience, set over against it in order to condemn it as incomplete.

> Green takes the bare fact that there is unity in moral experience, abstracts that unity from experience (although its sole function is to be the unity of experience) and then, setting this unity over against the experience robbed of its significance, makes of the unity an unrealized and unrealizable ideal and condemns the experience, shorn of its unity, to continual dissatisfaction. (*EW* 3: 169)

Dewey has put his finger on the fallacious methodology of absolute idealism, whether on an intellectual or moral plane. Ironically he had already detected the intellectual version of the fallacy years before when he rejected the Kantian synthesizing categories as vicious abstractions from human experience. His *Psychology* accordingly did not follow Green's notion of the intellectual absolute. Its replacement was the theory that knowing experience grew in the course of the inquiring activities of the self, where the "self" did not stand for anything apart from experience, but only for experience's analytic and synthetic movements during reasoning. The *Psychology* denied the primacy of the intellectual functions, subordinating them to the will, or purposive activity. The moral/practical will required supplementation by the absolute self postulated by the religious will in the act of faith. This meant that Dewey in effect had two psychologies, one for the processes of human inquiry and another to guarantee the religious identity of the human self with the absolute self. By 1891 Dewey had abandoned this religious quest, and he instead committed his philosophy exclusively to the ordinary self of human experience.

This commitment remedied the need in the *Psychology* to offer two absolutes, the absolute of ordinary human experience and the absolute of the perfect self. Both were conceived by Dewey as active experience, as discussed earlier. However, the former was fragmentary while the latter was fully harmonized, and only the bare act of faith could unite them. By 1891 Dewey could abandon the perfect self and the faith in it. Left with but one absolute, the absolute of socially active experience, a functionalist philosophy of the self could be formulated. This philosophy could truly integrate knowledge, feeling, and will without the distorting effects of the teleologically controlling absolute self. Just as the Kantian thing-in-itself *and* the synthesizing categories had to both be eliminated in order to understand human intellectual experience, so too did Dewey come to realize that the elimination of the permanently disorganized experience required the corresponding elimination of the perfectly harmonized experience. In moral/practical terms experience is never so disorganized that everything must be done all at once. The many stabilities of experience ensure that uninterrupted successful activity is the norm and not the exception. But because problem solving conducted in order to restore activity is still activity, the increased harmony that signals successful problem solving is but an aspect of that activity, and not some entity of "absolute harmony" imposed from beyond. Just as meaning can increase in experience without the interposition of transexperience-synthesizing categories, so too can it increase without being drawn forward by the perfected self.

The essential fallacy of absolute idealism, in short, is that it must ask us to take our experience in two contradictory ways. To begin with, unless our experience were able to display some coherence, we could never improve upon it, and unless we could experience that improvement, we could not enjoy its benefits. Now, in order to prove the existence of the absolute, the absolute idealist must demonstrate its workings in human experience. This illustration proceeds by arguing that human experience must be of such character as necessarily requiring the assistance of some power beyond ordinary human experience. But in order to prove that human experience cannot improve its coherence on its own resources, it must be shown that human experience is hopelessly fragmentary, lacking any internal methods of improving itself. How does the absolute idealist prove that human experience is so lacking? Only by contrasting it with an ideal of maximally coherent experience, of course. This ideal is, for the absolute idealist, the teleological guidance that human experience needs.

Now it must be noticed that the absolute idealist must ensure that this absolute avoids the fate of Kant's thing-in-itself, by proving that this absolute is actually revealed in human experience. But it cannot be revealed in just any human experience because only *increasingly harmonious experience* will do. Without a doubt we do experience such increased harmony, but we can only experience the absolute if we experience our experience as a manifestation of the perfect absolute experience. This implies that the absolute idealist must portray ordinary human experience (as it "really" is) as utterly fragmentary and incomplete, *lacking any coherence whatsoever*. The absolute idealist accomplishes this by reminding us of the perfect absolute, which stands in such stark contrast to our pitifully incomplete experience. The absolute idealist's dialectic therefore contradictorily requires us to experience the *same experience* as both utterly fragmented and increasingly harmonious.

Dewey had occasion in later years to apply this critique to other absolute idealists besides Green. For example, in a review of Josiah Royce's *The World and the Individual* (1900) he explains Royce's curious methodology.

> The dialectic is this: (1) Our experiences are meanings, purposes fulfilled. Then, since reality cannot be conceived apart from experience, the reality—absolute reality—is meaning fulfilled. (2) But our purposes are only partially, inadequately, merely universally or indeterminately, fulfilled. But since absolute reality is meaning fulfilled in experience, it must be exhaustively, eternally fulfilled. The Absolute experiences all at once, adequately and completely, that which we try to experience in pieces, in series and in distorted fashion. The gist of

my criticism is that the argument depends upon taking propositions (1) and (2) alternately. They cannot be taken together without destroying each other. (*MW* 1: 255)

Dewey's contributions to the 1903 *Studies in Logical Theory* attack Lotze's epistemology in the very same manner:

> How does it happen that the absolute constitutive and intuitive Thought does such a poor and bungling job that it requires a finite discursive activity to patch up its products? Here more metaphysic is called for: The Absolute Reason is now supposed to work under limiting conditions of finitude, of a sensitive and temporal organism. The antecedents of reflective thought are not, therefore, determinations of thought pure and undefiled, but of what thought can do when it stoops to assume the yoke of change and of feeling.... Why and how should a perfect, absolute, complete, finished thought find it necessary to submit to alien, disturbing, and corrupting conditions in order, in the end, to recover through reflective thought in a partial, piecemeal, wholly inadequate way what it possessed at the outset in a much more satisfactory way? (*EW* 2: 334)

Dewey similarly rebukes Bradley's dialectical proof of the absolute in "The Intellectualist Criterion for Truth" (1907).

> Much of Bradley's writings is a sustained and deliberate polemic against intellectualism of the Neo-Kantian type. When, however, we find conjoined to this criticism an equally sustained contention that the philosophic conception of reality must be based on an exclusively intellectual criterion, a criterion belonging to and confined to theory, we have a situation that is thought-provoking.... The curious character of the situation is that reality is an "absolute experience" of which the intellectual is simply one partial and transmuted moment. Yet this reality is attained unto, in philosophic method, by exclusive emphasis upon the intellectual aspect of present experience and by systematic exclusion of exactly the emotional, volitional features which with respect to content are insisted upon! Under such circumstances the cynically-minded are moved to wonder whether this tremendous insistence upon one factor in present experience at the expense of others, is not because this is the only way to maintain the notion of "Absolute Experience," and to prevent it from collapsing into ordinary everyday experience. (*MW* 4: 51)

Dewey's chapter on "Existence as Precarious and as Stable," in the 1925 *Experience and Nature* fully expresses his verdict on the absolute.

> [The Absolute] constitutes the most recent device for first admitting and then denying the combinedly stable and unstable nature of the world. Its plaintive recognition of our experience as finite and temporal, as full of error, conflict and contradiction, is an acknowledgment of the precarious uncertainty of the objects and connections that constitute nature as it emerges in history. Human experience however has also the pathetic longing for truth, beauty and order. There is more than the longing: there are moments of achievement. Experience exhibits ability to possess harmonious objects. . . . [T]he contents as well as the form of ultimate Absolute Experience are derived from and based upon the features of actual experience, the very experience which is then relegated to unreality by the supreme reality derived from its unreality. It is "real" just long enough to afford a spring-board into ultimate reality and to afford a hint of the essential contents of the latter and then it obligingly dissolves into mere appearance. (*LW* 1: 55–56)

The elimination of the absolute self required a transformation of the other primary factors in Dewey's philosophy: the ideals toward which we strive, the self in the process of realization, and the nature of growing experience. Absolute idealism, Dewey had begun to see, imposed a teleologically final end to forge a metaphysical unity of persons and God, but at the extreme cost of making human experience, both moral and intellectual, incomprehensibly contradictory. There can only be one philosophical absolute, Dewey decided, which is active human experience. All other realities must be understood as just functional phases of that absolutely ordinary experience.

This transition did not wrench his philosophy away from idealism, just away from absolute idealism. Like several other of his idealistic contemporaries (notably Bradley and Seth in Britain and Howison and Bowne in America) Dewey was searching for a new kind of idealism that could be true to actual human experience. The question of why Dewey did not proclaim his newfound realism, his newfound empiricism, ignores the philosophical atmosphere of the late 1800s. Realism stood for scientific materialism or its cousin, Cartesian/Kantian dualism. Empiricism stood for psychological subjectivism or its cousin, solipsism. Neither realism nor empiricism were acceptable options for those educated in post-Kantian idealism. In hindsight we know that Dewey did attempt a rehabilitation of empiricism and realism in the first two decades of the twentieth century and of naturalism in the last three decades of his career, but these brave endeavors were predicated on his successful formulation of a suitably revised functionalist idealism in the 1890s. The heart of these successes was his reconstruction of ideals, the self, and experience, after the elimination of the absolute self.

Self-Realization and Idealism

Dewey's functionalist and idealistic experimentalism of the 1890s was founded on the tenets that (1) active social experience is philosophically absolute, (2) the self is those aspects of this experience responsible for its organized growth, (3) intelligence is that aspect of the self representing the coordination of the self's activities, (4) reasoning is that process within intelligence which conducts inquiry during problematic situations in order to restore coordinated habits and hence harmonious active experience, and (5) the distinction between physical facts (what is taken for granted) and mental ideas (what is called into question) arises during inquiry and vanishes when harmonious active experience is resumed. That aspect of the self to which the responsibility of growing experience is assigned was no longer identified with the absolute self in its all-consuming perfection, but rather with the organizing factors of intelligent inquiry involved in learning. The functionalism lurking in the *Psychology* was now fully blossoming into an emergent theory of the social self. The *Outlines of a Critical Theory of Ethics* does not go very far in this direction, focusing on the ideal of moral community as the proper balance between hedonism and Kantianism. While the absolute self is absent and the requirement that moral ideals must progress is firmly emphasized, Dewey's theory of ethics is not explicitly portrayed as the correction of absolute idealism's errors. This task was left for two further explorations into the new territory of experimental idealism, his article of 1893 titled "Self-Realization as the Moral Ideal" and the 1894 *The Study of Ethics*.

Dewey argues in "Self-Realization as the Moral Ideal" that capacity should be understood not as a contrast between an actual divine power and a human potential, but between a person's activity as it may be understood in two or more differing ways. The recognition of capacity lies in observing actual activity, not in setting up some abstract ideal to compare human activity against. However, because the purpose of activity may be understood differently by the actor and observers or differently among observers or in multiple ways by the actor himself, contrasts between differing observations of capacity can arise. This permits the possibility of education. The observer who can organize a child's activities can control the development of his capacities toward the desired activities of adulthood. The purpose of activity may be understood differently by the actor himself because one's activity can be conceived as having multiple ends. This ability permits the possibility of learning by oneself since one can hypothetically set up an activity to be accomplished and formulate possible means of developing one's capacities toward the ability to perform that desired activity. This is highly significant for his theory of moral inquiry. Dewey's theory of moral deliberation as an imaginative vision of future activities is the fruition of his novel theory of self-realization.[27] It is also this sense of learning which is significant for the study of the development of Dewey's epistemology.

Dewey's theory of reasoning, in which thought is aroused by problematic experience (the interruption of activity), and aims at the restoration of harmonious experience (the resumption of activity), was described above. In Dewey's absolutist phase thought was one of the self's abilities which really owed its efficacy to its actual existence as a power of the absolute self. Now, in Dewey's experimentalist phase, thought has no such obligation and can instead be understood as just one of the self's capacities. As a capacity the ability to reason is itself an activity aimed at an end. Reason is also responsible for its own development since thought can be approached in a thoughtful manner in an effort to develop its own capacities. Put another way, thought can be made an object of thought since one can understand one's capacity for reasoning and also can question this capacity's ability to achieve satisfactorily the end of reasoning. Such questioning is the inquiry into inquiry, or logic, which defines the essence of Dewey's epistemology. Another person's evaluation of one's reasoning methods and reorganization of one's problem-solving techniques are the teaching of logic.

In Dewey's absolutist phase reasoning's goal of harmonious experience was taken to be already eternally in existence in the absolute self of perfect active experience. Now, in his experimentalist phase, the creation of more-harmonious experience is no mere duplication, but true novelty: an addition to reality that in no sense existed prior to that creation. Dewey's refutation of materialistic determination lay exactly in this rejection of the notion that future reality in some sense already exists in past reality. He also thus rejected teleological determinism by denying that present reality in some sense already exists in future reality. The types of necessity that each kind of determinism rely upon have only relative validity as a functional phase of inquiry but represent in themselves only incomplete achievements of thought. His article "The Superstition of Necessity" explains this instrumentalist understanding of necessity, which is discussed below. The identification by Dewey of experience with purposive activity, and his identification of the self with the growth of purposive activity, also implies that the creation of harmonious experience is the organic growth of the self. This last realization had many significant implications for his philosophy, of which two are central for the emerging instrumentalism of the early 1890s. First, the growth of harmonious active experience is the ultimate end of life, and as that growth is just self-realization, then the only completely moral end is the process of self-realization. Second, human freedom lies in such growth, in the self's control of its process of realization.

In *The Study of Ethics* Dewey uses the term "ideal" to refer to what he previously called the "rule." Rules/ideals guide conduct, not in the sense of dictating the good action, but as principles used in reasoning to discover what the right action is for a particular situation. When used, they are the ideals for the person using them and have no existence beyond such use. Against the hedonistic and the absolutist theories of ideals, which both fall into the error of setting up ideals as entities external to the activities of the self, Dewey asserts that ideals are really effective where they are factors in actual human experience, or "internal" to the self.

Fixed, transcendent ideals, whether conceived as pleasures to be attained or as perfect modes of conduct, pose six insuperable difficulties (*EW* 4: 257–262). First, transcendent ideals are independent from our scientific understanding of the world, making our efforts to grasp nature's workings completely irrelevant to moral conduct. Second, our efforts to match the ideal are irrelevant to their existence as ideal. Third, choice between competing ideals is rendered inexplicable and arbitrary. Fourth, there is no such thing as the development of ideals, or of moral progress, but only our conduct's distance from them. Fifth, our moral progress is always a negative matter, a lack, which never can be fully eliminated. Sixth, fixed transcendent ideals cannot help us to determine what should be done in any particular situation.

> The fixed ideal gives no instruction or information as to the particular thing needing to be done. It does not translate itself into terms of a concrete, individual act—and every act is concrete and individual. In other words, it does not and cannot become a working principle for what has to be done.... Such ideals are pure luxuries; only the sentimentalist and the pure theorist can afford them. The working man, of busy life, must have an ideal by which he can go in action, one which defines specific acts.... Again, our theory meets this need, because the ideal is nothing but the definition or mediation of the immediately acting, or impulsive, self. We conclude then, from our examination of abstract ideals, that true ideals are the working hypotheses of action; they are the best comprehension we can get of the value of our acts; their use is that they mark our consciousness of what we are doing, not that they set up remote goals. Ideals are like the stars; we steer by them, not towards them. (*EW* 4: 261–262)

Because Dewey's moral theory is at once a theory of the practical life, which is in truth the only life, his complaints against fixed ideals have a far wider bearing than just moral deliberation. Rules/ideals include every practical principle that can be used in actual deliberation. Every principle of knowledge or science is thus included as well. These six complaints against fixed, transcendent ideals are the maturation of Dewey's insistence from the start of his career that reason not be abstracted from experience and are the demonstration of his fully formed instrumentalism. Any philosophy which would abstract from deliberative experience its intellectual factors, blow them up into metaphysically perfected entities, and then claim that our task is gradually to approximate and duplicate in ourselves these external entities is condemned by Dewey's instrumentalist philosophy.

> The theory of experimental idealism (as we term the position here taken), because of its recognition of activity as the primary reality is enabled to give both thought and feeling their due. It does not attempt the impossible task of setting up for activity some end, whether a state of feeling or one of perfect reason, outside itself. It is content to note that activity, moving according to its own law and principle, becomes objectively conscious of its value in the ends which its projects (ideals) and subjectively conscious of its value in the emotions which accompany the realizing of these ends. As compared with the facts, then, both ethical rationalism and empiricism take a derived and secondary phase for the whole truth. As compared with each other, rationalism is right in so far as it asserts that feelings (or pleasure and pain) are mere abstractions apart from the objects (or rational contents) which give them their quality, while empiricism is right in asserting that an end which is not felt (that is, appreciated as part of the agent's own being) has no moral validity or claims. (*EW* 4: 264)

This statement of what Dewey calls experimental idealism is evidently not limited to the consideration of moral theory in the sense of ethical conduct but encompasses any practical conduct. It expressly orients us to the relationships among his metaphysics (activity as the primary reality), his psychology (the organic relations and movements of thought and feeling), and his epistemology (the inquiry into the role of rationally ideal principles in deliberative thought).

The opposition between ethical rationalism and empiricism in ethical theory is mirrored by the opposition between epistemological rationalism and empiricism in logical theory. Epistemological rationalism emphasizes the ideally rational principles to the point of erecting them into metaphysical realities transcending ordinary human experience while epistemological empiricism emphasizes the individualized aspect of experience to which any existence must answer. One says that knowledge really is *universal* knowledge which is known while the other declares that knowledge really is that knowledge known by an *individual*. Both rationalism and empiricism, by overemphasizing the universal and individual aspects of human experience, have set up themselves in a never-ending struggle that neither can win. Since each is partly right and since each can properly defend their view only by smuggling in the other side's preferred aspect of experience to give it life, they present an amusing spectacle for the instrumentalist. As absolute idealism faded and the "new" realism ascended into prominence in the early 1900s, Dewey found more than ample opportunity to condemn realism's similarly transcendental features. His analysis of the debate between realists and idealists and his attacks on all forms of transcendentalism are ultimately based on the six criticisms of fixed ideals enunciated in *The Study of Ethics*.[28]

Experimental idealism treats ideals as instruments of analysis available to a person that are to be applied in problematic situations, where "what is to be done" is the paramount question. Ideals are thus distinguished in Dewey's philosophy from moral judgments despite their conflation in ordinary language. If one says, "selfishness is wrong," he or she could be taken for expressing commitment to an altruistic ideal or passing a moral judgment. But in ordinary language passing a moral judgment such as "selfishness is wrong" makes sense only in a certain type of context, where one is judging someone's actual conduct (perhaps someone else, or oneself). Furthermore a statement such as "selfishness is wrong" made in that context is incomplete, as it does not specify exactly what aspect of that conduct is selfish and what adjustment to that conduct would make it right. The complete expression would be something like "Look at what he is doing; such selfishness is wrong, and he should instead share that candy with his brother." Dewey's terminology locates the ideal in "selfishness is wrong" and the moral judgment in "he should instead share that candy with his brother." A moral judgment is always a conclusion of what ought to be done in a particular situation in light of certain circumstances. In the example just given, the moral judgment concerns the unfolding conduct of another person. The ideal also can be used in one's analysis of one's own unfolding conduct and similarly may provoke an alteration of conduct. The use of the ideal fixes attention on certain aspects of the situation in preparation for the next step of formulating a moral judgment that proposes a resolution of the situation. This functional theory of the nature of the ideal ensures that it has an organic existence within the activities of the self. The living presence of ideals within the thoughtful deliberation of problem solving ensures that they do not suffer the fate of transcendent ideals, since Dewey has designed his theory of ideals to meet the six criteria set down in *The Study of Ethics*.

Of these six criteria, the ability of Dewey's theory of ideals to satisfy the "naturalism" criteria (our efforts to grasp nature's workings must be relevant to moral conduct) and the "progress" criteria (the development of ideals must be a possible aspect of moral conduct) deserve greatest attention. The satisfaction of the naturalism criterion amounts to a demonstration that the putative "is-ought" distinction preventing statements of fact from functioning in inferences to moral conclusions is an entirely false distinction, having no basis in actual human experience. The satisfaction of the progress criterion also relies on an appeal to actual human experience, which does display the modification and invention of ideals in the course of moral deliberation.

It must be kept in mind that Dewey uses "moral" synonymously with "practical." Any conduct involving self-realization requires the development of intelligence, which in turn requires the process of practical judgment. Instrumentalism should therefore be considered as the theory of the process of practical judgment in general, extending to its widest application experimental idealism's theory of the moral judgment. Dewey's resources in *The Study of Ethics* for proving that his theory of ideals passes his own criteria are quite limited. His later writings must be consulted to discover how he made up for this lack, particularly his 1903 works "Logical Conditions of a Scientific Treatment of Morality" and *Studies in Logical Theory*. For our purposes in this section, only the former work's account of the intertwined roles of scientific inquiry, the functioning of ideals, and self-realization need to be examined.

Dewey's expression of the relationship between intelligence and moral thinking is tersely and not always clearly expressed in this essay. Its primary goal is to portray moral thinking as the deliberate effort to control the process by which practical judgments are formed. Moral thought is therefore not directly aimed at habitually performing conduct (although such conduct is intelligent) or even at solving a problem in order to reestablish habitually performed conduct (although such problem solving expresses how the reasoning process uses ideals to produce practical judgments of what ought to be done). Rather, moral thought arises when the factors involved in the reasoning process, including ideals, are brought to conscious attention because the process of producing practical judgments is under question. Habitually performed conduct does not in itself expand experience. Problem-solving activity uses ideals to expand experience in a transition from a specific situation to a better specific situation. Moral thought improves problem solving and hence transforms ideals to improve one's general ability to transition a variety of situations into better situations. Put in terms of intelligence, habitually performed conduct is an expression of attained intelligence. Problem-solving activity is an expression of that aspect of growing intelligence called reasoning. Moral thought is reasoning brought to bear upon the factors involved in reasoning. Put in terms of knowledge, habitually performed conduct is possible as a result of already attained knowledge; problem solving is possible as a result of the capacity of knowing; moral thought is possible because of the capacity to control the process of knowing. Moral thought, since it permits the control of the process of knowing, permits control of the direction of self-realization, thus controlling the expansion of experience.

Moral thought, the control of the process of practical judgment formation, has three phases. First, the discernment of the possibility of moral thought brings to focus our ability to judge the value and priority of ideals. This phase is called by Dewey the science of ethics or the logic of conduct. Second, since moral thought can be viewed as an actor's deliberate active experience, psychology can be brought to bear on discerning the factors of that intentional experience. Third, since moral thought can be viewed as a certain type of experience occurring within certain environing conditions and having a certain kind of social value, sociology and all the other special sciences can be brought to bear on discerning the organic relationships between the actor and his environment.

Dewey's conception of philosophy is precisely the coordinated pursuit of these three phases of moral/practical thought. This conception of philosophy accounts for Dewey's claim that scientific inquiry is relevant to the ideals of moral conduct. Scientific inquiry can have two quite distinct senses for Dewey. In its primary sense it denotes any deliberately rational problem solving whatsoever.

> Our attitude becomes scientific in the degree in which we look in both directions with respect to every judgment passed; first, checking or testing its validity by reference to possibility of making other and more certain judgments with which this one is bound up; secondly, fixing its meaning (or significance) by reference to its use in making other statements. (*MW* 3: 4)

As Dewey emphasizes, a body of knowledge becomes scientific to the degree that its ideals (or, as he also calls them, "generic propositions" or "hypothetical laws") can be linked to form chains of inference leading to a specific practical judgment of what ought to be done in a particular situation. It is the *logic* of the body of knowledge, and not any actual content of the eventual practical judgment, which earns the title of "scientific." Moral thought in its first phase can rightly be called scientific. That is why Dewey can proclaim a "science of ethics."

In a secondary sense, scientific inquiry can denote a body of knowledge designed to produce a specific kind of practical judgment. The "special" or "descriptive" sciences, as Dewey calls them, bring to mind physics, chemistry, etc. These sciences are relevant to the sociological phase of moral thought, as mentioned above, but their significance extends far beyond the practical value of their conclusions for moral thought. Their ultimate significance lies in their common method of reasoning. Scientific reasoning, claims Dewey, is the paradigm of reasoning: the scientific method of problem solving is the pattern to follow in any problem solving. In a two-fold manner, then, the naturalism criteria (our efforts to grasp nature's workings must be relevant to moral conduct) is satisfied by Dewey's theory of the role of ideals.

The satisfaction of the progress criteria (the development of ideals must be a possible aspect of moral conduct) is established to the extent that Dewey can develop a science of ethics. It is one thing to describe, as he does in various writings, how social ideals actually have altered over time and across cultures. It is quite another to show that these transformations can be brought under conscious control. Dewey's demonstration of this possibility is virtually his entire theory of the democratic life as the collective inquiry into improved social harmonization. Again, Dewey draws sustenance from the example set by the physical sciences since the progress of a science lies in the transformations of its laws.

A close examination of his theory of the control of ideals, as it is directly concerned with the theory of the nature of science, is provided later.

An Experimentally Idealistic Epistemology

The reconstruction of Dewey's idealism called for by the elimination of the absolute self permitted the full emergence of his functionalist account of human self-realization. This functionalist account, set within in the larger context of the absolute of growing active experience, in turn set the stage for Dewey's progress toward instrumentalism. The epistemological doctrines of his experimental idealism are as follows.

1. Active social experience is philosophically absolute.

2. The self in its realization is just those developing aspects of this experience responsible for its organized growth.

3. Intelligence is that aspect of the self representing the coordination of the self's activities.

4. Reasoning is that process within intelligence that conducts inquiry during problematic situations.

5. Inquiry aims to restore coordinated habits and hence harmonious active experience.

6. Inquiry uses ideals to analyze the problematic situation and direct possible courses of action that may restore unproblematic experience.

7. Successful inquiry develops ideals and hence increases the fund of intelligence available.

8. The distinction between physical facts (what is taken for granted) and mental ideas (what is called into question) arises during inquiry and vanishes when harmonious active experience is resumed.

9. Functional psychology is responsible for examining the roles of intelligence and the logical processes of inquiry.

10. Functional psychology is essentially social psychology. Mind is present in behavior, moral relationships, and ultimately social institutions.

11. Morality and science are not entirely separate endeavors. They both are kinds of practical experience, and the logic of science is the same as the logic of morality.

CHAPTER FIVE

The Logic of Conduct

> *It is possible to recognize a function of philosophy which it belongs to the genius of Hegel to have made conceivable. Entities are but formulations of thought at different phases of experience. With every advance these formulations change. . . . Reality lies in immediate experience, and must be sought there. Thought can only make us conscious of how we act, and thus give us the advantage of a conscious technique.*
>
> George H. Mead, "A New Criticism of Hegelianism: Is it Valid?" 1901

It is highly significant that Dewey's *Psychology* distinguishes rational thinking from lower stages of knowledge, such as perception and imagination, and also from the highest stage of knowledge, which is intuition. Thinking has to do with knowledge using universal aspects of things in experience, while the lower stages deal only with things as particulars. Intuition involves knowing the concrete individuals that truly exist in experience; all lower stages of knowledge are abstractions by the psychologist, formulated for the purpose of understanding the human ability to know those self-sufficient organic wholes encountered in experience. Thought does not exist for its own sake in some self-sufficient realm of mind but arises out of more basic experiences and does its work only to be absorbed into a more important knowing experience. All of the entities of thought, those percepts, concepts, judgments, facts, inferences, etc., are but functional distinctions made in order to determine how learning, the growth of the self's powers, occurs. The activities of mind, the analyzing and synthesizing abilities, are but functional distinctions as well. Dewey emphasizes again and again that he must not be misunderstood to be describing actually existing mental entities or events. Only the harmonious whole really ever exists for experience; no distinct and separate mental existent or act can actually be immediately experienced apart from its whole context. The psychologist studies the mind's processes from lesser to greater harmony, which requires the mind's ability to idealize sensations. On Dewey's psychology this task has already been accomplished before thinking undertakes its work, through apperception and retention. Thinking takes for granted that all experiences possess meaning. They are not just ideas in the existential sense of a particular percept happening at a certain time and quickly gone, but ideas in the logical sense of enduringly related to other ideas. Psychology must therefore investigate ideas as logical functions as well.

Reasoning and Experience

Every mental state must be more than just a mere existence in the mind. It also has meaning, and we refer to a mental state's meaning as a concept. A concept is not tied down to any particular—it is universal. Also it is not a particular itself, like an image. Images are mere existing mental states, abstracted from their meaning. The meaning of an image is the conception. The dual nature of ideas, as mere psychical images and as relational meanings, is stressed by Bradley.[1] Bradley, however, declares that logic treats ideas as meanings, while psychology treats only ideas as mental events. This antipsychologism was of course untenable for Dewey, as was Bradley's early dualistic view that ideas "float" until attached to reality by the act of judgment. Dewey agrees with Bradley and other idealists on the distinction between the idea's existence and meaning because this distinction avoids the dangers of associationism. Associationism ignores the fact that a mere psychical existence, considered as independent of relations, cannot be experienced.

Knowledge as Idealization

In an 1887 essay, "Knowledge as Idealization," Dewey expands on many themes of *Psychology*'s chapter on thinking.

> Absolute nonsense and nonentity are synonymous as matters of conscious experience.... if we could strip any psychical existence of all its qualities except bare existence, there would be nothing left, not even existence, for our intelligence. Even the fact that there is an experience, aside from what it is, is not the sensation itself; it is the interpretation of the sensation. It is part of the meaning. If we take out of an experience all that it means, as distinguished from what it is—a particular occurrence at a certain time, there is no psychical experience. The barest fragment of consciousness that can be hit upon has meaning as well as being. Take away the meaning, and consciousness vanishes. (*EW* 1: 178–179)

Dewey always maintained that some degree of meaning is essential to experience. Only for psychological theorizing are the functional distinctions between an idea's existence and meaning established. Thinking's task is to increase the meaning of future experience, stimulated by the incompleteness and disharmony pervading present experience. As Dewey says in "The Intellectualist Criterion of Truth" (1907), experience

> ... is neither an affair of meaningless existence nor of existence self-luminous with fulfilled meaning. All things that we experience have some meaning, but that meaning is always so partially embodied in things that we cannot rest in them. They point beyond themselves; they indicate meanings which they do not fulfill; they suggest values which they fail to embody, and when we go to other things for the fruition of what is denied, we either find the same situation of division over again, or we find even more positive disappointment and frustration—we find contrary meanings set up. (*MW* 4: 53)

Because thinking's task is the transformation of experiences, knowledge as thought's product cannot be the mere reading off of givens in experience. Knowledge requires the establishment of more relations among experiences. It is always a matter of using experiences already having some meaning to create new experiences with greater meaning. Thought does not refer to a substantive entity, but an active process through time. Therefore the heart of thought, the concept, must be inherently temporal and subject to change. A concept, as the universal aspect of the experience of a thing, could not possibly serve any useful function in mind's activities if it were some timeless abstraction, but instead it must energize the thing with suggestive directions to other experiences which are not yet present. Because thought serves to increase the number of meanings of a thing, the concept of that thing will grow over time. The thing, considered together with its concept, is termed by Dewey the individual. Dewey declares in the *Psychology* that all knowledge "proceeds from the individual to the individual" (*EW* 2: 199). We are also told that the only things really ever experienced are individuals and that an individual is the organic union of the universal and the particular, the concept and the percept. Dewey borrowed this use of the term "individual" from F. H. Bradley, who defined the individual as that real thing to which a judgment refers a concept.[2]

Intuition is the intellectual act of grasping all of an individual thing's meanings. Grades of intuition correspond to the number of meanings, the quantity of relations with other things, embodied in the thing. Because thinking serves to increase those meanings, thinking's purpose is to improve the intuition of the thing. An improved intuition, as the result of more thought, always involves the establishment of relations between two things, and thus it is never really about only one thing. A higher intuition brings two previously separate things into organic relations with each other, which for Dewey is their synthesis into a greater whole. The upshot of this view of intuitional knowledge is that thought's work must improve knowledge of one thing only by eliminating its independence and uniting it with another thing. The process of union alters both things brought together. What once was distinct now must cohere, which requires that both things must be conceived anew. When individuals become better known, they must surrender their independence from each other at the price of altering what they really are.

This is why Dewey is careful to say of knowledge's growth not that it is of things but that it proceeds from the individual to the individual. He means that in order for knowledge of an individual to increase, that individual must suffer a change to its conceptual side. This change allows it to be incorporated with another individual, also undergoing conceptual alteration, to create a wholly new concept which may be now applied to both things which cannot be exactly the same as they were before. This is the nature of knowledge's organic growth. The things, as particular existences, of course do not change during this process of knowledge growth. However, these things in so far as they are conceptually known must alter as knowledge does its work. Thereafter they are not conceived in the same manner as before. Keeping in mind that Dewey holds that both the particular and conceptual are but aspects of experiences of individuals, we can see why he believes that knowledge must alter experiences by increasing their harmonious interrelations. Dewey later had occasion to remind realists of the fact that meanings of terms, and hence how we conceive objects, must alter over time as knowledge grows. In the 1910 "The Short-Cut To Realism Examined" Dewey attacks the new realists' view that the objects of knowledge are externally related to the knowing of the object. His analysis of this position forces the new realists to the untenable position that scientific investigation never results in the alteration of the conceptual meanings of scientific terms.

There is a reason why a biologist's experience of a particular plant is quite different from anyone else's experience of the same plant. The biologist experiences a very different individual because the conceptual aspect of that experience is so much more richer with meanings. For example, those meanings link this plant with other plants in a wide variety of ways, involving botanical classifications that each bring suggestive anticipations of what may be expected of this plant. When will it flower? How large can it grow? What is its root structure like? Which insects may pollinate it? The reader, if like myself not trained in botany, may substitute an area of expertise of their own to understand how their experiences of the familiar things in that area are quite different from the untrained eye. Perhaps you have car maintenance skills, unlike myself. I assure you that your experience upon opening the hood of an automobile is considerably different from mine if I were also gazing down on that car's engine. The many parts of the engine are much more clearly distinguished and interrelated in your experience than in mine, and your efforts to fix it would be commensurably more effective. Allow me to illustrate this point with a true story. My car had trouble starting one day, and on the supposition that my looking at the engine might not be a total waste of time, I examined the engine as best I could. I recall gazing a long while at the parts and their connections, looking for any sign of irregularity. At long last, finding nothing to do, I called for the tow truck. Later that day, a mechanic showed me what was wrong: an electrical wire had become disconnected. I now saw that this wire was not hidden but had been lying on top of the engine block in perfectly plain view, obviously detached. Two further things were immediately obvious as well. One, during my inspection I must have "seen" the detached wire. That is to say, the perceptual content of my experience of the engine was approximately the same as the mechanic's. Second, I must not have "seen the detached wire." I was unable to experience the detached wire as an individual. Although it was present existentially, I could not experience the wire as detached. The mechanic somehow knew that the wire was detached when it entered his perceptual field. The reason why the mechanic could know this must have to do with his superior conceptual knowledge of engines. This knowledge brings the engine's parts into an interrelated whole which, on the cue that the engine would not start, allowed the mechanic to trace the meanings of the parts to check their proper connections. It was precisely those meanings which I lacked, and hence my experience did not contain that detached wire.

Dewey's theory of knowledge uses a dramatically different notion of the concept than the older theory of deductive knowledge. In that tradition, a concept's intension (the number of qualities to which it refers) must be inversely proportional to its extension (the number of things to which it applies). But as Dewey points out, this tradition, which finds universals by abstraction, cannot account for a biologist's increasing knowledge of plants as she or he studies more and more of them. It is absurd to say that the biologist's concept of "plant" becomes thinner and thinner, standing for fewer and fewer meanings, as the biologist studies more plants. The mistake made by the deductive theory is to link concepts too tightly with qualities. Qualities may indeed be conceptualized, but hardly any concepts of great worth are of just qualities. There are universal qualities, but other universal meanings exist too. When a red rose suggests the emotion of love, no mere quality (of redness? of thorniness?) supplies the connecting relation of meaning. Dewey's theory of the concept demands a more thorough explanation of their origin and growth, which will come as he explicitly links mental activity with the nervous system on one side and the organism's purposive behavior on the other. A portion of that explanation is attempted in his "Reflex Arc Concept" essay. But such explanation would appear completely arbitrary and to no point for a reader who has not grasped Dewey's novel understanding of the nature of meaning/concept and its relation to individuals in experience.

The third edition of the *Psychology* and an article titled "How Do Concepts Arise from Percepts," both published in 1891, use the concept of "triangle" to illustrate Dewey's argument that as universal the mind must ignore the particular details of an existing triangular figure. The individual thing, the triangular figure drawn on paper, has both a particular aspect and a universal aspect. It is an error to suppose, as some philosophers do, that because the mental act of experiencing the figure is indeed a particular event as a mental state, no truly universal idea could exist. Their error lies in supposing that existence/experience must be exhausted by fleeting particularized mental states. Only the individual, the meaningful thing, possesses existence for Dewey. As aspects both the mental state and its meanings must be recognized. It is on the one hand quite right for philosophers to deny existence to mere concepts, but on the other it is very misguided for philosophy to refuse to have anything to do with concepts. A better theory of the concept will clear this up by making a concept a mode of mental action which has durable effectiveness through time and through many particular mental states.

> For example, take the percept of a triangle. So far as this is a mere percept, it is regarded wholly as a particular thing. Knowledge of it from this point of view would be exhausted in getting its exact shape, size, length of sides, degree of angles, stuff made of, color, etc. The mind would nowhere be led beyond the consideration of the bare thing present. Even if it were found that the sum of its three interior angles was equal to two right angles, this would be a trait of the particular triangle, a bare item of information, of no more general value than that the length of one side was 1 $\frac{2}{7}$ inches. (*EW* 3: 143)

This figure, with all of its particular factual details picked out, is not yet experienced as a triangle because the particular facts get in the way of focused attention on the one aspect of this figure which could define it as triangular. We, of course, understand what that aspect is because we possess the concept of "triangle." But what exactly is that aspect? It must be a mode of mental action, not a static quality. Attention to the triangle's static qualities only provides a list of particular details concerning just this one triangular figure. For the mind to attain a concept, it must define by setting aside particular facts and instead treating the triangular figure actively.

> The concept, "triangle," in other words, is the way in which three lines are put together; it is a mode or form of construction. Except as we know this mode of formation our idea of a triangle is exceedingly imperfect. Hence, the characteristics of a concept. It is (1) "ideal" not sensuous. That is, as a mode or way of mental action, it cannot be felt or seen or heard. It can be grasped only in and through the activity which constitutes it. The only way to know the concept triangle is to make it—to go through the act of putting together the lines in the way called for. . . . The concept is (2) general, not particular. Its generality lies in the very fact that it is a mode of action, a way of putting things or elements together. A cotton loom

is particular in all its parts; every yard of cloth produced is particular, yet the way in which the parts go together and work together, the function of the loom is not particular. (*EW* 3: 144)

The mind first analyzes the figure, distinguishes its various characteristics. Then it synthesizes a selected portion (the three straight sides), considering them as a whole which can be found in subsequent triangular figures. When putting together three straight lines in just the right way (ends touching, no overlapping) the mind is in a mode of mental activity which, when remembered and applied to a new perception of a figure, can allow the mind to classify this new figure as a triangle too. What the mind has put together once can now be noticed in any future experienced thing without having to start over and put that thing together too. After the mind has grasped the rule governing the creation of the triangular figure, it can ignore the particular details of future triangular figures and focus solely on its three straight sides. The mind has defined the triangle and may consider "triangle" as no longer a perceived object of temporary significance but a universal meaning that relates all triangular figures. That is the nature of a function: while it in itself has no actual existence, it is nevertheless really embodied in mental activity as the universal aspect of any experience.

Because the concept itself is never a proper object of knowledge, but only the individual, the expression of knowledge is accomplished by the judgment. All that is needed to make a judgment out of a concept is to consider the concept as actually referring to reality. Concepts are created by freeing ideal meanings from any reference to reality, but judgment reintroduces such reference. This reference must be identified, so in the judgment the reference is specified by the subject while the concept is the predicate. This means that judgment is both analytic and synthetic. It is analytic in that it requires the recognition of a difference or distinction between the subject and predicate, while it is synthetic as it also affirms an identity or connection between the subject and predicate (*EW* 2: 188). Because judgment is the result of meaning alterations occurring to at least two individual objects and because it requires at least two objects for the mind to abstract an aspect of one to discover the same aspect in another, judgment always links two or more individual objects with a universal concept. Judgment, by establishing links between multiple individual objects, must increase the meaning of all.

Starting in 1892 in the "Introduction to Philosophy Syllabus," Dewey began to distinguish the categorical and hypothetical functions of judgments. The 1915 "The Logic of Judgments of Practice" is his first comprehensive attempt to develop a theory of hypothetical judgment which supports instrumentalism. While Dewey's mature theory of judgment held that the various kinds of judgments represent thought's efforts at the various stages of inquiry, he never abandoned the basic notion that the final purpose of judgment is to transform the meanings involved in a specific, individual situation. All other judgments, regardless of the degree of their universal or general nature and no matter how they might refer to many things or an unlimited number of things, are only instruments which must eventually find their application in a particular situation. This is why Dewey later calls them "propositions," to distinguish them from judgments. One of the central principles of Dewey's epistemology was therefore set down very early on in his career: knowledge always refers to specific individual things in experience. The notion that knowledge is of reality simply and vaguely, or that knowledge refers to a lone relation between the knower and reality, was an utterly alien view for Dewey. The central significance of this principle came to the fore as he announced his rejection of "epistemology" in the 1903 *Studies in Logical Theory*. There Dewey complained that epistemologists attempt to conceive their task as determining how knowledge relates to reality, forgetting that knowledge in its primary sense is always a particular event occurring in a specific situation and concerns an individual known object.

Reasoning, Logic, and Verification

With a theory of judgment in place, Dewey offers a theory of reasoning. Reasoning is the explicit recognition of the relational processes of analysis and synthesis that make knowledge possible. Its nature can be seen when, given the proceeding exposition, we understand that knowledge is never simply immediate. Indeed, at every stage of mental activity, experience is mediated, or related to other experiences through concepts. "All knowledge implies, in short, a going beyond what is sensuously present to its connection with something else, and it is this act of going beyond the present which constitutes the mediate factor" (*EW* 2: 192). Reasoning is possible because the mind can attentively consider the mediating elements which make judgments possible. Reasoning is typically implicit, as in judgments such as "This fire will burn." However taken for granted in the moment of judgment, we can make such a judgment only by reasoning. We recognize in one experience a factor (analyzing), connecting it with recalled experiences (synthesizing), and then turn our attention to other factors attached to these recalled experiences. The fire is bright, there have been past bright things, many of those bright things also are hot, therefore this bright fire is also hot fire. This procedure relies on past experiences, and limited past experiences will cause error in judgment. Dewey uses an example of a child's judgment. "If all bodies which he had thrown in [water] had sunk he would conclude that a piece of cotton would sink likewise" (*EW* 2: 193). We do not usually notice the reasoning process, instead concentrating on the particular experience before us. But when we do, we can explicitly reason by focusing on the universal, connecting, synthesizing factor that mediates experiences.

Every judgment has both a universal and a particular element, accounting for the distinction between a priori and a posteriori knowledge. They are not really two different kinds of knowledge but are rather just two necessary stages in the development of knowledge.

> Empirical knowledge goes from one particular to another by means of the universal element which connects them, but is not conscious of the universal element. Reason recognizes the universal element, the relation, and uses it to connect one particular, one fact, with another. . . . A *posteriori* knowledge is simply the *unconscious* recognition of the universal element, or relation, the ideal significance; *a priori* knowledge is the conscious recognition of it. (*EW* 2: 195)

These two elements of knowledge permit the two kinds of reasoning. Deduction occurs when a universal is imposed upon a particular, as in the fire example above. Induction occurs when the mind finds the relations, the connections, between hitherto distinct experiences and thus discovers the universal. This is the synthesizing ability of the mind, when it is under conscious attentive control. We can now see the activities of the mind in a new light. The mind is always analyzing, yet it always uses the products of analysis to synthesize as many other experiences as possible. Thus there is no gap between fact and law. The particular fact is in self-consciousness only because it has meanings, and the universal law is just one of those meanings. Fact and law are but two ways of looking at the same mental state. "When we abstract its particular aspect, its definite side, we regard it as fact; when we abstract its universal side, its relation of identity, we regard it as meaning or law" (*EW* 2: 199).

Dewey's view that the reasoning factors in judgments may or may not be attentively recognized produces a rather intriguing perspective on the nature of knowing experience. While reasoning is the focused attention on the analyzing and synthesizing activities of mind, it is not necessary that one's attention be fixed on these activities in order for one to make a judgment. This distinction between explicit and implicit reasoning permits Dewey to shed better light on his pronouncement that all knowledge is mediate. In explicit reasoning the mediating factors in knowledge are noticed while in implicit reasoning the mediation necessary for knowledge is not noticed (*EW* 2: 193). On this view much of the knowledge we have of objects in the world really are cases of implicit reasoning because no notice is taken of the activities required to judge the object, and hence the mediating concepts are not consciously recognized as such. Dewey uses the example of seeing a man. The judgment that "this is a man" is the result of the mind's activities linking the present visual perceptions with similar past perceptions. The similarity of "manhood" and the recollection of previous perceptions do not have to be, and usually are not, paid any attention. Only the result matters: one simply immediately perceives a man. When "immediately" is used here, it is not meant that knowledge is not involved, because mediating knowledge must always be involved. Rather the immediate quality of the seeing of the man lies in the fact that no notice is taken of the mediating factors.

It is a good thing that knowledge of things can occur in this immediate sense. If we constantly had to pay attention to all the mediating factors involved in judgment, we would never have time actually to interact with things in the world. Reasoning in the explicit sense for Dewey occurs only in certain circumstances as needed. Most knowledge is of the implicit reasoning type, and that is why in these cases he says that knowledge is both immediate and mediate. Grasping the uses that Dewey makes of these terms is crucial for understanding his theory of knowledge, especially as he defended his immediate empiricism in the first decade of the 1900s. That defense required an explanation of how a perception could be both immediate, in the sense that it is the thing itself which is experienced and not a mental copy, and mediate, in the sense that the thing is known through its conceptual relations to other things. Dewey's critics tried to accuse him of self-contradiction because on their view the immediacy of an experience of a thing necessitated its complete isolation from any relations to other things. In this accusation Dewey perceived a return to the old sensationalist view of immediate experience, in which immediate experience, if it were to exist, must consist of completely disjointed and unrelated particulars. Its defeat lies in the recognition that while the knowing of a thing requires an attribution of meaning to it, which in turn involves mediating concepts linking it with other things, this attribution is usually (excepting cases of explicit reasoning) immediately experienced. That is to say, the meaning of an object is immediately had without any notice taken of any mediating factors or other experiences of things. The similarity between Dewey's view of perception as implicit reasoning and Peirce's theory of perceptual judgment should be noticed as well. Peirce found persuasive the notion that the act of perception involves mental processes. "Notwithstanding its apparent primitiveness, every percept is the product of mental processes, or at all events of processes for all intents and purposes mental."[3] Peirce also says that every perception contains within it an abductive inference.[4]

The distinction between implicit and explicit reasoning allows Dewey to subject the dualistic theory of knowledge to devastating criticism. On that theory, the investigation into the relations between thought and its objects must presume that thought is entirely separate from the experience of its object. This investigation assumes first the experience of objects and second the existence of thought, which is quite other than the experience of objects, so that the question of how ideas may correctly or incorrectly apply to objects may be pursued. Dewey rejects this dualism because it must hold that objects in experience can be inspected quite apart from any intervening thinking. In "Is Logic a Dualistic Science?" (January 1890) he argues that no such inspection is possible because of the admitted psychological fact that considerable mental processes are required for the observation of objects to occur at all.

The distinction between implicit and explicit reasoning rescues his position from some objections. If thought is always involved with every perception of an object, then why for the most part do we not actually have the idea that thought contributes before us and why do we not have its elements before us? The dualistic logician has an even more significant objection along these lines. If thought can never be distinguished completely from the experience of objects, how could we ever determine whether our thoughts are adequate to its object? What becomes of truth if no comparison could ever be made between our ideas of objects and the objects themselves? Are all of our ideas automatically true? Dewey takes up this problem of verification in the follow-up article, "The Logic of Verification" (April 1890). He first points out that the dualist cannot offer a sensible account of verification since she or he is in the dilemma that either we can know what the objects of experience are or we cannot. If we already may know the objects of experience, then there is no need to trouble ourselves with ideas at all, much less compare them with known objects. Alternatively if we cannot know the objects in experience, we could not possibly compare ideas to them, as comparison requires knowledge of these two things.

Fortunately ideas and objects are not two quite different sorts of things, but closely linked together in meaningful experience. Recalling Dewey's theory of the meaningful object, we can see how he uses the notion of the idea as the universal aspect of a thing to create a new theory of fact, idea, and verification. Because a fact is just a known thing, a known thing is known through its meaningful relations with other things, and the idea is but one of these relations; then when an idea changes, the facts involved with that idea must alter too. Sometimes there is a need for altering ideas, but when there is no need, our experience is simply of known things, and the fact/idea distinction does not arise. However, when there arises a need for a new idea, the thinking process which will undertake the alteration of an idea must also alter those facts which are involved with that idea. This is why Dewey says that the fact/idea distinction is only logical, not ontological. As the logical processes of thinking proceed, new ideas will be formulated by mental analyzing and synthesizing activities (distinguishing certain aspects of things and finding them in other things). By definition a new idea could not possibly fit those facts which were of the old idea's domain. When one entertains a new idea, those previous facts are in doubt because they are not considered as known any longer. But while the facts of the past are in doubt, so are the potential facts of the future. A new idea suggests that certain things encountered in experience will have certain characteristics.

At this stage of the thinking process, the fact/idea distinction is in full bloom. The facts are those uninvolved and hence unaffected known things that form the background to the thinking. The idea is this new universal meaning which proposes to transform the affected things into other known things, with different meaning. As this idea is considered (the novel known things are entertained), it will be noticed either that the total overall harmony of these things has increased or that it has decreased. The increase in harmony signals success; the mind's natural preference for increased harmony will lock the novel known things into firm knowledge, and all doubt will evaporate (and the fact/idea distinction evaporates with it). The reestablishment of knowledge is what Dewey called in the *Psychology* the act of intuition. A decrease in harmony, on the other hand, will cause a return to the process of searching for a new idea.

> The mind attacks the mass of facts which it suspects not to be facts piece-meal. It picks out some one aspect or relation of these "facts," isolates it (technically the process of abstraction), and of this isolated relation it forms a hypothesis, which it then sets over against the facts from which this relation has been isolated. The isolated relation constitutes, technically, the universal; the background of mass of facts is the particular. The verification is the bringing together of this universal and particular: if the universal confronted with the particulars succeeds in filling out its own abstract or empty character by absorbing the particulars into itself as its own details, it is verified. And there is no other test of a theory than this, its ability to work, to organize "facts" into itself as specifications of its own nature. But on the other side, the particulars attacked by the universal do not remain indifferent; through it they are placed in a new light, and as facts gain a new quality. Organized into the theory, they become more significant; what had previously been oppositions and even contradictions among them is removed, and we get a harmonious system. (*EW* 3: 88)

The successful harmonization of known things is the process of verification. In this process two occurrences stand out. First, objects which were known are known no longer in the same way because things have new meanings. Second, new known objects have been created. It is not the case that facts stand passively by while fixed, unchanging ideas are mechanically compared to them. Rather verification is always a process of learning. As things acquire new, better meanings, old facts are eliminated, and new facts are created. When verification is finished, experience loses any fact/idea dichotomy and returns to its ordinary state of having known objects. In "The Present Position of Logical Theory" Dewey defines this understanding of the processes of thought as "transcendental" logic and is eager to persuade his readers that this logic is just the logic of science, not some arcane metaphysical dialectic. Fulfilling his promise to show how Hegelianism is the only truly scientific philosophy, Dewey explains why the age-old inductive and deductive logics are captive to outdated models of thinking. Only transcendental logic, and its grasp of the real nature of verification, can account for scientific methods and results.

The Logic of Conduct

Starting from the infamous inability of deductive logic to foster real scientific learning because of its authoritarian and scholastic mode of organizing and transmitting only achieved knowledge, Dewey points out that inductive logic must also suffer. Since induction was designed to be as responsive as possible to particular human experience, in contrast to the complete indifference of the syllogism, it strove to be nominalistic and fell into the errors of atomistic sensationalism. Inductive logic then could not fully account for the stability and objectivity of scientific knowledge. Kantianism is but a sophisticated psychological revival of deductivism because Kant assumed sensationalism and used the categories to guarantee the universally valid aspects of experience. Transcendental logic, in its finest Hegelian sense, takes induction and deduction to be but the analyzing and synthesizing elements in the reasoning process. As elements they cannot provide knowledge by themselves. As Dewey has long argued before, sensations cannot really give knowledge because of their lack of meaning, but neither can universal concepts because they too are meaningless without an anchor in experience. Knowledge is neither a posteriori nor a priori but their unity since the final judgment of intuition that reveals the known object is always of the universally meaningful object in experience.

In the last analysis Dewey portrays Hegel as devoted to experience as it is actually lived. That experience will either reveal the patterns of thought's activities as described by transcendental logic, or it will not. Hegel, unlike Kant, rejects the notion of thought operating in a realm separate from experience in order to guarantee experience's features. Thought for Hegel is nothing other than the phases of progressively understood experience.

> [T]he very meaning of "transcendentalism" is not only that it is impossible to get valid truth from the evolution of thought in the scholastic sense, but that there is no such thought at all. Processes of intelligence which have their nature fixed in themselves, apart from fact and having to be externally applied to fact, are pure myths to this school. Types of thought are simply the various forms which reality progressively takes as it is progressively mastered as to its meaning,—that is, understood. Methods of thought are simply the various active attitudes into which intelligence puts itself in order to detect and grasp the fact. Instead of rigid moulds, they are flexible adaptations. Methods of thought fit fact more closely and responsively than a worn glove fits the hand. They are only the ideal evolution of the fact—and by "ideal" is here meant simply the evolution of fact into meaning. (*EW* 3: 133)

Hegelian transcendental logic thus preserves the relative stability and trustworthiness of known objects (the deductive requirement), while respecting the presence of this knowledge in human experience, and the ability of future experience to cause the overthrow of old knowledge for new knowledge (the inductive requirement). At bottom, transcendental logic is empirical, because its own ability to describe accurately the processes of human reasoning depends on its sensitivity to actual human experience. Empirical logic will thus coincide with the study of actual scientific methods, freed from the fear of a priori metaphysics (*EW* 3: 141).

By 1891 Dewey's instrumentalist theory of logic was already emerging. It is appropriate to refer to his logic of this early date as instrumentalist even though Dewey did not use that label in print until 1904 (*MW* 3: 317). However, he did contemplate writing a book that used this term, for J. H. Muirhead's Library of Philosophy Series. The volumes of this series, starting in 1892 and continuing for several years, advertised *Principles of Instrumental Logic* by John Dewey in a list of works in preparation. While it was never published,[5] his logic was recognizably instrumentalist according to Dewey's own later definition.

> Instrumentalism is an attempt to establish a precise logical theory of concepts, of judgments and inferences in their various forms, by considering primarily how thought functions in the experimental determinations of future consequences. That is to say, it attempts to establish universally recognized distinctions and rules of logic by deriving them from the reconstructive or mediative function ascribed to reason. (*LW* 2: 14)

The foundations of transcendental logic underlying instrumentalism, discussed above, have far more to do with his dissatisfaction with other logics than with his constructive efforts in functional psychology. Dewey's merger of a Hegelian theory of reason with a voluntarist theory of thought quickly flowered into a stunningly original philosophy of human intelligence.

Intelligence and Knowledge

In his early writings Dewey only briefly mentions the stimulus to thinking, a dissatisfaction with known objects, leaving much in obscurity. What exactly does such dissatisfaction consist of, and how does it arise? Dewey does not answer these questions in "The Logic of Verification" or "The Present Position of Logical Theory." The *Psychology* offers a few simplistic answers. Dissatisfaction is the experience of insufficiently related things standing in contrast to the already harmoniously related known objects of experience, and dissatisfaction will arise because as time goes on, new active experiences constantly bring insufficiently related things. As Dewey further developed his theory of knowledge in the early

1890s, the key link between active experience and thought's efforts to harmonize experience became the notion of "habit."

Habit, Inquiry, and Learning

In the *Psychology* habit is that aspect of experience in which one meaningful thing will trigger successive meanings leading to an action (*EW* 2: 102). Dewey curiously distinguished intellectual and volitional habits in the section on "Habit," isolated from the sections on thinking and intuition. Habit is not mentioned again until the book's last third, on will. There we are told that habit is control, and the ability of the individual to attain control is the will's origin. "Will" ultimately only refers to controlled actions. The October 1892 syllabus for Dewey's Introduction to Philosophy course states that the purpose of new ideas is to revive thwarted activity by reinstating harmonious active experience. In the 1896 "Reflex Arc Concept" article, all intellectual activities, including mental habits, are aspects of the effort to attain habitual behavior. These developments and many others occurred because Dewey was forced to consider the internal harmony of his own philosophical system. This growing harmony can now be observed from the side of his psychological examination of knowledge's role in self-realization.

From the previous section we recall that Dewey held that the subject of the judgment is the individual thing while the predicate is this thing's universal aspect, the meaningful relations to other things. A judgment is always a provisional affair, a beholding of things in a new arrangement of meanings, that may or may not increase the overall harmony of the situation to the required degree. The ability of a judgment to increase the harmony of an experience was, however, insufficiently connected to Dewey's notion of habit. His writings of 1892–1896 fill this gap. They start from the principle, first clearly enunciated in the February 1892 Introduction to Philosophy syllabus, that an organism is never performing only one act at a time in serial fashion. Rather activity is always a matter of the coordination of multiple acts all happening in an overlapping manner. This coordination is always a matter of degree, corresponding to the degree of success which these activities have in reaching their goals. Of the activities of an organism, the one primary goal which the organism appears to have can be selected. From this selection of the primary goal, the contributing minor acts of the organism can be discriminated. Among these minor acts is the reasoning involved in the thoughtful recoordination of habits. Judgment plays an essential role as the product of such reasoning.

Dewey's reconstruction of the reflex arc into the organic circuit as the basic unit of activity must not be conceived as so unitary that the organism can only undergo one organic circuit at a time. Instead any circuit can be selected out of an organism's activities as the primary mode of action, and within that primary circuit the coordinating subactivities can each be discriminated as having their own circuits. The "will" or "self" stands for the coordination of the contributing activities, while "intelligence" is the discrimination of the coordinating activities (*EW* 3: 212–214). The nature of meaning, insufficiently elaborated in earlier writings of his absolute idealism phase, is now transforming into a psychobiological entity so that it can contribute to Dewey's theory of conduct. His functionalist analysis of conduct has revealed that completed actions serve as the discharging conditions which set off other actions. The role of habit fits precisely here. An organism has a habit when a certain act automatically stimulates the start of another act, which when completed can also in turn stimulate a third act. A habit always requires some specific kind of act to serve as its stimulus, and it always proceeds to a specified end. Dewey uses the terms "sensation" and "stimuli" to refer to the act required to set off the operation of a habit. As a kind of action, a habit is an organic circuit with its coordinated subacts. Successful coordination is the experience of harmonious activity, in which each habit called for is provided with its proper stimuli, and together the habits are performed in a correctly coordinated way to achieve the organism's primary goal. In terms of meanings an act is fully meaningful when it properly serves to trigger the next required habit of an overall action. An act lacks meaning to the degree that it fails to trigger the required habit.

Dewey's insistence that the individual is the only true object of knowledge is now transformed into the tenet that the properly coordinated and completed action is the only true object of knowledge. Keeping in mind that knowledge is for Dewey the effort to make adjustments to the meanings of things so that more harmonious experience can emerge, we can now see that the process of knowledge has as its objective the adjustment of the stimuli to habits. Knowledge is that process of activities which examines the acts of the present problematic situation, analyzes those acts to ignore their unsuccessful meanings and focus on possible successful ones, synthesizes a novel view of the things in the situation to suggest other meanings which may trigger the needed habits, and tries out those new meanings to discover whether the triggered habits actually do successfully recoordinate to restore the primary activity desired. Meanings, the ideal aspects of actions, are in ordinary unproblematic activity not noticed as meanings apart from the things enjoyed. However, in a problematic situation when the primary activity has halted, things are scrutinized for their meanings as they had them before activity stopped, and then things have new meanings projected on them, transforming them for future possible use as triggers of habits. In the October 1892 Introduction to Philosophy syllabus Dewey relates knowledge to action.

> The postponement of the complete and direct activity is the same as the inharmonious adjustment, the rubbing together, of the various elements in it. This mutual resistance, or the activity in its direct

course arrested, constitutes knowledge. This knowledge, however, in calling attention to the various factors of the activity in their separateness, calls attention also to their relations to one another and thus points the way to a further reunion. . . . Knowledge, in other words, is, as disintegration and accompanying arrest of activity, a report or account of that activity; as readjustment of the distinguished factors to one another, it is the project or ideal of further activity; i.e., knowledge on its analytic side is reference to past action which it registers in its distinct conditions, thus objectifying it; on its synthetic side, it is reference to future or purposed activity, which it states as harmony or unity of the distinguished conditions, thus subjecting (rendering into its value for the self) the objective. (*LW* 17: 158)

Knowledge for Dewey has a definite, limited place within intelligence. Intelligence is one of the aspects of the self, which in turn is but a factor of active experience. The self arises in experience when habitual activity halts. At this stage, a distinction arises between the unity expressed by the desired resumption of unproblematic activity and the disunity of the current factors of the problematic experience. Intelligence is that aspect of the self expressing the subjective coordination of habitual activity while sensation is that aspect of the self which arises during problematic experience to express the diverse meanings of things suddenly under scrutiny. It is the function of knowing/reasoning to select which sensational meanings are worthy of attention and to reconstruct these meanings to restore habitual, harmonious activity.

It is very important to notice fully how Dewey distinguishes between intelligence and knowledge. In its usual sense knowledge has the connotation of stored-up facts and principles already learned; it is knowledge in this sense that he transfers to intelligence. To act intelligently is to be in possession of such a variety of habits appropriate for successfully conducting oneself in many different situations. Knowledge is but one aspect of intelligence: the learning aspect, which is capable of modifying and even creating new habits. This distinction between intelligence and knowing/learning is one which Dewey certainly depended on throughout his career, but on occasion he may not have taken sufficient care to keep them clearly separate. As he reflects in his reply to his commentators in *The Philosophy of John Dewey,*

> [T]he word "intelligence" represents what is essential in my view much better than does the word *knowledge,* while it avoids that confusion of knowing—inquiry—and attained knowledge which has led some of my critics astray in their accounts of my position. . . . I should, from the start, have systematically distinguished between knowledge as the outcome of special inquiries (undertaken because

of the presence of problems) and *intelligence* as the product and expression of cumulative funding of the meanings reached in these special cases. (*LW* 14: 6)

Learning is possible because one's reasoning habits can take charge during problematic situations. Without the ability to learn, to solve problems, any halt to activity could potentially be permanent. Such an organism would truly be unintelligent and also soon dead. Lower forms of life are provided with fixed habits, called instincts, which can deal with only a limited range of environmental circumstances. Higher forms of life, including human beings, have fewer instincts but can learn a wider range of habits to deal with more varied and complex circumstances. Human beings can also learn reasoning habits and develop them in the course of their use; this ability gives rise to the sciences, logic, and philosophy. The term "habit" is not synonymous with "instinct," denoting only the rigid and unchanging capacities of organisms. Dewey emphasizes in *The Study of Ethics* that higher animals rely less on instincts and must depend on more and more complex systems of flexible and continually readjusting habits (*EW* 4: 348).

Functionalism's Antidualism

If habits are just aspects of an organism's activity, then the functionally distinguishable elements of habit are all on the same ontological/metaphysical level with each other and with the organism. As Dewey argued in "The Reflex Arc Concept in Psychology," the reflex arc was infected by dualistic psychology, which in turn was inspired by a dualistic metaphysics of the physical and mental. On this model the stimulus exists on the border between body and mind, and the central connections are purely mental while the motor response stands on the border again. The theoretical distinction between stimulus, coordination, and response should not entirely be discarded, Dewey argued, but psychology's liberation from dualism requires that each element of action cannot be rigidly identified with ontologically separate entities having only mechanical relations. Only a functionalist theory of the reflex arc can both successfully avoid dualism and fully explain all of the features of human action called for by the theory, especially the ability to learn. To avoid dualism and its concomitant principle of mechanical causal relations, the distinction between stimulus, idea, and response must be teleological, meaning that such a distinction made within an act first requires a proper conception of the act, which requires a conception of the act's goal.

This conception may be formulated by an observer or by the actor (and Dewey reminds us that these may not coincide). However, there is no uniquely right answer to the question what is he or she (or what am I) doing? Of course, no conception of the purpose of activity may be formed, in which case only serial events are noticed, none having any more significance than any other. But where a purpose is defined, the act's teleological nature requires that mechanical causality be replaced by organic coordination of interrelated parts, each of which must be considered as relatively functional wholes themselves. Because in functional psychology the whole unit of behavior is the act, each part of an act A must itself be an act Aa, Ab, Ac, and so forth. The stimulus must be a sensori-motor coordination (for example, the focusing on a candle) and so must the response (the reaching for the seen candle). These acts may themselves be analyzed into their constituent acts, ad infinitum.

This functional theory of habit reconstructs the mechanical reflex arc so that there is no way, independent of specifying the purpose of an act, to define exactly what constitutes stimuli or responses for human beings. Dualism relies on such definitions because without a rigid designation of the stimulus or of the response, the metaphysical distinctions between the physical object and its effect on the experience of a human being, or between the experience of acting and its effect on a physical object, could not be made. In a similar manner absolute idealism relies on the metaphysical distinction between the stimulus as an isolated meaningless sensation and as the content of a meaningful experience. A rigid designation of "stimuli," for example, can be made for an activity only if the actor's interaction with his environment is conceived in a mechanical, serial fashion.

Let me return to the example of searching for the cause of engine trouble to illustrate Dewey's theory. My behavior as I leaned over the engine would be, from an observer's standpoint, not very much different from the mechanic's behavior. What might be observed? The leaning over the engine, the movements of the head, the glancing around of the eyes. Of course, the final acts of my behavior were to straighten up and turn away in frustration while the final acts of the mechanic were to reach for the loose wire, reconnect it in place, and turn away in satisfaction. How might the observer explain the two very different series of acts? The obvious answer must be that the mechanic saw the loose wire; this answer of course presupposes that the observer assumes that the mechanic's purpose must be to discover something correctable within the engine. Yet I had the very same purpose. If the observer did not know that I had the same purpose, how could he have guessed that the cause of our two behaviors' differing was the loose wire, much less the seeing of the loose wire?

Let us next say that the observer has supposed (correctly) that we both were looking for something correctable within the engine. Can the observer's original answer now hold good? This answer in effect says that the mechanic's final acts were caused by the stimulus of the sight of the loose wire while mine were not. But the observer must be very careful when specifying the nature of this alleged stimulus. Is the observer saying that I did not have the sight of the loose wire while the mechanic did, and, if so, what could he possibly mean? The loose wire was in some sense a part of my visual field, after all. What if the observer had to explain exactly what he meant by saying that he perceived in the mechanic's behavior that the mechanic had the stimulus of seeing the loose wire? What if the observer explains, "Well, the loose wire was sitting right there, after all, and how could the mechanic miss it?" This is a very unsatisfactory answer since the observer knows that when I looked over the engine the loose wire was sitting there, too. A more sophisticated answer would be, "A mechanic wouldn't miss the loose wire." This is a much better answer since it points to the mechanic's skills as contributing to the explanation. However, it also eliminates the original answer, since it confesses that we both "saw" the loose wire but it functioned as a stimulus for the mechanic while it did not for me. Dewey's functionalism treats an act (here, the seeing of a loose wire) as a stimulus only insofar as it functions as the trigger to further habitual action. The mechanic's behavior in this episode was far more intelligent than my own. What this means is that the mechanic's engine-problem-solving habits are far more extensive and coordinated than my own.

But this analysis does not go deep enough to reveal fully functionalism's radical treatment of the nature of the stimulus. Our observer might yet say that while the loose wire was a stimulus for the mechanic and not for me, the loose wire was still there as a potential stimulus before either one of us began to look for it. Functionalism rejects this stand on the preexisting loose wire because it is in the nature of a problem-solving stimulus that it cannot in any sense be said to *exist* as a potential stimulus. A problematic situation is problematic precisely because the stimulus required is not present; if it were, there would be no problem. But the observer will say, of course, for the problem solver the stimulus does not seem to be really there until the problem is solved, but *really* the stimulus must be there all along, otherwise how could it be discovered? Functionalism hardly denies the existence of things before or after problematic situations, but what is at issue is the loose wire's existence *as a stimulus* prior to the problem's resolution. How does the observer know that the loose wire is the stimulus required to solve the engine problem? There are only two possibilities: through the observer's own investigation into the engine trouble, or through carefully watching the mechanic's behavior. On the first scenario the observer has discerned the loose wire and then is not surprised when the mechanic does too; on the second scenario the observer has inferred from the mechanic's problem-solving success that the loose wire is the cause of the trouble. Both scenarios therefore place as the priority someone's undergoing the investigation and making the transition from not knowing what is needed to be done and not having the needed stimulus, to knowing what to do because the needed stimulus is now present. It makes no sense to say that anything exists as the needed stimulus prior to the problem's solution, except as a way to describe vaguely the whole scenario after its successful conclusion.

Those who would argue that stimuli exist as stimuli prior to the problem-solving activity are confusing descriptions of the serial sequence of activities formulated after they are completed with understandings of the intelligent process of problem solving. The former can be phrased in mechanical terms:

"The engine trouble causes the mechanic to look for the problem, which causes the mechanic to see the loose wire, and the loose wire then causes the mechanic to reach for it and reconnect it." The ordinary reflex arc concept is suited to such primitive descriptions. The latter, since they are fundamentally organic understandings, require teleological terms and relations: "The mechanic's desire to start the engine brings many habitual principles of engine repair to bear to analyze the situation, which suggest focusing on certain electrical aspects of the engine first, such attention in turn coordinating searching activities that select electrical connections for testing their soundness. When a particular electrical connection appeared unsound, the observed looseness of the wire harmoniously synthesized the conflicting elements of the situation to bring the mechanic to the judgment/hypothesis that reconnecting this wire would permit the engine to start. When tested, the judgment proved sound as the engine did start after the wire was reconnected."

Dewey considers this confusion, between a mechanical description of matters after the behavior has run its course and an understanding of the behavior as a purposive process, to be so prevalent in psychology that it deserves its own label as the "psychological" or "historical" fallacy. This fallacy is committed when "a set of considerations which hold good only because of a completed process, is read into the content of the process which conditions this completed result" (*EW* 5: 105). Functionalism avoids this fallacy because it takes the temporal and situational nature of learning seriously. Learning cannot be properly understood if it is assumed that matters stand for the learner just in the same way as they do for an observer. There are two important connections of this functionalist principle with Dewey's earlier philosophy. First, it echoes his rejection of those atomistically empiricist psychologies which assume that the seemingly permanent elements of sophisticated adult experience must also really be present in the child's experience. Second, it is an express repudiation of Dewey's absolute idealism of the *Psychology* since the notion of the eternal and perfectly harmonious self was read into actual fragmentary human experience. The most significant connection with Dewey's developing instrumentalist epistemology is that his theory of nature of knowing is organically one with his theory of the stimulus. Just as a stimulus could not exist prior to the problem-solving activity, so too a known object could not exist prior to the problem-solving activity because a known object is just (loosely put) the judgment made possible by the stimulus, which has proven itself satisfactory.

If learning is just one aspect of the activity of habit adjustment and recoordination and reasoning is the process of creative learning, then all of the features of reasoning's process are on the same ontological/metaphysical level as the organism's activity itself. Among the features of the reasoning process are the distinctions between objective facts (things taken for granted) and subjective ideas (things called into question). This objective/subjective distinction is not a harbinger of some sort of dualistic metaphysics. As George H. Mead's quotation at the start of this chapter proclaims, "entities are but formulations of thought at different phases of experience." Functionalism is antidualistic in another and even deeper sense because it locates the organism's activity within its social environment. Knowledge proximately solves immediate problems, but, perhaps more important, knowledge in a larger sense serves to expands the powers of the self, which in turn makes richer, more meaningful active experiences possible in the future. The expansion of experience is the ultimate end of life for Dewey. Because experience is socially active experience and the self is but a social entity, the expansion of meaningful social relations, or, in other words, the expansion of the self, is the only end toward which progress tends. Such is the social context and instrumental nature of knowledge.

In a 1897 essay, "The Significance of the Problem of Knowledge," Dewey places the question of the nature of knowledge in an extremely far-reaching social context, from the Greek search for self-knowledge to the modern search for scientific techniques. The history of Western civilization reveals how social issues of the greatest import reshape the age-old question of what is knowledge according to the needs of the times. It is Dewey's sociological thesis that the debate between empiricism and rationalism, between those who defend the primacy of the individual's varied experiences and those who defend the primacy of the culture's fixed principles, is an argument carried on by a civilization asking how to benefit effectively from the individual's released powers in a progressively democratic political arena. This is a worthy argument to which philosophy's efforts should be directed, but not if philosophy degenerates into mere epistemology. In Dewey's view philosophy as psychology and social ethics can contribute to the thoughtful appreciation of our culture's problems by asking after the practical conditions of successful social activity, but philosophy as an interminable struggle between the extremes of empiricism and rationalism cannot (*EW* 5: 21–23). The themes of "The Significance of the Problem of Knowledge" are a harbinger of Dewey's later social critiques of philosophy's purpose and method, notably those of *Reconstruction in Philosophy* and *The Quest for Certainty*. Its themes are also a preparation for Dewey's continuing claim that psychology must be oriented to the current social problems of democracy, whether applied to education as in "Psychology and Social Practice" (1899), *The School and Society* (1899), *How We Think* (1910), and *Democracy and Education* (1916); or to ethics as in "Psychological Method in Ethics" (1903), "Logical Conditions of a Scientific Treatment of Morality" (1903), and *Ethics* (1908); or to political deliberation as in *The Public and Its Problems* (1927) and *Individualism, Old and New* (1930).

Problem Solving

In several publications dating from 1900 to 1903, Dewey developed the theory of learning presented in "The Reflex Arc Concept" by reconstructing his earlier transcendental logic of the process of restoring harmonious active experience. The central writings are "Some Stages of Logical Thought" (1900) and his four chapters of *Studies in Logical Theory* (1903); his "Lectures in the Theory of Logic, 1899–1900" should also be consulted.[6] While the main goal of the first article is to display the greater value of experimental science over less advanced methods of problem solving (taken up in the next section), an overview of Dewey's basic scheme of problem solving is offered. The title of this article can be misleading since the stages referred to are not the phases of reflective thought per se, but rather various modes of thought, from the least to the most advanced, all of which display in more or less developed form the same phases. These phases are the same as those advanced in his earlier writings on reasoning. The list below gives the earlier and later version of each phase.[7]

> 1. The introduction of non-harmonious experience (halting of habitual activity, causing problematic doubt, because the needed stimulus is missing).

> 2. The attention on the contradictory elements in experience (reflective focus on the activity halted and missing stimulus).

> 3. The analysis of experience to select out certain meanings of things (the use of ideas to construe some features of the situation as especially significant).

> 4. The synthesis of experience to alter these meanings so that things suggest a more harmonious experience (the linking together of ideas, some of them new, concluding with a practical judgment that suggests how to restart the desired activity).

> 5. The restoration of harmonious activity (the practical judgment's testing successfully restarts the activity).[8]

Dewey's theory of inquiry is the functionalist version of the Hegelian dialectic of analysis and synthesis that was so influential for his early idealism. His own comments on this transformation are instructive.

> There was a period extending into my earlier years at Chicago when, in connection with a seminar in Hegel's Logic I tried reinterpreting his categories in terms of "readjustment" and "reconstruction." Gradually I came to realize that what the principles actually stood for could be better understood and stated when completely emancipated from Hegelian garb.[9]

Despite the effort by commentators beholden to the traditional story of Dewey's development who used this quotation to infer that he had rejected all Hegelian theories, the actual import of this quotation lies in choice of terminology, not in fundamental ideas. Dewey's functionalism understood mental events in terms of a teleologically dialectical circle or organic circuit. It was his superposition of dialectics onto biological psychology which made Hegelian terminology an outdated obstacle. In Dewey's 1897 lectures on Hegel, the parallel lines of thinking are evident. The first quotation concerns Hegel's psychology.

> In sensation, in feeling, the soul is at one with the object. But when self-consciousness rises this unity breaks into two, the object is set over against the subject, the subject against the object. But this division makes a contradiction in spirit, whose very nature is to be an active unity. The subject, therefore, sets to work to subdue the object to itself.... Having thus set nature over against itself, it then, as it were, turns [a]round and proceeds by knowledge, art and conduct, to transform this outer nature into a factor of its own activity.[10]

The second quotation concerns Hegel's philosophy of spirit and its superiority to Kantian rationalism and British empiricism.

> While rational psychology sets up a ready-made and abstract soul, empirical psychology begins with a lot of ready-made faculties, not attempting to show any necessary connection between these faculties and the nature of spirit itself. It resolves the soul into an aggregate of independent powers which stand in mechanical relation to each other. The philosophy of spirit shows that these so-called faculties of mind, and also all concrete empirical material, are simply elements in the development of the active unity of the spirit. We understand spirit, then, not when we begin by supposing a substance which we term soul or by supposing a lot of separate mental faculties, but only when we trace the varied processes by which spirit realizes itself. Our so-called faculties will then appear in their proper place as stages in its evolution. Thus the whole science becomes living, organic and systematic.[11]

If a substitution of "active social experience" is made for "active unity of spirit" and if the elements/processes of the "spirit's development" are functionally construed as the logical functions of thought, the pattern of Hegelianism is recognizably present in Dewey's functionalism and instrumentalism. This pattern is evident in both in his specific analysis of the phases of inquiry and his wider sociological treatment of the stages of logical thought.

The stages are serially distinguished by the degree to which they take the ideas of phase 3 to be assured and unchanging. The simplest stage does not question ideas at all. Indeed problem solving hardly notices them as ideas distinct from the nature of the situation. They seem to the users as paradigmatically real and permanent, so real that they make up the structure of the cosmos or the divine. More complex stages display some degree of questioning of ideas since they may either fail to apply to a problem or may prescribe contradictory judgments, but the aim of the analysis phase is to select the truly applicable idea to rule on the problem. Dewey labels this elevation of ideas to real and permanent things in their own right as the "Aristotelian" logic. The empirical stage is worthy of greater attention since it is the immediate and necessary predecessor to the highest scientific stage. In the empirical stage ideas are not given absolute jurisdiction. The rejection of universal principles in toto places all the value on immediate and particular facts at hand. The rigid deductivism of earlier stages is thrown over for the opposite mode of inductivist thought. Repeating his accusations against inductive logic made earlier in "The Present Position of Logical Theory," Dewey argues that the extreme nominalism fomented by inductivism may free things from the arbitrary rule of universal principles but strips things of meaning sufficient to permit valuable inference from things to other things (*MW* 1: 171).

The refreshing liberation of particular, contingent things is necessary for modern science, but by itself it only leads to sterile positivism. Natural laws are subsidiary and contingently related to the superior reality of individuated particulars. Not surprisingly the problem of induction forbids thought's reliance on nature's stable features: "thought is just a gymnastic by which we vault from one presented fact to another remote in time and space" (*MW* 1: 173). The recent philosophical reaction against inductivism, transcendentalism, returns to the Aristotelian conception of fixed ideals by locating them in the supremely real thought of the absolute. Dewey does not explicitly label the highest stage of logical thought besides identifying it with modern science's research into the means of controlling nature for "effecting the growth of experience" (*MW* 1: 171). Truly scientific inquiry fully realizes that thinking is a doubt-inquiry process in which *all* of thought's aspects are developed and modified. The other three logics hypostasize one or another phase of inquiry into a reality external to, and controlling of, the thought process (*MW* 1: 173–174).

Dewey's first opportunity to present his instrumentalist theory of inquiry to a wide philosophical audience is the *Studies in Logical Theory*. Its preface, written by Dewey, should not be overlooked for guidance toward his general approach to knowledge in the wider context of inquiry and, ultimately, growing experience.

> [J]udgment is the central function of knowing, and hence affords the central problem of logic; that since the act of knowing is intimately and indissolubly connected with the like yet diverse functions of affection, appreciation, and practice, it only distorts results

reached to treat knowing as a self-enclosed and self-explanatory whole—hence the intimate connections of logical theory with functional psychology; that since knowledge appears as a function within experience, and yet passes judgment upon both the processes and contents of other functions, its work and aim must be distinctively reconstructive or transformatory; that since Reality must be defined in terms of experience, judgment appears accordingly as the medium through which the consciously effected evolution of Reality goes on; that there is no reasonable standard of truth (or of success of the knowing function) in general, except upon the postulate that Reality is thus dynamic or self-evolving, and, in particular, except through reference to the specific offices which knowing is called upon to perform in readjusting and expanding the means and ends of life. (*EW* 2: 296)

Dewey's nominal adversary in the *Studies* was Göttingen professor Rudolf Hermann Lotze (1817–1881), whose later years brought fame as the preeminent and most popular German philosopher. This enormous influence extended beyond the borders of his native country. For example, his writings were in such demand elsewhere that they nearly all received the rare honor of translation into French and English. This fame brought the mandatory study of Lotze to philosophy departments. Santayana's desire to write his dissertation on Schopenhauer was set aside by Royce in favor of Lotze; Royce apparently had the practical inclination to yoke Santayana to the more significant cart of the day.[12] The wide popularity of Lotze in his own time, and his nearly complete obscurity today, can be attributed to his syncretic and sympathetic approach to philosophical speculation. No school wholly met with his approval, no doctrine received an unqualified assent, yet all other systems had a valuable aspect worthy of appropriation into his own thought. Impossible to categorize neatly and unable to found a philosophical school or organize disciples of his own, Lotze's writings provided fertile soil for diverse yet incompatible yields raised by Hegelians, personalists, dualists, materialists, and positivists.

There is very little sign that the young Dewey could be counted among those directly influenced by Lotze although Dewey was familiar with his major psychological, logic, and metaphysical works. In the *Psychology* Dewey remarks that "Lotze is difficult to class, having, upon the whole, an independent basis; he is indebted to Kant and to Herbart in about equal measures, while he is everywhere influenced by the physiological aspects of the science" (*EW* 2: 364). In his text on Leibniz, Lotze is mentioned as one who agrees with Leibniz that the mechanically materialistic aspect of the universe cannot be denied, yet it is not capable of accounting for the universe's spiritual harmonies (*EW* 1: 427). Lotze's logic was among the "modern" approaches that

Dewey taught in courses at Michigan (e.g., a course titled "The Logic of Scientific Methods" in 1890) and Chicago (e.g., a course titled "Theory of Logic" in 1899–1900). As the preface to the *Studies in Logical Theory* explains, the essays were the product of work done in the Theory of Logic course over the preceding years, work which critically focused on Mill, Lotze, Bradley, and Bosanquet.

Dewey's own contributions to the *Studies in Logical Theory* could have been on any or all of these important philosophers of logic. Lotze's preeminent stature and the structure of his logical and epistemological system made him an irresistible target for Dewey. That system managed to make just about every philosophical and psychological error that Dewey had been combating since his earliest idealistic phase. Lotze was enough of an sensationalist empiricist and a Kantian categorist to get completely ensnared in what Dewey had come to view as the cardinal sins: the notions that (1) pure logic, or "epistemology," should define knowledge as the proper relation between universally valid forms of thought and real objects, and (2) applied logic, the practical judgment of particular matters, is dependent on epistemology yet has no bearing on epistemology's concerns (*MW* 2: 302–303). While the *Studies in Logical Theory* have traditionally been viewed as Dewey's public notice of his full repudiation of idealism, his contemporaries would not have made any such assumption since few mistook Lotze's work for the paradigm of idealistic philosophy and no one considered it Hegelian at all. Furthermore Kantian and Cartesian dualists, scientific realists, and positivistic empiricists all would have read condemnations of their epistemologies in Dewey's broadside attacks. Peirce read a rejection of his own logical research in Dewey's functionalist and genetic approach to knowledge, and he complains (with some justification) that, by attacking only Lotze, Dewey does not clearly distinguish his philosophy from idealism.[13]

Dewey's criticisms of Lotze follow the same pattern as his previous criticisms of the Kantian "sense experience" versus "categorized knowing" dualism. Thought according to Lotze has two crucial tasks: to organize the otherwise unknowable sensations into forms permitting knowledge and to know only what is really there in sense experience without distorting it. The first task assumes that knowledge requires the application of universal and unchanging concepts to fleeting and unrelated particulars while the second task assumes that knowledge must not be the result of the imposition of thought's foreign influences but instead must perfectly reflect the reality found through sensation. Dewey's primary criticism of Lotze reveals how these two tasks are assigned to the pursuit of epistemology and why they are incompatibly contradictory. This critique was not unique to Dewey. For example, one Hegelian response to Lotze by Henry Jones made the same points in order to demonstrate absolute idealism's superiority.[14] B. M. Humphries has provided an excellent analysis of Jones's critique:

If you begin with raw data uncontaminated by thought, there is so far no knowledge but only brute (dumb, speechless) sensation (impressions); knowledge contains elements which certainly look like they are not given in sensation but are the work of thought. Does thought find or make these features? The former supposition makes the work of thought superfluous and is besides inconsistent with the acknowledgment that brute sensation cannot present such features. If, on the other hand, thought adds these features, then there is an arbitrary in knowledge on your view; such knowledge could be veridical only on the assumption of a corresponding spiritual principle in reality. Your view makes thinking either futile or falsifying, although this is concealed by an inevitable see-saw in your exposition: you are forced to attribute these problematic features sometimes to sensation (when you wish to guarantee that knowledge is genuine) and sometimes to thought (when you are aware that thought is not useless and that sensation is an insufficient ground for knowledge).[15]

Dewey acknowledges his indebtedness to Jones (*MW* 2: 333) but avoids Jones's preferred solution of the "corresponding spiritual principle in reality" by instead offering an instrumentalist account of thought's role in experience. This account agrees that it must be the purpose of thought to introduce greater organization into experience, and therefore it rejects the notion that experience prior to this development must be the verifying test of thought's value. Instrumentalism places the responsibility for testing thought's work on the developed experience. This sounds like a return to Kant since it would seem that the test of truth really rests with thought itself. However, because Dewey holds that experience is always active experiences occurring through time, the real test of judgment lies in the new activity brought about by thought's work. This understanding of knowledge as judgment's test must reject the assumption that knowledge's task is the reproduce features of the world as it is experienced. Instead knowledge creates new activities. Obviously the only way for Dewey to place differential value on judgments is to place differential value on activity. Unless some activities were more valuable than others, there would be no basis from which to assign to judgments different values (as more or less verified). Activities are neither true nor false, they only exist. Thought, relieved from the responsibility of reproducing them, could hardly falsify or distort activities. Thought thus stands for the organization of experience that makes successful activity possible despite the variability and contingency of the conditions of activity. Knowledge stands for the developing aspect of thought. Its resolution of particular problems increases thought's capacities to deal with future similar situations.

This all-important distinction between thought (or intelligence) and knowledge (or knowings/learnings) shatters the assumptions of epistemology as conducted by other philosophies. Dewey is not as careful with this distinction as he should be in the *Studies in Logical Theory*. His use of the term "thought" sometimes means "intelligence" but usually it means "reflective thought" or inquiry. Other philosophies clearly conflate intelligence with knowing, assuming that the available stock of concepts for thought does not alter through time. Thus they easily imagine how thought must be separate from experience since there is never any guarantee that new experience will be corralled by the concepts. Dewey's instrumentalism suggests that it is thought's task to deal with new experience, and where thought cannot succeed, reflective inquiry creates new concepts to produce knowledge that will. In thought, concepts are submerged in the sufficiently meaningful experience of unproblematic activity. No notice is taken of the concept of a thing since we know what to do with it and what to expect from it, and thus we use previously established knowledge without being consciously aware of our dependence. In inquiry, experience is not sufficiently meaningful, and things suddenly become doubtful. Their meanings (thought's concepts) are brought to our attention because they do not work, and new meanings are demanded if activity is to resume. Hence reflective inquiry must alter their meanings to produce a testable judgment of what activity will work.

In this way instrumentalism offers a new theory of knowledge verification. Dewey agrees with empiricism that experience must always be the test of knowledge, and he agrees with idealism that reflective thought's duty is to transform experience. These are not contradictory aims because it is only *future* experience, after reflective thought has transformed past experience, that is entitled to serve as the test of thought. Inquiry and knowledge look forward, not backward. It is the future needs of the thinker, not the past experiences of the thinker, that knowledge serves. Thought as stored-up intelligence has the sole responsibility for dealing with present experience, but thought in this sense does nothing; thought is but a convenient name for the meanings inherent in unproblematic things that we use in our activity. However, things have those meanings now only because inquiry has done its work in the past. The Lotzean dilemma seems now to reappear: how can present experience ever test the meanings imposed by past inquiry? If it cannot, then no need for any further inquiry would arise, and then thought would thereafter prevail untested.

Dewey's answer is that experience tests meanings constantly, as we always run the risk that a reliable thing suddenly becomes unreliable. This easily recognizable feature of experience is the eruption of disorganized experience into harmonious experience. It is not the appearance of completely meaningless experience; everything always has some, if few, relationships with other experience. Rather it is a thing's insufficient meaning that calls for inquiry and serves as materials for the creation of new meanings. Those new meanings transform the previously problematic thing out of existence when a new usefully meaningful thing replaces it to serve as the test of the new meanings. This transformative function of inquiry means that knowledge always creates its object. And the Lotzean dilemma emerges once again: how could the object of knowledge serve as a real test of the knowledge which created it? Dewey's reply is that it really is not the object of knowledge which serves as its test since that object was created only in the inquiry process whose final end is to judge what activity will resolve the problematic situation. It is this activity, using the new object of knowledge, which is the real test of that knowledge and that object. This new activity lies beyond thought in a way that the object of knowledge could not. If this activity fails to restore unproblematic activity, the supposed object of knowledge will be abandoned as unreal, and inquiry will start all over again. Experience thus tests thought in two ways. New experience may prove intelligence to be inadequate, and prove knowledge produced by prior inquiry to be inadequate.

Dewey turns the tables on the epistemologist by asking how epistemology makes the testing, the falsifying and verifying, of knowledge possible. So long as experience and thought are held to be intrinsically different things (as opposed to their unity in meaningful experience), fruitful comparison is impossible. No one else, from the layman to the scientist, takes much notice of that division between things and thought upon which the epistemologist is fixated (*MW* 2: 305–306). Furthermore how will the epistemologist conceive of the relationship between experience and reality? Even if experience is held to be perfectly transparent of reality, or actually reality itself, the impossibility stands. If reality is beyond experience (and hence possibly, for all we know, different from experience's testimony), as Lotze assumes, then an additional mystery is created.

> Now, Lotze is committed once for all to the notion that thought, in any form, is directed by and at an outside reality. The ghost haunts him to the last. How, after all, does even the ideally perfect valid thought apply or refer to reality? Its genuine subject is still beyond itself. At the last Lotze can dispose of this question only by regarding it as a metaphysical, not a logical, problem (*Logic*, II, 281, 282). In other words, logically speaking, we are at the end just exactly where we were at the beginning—in the sphere of ideas, and of ideas only, plus a consciousness of the necessity of referring these ideas to a reality which is beyond them, which is utterly inaccessible to them, which is out of reach of any influence which they may exercise, and which transcends any possible comparison with their results. (*MW* 2: 365–366)

In metaphysical speculation, of course, Lotze offers an account of how reality causes sensations to occur in just the right manner to ensure that thought's organizing of sensation reproduces in universal ideas the structure of reality. Dewey is hardly interested in pursuing Lotze into that realm of philosophy since similar dilemmas recur. How could a causal relationship stand between reality and sensations, and how could reality guarantee the right production of meaningless sensations in a mental medium? Answers to these questions could never, by definition of knowledge in this metaphysics, be known. Such a transcendent reality, like the absolute of idealism, is given a heavy responsibility to arrange matters perfectly so that human thought must go to the trouble of reproducing it. If reality is already so rationally structured (realism) or so structured by reason (absolute idealism) and if it helps to determine what sensational experience is like, then why does it not just manifest itself as fully rational in experience, instead of the disjointed, chaotic manner of sensations? "Why and how should a perfect, absolute, complete, finished thought find it necessary to submit to alien, disturbing, and corrupting conditions in order, in the end, to recover through reflective thought in a partial, piecemeal, wholly inadequate way what it possessed at the outset in a much more satisfactory way?" (*MW* 2: 334).

The same hypothetical question awaits the transcendental realist. Why should reality have to produce only sensations in us, forcing us to rely on thought, instead of producing (reproducing?) itself as it really is? Both the realist and the absolute idealist have an available reply: the human variable forbids the simple and easy transference of the structure of reality into human knowledge. The appeal to the human variable reduces human experience to a subjective realm, separate from both reality and thought. Unfortunately, as human thought has only experience to work with, no one could ever determine whether the structure of human thought actually matches the structure of reality or even the extent to which experience differs from reality. For all we know, on this metaphysical theory, reality may really be utterly chaotic, and hence human thought is always false to it. This hypothesis seems strange, but it is, for we all know, just as possible as its counterpart notion that reality is perfectly structured and human thought is always false to it.

It is here that the empiricist steps in. He or she refuses to have anything to do with a transcendent reality and claims that it is not reality beyond experience that tests thought, but just experience itself. So far Dewey is in complete accord with this sentiment. However, traditional empiricism curiously also takes experience to be quite chaotic and disconnected, requiring thought to supply meaningful relations. Hence the empiricist runs the same risk of committing the fallacy of rationalism as Lotze (*MW* 2: 348). The empiricist's only recourse is the extreme claim that thought should not transform experience in any way. On this claim, experience arrives sufficiently self-luminous for most purposes, and if thought is used, it must be kept safely out of experience's way. This treatment of thought is rationalism in the extreme; a purified logic of symbols lacking any reference whatsoever can be the only result. Dewey's opinion of that exercise's value may be safely left to the imagination of the reader.

Interestingly Dewey's selection of Lotze as his foil appears quite prescient in the light of subsequent philosophical developments in Anglo-American philosophy.

Those developments include the emergence of pragmatism as a movement of thought, but Peirce's role would be muted and generally influential only through William James. Peirce himself was confident that Dewey would not have an impact on philosophy's progress, since philosophy should serve science's need for pure logic.

> The Chicago school or group are manifestly in radical opposition to the exact logicians, and are not making any studies which anybody in his senses can expect, directly or indirectly, in any considerable degree, to influence twentieth-century science.[16]

Experimental Science

Dewey's views on the nature of scientific concepts, rules, and inquiry have been briefly mentioned in previous sections of this chapter. In a few scattered writings from 1891 to 1897 he developed these views in the course of criticizing other philosophers.

Chance, Necessity, and Causality

The first example is the 1891 "The Present Position of Logical Theory," in which Dewey rejects Kant's theory of the ground of physical causality in favor of Hegel's. According to Dewey, Kant separated causality from experience as something foreign to it yet necessary for experience to be synthesized into knowledge while Hegel considered causality to be an essential aspect of knowing experience that only analysis would discern (*EW* 3: 138). The only valid sort of necessity is organic necessity. Mechanical necessity signifies only a partial degree of understanding and a need for further learning. Organic necessity is recognized best in analysis because the relations between cooperating elements of a whole are not ordinarily noticed, but just the whole thing/act/event.

Knowledge is always of a whole and only in a derivative sense of the relations between its parts. If one has noticed external relations between wholes, this is an essential beginning to knowledge (the result of analysis), but it is not completed knowledge, because full knowledge is never of merely external relations, but only organic relations. If one notices organic relations between parts of a whole, this is the explicit sign that one fully knows the whole. Knowledge is always a matter of explicitly experiencing a harmonized whole, never of experiencing multiple wholes only contingently and externally related or even of explicitly experiencing the organically related parts of the whole.

For Dewey all proper principles of knowledge must serve the discovery of internal, organic relations. We saw this viewpoint at work in his dismissal of fixed, transcendent ideals for his moral theory. Moral necessity, he argued, could never be simply a matter of obeying a drive to achieve a pleasure external to the self, nor could it be an ideal of conduct imposed from beyond the self. Obligation or duty can only be an aspect of the self's own activity, a matter of organic relations between one's conception of the end to be achieved and the available means to accomplish it. Scientific necessity too must be only a matter of the self's achievement of its own ends, arising in the course of knowing. The same applies to the correlative concept of contingency. Both contingency and necessity are notions arising in the course of inquiry. They arise during the process of learning, as reasoning first notices purely contingent occurrences in a problematic situation, analyzes distinct aspects of separate things so that they appear to be externally related, and then synthesizes these aspects of things so that a new harmonious whole emerges to organically encompass the previously externally related things, which now seem to have no real independent existence of their own at all.

A second example of Dewey's criticism of another philosopher on these matters is "The Superstition of Necessity," stimulated by his reading of Peirce on scientific causality and necessity.[17] While Dewey declined to address Peirce's views directly, this article is nevertheless an excellent opportunity to compare the thought of two pragmatists on the nature of science and scientific inquiry. Peirce and Dewey each affirmed the reality of contingency, but they disagreed whether it could be scientifically supported. Peirce's theory of scientific method accepted chance, treating it as a scientific hypothesis. Dewey rejected both theses and sustained this rejection in his later work. However, because Dewey did not hold that scientific knowledge should be taken as the uniquely correct account of reality, he had no difficulty affirming the reality of contingency at a prescientific level of experience. Is science compatible with chance? Peirce argued that chance is ontologically real and that it is as real as any entity described by science. The actual practice of scientific method reveals this, as empirical considerations point only to "an element of regularity in nature," despite rampant a priori prejudices favoring "exact and universal" laws of nature. Furthermore chance has value as a scientific hypothesis in its own right.[18] Dewey held that chance and its counterpart notion of necessity have only a limited role in scientific inquiry and do not denote anything scientifically real.

Peirce's approach to chance originated with his career in science. It is perhaps too much to say with Ian Hacking that because statistical science had gained considerable stature by Peirce's day, "his conception of chance was oddly inevitable."[19] Hacking supplies the correcting factors, noting that Peirce was trained as a scientist and for thirty years pursued a wide variety of scientific investigations, most requiring accurate measurements of physical phenomena from light wavelengths and gravitational forces to geographical distances and astronomical positions. This firsthand understanding of measurement's importance to science was joined by a recognition of the essentially statistical nature of the measurements of continuous quantities.[20] Peirce was also impressed by the explanatory power of the essentially statistical thermodynamic theories coming into full flower in the work of Joule, Clausius, and Maxwell in the mid nineteenth century. Science is thus limited because its laws are only statistical in nature; as descriptions of event probabilities only, they cannot be used to formulate necessities.

The denial of necessary scientific laws allowed Peirce to reject determinism, which he defined as the view that the position and velocity of an object at any time can be theoretically predicted with certainty by using one or more necessary physical laws and the positions and velocities of that object and some set of additional objects at any other time. Any prediction with certainty would require that neither scientific constants nor physical quantities could vary over time. This is why Peirce declares that "the essence of the necessitarian position is that certain continuous quantities have certain exact values."[21] Peirce's alternative is tychism, the purely spontaneous and contingent deviation from natural laws, which happen to some degree at all times to all laws. Peirce offered tychism as a scientific hypothesis and evaluated it highly according to its ability to explain the phenomena of consciousness, free will, growth, variety, and regularity, all of which present great difficulties for the determinist, who either denies their existence or accepts them as inexplicable.[22] Peirce found his understanding of scientific method to be quite congenial to the existence of real contingency in nature.

Dewey's response to Peirce, "The Superstition of Necessity," also offers an argument against determinism, but Dewey never acknowledges statistical science or probabilistic laws. Indeed the very enterprise of law formulation is held to be only a stage in the process of scientific learning, one which must be superseded.

> All science can ultimately do is to report or describe, to completely state, the reality. So far as we reach this standpoint, regarding any fact or group of facts, we do not say that the fact *must* be such and such, but simply that it *is* such and such. . . . Only as the consciousness of the unity grows still more is it seen that instead of a group of independent facts, held together by "necessary" ties, there is one reality, of which we have been apprehending various fragments in succession and attributing to them a spurious wholeness and independence. (*EW* 4: 20, 21)

Science, as a branch of conceptual knowledge, must have as its goal the most complete and inclusive judgment of what exists, but this judgment will not involve any distinct enumeration of facts. The only true whole is the whole of all reality, and it is science's ideal task to express its nature. This task will proceed according to the mind's own proper intelligent growth, which emerges gradually during its attempts to reach goals. The first step in these attempts is to break up experience into manageable pieces of greater importance (*EW* 4: 24). The second step is the realization that some objects are dependent on others. At this stage the mind innately retains the notion of the objects' independence and expresses their relation as an external necessity linking them (*EW* 4: 24). The conception of law or regularity belongs to this halfway stage. Dewey is arguing that both notions involved here, law and the whole but related object, require each other. Put another way, both the nominalist, who stresses the whole objects, and the realist, who stresses the regular relations, are locked into an endless dispute since neither will be able to banish the other without at the same time dissolving their own favored element. The determinist, who retains both as necessary to a complete description of the world's workings, is also trapped in this halfway stage of understanding (*EW* 4: 28–29).

Necessity for Dewey is manufactured by the mind during a teleological, purpose-driven process. It has only relative validity at one stage of the learning process but will evaporate when the mind is ready to proceed to the final third step. There the necessarily related objects are stripped of any conceptual independence and are merged together to form a larger, inclusive organic whole, which can be understood with one concept and is in itself one fact. Chance, like necessity, also evaporates as the final step is taken. This explains Dewey's assertion that chance is related to ignorance, not in the sense that chance would disappear if we could only discern all the necessary laws relating everything, but in the sense that complete knowledge would remove any need for the notions of chance or external necessity. Contingency and causality, like other relations, must be then understood as teleological functions of the learning process. Dewey places the examination of both cause and effect in its proper logical context by asking how these categories arise in the gradual learning process toward a complete understanding of the whole fact, of which both the effect and the cause are only organic portions. Dewey retained this understanding of the functional role of causal necessity for his mature work, as the following quote from his 1938 *Logic* shows:

> The determination of "causal" linkage between any two events is not final nor logically complete. It is a means of instituting, in connection with determination of other similar linkages, a single unique *continuous* history. As a result of scientific inquiry, events that had previously been experienced as separate and independent become integral constituents of one and the same continuous occurrence. . . . Reference to causation recurs only when there are grounds for doubt as to whether the spatio-temporal linkage in the case of some set of events is such as in fact constitutes an existential continuum.(*LW* 12: 440–441)

Dewey eventually did come to appreciate the statistical nature of many scientific inquiries, but he interpreted probabilistic laws as having only a functional existence: they cannot be really existing "habits" in nature (*LW* 12: 465–473). The fundamentally identical evaluations of causality, of the proper goals of scientific inquiry, and of the search for wholeness and continuity across forty-seven years of Dewey's career is good evidence that he had permanently settled upon a functionalist understanding of scientific principles, such as necessity and causality, as early as 1891. This understanding was in turn based on a functionalist notion of thought's concepts from his earliest idealistic philosophy.

Dewey deeply disagreed with Peirce over the issue of necessity's role in scientific inquiry and its real existence. The next question must be what is the bearing of this disagreement upon the larger question of the proper philosophical understanding of the reality of chance and growth? This is a question of great importance, because both philosophers believed (1) that determinism is an indefensible thesis and (2) that growth is a real feature of experience and reality. Peirce's efforts to show how science could rationally defend the real existence of contingency were an essential part of his larger goal to establish a philosophy of growth and evolution. Such efforts must therefore rely on the supposition that science is capable of revealing how reality really is. Peirce does hold this to be true: if a scientific hypothesis can survive unlimited inquiry, it correctly describes reality. But Peirce was not completely dependent on science to defend the reality of contingency since his phenomenological study of experience revealed the presence of the truly contingent, the realm of pure possibility, or firstness.

From Dewey's perspective it is inquiry's task to eliminate contingency wherever it is found to be problematic and therefore to offer us a vision of the fullest fact possible. At its logical limit, then, science would present us with the fullest experience of what is in its entirety. This ultimate experience would not include any contingency (or necessity), for these signify a lack of full knowledge. There is more than a superficial resemblance of this scientific vision to the "Hegelian block-universe," the "absolute whole of wholes," so dreaded by William James. Dewey would indeed fit this rationalistic mold, save for three considerations. First, science operates only where it is needed to transform experience. Second, contingency will never be eliminated from human experience, and there is not even any good reason why it should be. Third, because active experience is for philosophy the reality, where contingency is experienced then reality really is contingent. Dewey held that the understandings supplied by ideal scientific knowledge should not be mistaken for a uniquely correct description of "the way reality actually is."

This stand on the limitations of science was not taken by Dewey only after he abandoned absolute idealism since he never believed that experience or reality could ever be only as conceptual knowledge portrays it. While science pursues and captures stabilities, experience is always wider than the fruits of science. Like Peirce and James, it was at the prereflective level that Dewey perceived the truly possible, potential, and contingent. They are agreed that any attempt to banish it as illusory must rely on an incomplete and illegitimate understanding of the nature and purpose of science, conjoined with the unwarranted license for such scientific knowledge uniquely to describe the way reality is. That is why the question with which we began, is science compatible with chance, was answered in the affirmative by Peirce while Dewey consistently held that this question masks the real issue: what functional role does the conception of chance, along with necessity, play in the progress of scientific understanding? As asked, the first question would be answered with Dewey's statement that ideal scientific knowledge has no place for either contingency or necessity and that there can be no such thing as scientific chance. This contrasts sharply with Peirce's view. However, this disagreement should not be used to infer any divergence on the wider issue: is contingency a real element or trait of existence? Dewey did believe that in a larger sense, scientific knowledge is perfectly compatible with contingency since experience is expansive enough to include both. Peirce and Dewey's affirmations of contingency should therefore not be viewed as dependent on their divergent views of scientific logic.

A third example, found in *The Study of Ethics,* of Dewey's criticisms of a philosopher's improper use of the concepts of necessity and causality is his rejection of James Martineau's defense of human free will and indeterminism (*EW* 3: 345–350). Along the same lines is Dewey's 1894 "The Ego as Cause," in which he shows that libertarians, William James included, are engaged in a contradictory effort to establish human free will. They want a substantial "ego" or "will" to be free from causes so that the human being can be free from causes in decision making. But on the other hand they can give positive content to their notion of the ego only by making it just another cause of decision making (*EW* 4: 94–95).

The centerpiece of Dewey's philosophy of organic relations as applied to psychology is of course "The Reflex Arc Concept in Psychology," which forms the basis of his later psychological texts, *How We Think* (1910) and *Human Nature and Conduct* (1922). Dewey again uses the same argumentative procedure against mechanistic causality in the 1897 "The Psychology of Effort" to critique the prevalent psychological notion that the self is revealed in experience as the sense of struggle, of effort, to accomplish an act. Erecting a specious psychological entity such as "effort" and then exclusively identifying it with the "real self" over against the external "obstacles" commits the fallacy of erecting functional factors of activity into an artificial dualism of competing ontological entities (*EW* 5: 151–163).

Scientific Explanation, Teleology, and Darwin

Dewey's conception of the other special sciences followed that of psychology. Neither mechanistic causal relations between essentially independent existences nor final causes drawing real essences toward their perfection can stand as the last word of any scientific knowledge. While an improvement over the medieval reliance on final causes, the modern conception of externally related forces appeared to banish quality and value from the universe if such human concerns could be ontologically reduced to moving matter. Such a reduction, Dewey argued, misses the real import of modern science, which is the liberation of nature from final ends for the harnessing of nature's forces for human purposes. Nature is not alien and remote from human concerns but is just the prevailing conditions of possible human achievement which are directly present in human experience (*MW* 12: 119–120). The fundamental relation between the forces of nature and the forces of humanity is not one of mechanically blind cause and effect, nor is it one of teleologically all-seeing harmonization. This relation is one of relatively organic cooperation played out in our experimental efforts to reach goals. In this arena of purposive activity, human values are regnant and ineliminable.

"The Influence of Darwinism on Philosophy" (1909) credits Galileo in physics and Darwin in biology for establishing a model of scientific explanation that shuns final causes. This model permits new scientific concepts liberated from permanent forms to deal with the changing and impermanent. Darwin's reconstruction of the term "species" is more instructive, retaining the requirements that (1) changes must be understood in their specific environing conditions, (2) nothing in nature answers to any universal definition of an essence of a thing, and (3) a priori definitions using fixed concepts must be replaced by provisional definitions using flexible and revisable concepts. These three principles, applied in philosophical inquiry as Dewey himself attempted, would result in a philosophy that "forswears inquiry after absolute origins and absolute finalities in order to explore specific values and the specific conditions that generate them" (*MW* 4: 10).

Furthermore the progress of scientific thought in the late nineteenth and early twentieth centuries, especially in physics, eliminated the fundamental concepts required by a metaphysical philosophy of mechanistic causality: the absolutes of space, time, and motion, definable in terms independent of human experience. Dewey gives us a tantalizing insight into the possible effects of such revolutionary scientific changes on his own philosophy. In a 1946 letter to Arthur Bentley he described how he had read James Maxwell's *Matter and Motion*, while he was at the University of Michigan. "I remember thinking it was the only thing on physical science principles I could understand."[23] The book was also memorable for Bentley, as he recalled how Maxwell's use of the concept "transaction" captures Maxwell's belief that natural processes must now be viewed as a system and that all physical terms must receive their definitions from their role in that system. Bentley declares that Maxwell's views are a "positive and wide parallel to what we are trying to inaugurate,"[24] referring to his and Dewey's nascent work, *Knowing and the Known*. Maxwell's text has numerous examples of revisions to scientific methodology in this direction. For example, article 102, "Relativity of Dynamical Knowledge," begins as follows:

Our whole progress up to this point may be described as a gradual development of the doctrine of relativity of all psychical phenomena. Position we must evidently acknowledge to be relative, for we cannot describe the position of a body in any terms which do not express relation.[25]

In the twentieth century Dewey took the emergence of relativity theory, and its operational definitions of basic terms, as the victory of the instrumentalist standpoint. Relativity

signified that local or individualized times are not the same as a generic common time of physics; in short, it signified that physical time designates a *relation* of events, not the inherent property of objects. . . . [I]t marked the end, as far as natural science is concerned, of the attempt to frame scientific conceptions of objects in terms of properties assigned to those objects independently of the observed consequences of an experimental operation. (*LW* 4: 116)

Dewey's rejection of mechanistic and teleological science in favor of a conception of science as experimental inquiry allowed him to incorporate scientific inquiry into his general model of practical problem solving along with moral inquiry. Dewey thus achieved the primary goal of developing a logical theory of human inquiry sophisticated enough to resolve the continuous nature of moral and scientific inquiry. Dewey's instrumentalist theory of inquiry and knowledge as it was refined during his last years at the University of Chicago culminated in the publication in 1900 of "Some Stages of Logical Thought," in 1902 of "The Evolutionary Method as Applied to Morality," and in 1903 of "Logical Conditions of a Scientific Treatment of Morality" and the *Studies in Logical Theory*.

The only alternate notion of explanation, after mechanism and final-cause teleology has been set aside, was for Dewey the "genetic" explanation. The term "genetic" came to stand for what is earlier writings received the label "organic." The organic nature of a thing was understood when its whole-part essential relations were understood by grasping how each of the thing's parts functionally related to every other part and to the proper functioning of the whole. The genetic nature of a thing is for Dewey an expansion of the organic nature along the temporal dimension and the environmental dimension. The temporal dimension permits the understanding of a thing's growth. The environmental dimension locates that growth within a larger set of environing conditions for the thing's growth.

Dewey's primary inspiration for this notion of the genetic understanding of a thing was not Darwin's theory of evolution. Despite the oft-heard claims in the traditional story of his philosophical progress, Dewey did not abruptly convert into a believer in naturalistic evolution in the 1890s. Because there was no such conversion, Darwinian evolution cannot be used to account for the transformation of his absolute idealism into instrumentalist empiricism. It certainly is the case that he discovered how evolutionary science delivered on all of the promise of Hegel's, Trendelenburg's, and Wundt's organicist thought, forging a functionalist psychology that meshed well with Hegelian dialectical reasoning. The immense role of organicism in Dewey's philosophy has been previously noted, but the convergence that he saw between evolution and Hegelian reason is not as easy to see. In Dewey's theory reason proceeds as the effort to reconcile the struggle between the contradictories of the harmony of learned experience with the disharmony of novel experience. In his functionalist phase Dewey expressed this contradiction as the clash between the gained working habits of an organism and the novel conditions testing the adequacy of those habits. The evolutionary notion of an organism's traits undergoing the testing of a relatively hostile environment is quite similar; so similar, in fact, that he had a very easy time shifting his vocabulary to match. Dewey also had a precedent to follow, as William James had already discovered how to express his psychological theories in terms of evolutionary biology. As the "Biography of John Dewey" explains, "James's influence on Dewey's theory of knowledge was exercised not by the *Pragmatism*, appeared after Dewey's theory had been formed, but by chapters in the *Principles of Psychology* dealing with conception, discrimination and comparison, and reasoning."[26]

Those influential portions of James's *Principles*, as already mentioned, presented a functionalist theory of conceptual reasoning in the larger context of an organisms's struggle to survive. The foundation of Dewey's and James's agreement on the possibility of an evolutionary understanding of human psychology was the notion of organic, self-unfolding teleology, which they took to be the only alternative to mechanistic and final-cause explanation models. As H. S. Thayer has explained, the extensive overlap of fundamental notions which Dewey observed between Hegelianism as applied to reasoning and Darwinian biology as applied to psychology was predicated on the common centrality of the categories of continuity, growth, and creativity.[27] The centrality of these categories eventually condemned absolute idealism and, not surprisingly, continued to play a very large role in Dewey's metaphysics of experience.

In summary Dewey used Darwinian notions, with James's help, to flesh out a robust organically functionalist theory of experience, mind, and intelligence only *after* he had rejected absolute idealism and arrived at a fully empiricist metaphysics. The traditional story's demand for a much larger role for Darwin, however deflected by the revised account given here, certainly meets its doom by listening to Dewey's own reflections on his earliest intellectual interests. In the course of depicting the education he received at the University of Vermont, Dewey makes a point of noting how evolution was extensively taught, despite the "orthodox environment" of the times. No repulsion on Dewey's part toward evolution was the result. On the contrary Dewey says that the controversy over evolution only stimulated him to read absorbingly all he could on this and other issues arising from the conflict between the natural sciences and religion.[28] There is no reason to find in Dewey's graduate education any antipathy toward evolution since Morris's absolute idealism simply absorbed humanity's ascent from lower animals into the all-encompassing teleology of the universe and Hall's psychology lectures assumed evolution as a matter of course. While there is precious little documented evidence to support the very plausible idea that young Dewey abandoned biblical creationist beliefs when he fled from his dualistic and repressive Congregationalist upbringing, there is from the very beginning neither a repudiation of evolution nor a celebration of creationism anywhere in his published work.

While Dewey had no difficulty with humanity's evolution from primates, his early teleological philosophy did repudiate the mechanistic materialism that undergirded some intellectuals' understanding of evolution's larger philosophical implications. Dewey attacked the ability of materialistic evolution to account for biological purposiveness in general (see the 1886 "Soul and Body," *EW* 1: 102) and moral conduct in particular (see the 1887 "Ethics and Psychical Science," *EW* 1: 217). But in neither of these essays does Dewey reject evolution itself as an established scientific theory of the origin of life and human beings. In "Ethics and Psychical Science" the advancement of the moral life envisioned by Dewey relies on evolution's statement of the environmental conditions for human existence. Still, mechanistic evolution cannot explain the origin of social community that grounds moral behavior.

> ... a theory of evolution may tell us much as to how this moral order has been realized in social and individual life in the past,—it may give us suggestions as to the use of means of further realization in the future; but it is forever helpless in calling into existence the moral order. (*EW* 1: 217)

Evolution's "survival of the fittest" directive cannot become a moral end for human beings either. Even if evolution correctly portrays humanity's future advancement as a stage toward higher forms of life, this factual prediction could not arouse anyone's interest as a moral aim (*EW* 1: 219–220). Dewey expands on both of these objections in the 1908 *Ethics* (*MW* 5: 333–335).

Dewey's undoubted growing interest through the 1890s in evolution's ability to shed light on human conduct and intellectual processes was not matched by any movement toward accepting mechanistic materialism. His mature philosophy, while naturalistic, never welcomed materialism. Dewey's philosophy of human nature was from the beginning teleologically oriented. After he rejected the all-encompassing teleology of the absolute, he quickly saw, largely thanks to

James's *Psychology*, that the evolutionary explanation of the individual's goal-directed behavior toward survival in a precarious environment of unstable values was completely compatible with Wundtian psychology and experimental idealism's theory of the growth of the self.

With this background of Dewey's genetic method in place, his theory of inquiry can be set into its context. If the genetic explanation of a thing is desired, then inquiry must go into its growth conditions. As Dewey explains in "The Evolutionary Method as Applied to Morality,"

> The essence of the experimental method I take to be control of the analysis or interpretation of any phenomenon by bringing to light the exact conditions, and the only conditions, which are involved in its coming into being. (*MW* 2: 4)

But what is the connection between the value of a thing's genetic explanation and the process of problem solving? How does an account of the growth of a thing assist in practical questions of conduct? If we recall that problem solving aims to direct conduct in problematic situations, then the role of means-end thinking takes center stage. Problem solving is essentially the formulation of a means to reach the desired end. Since the desired end of problem solving is the restoration of unproblematic activity while the desired end of using the genetic knowledge of a thing is just the creation of that thing, it seems that the experimental method is not the same as the problem-solving process. However, if the experimental method is viewed as an aspect of problem solving, their relationship comes into focus. The experimental method cannot be blankly identified with problem solving, for problem solving is the wider mode of human activity. Since the creation of something is typically the means for restoring unproblematic activity, ideas must be at hand telling one how to make that thing. These ideas may function well, or they may function poorly, depending on the current environing conditions. When the ability of one's ideas to function well comes to be questioned, the role for the experimental method emerges.

The experimental method is valuable for only one kind of advanced problem solving, as Dewey's "Some Stages of Logical Thought" (1900) explains. Here, Dewey uses the term "idea" to refer not to what may otherwise be called concepts or mental states (though these are aspects of ideas), but rather to what he previously has called the "ideal" or "principle" and what in later writings he calls the "hypothesis" or "law." Ideas are used in problem solving to analyze a problematic situation in order to focus only on certain features, which will then be adjusted in meaning in the synthetic phase of problem solving to reach a judgment of what is to be done. Ideas direct us; their task is to suggest what really is going on in a doubtful situation.

In the simpler modes of logical thought, problem solving assumes that the stock of ideas at hand is permanent, certain, and largely beyond our control.

Corresponding to this apprehension of ideas is the notion that every situation that can be encountered must fall under the covering jurisdiction of at least one idea. The unique characteristics of a situation are ignored as irrelevant, especially any factors in the process of change, since they cannot be dealt with by fixed ideas. The highest stage of logical thought, that of modern experimental science, arises when interest is taken in a situation's unique and changing conditions, and thus it requires a major alteration of standpoint taken toward ideals. When a thing is studied not for the purpose of subsuming its "essence" under a "category," but for the purpose of discovering its own particular usefulness and the means to control it, then it is the ideals that must be designed to fit the particular thing in this process of discovery. The experimental method in effect tests the ideas' usefulness for formulating practical judgments of what should be done to create a specifically desired thing in certain environing conditions.

Dewey uses the example of the experimental study of water to illustrate this revised role of ideas in science in "The Evolutionary Method as Applied to Morality." In order for water to be useful, its genetic conditions must be understood, and thus modern science has analyzed what has been taken to be the purest of waters into H_2 and O. With this discovery of the conditions necessary and sufficient to produce some water, the term "water" gets scientifically defined as that substance which "really" is H_2O. Other liquids that look like water but are not solely composed of molecules of H_2O are henceforth declared to be impure mixtures of water and other substances. "Water is H_2O" stands for a procedure of creating water using H and O or for a procedure that removes all non-H_2O from what looks to be water and hence is just a shorthand equation for water's creation. A comparison with Peirce's theory of a scientific concept's meaning, like "lithium," is quite apt here, as he declares that the method of experimentation "tells you what the word lithium denotes by prescribing what you are to do in order to gain a perceptual acquaintance with the object of the word."[29] Dewey fully agrees and would only add that the meaning of Li, like the meanings of H and O, are but the sum of all of the possible procedures of lithium genesis.

Dewey posts two crucial warnings of possible misunderstanding of this theory of scientific method, perpetuated by inferior stages of logical thought. First, it might be thought that science's task is to discern the nature of water in general since the formula H_2O applies universally to any water anywhere. This basically Aristotelian description of science's task forgets that water in general is never humanly encountered because only this or that particular body of water is confronted. It also forgets that the formula will not help to produce water in general, but only some completely individual and unique splash of water. If the Aristotelian-minded philosopher were to reply that H_2O is completely universal and since water really is H_2O, then water must be universal, Dewey responds that this argument mistakes a hypothetical proposition for a categorical proposition.

The proposition "water really is H_2O" appears to have categorical form, but as it is only shorthand for "if you combine pure hydrogen and pure oxygen under certain conditions of temperature and pressure, then some water will be created," this proposition is simply an "if-then" hypothetical proposition. Furthermore an Aristotelian-minded philosopher converts the notion that "H_2O is a universal" into an ontological statement having a bearing on reality. It cannot have any such bearing, since H_2O is a universal or generic idea in only a hypothetically conceptual, not a rigidly ontological, sense.[30]

The second warning of possible misunderstanding protests against the notion that science's task is to discover what *really* exists, independent of our acquaintance with things in experience and hence independent of how we come to know what really exists. This medieval and early modern notion assumes that those resolved elements which science has shown to make up a thing must have an ontological and valuational existence prior to and independent of that thing. We have seen Dewey protest against this view as it was imbedded in empiricist psychology, leading philosophers to make the "psychological fallacy." Applied to the case of water, this notion would lead a philosopher to conclude that science has revealed what truly exists: just H and O. The argument for this conclusion proceeds as follows. Wherever water is, H and O necessarily must really be, and as H and O are causally necessary for the existence of water, then it is H and O which possess an independent existence prior to and independent of water (and to our investigation of water) and not the other way around. Dewey's critique of this argument complains that, in addition to misunderstanding the truly hypothetical nature of this argument's first premise, this philosopher has given the wrong sense of "causally necessary" to the second premise. There is an older sense of causal necessity being applied here, which originated with the mechanistic model of explanation. In that model the components of a thing were thought to relate only in an external and contingent way, and the components retain their own characters despite comprising the larger whole. In addition, on that model, these characters fully account for any properties which that whole exhibits. As explained above, the mechanistic model therefore commits the "historical" or "materialistic" fallacy, in which it is assumed that

> the earlier fact somehow sets the standard of reality and of worth for the entire series. In practice, though not in express formulation, it is assumed that the earlier stages, being "causal," somehow are an exhaustive and adequate index of reality, and that consequently all later terms can be understood only when reduced to equivalent terms. (*MW* 2: 10)

In opposition to the mechanistic model, Dewey claims that even if the chemical properties deemed inherent to H and to O were understood, they could not in any way be used to infer the characteristics of water, any more than the chemical properties of water could be used to infer the chemical properties distinctive of oxygen or hydrogen (which is the error of the idealist). The emergent properties displayed by water in its creation are a genuinely novel and mysterious fact. This tends to be forgotten by philosophers

> because an older, purely metaphysical conception of causation survives, according to which the cause is somehow superior in rank and excellence to the effect. The effects are regarded as somehow all inside the womb of cause, only awaiting their proper time to be delivered. They are considered as derived and secondary, not simply in the order of time, but in the order of existence. Materialism arises just out of this fetich-like worship of the antecedent. (*MW* 2: 12)

The tightly supportive bond between the Aristotelian notion of essences and the mechanistic notion of contingently related and independent realities would push to the forefront of American and British philosophy in the first decades of the twentieth century in the form of a revived realism. Dewey's criticisms of this realism are based on these defenses of the genetic method's superior ability to describe actual scientific practice.

To summarize, Dewey understood the experimental method in science to be aimed toward discovering the genetic conditions of something's creation. The experimental method formulates scientific ideas, those principles that direct the analysis of a present situation for the formulation of actions that accomplish the creation of a thing. The testing of the ability of these actions to create the desired thing tests not merely the actions as means but ultimately the principles that directed the trial of those actions. In the experimental method thought must not take any ideas for granted but must creatively adjust ideas and even generate novel ideas. These ideas are scientific to the degree that the meanings of the terms involved (hydrogen, oxygen, water, etc.) are kept the same in all ideas using them.

This scientific demand for the stability of meanings is not absolute, however, lest it prevent the creation of new ideas. This demand only states that where a meaning of a term is adjusted as an idea is altered, the instances of that term in all the other ideas of that science receive the same adjustment in meaning. This demand for the stability of meanings is just the logical command to avoid the fallacy of four terms. In deductive logic valid inference will be vitiated by a middle term having two different meanings in the two premises. In Dewey's theory of scientific method, the ability of ideas to direct the chain of actions necessary for a thing's creation is the deductive aspect of thought. Deduction cannot be the only aspect of scientific thought because in modern science ideas are not assumed as certain, categorical premises to be arranged in a coherent, fixed system, but only as hypothetical and provisional premises to be arranged in flexible, alterable chains. Dewey's logic of science has no place for categorical propositions; only lower grades of problem solving may take ideas as fixedly certain. The logic of the experimental method in its deductive aspect is a logic pertaining to the chain of inferences between hypothetical or generic propositions, concluding with a practical judgment of what is the last thing to be done to produce the desired thing. Dewey's account of scientific inquiry in "Logical Conditions of a Scientific Treatment of Morality" makes this clear (*MW* 3: 9–10).

Dewey is always careful to emphasize that the meaning possessed by any universal idea rests solely in its functioning contribution to the concluding practical judgment and hence in the eventual act signaling the outcome of the process of logical thought. "There is no road open from any generic formula to an individual judgment. The road leads through the habits and mental attitudes of the one concerned in judging. The universal gets logical force, as well as psychical reality, only in the acts by which it is invented and constructed as a tool and then is employed for the purpose for which it was intended" (*MW* 3: 12). This theory of the purely instrumental function of ideas to facilitate successful conduct can be viewed in two ways: first, as the outcome of Dewey's reconstruction of transcendental logic, and second, as the basis for his mature theories of reflective thinking, instrumental logic, and scientific inquiry.

As the result of Dewey's functionalist transformation of transcendental logic, his instrumentalist theory of scientific inquiry fulfilled the promise of his early claim that the Hegelian portrait of thought matched actual scientific practice. This point is not contradicted by Dewey's regular denouncement of transcendentalist logic in writings around the turn of the century and thereafter. These statements refer to the use of the final cause, the transcendent absolute, as the mode of explanation. Transcendentalism

> claims, by analysis of science and experience, to justify the conclusion that the universe itself is a construction of thought, giving evidence throughout of the pervasive and constitutive action of reason, and holds, consequently, that our logical processes are simply the reading off or coming to consciousness of the inherently rational structure already possessed by the universe in virtue of the presence within it of this pervasive and constitutive action of thought. (*MW* 1: 172–173)

This kind of "transcendentalism," of course, Dewey had rejected by 1891. But there were other ancillary aspects of Hegelian transcendentalism which Dewey's functionalism and instrumentalism retained as their foundations. As recounted earlier, by the start of the 1890s Dewey held that ideas are but those meaningful aspects of an experienced thing that suggest other experienceable things. The purpose of reasoning is first to select out some of those meanings, next to adjust those meanings by projecting them onto future possible experiences, and finally

The Logic of Conduct

to act on the suggestions that these new meanings provide. The selective, or analytic stage, of reasoning was termed the inductive phase while the projective, or synthetic, stage of reasoning was the deductive phase. The recognition of the functional roles that the inductive and deductive phases had in the restoration of harmonious active experience was seen by Dewey as the victory of transcendental logic. Instrumentalism retains this basic pattern for reasoning. In problem solving, ideas (universal propositions) are brought to bear upon certain features of a situation in order to select out their salient meanings, those meanings are transformed by imposing a new suggestive relationship that offers a judgment of the means to the desired end, and finally that means is acted out to see if the desired end is produced.

By 1903 Dewey also had fruitfully united his earlier theory of the concept of a thing as the procedure for its construction with his general problem-solving schema by recognizing that construction directions are practical hypothetical propositions of the form "if X is desired, then do Y under conditions Z." *If* the universal aspect of a thing provides instructions for its creation, *if* such instructions are in hypothetical propositional form, and *if* hypothetical propositions can be linked in chains (provided that their common terms have sufficiently similar meaning), then the ideas which can be brought to bear upon a problematic situation can supply the needed recognition that certain features of the problematic situation may be the means to accomplishing the desired end. Science's methodology aims at formulating and testing ideas to increase their conditional reliability in problem solving. To do so, it focuses on a particular thing to try to discern its generating conditions. In Dewey's water example, water is not treated as a special end unless its availability becomes problematic for other purposes. But when water draws such attention (for example, during a drought) the means for creating water that have been previously taken for granted are now questioned, and the realization that new ideas about water are needed provokes special scientific inquiry into water itself. In this scientific inquiry it is precisely because few ideas about water can be taken for granted that novel ideas must be created.

Dewey does not offer a logic detailing how such ideas can be created. Could any logic specify how to go about the creativity of genius? However, his logic of scientific inquiry specifies how new ideas are tested: using them to infer a practical judgment of what to do, actually going through the procedures they suggest, and seeing if the desired end is produced. The desired end may result as planned, or it may not; if not, the actual results become suggestive of how to revise the ideas as the inquiry process is begun again. If the desired end does result as planned, then not only has the concluding practical judgment been verified, but the idea(s) that proposed this judgment are indirectly appraised as warranted as well. Of course, all verification is provisional, since future inquiry may demand their adjustment or replacement. If the term "true" or "verified" suggests a certainty, a guarantee that a judgment or idea is absolutely true and never to be crossed by actual experience, then Dewey's use of these terms seems inappropriate. No judgment or idea ever deserves such faith in their usefulness. Verification is relative to situation and context, and we can only say of any idea that it has proven reliable so far.

An Instrumentalist Epistemology

The oft-asked and oft-answered question raised by Dewey scholars—when did Dewey stop being an idealist and become a pragmatist?—can be answered anew using this analysis of the development of his theory of knowledge, together with the preceding discussions. This question's two parts must be answered separately. First, Dewey's relationship with idealism has six essential components: his views on idealism's treatment of experience, reality, the self, thought, physical and mental objects, and principles of knowledge. Second, his relationship with pragmatism has eight essential components in addition to the previous six: his views on meaning, concepts, judgment, reasoning, inquiry, knowledge, scientific method, and intelligence. Only after Dewey's relationships with idealism and pragmatism are well defined can our primary question be answered.

On experience and reality Dewey agreed from the start with idealism that experience is metaphysically ultimate, and he never lost that belief. Unlike most other idealists, Dewey always characterized experience as *active* experience. Against absolute idealism Dewey around 1891 no longer held that a perfect self of absolute experience, holding all human selves in its teleologically grasping end, is the true reality. By 1891, then, Dewey held that the only reality is that of ordinary human experience. On the self Dewey from the start agreed with idealism that the self is but an aspect of experience. With many other idealists Dewey agreed that the self is but an aspect of social experience, and he never lost that belief. After 1891 Dewey's philosophy, freed from the absolute self, proclaimed that ordinary human experience is always and only social experience. This experience is always in the process of growth, which means that the social self is in a process of realization. On thought Dewey from the start agreed with most idealists that thought is an aspect of the self's growth and hence is responsible for providing order and cohesion to experience. Also agreeing with idealism, Dewey from the start held that knowledge is responsible for creating its objects and does not passively register or reproduce them. These two agreements with idealism were never abandoned in his later philosophy. Unlike most other idealists Dewey held that thought was organically related to feeling and volition and hence organically a part of active experience. Thus Dewey never agreed with idealism that thought's essential function was to serve the process of practical conduct. After 1891 Dewey's psychology, freed from the absolute self, explored how thought was responsible for its own developing powers in the process of learning. On physical and mental objects Dewey always agreed with idealism that physical objects could not have a reality independent from mental objects or experience in general. Unlike many idealists Dewey never reduced physical objects to mental objects, instead claiming that both arise within experience as functional products of reasoning. Unlike most other idealists Dewey, through his functionalist psychology emerging in the *Psychology* and evident in writings after 1890, demanded that the physical/mental distinction is relative to the inquiry situation and vanishes as inquiry concludes with the return to ordinary unproblematic experience. On principles of knowledge Dewey agreed with idealism that thought uses such principles to organize new experience harmoniously with previously organized experience. With absolute idealism (and against Kantian idealism) Dewey also agreed that knowledge's principles undergo transformation over time as intelligence develops with the self's realization. He never abandoned these two agreements with idealism. With Dewey's rejection of the absolute self in 1891, he located the real existence of ideals within human intelligence and placed the responsibility for the development of ideals within problem-solving inquiry.

Let us now turn to Dewey's relationship with pragmatism. Dewey always located meaning at the basic level of human experience since all experience is to some degree meaningful and the process of active experience can increase that meaning. Dewey always held that meaning can never be explained in terms of things beyond human experience and that the growth of meaning is explained in terms of human activities. Meanings always project forward toward future possible experiences; a thing's meaning is just those activities in which the thing may play a role as a means. Dewey's position that concepts/ideas are just the meanings of things considered in their universal aspect implies that concepts are inherently teleological as well. The essence of a concept is the hypothetical proposition: "if X is done under conditions Y, then Z will result." Dewey refers to the judgment as the concluding proposition of an inferential chain of hypothetical propositions. Judgments are practical, as they specify what is to be done to produce something valuable, and hence judgments are statements of what to be done in a particular circumstance. In ordinary unproblematic experience only meaningful experience is had, as activity proceeds from things to things in a habitual way. In problematic situations, when inquiry focuses on things' meanings in order to adjust or create ideas for the purpose of proposing a new course of action, knowledge is created as new things are created to permit the restoration of habitual activity. Dewey considers knowledge to be the novel knowing of things which solve a particular problem, some of which are modified or replaced in this inquiry process. Scientific method is the deliberate focus on the conditions required for the creation of a thing; in science, inquiry is not immediately directed at resolving a problematic situation, though its stimulus and its results are located in such problems. Scientific inquiry tries to discover those stable features of nature that permit human activities reliably to create a thing under a variety of conditions. Problem solving and scientific inquiry together develop the fund of ideas that can be used to perpetuate human activities despite novel events and conditions. Intelligence for Dewey is just the name for the sum of available ideas, the total quantity of coordinations among our habits, for both problematic and unproblematic activity. The epistemological doctrines of Dewey's instrumentalism may be summarized as follows:

1. Cognition is the effort to form judgments, which are new links of meanings aimed at the resumption of habitual activity. Knowing is the experience of accomplishing this goal using these judgments.

2. All cognitive judgments are practical: they come into existence due to a problem, and function to eliminate the problem. All intellectual functions are practical and temporal, having a specific natural origin and a definite termination.

3. Truth, as a collective label for knowings/verifications, exists within experience. The correspondence theory of truth, when construed as a correspondence of subjective ideas with objective experience-independent things, must be rejected.

4. The known object is created by the process of cognition. It is impossible to know something as it is prior to the knowing of it.

5. Knowing an object is surrounded by other kinds of experiences of it. These other experiences serve as the materials for cognition and its verification.

6. All experiences, and especially their physical and mental aspects, should be understood as natural events on an ontological par.

7. An empiricism which places human active experience as absolute is the preferable alternative to absolute idealism or dualism.

To bring Dewey's relationship with pragmatism into better focus, a closer look should be taken at a few of his agreements and disagreements with Peirce and James. The traditional story of pragmatism typically alleges that Peirce influenced Dewey towards these tenets: (1) doubt arouses inquiry which seeks satisfaction; (2) the meaning of concepts is their use; (3) truth is the result of ultimate inquiry. All three of these views are in fact present in Dewey's 1886 *Psychology*, well before Dewey seriously read Peirce (1893 at first, then later circa 1916, then finally after 1930). While Dewey took no early inspiration from Peirce, his later study of Peirce did help him to refine his positions on experience, inquiry, and logic.

Regarding Dewey's relationship with James, we have already seen why the alterations Dewey made for the third 1891 edition of the *Psychology* concerning sensations cannot be taken as evidence for the view that James drew Dewey away from idealism. The traditional story also typically alleges that James influenced Dewey toward these tenets: (1) the mind is not a substance, but a process in experience; (2) concepts are teleologically functional; (3) brain and mind must be understood through evolution. The first two were also well expressed in Dewey's *Psychology*. James's *Principles of Psychology* came out in 1890, too late to influence Dewey on these vital pragmatic views. On the second point concerning the functionality of concepts, it is true that Dewey offers in later editions a much better developed description of the function of concepts in knowledge. The first edition was content to say that concepts are the universalized aspect of individually experienced things, which are responsible for their meaning. By the third edition this universalized aspect is the rule for constructing the meaningful thing. The idea that James should be credited for this now recognizably pragmatic view does not hold up, however. First of all, Dewey was developing the constructively functional theory of concepts in articles published before 1890. Second, James's *Psychology* nowhere describes concepts as the rule for generating the meaningful object. To summarize, Dewey and James arrived at their views on experience as a whole and concepts as functional quite independently of each other. To explain how Dewey became a functionalist is to tell the story of his earliest idealistic views, views which he reconstructed but never abandoned. Those who do not a firm grasp of Dewey's own type of early idealism are prone to locate his functionalist or pragmatic views in Peirce or James or both.

The third alleged debt to James, the evolutionary view of brain and mind, actually did contribute to Dewey's epistemology. But this by itself is insufficient evidence, especially in light of the foregoing, to conclude that James's *Principles of Psychology* was the attractive magnet that drew Dewey away from idealism. The primary contribution of the *Principles of Psychology* was to suggest to Dewey how better to express his functionalist account of thought in solely biological terms. His functionalist epistemology, however, was already evident in his own *Psychology*. Hence James deserves no credit for converting Dewey from idealism to pragmatism. Dewey's rejection of the absolute of idealism had everything to do with his internal reconstruction of the logic of idealism, and not with James's contributions to evolutionary psychology.

Dewey's relationship with pragmatism can also be examined in terms of his disagreements with Peirce and James. The traditional view of Dewey's intellectual debt to Peirce and James naturally tends to overlook fundamental disagreements between them. Dewey's disagreements with Peirce include the following:

> 1. Peirce held that reality is equivalent with the ultimate truth while Dewey held that reality is experience. Peirce defines the real as that

which would be known by inquiry carried out to its ultimate limit. While Dewey in the 1938 *Logic* accepts Peirce's definition of truth as what would be known by ultimate inquiry, Dewey does not use this definition of truth to define reality. As Dewey said in his 1886 *Psychology* and continued to believe for the rest of his career, the world as known cannot be equivalent to the world as experienced and hence could never be equivalent to the world itself.

2. Peirce held that in knowing the world, the knower does not alter the reality known. Dewey held the instrumentalist view that for humans to have knowledge, the known object had to be created by the knower's actions altering the environment. In other words, the known object could not possess existence prior to being known.

3. Peirce believed that scientific discovery essentially involved the formulation of statistical laws. Dewey held that statistical laws represented the results of an inferior stage of scientific inquiry, to be surmounted by the discernment of organic relations in nature.

4. Peirce was a staunch proponent of antipsychologism in logic, rejecting the notion that the logician must study the actual thought processes of human beings. Dewey held that logic is the inquiry into human inquiry, conducted with an aim toward improving the effectiveness of reasoning procedures. While Peirce and Dewey were both fallibilists and hence rejected any sort of absolutism concerning the truth of logical theorems, their attitudes toward the logician's function is quite different. Peirce himself rejected Dewey's 1903 *Studies in Logical Theory* as completely opposed to his own logical efforts.

Dewey's disagreements with James include the following:

1. James often confused the notion that the satisfactoriness of experience brought about by an idea constitutes its truth with the quite different notion that the satisfactions brought by the consequences of the belief in an idea are signals of its truth. In the first notion ideas are means created, and thus truths are created, for the purpose of improving experience while on the second ideas have a prior existence and a prior validity before the consequences are tested to learn their truth. Dewey argues in 1908 ("What Pragmatism Means by Practical") that he can agree only with the first notion while the second gives aid and comfort to rationalists and intellectualists who are content to find in pragmatism just an account of how humans

discover eternal truth. Dewey also says that he would like to see pragmatism as a philosophical movement dissolved so that the various allied tendencies could freely pursue their separate interests and problems.

2. James's pragmatism placed a great deal of emphasis upon the question of the satisfactoriness of an idea for the individual using that idea and hence often offered a definition of truth that reduced it to a personal level. James rarely treated truth as a matter of social or universal satisfaction, in contrast to both Peirce and Dewey's view that inquiry and knowledge can only be understood as a social process and result.

3. James's membership in the long tradition of empiricism is exemplified in his insistence that experience can provide direct knowledge of objects without that knowledge constituting the object. His rejection of idealism thus follows the traditional path by claiming that knowledge is a matter of external relations and that knowing is not essential to the existence of the object known. This epistemology inspired many of his students, for example, Ralph Perry, to develop a realism that asserts the independent existence of objects apart from their entering into the relation with that consciousness called knowing. Dewey perceived the contradiction between such an epistemology and James's radical empiricism, and he asserted instead that the known object cannot be independent of the knowledge of it. Dewey's instrumentalism holds that knowledge creates the known object while James's epistemology was expressly designed to reject such an idealistic position.

The initial question, when did Dewey abandon idealism and become a pragmatist, must itself be abandoned because it is poorly phrased in the light of the complex relationships Dewey had with both philosophies. The better question is when did Dewey abandon the absolutism of his idealism, develop a functionalist psychology, and establish an instrumentalist version of pragmatism? The answer to this question finds that the time periods of these three events overlap. Dewey gradually abandoned absolute idealism from 1887 to 1891, he gradually developed functionalist psychology from 1884 to 1896, and he established instrumentalism from 1891 to 1903. All three of these events were based on some idealist and voluntarist principles accepted in the earliest years of his career, from 1883 to 1886. Dewey never rejected two central principles of idealism: experience is philosophically absolute, and knowledge transforms experience to creates its objects. Dewey from the start of his career accepted two central principles of pragmatism: thought is inextricably involved with the desires and volitions, making up purposive conduct, and thought thereby serves the needs of successful activity by an individual in a natural environment. Finally Dewey always held that there are existences independent of inquiry and its logical elements such as ideas, judgments, knowings, knowledge's objects, etc. These existences are responsible for stimulating and terminating inquiry but cannot be taken to be transcendent of all possible human experience.

The paramount transition in Dewey's career was his rejection of the absolute self, which permitted his functionalist account of the emergence and growth of the human self finally to be told solely in terms of the events of ordinary human social conduct and not in terms of a teleologically controlling, spiritually final cause. As this functionalist account was freed, so too was his study of human intelligence, permitting the start of Dewey's instrumentalist phase. The traditional story, eager to discern a thorough repudiation of idealism in Dewey's philosophical development, usually gets the all-important year of 1891 right, but mostly for the wrong reasons.

CHAPTER SIX

The Reconstruction of Epistemology

> Special theories of knowledge differ enormously from one another. Their quarrels with one another fill the air. . . . But they all make one common assumption. They all hold that the operation of inquiry excludes any element of practical activity that enters into the construction of the object known. . . . The common essence of all these theories, in short, is that what is known is antecedent to the mental act of observation and inquiry, and is totally unaffected by these acts; otherwise it would not be fixed and unchangeable.
>
> John Dewey, *The Quest for Certainty*, 1929

Dewey's psychological, logical, and metaphysical commitments as expressed in the *Essays in Experimental Logic, Experience and Nature,* and other works of his mature philosophy required the reconstruction of epistemology, replacing the fruitless exercise of surveying knowledge in general with an empirical study of actual human inquiry. His understanding of the nature of meaning required a reconsideration of the object of knowledge, and this reconstruction of knowledge in turn required a new theory of truth. The coherence of these views in turn arguably establishes Dewey's empirical philosophy as a genuine and significant alternative to positivism, dualism, materialism, and idealism, despite many philosophers' opinions to the contrary.[1] Dewey effectively undercuts the realist-idealist debate by exposing them both as transcendentalist philosophies and attacking their common premises.

Dewey's move from the University of Chicago to Columbia University in 1904 marks a significant turning point in his career, as he made a sharp transition from one type of professional activity to a quite different type. The collegial interactions that he enjoyed before 1904 were largely of a collaborative and insular nature. For example, only four of his articles from that period offered replies to published criticisms, indicating how his attention was then securely focused on the internal development of functional psychology and instrumentalism. After 1904 such focus would drastically alter. Dewey's active participation in the ongoing heated philosophical debates impacted both his own position and those of his interlocutors as they together tackled many issues in psychology, epistemology and metaphysics. These issues often revolved around this question: was pragmatism compatible with realism?

Dewey became a colleague of three realists at Columbia: Frederick J. E. Woodbridge, Wendell T. Bush, and William P. Montague. Perhaps almost as important, he was also introduced to a journal whose pages were very hospitable to realism and pragmatism. In 1904 Woodbridge had undertaken the editing for the new *Journal of Philosophy, Psychology and Scientific Methods*, with Bush joining him in 1906. This journal was conceived partly as a realist alternative to the older *Philosophical Review* at Cornell, a stronghold for idealism. While respectfully appreciative of Dewey's philosophical and pedagogical eminence, the Columbia faculty, being far more academically heterogeneous, were naturally less sympathetic and supportive than his previous colleagues. They did, however, take great interest in his version of pragmatism, recognizing an important contribution to the heated debates then engaging most philosophical minds. Dewey's 1903 *Studies in Logical Theory* and the 1905 articles "The Realism of Pragmatism" and "The Postulate of Immediate Empiricism" abruptly thrust him into the middle of a discussion of idealism and the merits of some newly minted rejections. As their principal source and inspiration these new voices had William James, who had long struggled with the attractive and repulsive aspects of the dominant idealism flourishing in the United States and England, especially as it was expounded by his friend and colleague at Harvard, Josiah Royce.[2] James was among the first to make argumentative challenges to idealism, and two Harvard graduates then defended realism in their influential responses to Royce's 1899 *The World and the Individual*.[3] James's own "Does 'Consciousness' Exist?" offered a key spark in 1904, helping to touch off the flames of controversy that quickly consumed much of subsequent volumes of philosophy journals in the United States and England.

The many defenses of realism against idealism were then generally of two sorts, depending on whether they relied on the pragmatist viewpoint. A triangle of idealism, realism, and pragmatism gradually emerged in the first decade of the twentieth century, as each developed serious objections to central views of the other two. They rarely diverged completely. Many idealists and realists shared epistemologies but not a metaphysics, and many idealists and realists found a great deal of worth in the pragmatist theory of the acquisition of knowledge. Pragmatists generally claimed to be realists, although some did not leave idealism's orbit. The controversies surrounding Dewey's doubtful departure from idealism were typical of the innumerable attempts during this period to delineate philosophical territory. The three works by Dewey mentioned above immediately drew critical review, both from established idealists and the upstart corps of self-proclaimed realists. Dewey did not fail to respond. Indeed most of his published articles would henceforth recognize and respond to others' interpretive and critical efforts directed at his own philosophy. Dewey's relationships with idealism have been explored, so here we are concerned with realism.[4]

An Empirical Theory of Meaning

The introduction to the 1916 *Essays in Experimental Logic* offers the most comprehensive integration of his central theses with his objections to historical positions

The Reconstruction of Epistemology

and current schools that he would write during this period. Its compressed and terse style engenders blunt statements of his views and sharp rebuttals to critics. If readers bracket their own philosophical sophistications, they can hear how Dewey tries to portray thinking in the pursuit of knowledge in the context of natural existences. And if labels are necessary, he provides them. After noting that analytic realism takes the known objects of the sciences as *the* reality independent of thought and demotes the study of human inquiry to the status of mere psychology irrelevant to logic and knowledge, Dewey points out that his instrumentalism will seem idealistic in comparison. "In so far as it is idealistic to hold that objects of knowledge *in their capacity of distinctive objects of knowledge* are determined by intelligence, it is idealistic." However, any truly idealistic overtones are decisively silenced: "Thinking is what some of the actual existences *do*. They are in no sense constituted by thought." Intelligence itself is for Dewey but a term referring to natural acts and events of thinkers, and its production of known objects is also completely natural. "The reorganization, the modification, effected by thinking is . . . a physical one. Thinking ends in experiment and experiment is an *actual* alteration of a physically antecedent situation in those details or respects which called for thought in order to do away with some evil" (*MW* 10: 338, 339). Statements of this sort asserting his realism are not rare. It is a simple matter to find Dewey asserting his position to be realistic, long before *Essays in Experimental Logic* was published.

Naive Realism and Immediate Empiricism

A primary example is the 1905 "The Realism of Pragmatism," which responds to an accusation that pragmatism is subjectively idealistic. Dewey states that pragmatism's theory of knowledge holds that mental states do have a role in the origin of knowledge, but when knowledge is attained, the known object is "present to the agent in the most naively realistic fashion" (*MW* 3: 153). Mental states are also to be conceived realistically. "Their origins as existences can be stated and must be stated in terms of adjustments and maladjustments among habits, biological functions" (*MW* 3: 155). Critics who find subjectivism in pragmatism have not learned that it realistically reinterprets cognition and its components and hence it rejects the representative theory of knowledge and its accompanying mind-matter dualism. When distinctions are retained between things and things functioning as representations of other things, a dualism in a practical and instrumental sense is offered, and not a dualism "indicating a radical existential cleavage in the nature of things" (*MW* 3: 155). The latter metaphysical dualism, and its representational theory of knowledge, asserts that ideas must be capable of transcending the mental realm so that they may represent their objects. Dualism is not alone in taking ideas to have a subsistent reality of their own; Dewey understands idealism to be grounded on the same view. This presupposition's denial is accordingly the liberating stride away from both dualistic realism and all forms of idealism.

Dewey's choice in this article of the term "naive" to qualify "experience of known objects" is repeated in "Naïve Realism vs. Presentative Realism" (1911).[5] In this article naive realism holds that perceptions are just natural events, in contrast to any other realism which holds that every perception is a case of knowledge. Dewey's argument, explained in the next section, shows that such a treatment of perception invariably slides into representationalism. Thus naive realism is designed to stand as the only viable alternative to representationalist notions of knowledge. In naive experience only objects are present. Even if the ability to experience an object is the result of knowledge, its heritage drops from view; what is thereafter experienced is not a representation of the thing, but just the thing itself. Dewey's label for his realism is somewhat problematic since other realisms have also been called "naive." However, with exceedingly few exceptions, these realisms claim that special kinds of perceptions can serve as knowably certain data in a foundationalist epistemology. This claim makes such realisms what Dewey called "presentative" realisms. G. E. Moore and the new realists must be included among them, for example. Dewey, as we have seen in previous chapters, was not tempted toward such sense-data foundationalism and its integral assumption of deductivism. Infallible certainty could never be a component of Dewey's epistemology.

Another essay written in 1905, "The Postulate of Immediate Empiricism," attracted more criticism from both realists and idealists. One of its tasks is to provide an alternative to the dualistic, representationalist thesis by claiming that a thing is what it is experienced to be. This claim is capable of providing a viable alternative by the following reasoning. Only if someone thinks that an experience cannot be of that thing of which it has been taken to be would the notion arise that this experience could not have the same sort of reality which the thing has. If no one ever has any reason to suspect that a thing may not be what it has been experienced as, then all experiences will retain their status as experiences of things.

Now, we all have experiences of things that have no such taint of suspicion or doubt. While some experiences include doubt and some include surety, it would be a logical leap to infer that all experiences of things should or even could contain doubt. This leap Dewey evidently rejects. While he does not mention Descartes in this essay, his contempt for the notion of universal doubt, and the corresponding notion that experience consists of a veil of ideas separate from all things, is a familiar theme of his writings. Also evidently rejected is the problematic solution that only doubtful experiences are mental ideas while assured experiences are of physical things; after all, a thing can be doubtful in one context and assured in another. Dewey is resolved on the stance that all experiences are just experiences of things, labeled in this essay as "immediate empiricism."

The Reconstruction of Epistemology

There is a close relationship between immediate empiricism and naive realism, as naive realism is the result of applying immediate empiricism to the question of the status of perceptions of things. As "The Need for a Recovery of Philosophy" (1917) explains, immediate empiricism finds everything to be real and natural.

> It is often said that pragmatism, unless it is content to be a contribution to mere methodology, must develop a theory of Reality. But the chief characteristic trait of the pragmatic notion of reality is precisely that no theory of Reality in general, überhaupt, is possible or needed. It occupies the position of an emancipated empiricism or a thoroughgoing naïve realism. It finds that "reality" is a denotative term, a word used to designate indifferently everything that happens. Lies, dreams, insanities, deceptions, myths, theories are all of them just the events which they specifically are. Pragmatism is content to take its stand with science; for science finds all such events to be subject-matter of description and inquiry—just like stars and fossils, mosquitoes and malaria, circulation and vision. It also takes its stand with daily life, which finds that such things really have to be reckoned with as they occur interwoven in the texture of events. (*MW* 10: 39)

Despite Dewey's attempt in "The Postulate of Immediate Empiricism" to "do my little part in clearing up the confusion," his definition of that postulate and his uses for it brought down upon him a hailstorm of protest that lasted for years afterward. By tendering his support for James's radical empiricism while recasting these issues in his own post-Hegelian perspective and terminology, Dewey engendered attention that escalated to a far higher level than ever before. Dealing with such criticism did have a benefit, as he was able to perceive the difficulties others were having with both his own and James's proposed alterations to widely cherished notions of reality, truth, and knowledge. He did try to predict the source of many such problems. "Now, this statement that things are what they are experienced to be is usually translated into the statement that things (or, ultimately, Reality, Being) *are* only and just what they are *known* to be or that things are, or Reality *is* what it is for a conscious knower. . . ." (*MW* 3: 159).

Dewey's prediction was accurate. His critics did not quietly accept the notion that some experiences come unaccompanied by the self-consciousness of knowing that "I" or my "self" is having these experiences. Furthermore they quickly detected and deplored his explicit denial in this essay of a uniquely determinate or permanent reality in favor of a process metaphysics. Hence they would not agree to Dewey's employment of the terms "knowledge" or "truth" since such lack of unique determinateness and permanence must for Dewey attach to these two concepts as well. His abandonment of what were commonly taken to be philosophical axioms about consciousness, experience, reality, and truth understandably attracted intense scrutiny.

Frederick Woodbridge was the first realist to question Dewey on these matters, and his queries met Dewey's expectations.[6] Woodbridge complains that if the transcendence of knowledge is denied, as Dewey requires, then the cognitive experience of things is going to be different from other experiences of these things since "in the cognitive experience all other experiences become altered" (*MW* 3: 397). Put another way, the knowledge of something will change it; such knowledge must *really* change it and make it different from what it also *really* was in a different sort of experience. So far, Woodbridge is correct. His next comment, that this position is indistinguishable from idealism, indicates that he understands Dewey to be committed to holding that the mental cognition of a thing is responsible for that thing's reality. This commitment would proceed from the principle that if X changes when Y is in operation, in the supposed absence of other goings-on, then X is somehow dependent on Y. Needless to say, this is a highly questionable method of argumentation, but it is typical of the sort used by many idealists, and Woodbridge hears an echo in Dewey's statements. However, Dewey would have nothing to do with such reasoning since his and idealism's conceptions of "mind" are quite distinct. Still, Woodbridge was right to point out that Dewey's epistemology holds that when a thing becomes known, it is really altered.

Dewey's response, "The Knowledge Experience and Its Relationships," points out that precisely because the account of things provided by knowledge differs from other types of accounts in experience, philosophers should take up the task of arbitrating the conflicting claims. His preferred resolution is the establishment of harmony rather than doubt or the elevation of one over the rest. This does require, as Woodbridge's comments show, an explanation of the relationship that the cognitive experience has with other kinds of experience. Dewey's resolution states that the mere existence of an experience's distinctive features has nothing to do with knowledge, but the connections between two experiences might if "one thing may be found subsequently to affect, influence or control, favorably or unfavorably, the quality of some other present thing" (*MW* 3: 174). This connection is itself an experience and qualifies as a cognitive experience since it takes place during a "doubt-inquiry-answer experience." It will result in the transformation of things for the purpose of giving them a stable reference, which in turn permits the erasure of doubt. In this way cognition can be contingently involved with other experiences as they contribute toward a solution to a practical problem. In one sense cognition alters things permanently, but the noncognitive things have not disappeared forever—they are always available in further noncognitive experience. While a new cognitive experience does go beyond or transcend the elements which went into it, it nevertheless always remains within experience (*MW* 3: 177).

Dewey is providing in abbreviated form the theory of knowledge presented in *Studies in Logical Theory,* discussed previously.

From the positions taken in "The Realism of Pragmatism," "The Postulate of Immediate Empiricism," and "The Knowledge Experience and Its Relationships," it should be recognized that Dewey is grounding their plausibility on the notion that things can really and inherently represent other things. Put another way, it is a mode of their existence that they can have meaning by standing as signs for other absent things. Dewey is hardly unaware of the fundamental role which this notion plays in his philosophy—he is careful to assert it in both essays mentioned above and others. In the introduction to the *Essays* he phrases this notion as follows: "It is as certain an empirical fact that one thing suggests another as that fire alters the thing burned" (*MW* 10: 349).

Dewey appreciates that he is contradicting a time-honored established philosophical theory attempting to explain the existence of meaning. This transcendental theory of meaning, widely adopted at least since Descartes, asserts that meaning adheres to things only as a result of some distinct process, some mental operation, responsible for transforming the intrinsically meaningless thing into an experience with a reality somewhat different from that of the thing itself. Kant and most subsequent idealists (notably excepting Hegel) treated original sensations as inherently meaningless, so that an individual's experience must be the result of mental transformations of sensations into knowledge of objective things. Realists, asserting the mind-independent existence of objects, also assign to mind the task of establishing meaning. The realists' distaste for the idealistic mental construction of objective things typically encourages them to hold that sensations by themselves are able to enfuse experience with sufficiently meaningful objects without any intellectual processes involved. This sounds like Dewey's view; however, the realists conflated it with the sort of naive realism that Dewey repudiated.

The Transcendental Theory of Meaning

In Dewey's thought a philosophy is classified as "transcendental" if it holds that a mind/mental state is necessarily present in every meaningful experience of a nonmental thing. The label of "transcendental" is presently quite outdated, and there is no intent to use the term here as Kant did, in the sense of a "transcendental deduction." Dewey did not use the term "transcendental" in the pejorative, metaphysical sense that is intended here, either. He applied a wide variety of other labels to his opponents, including "intellectualist," "rationalist," and "dualist," which point to how they give excessive ontological independence to minds and their alleged mental contents. Ultimately Dewey's antagonist is the legacy of Descartes, who bequeathed to philosophy the notion that physical reality in some sense transcends human experience.

Dewey's refutation of transcendental philosophies requires the refutation of the transcendental theory of meaning, which proceeds in his writings on two fronts. First, since for Dewey it is simply an empirical fact that things suggest other things, he often admonishes his readers simply to experience things for themselves. One is supposed to be able to notice that many experiences carry no awareness of the operation of any mind or mental state since only the meaningful thing is in their experience. While many observations of things carry the content "I am observing that thing," many others do not. Second, for those who are unimpressed by empirical observation and still insist that such egoless meaningful experiences must be the result of the operation of nonexperienced mental processes, Dewey directs the reader's attention to all the paradoxes and mysteries involved in the alternative transcendental notion that meaning requires an explanation involving the supposition that things are inherently meaningless. The transcendental theory of meaning at the core of nearly all realisms and idealisms is responsible for their transcendental theory of knowledge, which results in their joint engagement in the futile struggle called "epistemology."

The transcendental theory of meaning asserts that meaning (1) resides in a mental state and (2) refers to some other thing, which (3) resides entirely beyond human experience. Dewey agrees that a meaningful thing refers to some other absent thing, but disagrees with points 1 and 3. He recognized that traditional eighteenth-century psychology constructed the transcendental theory of meaning to correspond with metaphysical dualism. His rejection of this transcendental theory starts with his denial of point 3 since it relies on that problematic dualistic notion of the thing-in-itself. Dewey replaces point 3 with "resides beyond the present experience but within possible experience." This replacement occasions the need to reject the transcendentalist understanding of point 1, which takes mental states to be of an ontological category distinct from objects beyond experience. Dewey retains the terms "mental," "psychological," and the like but reconstructs them in a completely naturalistic way by endorsing behaviorism. His effort to carry out this reconstruction in his later writings is beyond the scope of this book, but it cannot be stressed too highly that his rejection of the transcendental theory of meaning amounts to a revision of the notion of "the object of meaning." Meaning for Dewey does not have an object, if by object we mean something outside of possible experience. Meaningful things are "leadings" to other experiences by suggesting what is now absent but could be present.

The transcendental realists attacked Dewey's immediate empiricism (and James's radical empiricism) by asking how it could be possible for an immediate experience to refer to another experience. On their view the very nature of an immediate experience by definition prevented it from making such a referral since the immediacy of an experience strips it of all qualities except its purely subjective, sensuous character. Both James and Dewey were thus roundly castigated for capitulating to subjectivism. Idealists, such as Charles Bakewell and Boyd Bode, also raised this question, accusing Dewey of confusing an object as conceived in its relations with an object immediately experienced.[7] They all argued that since the object as conceived is the result of knowledge, but the object immediately experienced is not a known object, then immediate experience must be devoid of any relations and any meaning. This controversy is grounded on the transcendentalist need for a category of immediate experience that lacks meaning or relations, so that thought can do its proper work: to transform such experience into an objective knowledge experience of a known object. Dewey recognized the common ground of the realists' and idealists' objections in their willingness to commit the "psychological fallacy" of granting to a transient mental state discerned by analyzing experience an existence independent of thought.

Dewey's response in "Immediate Empiricism," in agreement with James's view, argues that we actually are able to experience directly something as mediating between other experiences (MW 3: 168–170). Even if we locate in thought the ability to give meaning to experience, what would the meaning of thought itself be unless we could experience thought's results? And what would such an experience be if not an experience of an object's meaning? This direct experience of the object's meaning, as yet unmediated by any further thought, is precisely what Dewey understands as an immediate experience of a thing's meaning and hence of just that thing itself since it is impossible to experience a meaningless thing. Dewey sees in the transcendental theory of meaning an effort to bring together inherently meaningless experiences and inherently unexperienceable thought so that their entanglement can somehow produce meaningful experience. His rejection of this kind of explanation involves the rejection of meaningless experience and unexperienceable thought and the retention of the only sensible component: the direct experience of meaningful things. Dewey's Hegelian critiques of Kant and Lotze, explored earlier, have culminated in this empiricist stand on the nature and growth of ordinary human experience.

As Dewey explains in "The Knowledge Experience Again" (MW 3: 178–183), the recognition of the full meaning of an experience cannot itself be beyond experience; it is simply another type of experience. Of course, readers who equate "experience" with "subjective ideas" would have difficulty interpreting Dewey as anything but a subjective idealist. His contemporary critics, realists and idealists alike, nearly uniformly did just that. Many of his writings on this subject supply corrections to this distortion. For example, in the note appended to this essay for a later reprinting, Dewey says that "there is nothing in the text that denies the existence of things temporally prior to human experiencing of them. Indeed, I should think it fairly obvious that we experience most things *as* temporally prior to our experiencing of them" (MW 3: 167). How could such explanations fail to assuage the apprehensions of his critics? They failed because Dewey does not explicitly affirm the existence of things apart from human experience. He instead inferred the preexistent reality of things, using the postulate of immediate empiricism, only from our experience of things as preexistent.

The Thing-in-Itself

Dewey had no role in his philosophy for a realm of existence beyond human experience. At the heart of his rejection of any dualistic philosophy lies his refusal to countenance a Ding-an-sich. This refusal arose time and time again in the course of his debates with realists and occasionally with some idealists. He notes that "The opponents of pragmatism have been forced by the exigencies of their hostility to resuscitate a doctrine supposedly dead: the doctrine of unexperienceable, unknowable 'Things in Themselves'" (*MW* 6: 4). The thing-in-itself can be construed in two different ways, which were both repugnant to Dewey: (1) the thing forever beyond experience which possesses none of the traits which things can have as experienced; (2) the thing forever beyond experience as possessing traits found in experience. Dewey affirms the independent object, retaining it experienced traits even when not actually experienced, as a commonsensical notion. But this is no thing-in-itself.

Concerning the first attempt to conceive the thing-in-itself, Dewey finds that such a conception is necessarily empty. Even if somehow this thing were conceivable in a negative manner (for example, "that thing which has no experienceable traits"), it could never play any explanatory role in a theory of meaning, belief, or knowledge. Concerning meaning, how could we be sure that an idea's meaning is accurately directed toward its transexperience object? Whether a philosopher attempts to locate the guarantee of meaning in the idea's relation to sensations prior to thought or in the idea's relation to a reality beyond thought, the utter mystery of such a relation is apparent. In the course of attacking Lotze, whose epistemology happens to require both guarantees, Dewey simultaneously attacks any system requiring either.

> In other words, logically speaking, we are at the end just exactly where we were at the beginning—in the sphere of ideas, and of ideas only, plus a consciousness of the necessity of referring these ideas to a reality which is beyond them, which is utterly inaccessible to them, which is out of the reach of any influence which they may exercise, and which transcends any possible comparison to their results."(*MW* 2: 365–366)

A specific example of the mysteries involved in a supposed transcendent relation between true belief and its object can be found in beliefs about the past. If the effects of the past on the present are deemed irrelevant to belief about the past, how can a current belief relate to a past event, and how could one belief attain truth while another fails?

The Reconstruction of Epistemology

> How can the present belief jump out of its present skin, dive into the past, and land upon just the one event (that *as* past is gone forever) which, by definition, constitutes its truth? I do not wonder the intellectualist has much to say about "transcendence" when he comes to dealing with the truth of judgments about the past; but why does he not tell us how we manage to know when one thought lands straight on the devoted head of something past and gone, while another thought comes down on the wrong thing in the past? (*MW* 6: 6–7)

Hilary Putnam has sarcastically attributed the uncanny accuracy of transcendentally correct beliefs to those "noetic rays" shining from mind to reality. This problem is of course generalizable in such a way as to make the correspondence, or transcendental, theory of reference very problematic. On that theory of reference, the way the world really is, independently of our experience of the world, guarantees that some words and sentences really do accurately refer. Putnam, like Dewey, rejects such a theory, calling it a "magical theory of reference."[8]

The second way to construe the thing-in-itself is the attempt to conceive the thing forever beyond experience as possessing traits found in experience. This attempted conception is for Dewey purely gratuitous. Such an assumption cannot by definition be proven, and even if it happened to be valid, it could not contribute to an adequate theory of meaning or knowledge. Some realists claim that theoretically postulated entities exist beyond experience, but only circular reasoning results if the existence of such an entity is used to explain how it has become known. A logical or analytic realist's claim that reflective analysis discerns simple elements in experience that existed prior to and independent of analysis similarly relies on such circular reasoning. Furthermore this claim runs aground on the fact that such discovered elements possess meaning which certainly did not exist prior to the reflective efforts of thought. Their acquired meaning might be set aside as incidental, save for realism's insistence that, far from being meaningless, such elements are known objects (*MW* 10: 344–345).

A realist might reply that a known object's meaning is but the invariable veneer of experience laid on by the process of knowing, having nothing essential to do with the thought-independent object's own traits. This reply for Dewey only displaces the mystery. How interesting that irredeemably subjective experience is nevertheless necessary to a thought process which, when it happens to yield knowledge, latches onto an object as it "really" is if no experience were present. And since not just any haphazard examination of experience produces known objects, how does one determine the proper method of analysis? Realists all too glibly repeat the articles of faith, that logical analysis yields only known objects and that real and true objects are just those which logical analysis displays. Unfortunately, defining knowledge and known objects exclusively in terms of each other does not assist the human effort to gain knowledge about anything in particular.

> To be a realist and to be immune from error in particular cases of knowledge are not synonyms—which is to say that to know what valid knowledge is not necessarily to know what *a* valid knowledge is.... For note what is required of this same subjective experience. It must catapult upon the scene of an object, while (by a sort of rebound) it modestly withdraws far behind the scene.... in cases of genuinely scientific knowing, experience must affix to the object some special sign witnessing that this object is free from its own influence. (*MW* 6: 82)

Dewey's refusal to embrace any notion of the thing-in-itself was, like his doctrine of immediate empiricism, repeatedly construed by realists as a collapse into idealism. In an exchange with E. B. McGilvary, who asks Dewey whether he regards "all reality as embraced within experiences or Experience," Dewey emphatically makes his denial if "embraced" is taken in any existential sense. Experience is real but does not ontologically exhaust reality. Philosophy must abandon any effort to describe all reality as it is "in-itself" and must instead be *empirical*. The methodological commitment to the empirical study of things, at the philosophical level, entails the repudiation of transcendentalism:

> ... philosophy, like science, proceeds intelligibly and fruitfully to verifiable results only by taking experienced, not transcendental, things, and by discussing them in the characters they empirically possess, not in the characters which, according to some *a priori* method, they *ought* to possess.... I know shamefully little about 'all reality,' since my empiricism is precisely that the only realities I do know anything about or ever shall know anything about are just experienced realities.... (*MW* 4: 154, 155)

Dewey found occasion to reassert his empiricist methodology time and time again. Bertrand Russell complained of Dewey's *Logic: The Theory of Inquiry* that "... we are told very little about the nature of things before they are inquired into."[9] Dewey responded that such an attempt would be "... completely contradictory to my own position .. [and] completely absurd." (*LW* 14: 31).

Dewey's willingness to suffer the charges of idealism aroused by such declarations was grounded on his staunch rejection of the transcendentalist theory of meaning. In summary the transcendental theory of meaning requires contradictory stands on the nature of meaningful experience. On the one hand, the mind-independent object is supposed to possess meaning thanks only to the operations of a mind. Nevertheless this mysterious object is somehow supposed to guarantee that a mind's reference to it successfully lights upon it and only it without any assistance from the mind performing the operations and indeed despite that mind's complete inability to discern whether its efforts to refer actually succeed. Such mysteries only deepen when the transcendentalist turns to the nature of knowledge since a known object must at least be a meaningful object.

An Empirical Theory of Knowledge

Dewey's efforts to extricate himself from the charge of idealism should not obscure the fact that he had several points of agreement with the idealists. Foremost among these points are the views that thought increases the meaning of things and that this increase of meaning involves the establishment of more relations among things. Following from these points, they together also agreed that the experienced known object cannot be the same thing as any experienced object which was transformed by thought in the process of the creation of that knowledge. Both Dewey and idealists therefore maintained that the humanly known object could not possibly exist prior to the formation of such human knowledge. This position for Dewey follows from his postulate of immediate experience and his instrumentalist theory of the transformative function of thought. Since the object really is what it is experienced to be, then the known object cannot be experienced prior to a knowing experience of the object. This tenet, while practically tautologous, has a far more significant implication if taken seriously: there is no philosophical justification for asserting that the known object exists before it becomes humanly known. This implication is of course a restatement of Dewey's rejection of any sort of thing-in-itself, but it is this radical conclusion which most clearly places his philosophy entirely at odds with both absolute idealism and dualistic realism.

Absolute idealists (the later F. H. Bradley excepted)[10] believed that human knowledge was solely a matter of our mental recreation of the known object as it eternally truly exists in the absolute mind. They could not agree with Dewey's reduction of thought to the directly experienceable and found abhorrent the notion that mere human beings, and their purely subjective experiences, were responsible for the creation of knowledge. Dualistic realists also determined that Dewey fell into subjectivism since they, like the idealists, held that human knowledge must conform to the transcendent object as it really exists prior to, and independent of, any human experience. Both philosophies, because of their transcendentalist foundations, relied on the fundamental principle that the existence of the known object does not depend on whether the object is ever known by any human mind. In response Dewey argued that the only way properly to comprehend human knowledge requires the view that the existence of the known object is dependent on its being known by a human mind.

The transcendental theory of meaning contributes directly to the establishment of the transcendental theory of knowledge. Let us begin with one of the simpler approaches to this theory which, while not complex, lies at the heart of many realisms and idealisms. If knowledge requires of a certain kind of meaning a relation between a mental state and the mind-transcendent known object and if all mental states are states of a mind, then knowledge requires that known objects stand in a transcendent relation to a mind. Dewey's claim that his philosophy is realistic appears to run aground on the realists' requirement that the known object's existence is not dependent on its being known by a mind.

However, transcendental realists have long been internally divided over the nature of the knowledge relationship because there are three primary options: (1) admit that the known object in every respect completely and permanently transcends human experience; (2) argue that known objects can sometimes lead a double life, capable of simultaneously existing as mind-independent objects while existing in human experience as well; (3) accept the existence of mental duplicates or copies of the known object, which mediate between the mind-transcendent object and the human mind. That there are three very different options is a sign of transcendental realism's incoherence, which Dewey fully exploits.

The inadequacies of the first option have been thoroughly examined already. Dewey's strategy to counter the attractions of options of two and three is to prove that option two, together with other realistic suppositions, inevitably slides into option three. Dewey then shows that option three avoids a collapse into the dreaded position of idealism only by reverting back to option one. In the end transcendentalist realism really only differs from idealism by asserting the existence of the thing-in-itself. Dewey's immediate empiricism is designed to rescue philosophy from these unpalatable options by reconstructing the theory of knowledge.

We should therefore start with Dewey's difficulties with option two. Because option two portrays the known object as a visitor to the realm of human experience, free to come and go without allowing its existence to become dependent on experience, option two offers a theory of the elusive perceived "given" to experience.

Naive Realism and the "Given"

Dewey attacks the notion of the "given" in many of his writings; the sternest and most elaborate argument is contained in his 1911 "Brief Studies in Realism, Part One. Naive Realism vs. Presentative Realism" (*MW* 6: 103–111). Naive realism is Dewey's label for the stand taken on the nature of perception by his immediate empiricism. Naive realism holds that perceptions of things are natural events on an ontological par with all of nature. As natural events they in themselves are not cases of knowledge, although they have a central role to play in the knowledge

The Reconstruction of Epistemology

process. "Presentative realism" is Dewey's label for option two, which holds that some special kinds of perceptions are knowing perceptions of known objects.

By taking perceptions to be knowings, presentative realism must answer the question of what exactly is known in a perception. Dewey's example is a perceived star: let us consider the star and the seen light. As realists we should of course regard them as numerically distinct. Dewey's naive realism does so: on that theory the visible perceived light is part of a continuous natural process which includes the star. And as realists we had better be able to know how the components of this process operate together, which enables us to explain the perception of star. After all, idealism lurks nearby whenever a realist confesses to ignorance of the operations of natural processes. Dewey defends naive realism as the only adequate realism by accusing presentative realism of being incompatible with knowledge of natural processes involving perception. An ordered analysis of his argument proceeds as follows:

1. A perception is a knowing of a mind-independent object. (Assumption: made by presentative realism.)

2. Knowledge always has as its object some really existing object with its own characters. (Assumption: agreeable to nearly all idealists and realists, but not Dewey, that there is a uniquely "real" object of knowledge.)

3. The real star to be known possesses characters C. (Specific example, from 2.)

4. A perception of a star does not present all of C, but only the perceived C. (Assumption: agreed upon by both Dewey and presentative realists. For example, the perception of star does not present knowledge of the temperature at the star's surface or of the velocity of the light emitted.)

5. The perception of the star cannot be a complete knowing of the real star: it is never a knowing of all of C. (From 3 and 4.)

6. The star stands in natural relations with any perception of it. (Assumption: agreeable to both Dewey and presentative realists.)

7. The real star cannot naturally cause perceptions that are knowings of the unperceived characters of the star. (From 5 and 6.)

8. The natural relations which stand between the star and the perception of it cannot by themselves account for the complete knowledge of the star. (From 7.)

9. Knowledge of some of the unperceived characters of the real star must be a necessary component of a known realistic explanation of any occurrence of the perception of it. (Assumption: agreeable to both Dewey and presentative realists. For example, knowledge of the velocity of the star's emitted light is essential to a realistic explanation of how a spatially distant star is responsible for the occurrence of a particular perception of the star.)

10. Either the unperceived characters of the real star cannot be known (and hence no adequate natural explanation of a star's perception can be known), or, if they are to be known, they must be known as through some process besides the natural relations between the real star and perceptions of the star. (From 8 and 9.)

11. There is a satisfactory realistic explanation for the perception of stars. (Assumption: agreeable to both Dewey and presentative realists.)

12. The unperceived characters of the star are known. (From 9 and 11.)

C. A non-natural process is responsible for providing knowledge of the unperceived characters of the real star. (From 10 and 12.)

The establishment of this conclusion finds presentative realism well on the way to a forced surrender of its posture of being thoroughly realistic. The assumptions unique to presentative realism, (1) and (2), conjoined with its aim to provide a naturalistic account of knowledge, have been shown by Dewey to require a commitment to the conclusion. This intervening nonnatural process has been understood by eighteenth- and nineteenth-century psychology and philosophy as the reflectively self-conscious thoughts of a knowing mind. Following Descartes, Locke, and Kant, the knowing mind has been categorized as the paradigmatically nonnatural substance or process.

Dewey's argument above confronts transcendental realists who prefer the presentative realism of option two with a difficult question: if perception is taken to be a knowing, then there must be an object known. What is the object known in perception? The presentative realist must confess that whatever is known *in perception*, it is not the real star. Through *mental inference* the unperceived characters of the real star may be an object of knowledge, but not in perception. Since the presentative realist holds that any knowledge must have its real object (premise 3), the perception, as a perception, cannot really be of the

The Reconstruction of Epistemology

star, but of something else. The conclusion of the above argument invites the presentative realist to construe the perception as something nonnatural, existing only in the nonnatural mind. Option two, asserting the given known object, has collapsed into option three, which hypothesizes the existence of mental duplicates of the known object.

Several embarrassments now confront the presentative realist. The presentative realist has admitted six key points: perception by itself cannot have the real star as its object, the star cannot naturally cause perceptive knowings of it, only in the mental realm can perception have any meaning, only through mental inference can perception contribute to knowledge, only after mental inference has done its work can the perception be additionally and superficially taken to be of the real star, and therefore all knowledge of the real star comes into existence only as a result of the mental inferences of a knowing mind. The idealist completely agrees with these six admissions (since she or he agrees with premises (2) and (3) of the above argument) and deduces the general idealistic conclusion that objects can only exist as real if they stand in a knowledge relation to a mind.

Idealism can also be applied to easily subvert the remaining option for the presentative realist: to assert that the object known in perception is only the sum of the characters initially present in perception. This assertion is the essence of what Dewey terms epistemological realism in "Brief Studies in Realism, Part Two. Epistemological Realism: The Alleged Ubiquity of the Knowledge Relation" (*MW* 6: 111–122). Epistemological realism is grounded on the notion that perceptions, and hence all knowing mental states, are knowing states only because their objects stand in only one relation: to a knowing mind. That most idealists are epistemological realists is hardly a surprise, but to Dewey's neverending astonishment, many realists also affirmed epistemological realism. Only the bare ungrounded faith in the existence of things-in-themselves remains to distinguish epistemological realism from idealism. This is why option three ultimately must collapse into option one.

Dewey is not interested in agreeing with idealism's conclusion that the existence of real objects depends on knowing minds, although he is eager to highlight the fact that presentative realism inevitably tends to logically slide into such idealism. The above argument shows that presentative realism cannot offer a naturalistic understanding of how a physical star can stand in a causal relation with a perception that gives knowledge of it. The presentative realist's retort that no claim was made for perception's ability to supply complete knowledge of the star rings hollow. As we have seen, the perception cannot have *any* character of the real star as its object except by "second intention" after mental inference has done its work. Realists who resort to attributing to perception abilities that properly belong only to inference are therefore trapped. They cannot treat perception or inference as natural, and their transcendentalism is shrouded in unsolvable difficulties. This trap is inevitable if realists commit the fallacy of converting eventual functions into preexisting realities, as Dewey puts it.

Dewey's alternative to dualistic realism and idealism is the notion that the thought process yielding knowledge, including the gathering of perceptions, should be understood as entirely and perfectly natural. Specifically perception can yet be understood as a natural event and part of a continuous process that includes its cause, if it is the natural result of an organism-environment interaction. Naive realism accordingly rejects what Dewey called the "spectator theory" of knowledge by arguing that perceptions are not in themselves knowings of some object, and knowledge is not merely of some really existing object with its own characters.[11]

Inspired by the actual methods of science, which suffer from no ontological chasm between laboratory experiments and the objects of experimentation, naive realism reconstructs the purposes for the components of thought in the natural context of meaningful things. Dewey analyzes this inspiration from science in *Reconstruction in Philosophy* (1920).

> The division of the world into two kinds of Being, one superior, accessible only to reason and ideal in nature, the other inferior, material, changeable, empirical, accessible to sense-observation, turns inevitably into the idea that knowledge is contemplative in nature.... But in the actual course of the development of science, a tremendous change has come about. When the practice of knowledge ceased to be dialectical and became experimental, knowing became preoccupied with changes and the test of knowledge became the ability to bring about certain changes. Knowing, for the experimental sciences, means a certain kind of intelligently conducted doing; it ceases to be contemplative and becomes in a true sense practical. (*MW* 12: 148)

It cannot be perception's purpose, Dewey argued, to assist the mind in closely duplicating an ontologically separate unchanging reality using static ideas. Perception is the actively attentive response to the problematic instabilities of natural things, for the purpose of discovering these things' behaviors under controlling conditions. Perception has natural deficiencies to be sure, but unless its proper object is assumed to be fixed, finished, and independent, there is no need to denigrate perceptions as subjectively inferior existences requiring nonnatural supplementation. Things are what they are experienced as; if known, their meaning as known naturally inheres in them, not in minds. In Dewey's terminology perceptions are "cognitive" because they are a necessary part of the knowledge process, but they cannot be self-sufficient cognitions.

In summary, while Dewey is a sworn enemy of dualism, "Naive Realism vs. Presentative Realism" and "Epistemological Realism" display dualism as only a halfway pause in a slide toward idealism. Once the dualist has admitted the existence of a nonnatural knowing mind, the idealist can easily oppose dualism by asking for the problematic grounds of our knowledge of allegedly independent natural objects. From Dewey's perspective debates between realists and idealists who both hold that the only relation that a knowing mental state may have is a relation to a knowing mind are just endless exercises in smuggling in additional premises. The absurd spectacle of realists arguing that ideal knowledge must always be of known things, and of idealists counterarguing that known things can only exist through ideal knowledge, could be an ongoing dispute only because *both* hold that knowledge, as a special kind of meaning, must consist of ideal representations distinct from the object of knowledge.

It is important to emphasize that it was not Dewey's view that idealism can prove superior to dualistic realism. Rather Dewey found such debates hopelessly stalemated, and he based a new philosophical solution upon the denial of their common principles. The most important principle that must be denied is the conclusion of the above argument, that a nonnatural process is responsible for providing knowledge of the unperceived characters of the real star. Dewey's naive realism affirms that all experience is continuously one with the natural processes to which experience's objects also belong. This means that the knowing experience stands in many relations, not one; specifically the knowing experience has relations to other nonknowing experiences of things. There simply is no ontologically separate knowing mind to hold knowing experiences in its unclenching grasp.

A good example of Dewey's rejection of the given and his reconstruction of perception is provided by his exchange with a realist, E. B. McGilvary.[12] McGilvary complains that Dewey obliterates the all-important distinction between mental ideas and the bare facts or givens of experience. These givens, contra idealism, have a sufficient existence on their own in experience without any need for relating ideas or thoughts. Dewey's response, "Objects, Data, and Existences: A Reply to Professor McGilvary" (*MW* 4: 146–155), attempts to explain that the "given" which McGilvary so firmly grips onto is just what Dewey means by prereflective, alogical, noncognitive experience. McGilvary is clearly in the camp which believes that this given must be a known given, lest it disappear into nonexistence, like the despised Kantian thing-in-itself. He thus thinks that when Dewey refuses to read back into prior existence (prior experience, for Dewey) a known object like the visible hemisphere of the moon, then Dewey must be denying the existence of any givens before or after thought, and therefore McGilvary concludes that Dewey is an idealist because all must be dependent on thought.

Dewey counters by explaining that McGilvary is failing to recognize that this "bright something occasionally in experience, growing from slender crescent to full orb" which happens "whenever any one constituted like us opens his eyes and turns them in the right direction at an opportune time" (*MW* 4: 326) completely constitutes the prereflective act/experience. This type of experience can exist as it does without any thought intervening. Thought will intervene eventually but not permanently since the original experience is not thereby rendered forevermore inaccessible. Science informs us about what we are seeing, for example a spherical moon, but this *known* object was not what we experienced originally. To posit that it is what we did see would only make the relationship between the "bright something" and the spherical moon thoroughly enigmatic. Now, most adults only see the sphere, but that does not mean that this sphere, as known, has anything to do with the process by which during childhood they came to understand that it is actually a sphere. The assumption that it did makes for hopeless psychological and epistemological puzzles. Furthermore the meaning and verification of science's theories about the shape of the moon, the nature of the far side, etc., all rest at bottom on our ability to return to nonreflective but potentially cognitive experience.

The Creation of the Known Object

Josiah Royce helped to shape the origins of the realist movement in the United States with his infamous definition of the basic tenet of realism: "to be real means to be independent of an idea or experience through which the real being is, from without, felt, or thought, or known."[13] Royce's attack takes the term "independence" in an absolute sense, as excluding all relations to experience from a real being. The resulting real being is hence for Royce even more conceptually remote than Kant's noumenon, as the noumenon is at least supposed to have some relation to sensory experience. Two realists, Ralph B. Perry and William P. Montague, immediately objected to this interpretive maneuver, and several other realists picked up the phrasing involved in their objection. These realists preferred to interpret "independence" as signifying that a real being can *contingently* come into relations with experience, but it has no *necessary* relations to experience.

The crux of the matter is whether a real being *must*, in keeping with its own nature, always maintain a relation with experience. Idealists answered in the affirmative. Realists instead declared that no necessity, only possibility, pertains to a real being's relation to experience. This distinction was usually formulated in terms of the distinction between a real being's internal and external relations. Those relations of a real being pertaining necessarily to that real being are internal relations. All other relations, including for the realists any relation to experience, are external relations. Six philosophers picked up this line of opposition to idealism and jointly published in 1910 "The Program and First Platform of Six Realists."[14] The new realists were Edwin B. Holt, Walter T. Marvin, William P. Montague, Ralph B. Perry, Walter B. Pitkin, and Edward G. Spaulding.

Concerning known objects, Montague's first principle is unambiguous. "Realism holds that things known may continue to exist unaltered when they are not known. . . ." Marvin declares, "the proposition, 'This or that object is known,' does not imply that such object is conditioned by the knowing." Perry echoes with ". . . consciousness selects from a field of entities which it does not create." Spaulding's version says that ". . . the entity is known as it would be if the knowing were not taking place." Additionally the new realists all asserted that objects are in many external relations besides the experience relation. Two realists decided that the very notion of internal relations should be rejected completely, effectively equating idealism with their acceptance. Holt finds that internal or organic relations are incompatible with any satisfactory system of logic, and Marvin states that logic, which is prior to all science and metaphysics, requires that all relations must be external relations. Much later Russell echoes these complaints against Dewey, arguing that without the express recognition of "logically separable particulars," Dewey's logic of situational inquiry must resemble F. H. Bradley's idealism.[15]

Interestingly Perry attributes to William James the notion that idealism can be effectively sabotaged by rejecting its principle that internal relations exhaust any real thing's relations.[16] For James such opposition to idealism's rationalistic reliance on internalism lent plausibility to his pluralistic empiricism. His philosophy is pluralistic because things can have their own particular existence regardless of its external environment and is empirical because the question of whether a thing stands in any relation must be decided by appeal to experience alone. James accordingly asserted that many relations can be experienced that do not depend on any activity of thought. The new realists followed James on these matters, each stating that only empirical evidence can establish whether a relation pertains between things. For example, Holt says that "the degree of unity, consistency, or connection subsisting among entities is a matter to be empirically ascertained." Unfortunately Dewey's agreement with James's empirical pluralism was not recognized by the new realists because they made the additional presumption that knowledge must be characterized solely by external relations between the knower and the known.

Dewey's 1910 "The Short-Cut To Realism Examined" opens the debate between the new realism and pragmatism by characteristically agreeing that "knowledge always implies existences prior to and independent of their being known" (*MW* 6: 138). This nominal agreement leaves a great deal unsaid since Dewey does not believe that the known object, as it is known, could be among the independent prior existences. The realists' use of the notion of external relation brings this disagreement to a focus. What do realists mean by saying that the real object is externally related to knowledge of it? Let us consider the proposition "the offspring of organisms of a species may mutate to become a distinct species." The real object of knowledge in this case is presumably the offspring of organisms, and an ability to mutate into a species different from that of their ancestors is being predicated of them. How does Dewey go about casting doubt on the realists' notion that knowledge such as this does not affect the known objects? Does he mean to say that the knowledge which Darwin formulated after his return to England somehow materially altered the birds on far-distant islands that he had observed during his voyage on the *Beagle*?

If the realists hold that the known object, as the result of successful inquiry, does not change when it is referred to in a proposition, this is obviously true. Darwin cannot cause any physical changes to those observed birds by uttering statements about them. However, the realists must be saying more than this truism. If instead what is meant is that the meaning of a term as used in judgments does not change during the process of inquiry, this is false. The meaning of the term "species" altered for Darwin during his inquiry into the distribution of birds varying in physical features across several islands. At one stage in Darwin's mental development (matching science's then-current understanding) the term "species" meant an unchanging natural order such that every organism's offspring must be of the same species as its parents. At a later stage in Darwin's mental development (which other scientists have subsequently matched) it came to mean a rather looser natural order occasionally permitting offspring to be of a different species. Those among Darwin's opponents who argued a priori that by definition species cannot give rise to other species simply displayed their ignorance of the methods of scientific advancement.

All scientific inquiry involves alterations to the meanings of terms. Dewey's other examples are "mammal," "metal," "orchid," and "circle." A current science textbook's definition of "metal" would hardly be understood by a scientist a hundred years ago. This is the essence of scientific progress, and it explains why Dewey finds that knowledge requires the alteration of the object known in the process of inquiry. In Darwin's case he initially knew the birds as members of a species having variations and similarities, and he concluded his inquiry by knowing birds of different species that descended from ancestors of a single species. In the case of metals, scientists initially knew a wide variety of metals with some common observable properties, and scientists presently know metals as composed of atoms with certain valence values. In the former case the alteration of the objects known is a conceptual matter. In the latter case the alteration is conceptual, but the conceptual changes are driven by physical alterations made to the metals in the course of determining their atomic structure. Present-day investigations into species are more like that into metals since analysis now proceeds on the genetic level (in both senses of the term "genetic").

> Now the realist in ignoring the distinction between knowing, between active thinking or investigating, and achieved knowledge ignores also the problems of doubt, hypothesis, and error. He wins an easy victory because he assumes a completed ideal without telling by what criterion he distinguishes between the static ideal of possessed

knowledge in which meanings do not undergo change, and the active process of getting knowledge, where meanings are continuously modified by the new relations into which they enter. (*MW* 6: 139)

Dewey then raises serious doubts about the realists' ability to justify their contention that known objects are not altered by being known. What sort of empirical evidence can they muster? After all, the realists should not want to follow in the idealists' rationalistic footsteps by drawing conclusions about existences merely from an analysis of the terms of propositions about them. Nor should realists simply replace the idealists' logic of internal relations with external relations only likewise to set it apart from, and prior to, empirical knowledge. Dewey finds that the empirical evidence mustered by looking at how science actually proceeds supports his view.

The new realists could not agree. They typically claimed empirical support for external relations by arguing that mathematics or physics, as actually practiced, analyzes complex things to discover knowledge of parts which only have external relations to each other and the whole. Spaulding specifically addressed the sorts of examples to which Dewey often appealed, concerning chemistry and to physiology. For Dewey a molecule, or an organism, exhibits properties which its constituent atoms, or cells, do not have. Spaulding claimed that while the study of such things seems to reveal that the constituent parts must creatively synthesize when brought together to form the whole, such study may be incomplete. Further study may show how to derive the properties of the whole from those of its parts and so satisfy the demands of externalist logic.[17] However, this disagreement of whether science gains complete valid knowledge using external or internal relations is apparently impossible to settle on empirical grounds since Spaulding is eager to dismiss summarily any scientific use of internal relations as just an indication that such a science is at an immature stage. Dewey's study of scientific method and causal necessity persuaded him of the reverse.

Leaving science aside, the new realists agreed that the knowing experience is not a representational relation between knowledge's object and the knowing. Instead, in knowing, the known object is directly present to the mind, requiring no mediating idea. Perry understood new realism to be a denial of dualism because of its two primary tenets.[18] "Epistemological monism" holds that when a thing is known, it enters a relation which constitutes it as the idea or content of a mind. "Independence" declares that a thing's own nature is not dependent on any knowledge relation with a mind. Since Perry and the other realists assumed that knowledge is the mind's only relationship with things, this tenet really asserts "transcendence." Dewey's difficulties with the notion of transcendence (external relations, things-in-themselves, etc.) have already been noted above. While Perry thought that any philosophy that denied transcendence to known things must by definition be an idealism, Dewey saw that a denial of the ubiquity of the knowledge relationship permitted the natural nonknowing relations that establish naive realism.

Experience and Reality

Dewey expressed his immediate empiricism and naive realism in many different ways, depending on the argumentative purpose at hand. As we observed above, Dewey asserts that "a thing is what it is experienced to be." Elsewhere, he defends the "assimilation to each other of the ideas of experience and reality" (*MW* 3: 101) and states in *Experience and Nature* that experience means "something at least as wide and deep and full as all history on this earth, a history which, since history does not occur in the void, include the earth and the physical relatives of man" (*LW* 1: 370). Another way of stating naive realism, which Dewey finds useful for distinguishing it from epistemological realism, declares that the knower has natural relations to other things besides known objects (*MW* 6: 111–122). These relations, constructing the naturalistic setting of experience, situate the knower as an organism interacting with the environment. Dewey is well aware that he is contravening the time-honored metaphysical position that experience could not possibly be part of natural reality.

One of the most popular arguments against the claim that experience is part of natural reality proceeds from the fact that we know of historical periods before any human experience existed anywhere on the earth. This argument is only effective against full-blown idealism's assertion that reality and experience are coextensive. Dewey's metaphysics has no intention of making everything both experience and reality; it only claims that some portions of reality are experience. Dewey argues in "Reality as Experience" that the view of experience as naturally real is not refuted by scientific knowledge of time periods in the far past which lacked life and hence experience. His method of argument begins by denying any relationship between experience and a soul, mind, or consciousness (these having been discarded as metaphysically tainted). Without a duality a monism (though not a Parmenidean monism) remains: there is no recourse but to find experience and reality together in the same realm, permitting "experience" to be just a label for a distinctive kind of reality.

The existence of time periods prior to experience are quite compatible with this naturalistic view of experience. "Unless some heterogeneous kind of reality is shoved in, then the early reality is at any and every point on its way to experience. It is only the earlier portion, historically speaking, of what later is experience" (*MW* 3: 102). He confusingly speaks of their "assimilation" or "identification," but his purpose is actually not so bold. Experience is just an appropriate name for some portions of reality and not all reality. Reality is not marred by any discontinuities (only change) when it becomes an experience—it is always "continual-transformation-in-the-direction-of" (*MW* 3: 103). The principle of continuity of his process metaphysics is apparent here though Dewey does yet refer to these notions in such a manner.[19]

Dewey next tackles the real question lurking behind the dualist's interest in scientific knowledge. "What is the better index, for philosophy, of reality: its earlier or later form?" (*MW* 3: 103). Should philosophy, in order to be empirical, avoid a stance that denies scientific results? To do this, should it adopt as ultimate reality the portrait of reality drawn by science, in this instance, the scientific understanding of the past? Such questions attempt to confront Dewey with the horns of a dilemma, but he uses the postulate of immediate experience to go between them. Since reality is only what it is experienced as, Dewey will not deny the existence of times past since we can experience things as having existed in the past, as independent of human experience. The geologist experiences rock formations or sediment deposits as known to be very old. But the geologist can also experience them in a wide variety of other ways, as the ditch digger does, which are not part of knowledge. Should philosophy declare that the ditch digger fails to experience, to have, true reality?

Dewey believes that an affirmative answer is incorrect. Paraphrasing liberally, he asks us to consider whether, say, the occasion of the formation of the earth should be considered as entirely distinct and separate from our present experience of the earth. By the principle of continuity, the past earth could hardly be separated from its *present* state through its history, save in temporal distance. By the absence of a mind or consciousness, the past earth could not be separated from the *experience* of its present state. But could our *knowledge* of the past earth be distinct and separate from our present experience of the earth? This must be impossible, in the sense that only through a careful, reflective examination of present experience could we ever gain such knowledge of the past. This examination, this selective and attentive analysis, always takes place within experience and relies upon the *full* reality of experience. Furthermore whether this analysis will result in successful practice and hence knowledge also must depend on the full reality of experience. Finally scientific theories would never be found lacking and no scientific progress would be called for, if it were not for the fact that scientists expect their knowledge to always be compatible with the extra-scientific aspects of experience.

In brief science as it is actually practiced never questions in any way the full reality of experience in all its characteristics. Why then should philosophers doubt it and demote it to an inferior status? When philosophers do so, the non-knowledge aspects just do not disappear; the philosopher must put them somewhere out of the way of true reality. Unfortunately this alternate place becomes a second reality, and then inevitable questions arise about their relationships and interactions. Plato's and Descartes's metaphysics are paradigmatic examples of the results of this sort of reasoning. Plato's respect for the intelligible aspects of things, and Descartes's respect for science's description of nature, led to a reality separation (the realm of the Forms versus ordinary opinionated experience, and objective physical reality versus subjective consciousness). To repair such dualisms, one must leave ontology and practice epistemology—not what passes itself off as epistemology after a metaphysical dualism has been assumed—but the study of the actual methods of gaining knowledge of the world. Dewey believes that he has a good understanding of this knowledge process by way of functional psychology. As he tries to show in this article and elsewhere, this process is completely grounded at every stage in the conviction that the present experience of things is as they are.

The realists had serious reservations over Dewey's theory of knowledge and its implications for realism. As McGilvary points out in "Pure Experience and Reality,"[20] Dewey stated in the *Studies in Logical Theory* that the object of thought should not be read back into the time prior to its creation. There are very few other assertions that Dewey made during his career that created as much confusion and consternation. McGilvary's own reading of Dewey provides a corollary: "no truth made out by intellectual labor is to be held valid of anything real that may have existed before that labor was ended" (*MW* 4: 297). He infers from this that Dewey does not believe in any experience-independent reality and therefore must be an idealist of some sort. Montague's inference is incorrect. Accurately stated, Dewey does not believe in the existence of any experience-independent *known* reality, which is a very different belief. To say that the knowledge of a real thing is dependent on experience, and to say that this real thing's existence is dependent on experience, is to make a commitment to quite different propositions. When Dewey refers to the "known object" or the "knowledge-object," as he is usually careful to do, he is speaking of this object qua known, and not as it is experienced in other ways, or even as it is "in itself."[21] He has very little to say about things prior to their being experienced.

Such reticence is perfectly consistent with his adherence to the postulate of immediate experience. Ironically it is not really what Dewey is willing to say about reality that brings down the "idealist" accusation upon him, but rather what he is not willing to say. Here is the exact crux of this central problem that pragmatism presented for the American realists. McGilvary does approve of Dewey's so-called epistemological idealism, which holds that "no thinker, no thought-object; no experience somewhere and somewhen, no meaningful reality anywhere and anytime" (*MW* 4: 303). But Dewey's theory is unable commit to transcendental realism: the assertion of the mere existence of the real object, irrespective of whether it is ever thought of or ever experienced. McGilvary is all too aware that Dewey could reply, as he does in his response, that since we do experience things as having existed prior to our experience of them, we should also, by the postulate of immediate empiricism, believe that they really did exist in that past (*MW* 4: 120). But that was insufficient proof for McGilvary that

The Reconstruction of Epistemology

Dewey deserves to be a realist. What more could McGilvary have possibly desired from Dewey?

McGilvary held, with most other realists of that time, that although reality can enter into or have relations with consciousness, its existence is in no way dependent on such occurrences. The proper tenet defining realism was, as Montague declared, "the view that things do not depend for their existence upon the fact that we know them, and that consequently they can continue in what is called *existence* during those intervals of time in which no subject is aware of them."[22] Dewey's membership application into the realist party would hinge on an unqualified allegiance to this doctrine, but he placed too many qualifications on it as he attempted to clarify the nature of subjects, awareness, knowledge, and so forth. Such clarifications only served to raise clear warning signs for the realists because these seemed to justify various idealist readings of Dewey's pragmatism, as we have seen. McGilvary, like the rest of the realists, thus had tremendous obstacles impeding a clear review of Dewey's application. They consistently disqualified him from membership not for any simple denial of the requisite article of faith, but for his elaborate and irregular affirmation.

McGilvary was doggedly persistent in his pursuit of Dewey. He defined idealism as "any theory which regards all reality as embraced within experiences or Experience.... A clear unambiguous answer from Professor Dewey to the question whether he is an idealist in the current sense of idealism as defined above would, I am sure, make his view much more intelligible."[23] Montague suspects that Dewey must answer in the affirmative since he is so very quiet, unlike the realists, about anything that is not within experience. Dewey's answer claims that philosophy, like science, should inquire only into the empirical, the things and characters of experience, and never the transcendental. "I know shamefully little about 'all reality,' since my empiricism is precisely that the only realities I do know anything about or ever shall know anything about are just experienced realities" (*MW* 4: 155). Dewey's empiricist philosophy could hardly prove the existence of a reality forever locked off from the possibility of being experienced in some way, and therefore it does not affirm it. The Kantian thing-in-itself lurks behind these discussions of realism and idealism, and it still haunts them today. Dewey felt that it would hardly be just to require any realist to assert the thing-in-itself, though many more of his critics sought his conviction and banishment to idealism on that refusal.

Could Dewey accept epistemological monism? Perry relied on this tenet to escape the skeptical tendencies inherent in epistemological dualism and to replace the substance notion of mind with a relational view (situating Perry as an heir to James's rejection of consciousness). Epistemological dualism, by asserting that knowledge can be only of the effects which the independent, physical object has on the mind, is the view that Dewey refers to as epistemological or transcendental realism. Dewey disposes of this kind of realism by pointing out that it, of all the realisms, is the most vulnerable to dissolution into idealism. Once it is confessed that knowledge both exhausts all relations to reality and exists only for mind, the "short-cut" to idealism has been taken; the dismissal of the thing-in-itself is the only remaining step to complete idealism. The critical realists, by reviving transcendental realism and epistemological dualism, accordingly provoked Dewey's criticisms.[24]

Similarly the sense-data epistemology of Bertrand Russell, by taking perceptions to be instances of knowledge and making them the logical ground for all other kinds of knowledge, was untenable for Dewey. When Russell asks whether we can "know that objects of sense . . . exist at times when we are not perceiving them,"[25] he is calling into question whether we can know the external world. To the extent that Russell is able to show, on the basis of his premises, that the external world cannot be known, he is beckoning us to take the shortcut to idealism. Dewey responds to Russell by arguing that the category of internal mental states cannot possess meaning except where contrasted with a category of external things. There is no logical way to establish the existence of momentary knowing perceptions without assuming the existence of external things standing in various natural relations to the perception. Furthermore, to conclude that the quest for a logical inference from things in one category to things in its correlative category must result in failure is necessarily an exercise in self-contradiction.[26]

Dewey's naive realism is the rejection of an absolute ontological internal/external distinction. Its replacement is the contextually functional distinction between the environment and organism, where both kinds of things are completely natural. Can Dewey's rejection of epistemological dualism be construed as an acceptance of epistemological monism? He also agreed with James's rejection of consciousness as a substantive entity with mental contents, but as radical empiricists, Dewey and James retained the notion of experience in their philosophies. Mind can be discussed, but only insofar as it is a term denoting intelligent activities taking place within experience. Not only was Dewey unwilling to discuss physical entities independent of experience, he was unable to conceive of mental activities occurring independently of experience. Experience is therefore logically and actually prior to knowledge activity for Dewey.

Other realists, Perry included, rarely recognized that Dewey relied on this principle. Many consistently assumed that experience must exist only in relation to the knowing mental activity. Dewey's protests to the contrary notwithstanding, realists could not see that his explanation of knowledge in terms of experienced things was a rejection of idealism. This explains why Dewey could not eagerly proclaim an acceptance of epistemological monism. If Dewey were to agree that when a thing is known, it enters a relation which constitutes it as the idea or content of a mind, then this agreement would be construed by other realists as an acceptance of their understanding of "idea" and "relation." His functional psychology radically revised these notions because this psychology replaced the realists' static notions of "idea" and "relation" with active, teleological notions. This replacement is the basis for Dewey's persistent contention that knowledge must involve a change induced in the known object.

The Object of Scientific Knowledge

To coordinate Dewey's naive realism with current notions of realism, we can apply Michael Devitt's terminology provided in *Realism and Truth*.[27]

Weak Realism: Something objectively exists independently of the mental.

Realism: Tokens of most current common-sense and scientific physical types objectively exist independently of the mental.

Common-Sense Realism: Tokens of most current observable common-sense and scientific physical types objectively exist independently of the mental.

Scientific Realism: Tokens of most current unobservable scientific physical types objectively exist independently of the mental.

On these terms Dewey is a weak realist since he believes that cognitive experiences of things are but a very small portion of all our experiences of things. Alogical, noncognitive experiences of things thus objectively exist independently of the mental since as naive realism proclaims, such experiences presents things as they are, irrespective of any way in which they might be considered as ideas or as known objects in other experiences. Devitt would undoubtedly object since he treats all experience as inherently mental and hence treats any things presented in experience as mental too. His terminology is throughout infected with this transcendentalist assumption, vitiating his ability to appreciate Dewey's empirical realism.

There is a more powerful objection to Dewey's claim to weak realism. Since, as Dewey claims, knowledge is responsible for increasing the meanings of things and since he also claims that all experience must possess some minimal degree of meaning, then mental knowledge is bound up with all experience, and thus nothing could be said to exist without the mental. Dewey's response is twofold, First, many of our ordinary noncognitive experiences of things have never been inquired into and hence have never received any mental reworking of their meanings. Second, simply because in *one* context we do experience a thing as known does not mean that in *all* contexts we must experience that thing as known. Compare a biologist's experience of coming across a wild rose during a field study with the same person's experience of coming across a wild rose while on a romantic walk with a lover.

Naive realism rejects the ubiquity of the knowledge relation. We have many relations with things apart from knowing them. Transcendentalism instead assumes that once a concept has attached to a thing, they are bonded together permanently in human experience. Instrumentalism's theory of knowledge requires that we must have more relations with things to serve as the impetus and test of knowing that just the knowledge relation. This requirement also implies that Dewey's philosophy satisfies Devitt's definition of commonsense realism. We do experience chairs, bats, and stars as being the sorts of things that exist regardless of whether we have knowing experiences of them.

Whether Dewey's naive realism qualifies as scientific realism in Devitt's sense is much more problematic since the question now turns on Dewey's understanding of the reality of unobservable entities postulated by successful scientific inquiry. Let us use the example of the star. The analysis from the previous section of the process of knowledge of a star reveals a very significant confusion at the heart of Devitt's definition of scientific realism. Consider the experience of a star by an astronomer as compared with the experience of a star by a six-year-old. Both can orient their eyes upward on a dark, cloudless night and see the same star (let us say that the star is Polaris, the North Star). Suppose the astronomer asks the child to tell how far away Polaris is, and the child replies that this star must be about a mile away, bringing a smile to the astronomer's face at the child's naïveté.

What analysis of this situation can Devitt's definitions bring to bear? Let us suppose that this astronomer is a scientific realist by Devitt's definition. Now, the real star as known in astronomy is many, many light-years away (let us say that Polaris is 300 light-years away). Interestingly, it is manifestly impossible for anyone, astronomers included, to experience directly a star as light-years away. Still, the astronomer's experience of Polaris as *very* far away in contrast to the child's experience of the star as a little bit distant causes the astronomer's gentle mirth. The cause for the two different experiences of Polaris can presumably be attributed to the astronomer's experience of this star as a scientifically known star while no knowledge of the real star can be attributed to the child (beyond perhaps knowing its astronomical name of Polaris).

The important question for Devitt is are stars unobservable scientific objects? We have shown that the astronomer cannot observe Polaris as it really is since the astronomer cannot observe Polaris's three-hundred-light-year distance (or, if another example is required, Polaris's surface or core temperatures, or its actual diameter). Very few characteristics of the real Polaris are observable. In fact only those characteristics that manifest themselves very far away from the star are observable, such as Polaris's apparent diameter in earth's night sky and its apparent brightness and apparent color through earth's atmosphere. It is hardly any

The Reconstruction of Epistemology

inferential leap to say, given Devitt's transcendentalist leanings, that he would have to admit that Polaris is an unobservable scientific object. Or would he make this admission? Suppose Devitt were to say, "How could I confess to Polaris's unobservability, after its observable characteristics were so ably enumerated?"

Now we have the ingredients to impose a dilemma on Devitt. Either Polaris is an unobservable scientific object, in which neither the astronomer nor the child can observe Polaris, or Polaris is an observable scientific object, in which case the astronomer and the child are both capable of observing Polaris. The first horn reaches the undesirable conclusion that the astronomer cannot observe Polaris despite having scientific knowledge while the second horn reaches the undesirable conclusion that the child can observe Polaris despite lacking scientific knowledge. In neither case, then, is the astronomer's mirth justified since the astronomer's situation is no different from the child's. Devitt may go between the horns by pointing out the third option: the astronomer observes Polaris as a result of scientific knowledge while the child does not observe Polaris for a lack of scientific knowledge. Aside from the difficult but common transcendentalist problem of explaining exactly what the child does see if not Polaris, Devitt must admit that the only reason why the astronomer can observe Polaris, and hence the only reason why Polaris is an observable scientific object for astronomers, is because the available perceptions of Polaris (which anyone who can look up into the night sky have access to) have been transformed by the astronomer's scientific reasoning into an observation of Polaris.

This process of perception transformation by reasoning is not mysterious—it is all of a kind with ordinary, everyday inference. The other day I reached with a mitt-covered hand for a pan taken straight from a hot oven, just as my small daughter also reached for the pan with her bare hand. What accounts for the different means chosen of grabbing the pan? The perceptions of the tray seemed to be the same for me as for her: a circular shape having a shiny surface. The explanation lies in the fact that I saw the very hot pan while my daughter saw the pan. To call my instantaneous inference (from my knowledge of where the pan had been to the heat of the pan) an example of scientific reasoning seems too much, but there is only a matter of degree, not kind, separating astronomical inferences from kitchen inferences. The same trilemma for Devitt arises in the kitchen, too; either the hot pan was unobservable to both me and my daughter, or the hot pan was observable to both of us, or the hot pan was only observable to me while my daughter only saw the pan.

The first two options are clearly unacceptable to Devitt and to Dewey. Common sense demands some explanation for the different means chosen to grab the pan since neither I nor my daughter knowingly grab hot things. The third option supplies the satisfactory explanation: my mental reasoning on my perceptions supplied an observation of the hot pan while my daughter's simple perceptions supplied an observation of the pan. The same option of the star trilemma seems similarly satisfactory. All seems well, but now notice that Devitt must take the following position on observable scientific objects:

> (1) A scientific object is observable only where and when the observer is able to use scientific inferences to transform available perceptions into a scientific observation of the object.

Nowhere in *Realism and Truth* does Devitt carefully define "scientific object." From the various contexts in which he talks about them we can only gather that X is a scientific object if a theoretically successful scientific theory T mentions X. Let P stand for any scientific object, like Polaris. P is a scientific object because a theoretically successful scientific theory T mentions P. Combine this with principle 1 above and we get:

> (2) A scientific object P is observable only when and where the observer is able to use the inferences of a theoretically successful scientific theory T that mentions P to transform available perceptions into a scientific observation of P.

and

> (3) A scientific object P is unobservable whenever and wherever P is not observable.

Principle 3 is inappropriate when considering Devitt's understanding of scientific reasoning since by "unobservable" he sometimes means "not presently observable" and other times he means "never, ever observable." Because Devitt likes to use the example of electrons and because from his writings I gather that he would likely put electrons in the latter category, we should also list

> (4) A scientific object P is totally unobservable if and only if no observer could ever use the inferences of a theoretically successful scientific theory T that mentions P to transform available perceptions into a scientific observation of P.

Now let us add one more principle concerning belief in scientific objects. Let us say that

> (5) A scientist has a justified belief in the existence of scientific object P if either (a) the scientist can reliably scientifically observe P, or (b) the scientist uses a theoretically successful scientific theory T that mentions P to scientifically observe Q, where Q stands for the sort of observable thing that theory T is designed to explain.

If we carefully examine principles 2, 4, and 5, we can deduce that

The Reconstruction of Epistemology

(6) A scientist has a justified belief in the existence of scientific object P if either (a) the scientist uses scientific inferences to transform available perceptions into a scientific observation of P, or (b) the scientist uses scientific inferences to observe Q scientifically.

Principle 6 tells us that any justified belief in the existence of *any* scientific object *requires* the use of scientific inferences. Now let us apply 6 to the distinct questions of how a scientist may have a justified belief in an observable P and an unobservable P.

(7) A scientist has a justified belief in the existence of observable scientific object P if and only if the scientist uses scientific inferences to transform available perceptions into a scientific observation of P.

(8) A scientist has a justified belief in the existence of unobservable scientific object P if and only if the scientist uses scientific inferences which mention P to scientifically observe Q.

Principles 7 and 8 report that

(9) To be justified, a scientist's belief in a scientific object P must involve the use of inferences, either inferences leading to P or inferences mentioning P leading to Q.

Since using an inference is a paradigmatic case of using the "mental," principle 9 may be rephrased as

(10) To be justified, a scientist's belief in a scientific object P must involve the use of the mental.

What is the bearing of this result on Devitt's conception of scientific realism—that tokens of most current unobservable scientific physical types objectively exist independently of the mental? Consider that a person may have a justified acceptance of scientific realism only if this person has a justified belief in the mind-independent existence of unobservable scientific objects such as P. Applying principle 10, it can be inferred that

(11) A person may have a justified acceptance of scientific realism only if this person necessarily must use the mental to have a justified belief in the mind-independent existence of unobservable scientific objects such as P.

Principle 11 is based on Devitt's own positions. It should sound somewhat self-contradictory or at least a bit strange. How could a person be expected to say, "I am justified in believing in the mind-independent existence of P since I am only justified in believing that P exists because of my use of the mental"?

By 11 no one should be a scientific realist, least of all Devitt. Dewey avoids principle 11 since Dewey's instrumentalism claims that the scientifically known unobservable object P could never exist independently from mind because P possesses only a theoretical/hypothetical, and not a categorical, existence.

The response available to Devitt is to object to my inference from "the use of inferences that mention P" to "the use of the mental to justify a belief in P." He could say that while P is a theoretical entity, a concept of the mind, it can also be a real entity, as the two categories are not mutually exclusive. And this response is just right, except for a small problem: to be justified in accepting scientific realism and not merely weak realism, one must have sufficient justification for believing that a theoretical concept has a real instantiation. What sort of justification can Devitt offer? Devitt offers four arguments in pp. 129–131 to escape the bull's horns of this dilemma.

First, Devitt claims that reasons why one should think that P exists are irrelevant to whether P exists. This dust raising will not deter the bull since the real question is whether anyone could justifiably accept scientific realism (unless Devitt supposes that one should base scientific realism on some irrational or alogical source). Second, Devitt tries to scare the bull (and his readers) by raising the twin specters of verificationism and positivism. Instrumentalism, he claims, holds that the meaning of theoretical terms is exhausted by their verification or sense-data conditions. This specter is quickly deflated by two considerations. Dewey's instrumentalism is neither verificationism nor positivism since Dewey holds that the meaning of theoretical terms is exhausted by their inferential power functioning in hypothetical propositions. Furthermore Devitt's understanding of reference is tightly circumscribed by his transcendentalist theory of meaning. Devitt thinks that the only way for a term to have meaning is for it to light successfully upon just the right sort of really existing mind-independent physical object that the term is supposed to mean. Unfortunately for Devitt, on his own transcendentalist assumptions he must confess that no one could ever really figure out whether any theoretical terms accomplish this tremendous feat (and thus must confess that there is no justification here for an acceptance of scientific realism).

This is why Devitt offers his third argument. He tries to lull the bull to sleep with the transcendentalist song telling the tale of how the scientists really do believe in unobservable scientific objects because that is the only way really to believe in successful theories. Despite the trance that this popular song can induce (the entranced realists are far too many to begin to enumerate), it utterly begs the question against instrumentalism's account of how scientists actually use theories to control and predict natural events. By Devitt's logic one might as well argue that we ought to be celestial dragon realists since many millions of Chinese successfully have ensured the sun's survival of the dragon eclipse by sincerely beating loudly on drums and setting off fireworks to scare the celestial dragon. This correspondence theory of belief may be popular with realists (and many rural Chinese), but it is quite inadequate to deal with the very complex attitudes that scientists take towards electrons. Scientists do not take such a reverential attitude towards theoretical entities. If Popper and Kuhn have had anything interesting to say about scientific practice, they have spotlighted the highly critical and skeptical attitude at the heart of scientific method. Scientists are well aware that much more scientific effort goes into proving the nonexistence of theoretical entities than proving their existence, and scientists certainly seem much more resigned, if not complacent, about the eventual dismissal of once "proven" entities than are philosophical realists. Besides, the notion that electrons really exist is much easier to perpetuate in a philosophy classroom with a diagram involving little circles on the chalkboard than in a physics classroom with an immense array of equations involving dozens of variables on the chalkboard. "Where on the chalkboard is the electron, professor?"

Fourth, Devitt tries to run away from the bull by arguing that unless scientists really believed in the existence of theoretical terms, they would not take any interest in unifying theories or underlying mechanisms. The counterargument to his third point applies again here. Dewey's theory of scientific inquiry fully accounts for the pragmatic value, and hence high scientific interest, in trying to establish a conformity of scientific terms and a high degree of coherence among scientific propositions.

In conclusion Devitt's transcendentalist attempts to defend scientific realism boil down to the fundamentally corrupt notion that an experience-transcendent reality can be used as an explanatory term to explain why we experience what we do. Its curious logic amounts to saying, "Since successful theories are so pragmatically useful, we ought to believe in the theory-independent existence of their theoretical objects, but only because we must believe that our theories really do refer to them, and not just because such talk happens to be pragmatically useful." Dewey rejects such transcendentalism in favor of an empirical theory of meaning, of knowledge, and of truth. Dewey's empiricism entails weak and commonsense realism but not scientific realism since instrumentalism cannot hold that permanently unobservable scientific objects really have a mind-independent existence. On instrumentalism it is of course possible that presently unobservable scientific objects can become observable with improved inferences and technology.[28] However, the realistic argument that the occurrence of such novel observations (for example, of the planet Pluto or of individual atoms in the famous IBM photograph) can be used to infer the reality of many or most of the other presently unobservable theoretical entities is extremely weak since their occurrences are relatively rare and never outnumber the disproofs of other theoretical entities during any given time period. Labeling this sort of argument as "abductive," as Devitt does (pp. 111–113), uses Peirce's term but displays little acquaintance with his penetrating studies of the science of statistics with which his theory of abduction is related. Dewey had no difficulty admitting the possibility that presently unobservable entities may become instrumentally observable. However, this possibility cannot be used to conclude that scientists or philosophers are rationally justified in believing that all or many of the theoretical entities postulated by currently successful theories actually exist as well.

Like Peirce, Dewey thought that science does inquire into the stable structures of nature. Both should be classified as realists in the medieval sense of accepting the reality of universals, of relatively constant natural patterns pervading the universe. And, like Peirce, Dewey held that science could hardly be a profitable exercise in the absence of such natural patterns. The mistaken idea that there is a privileged language that accurately describes these patterns is also medieval, but it is an idea that lives on only in some philosophical circles.[29] William James explains, much as Dewey does, why the experimental sciences spelled the doom for transcendental realism.

> As I understand the Pragmatist way of seeing things, it owes its being to the breakdown which the last fifty years have brought about in the older notions of scientific truth. . . . Up to about 1850 almost everyone believed that the sciences expressed truths that were exact copies of a definite code of non-human realities. But the enormously rapid multiplication of theories in these latter days has well-nigh upset the notion of any one of them being a more literally objective kind of thing than another. There are so many geometries, so many logics, so many physical and chemical hypotheses, so many classifications, each one of them good for so much and yet not good for everything, that the notion that even the truest formula may be a human device and not a literal transcript has dawned upon us.[30]

An Empirical Process of Verification

Realism can be defined in starkly metaphysical terms, using some variant of the thing-in-itself to ensure that knowledge and truth transcends human experience, but this is not the only method available. Many self-proclaimed realists have alternatively defined realism epistemologically or logically, similarly ensuring that truth is transcendent of the human realm. The epistemological tactic ultimately rests on a metaphysically dualistic view while the logical tactic does not require that basis, however metaphysical its inspiration might be. Dewey's empiricist philosophy rejected all three kinds of realism, disputing the cogency of their notions of truth.

The Transcendental Theory of Truth

Interestingly, the first to criticize pragmatism's connection between truth and practical effectiveness, and its disconnection of truth and a fixed reality, were not realists but idealists.[31] When realists picked up these topics, their difficulties were best expressed first by Arthur K. Rogers, who found pragmatism to be

> a theory which holds that the stars, *e.g.*, and every reality for which the stars stand, come into existence with the human need which leads to their discovery, or that the earth really was flat, in any valid sense of the word real, so long as men found it satisfactory to believe it so, which denies, in a word, any meaning to the reality of an encircling universe in which our human experience and our human thought are set.[32]

Another way of putting the same matter is to argue that the object of belief is always firmly and commonsensically considered to be quite transcendent from one's mental states of experience, belief, knowledge, etc.[33] Rogers complains that pragmatism runs afoul of this belief since, on that theory, any object of belief is just an experience. The reader by now should recognize that here we have an problem generated by a misunderstanding of Dewey's "knowledge-object" and his genuine attempt at a nonsubjective, nonmental notion of experience.

When realists set down their own theory of truth, they typically used some variant of a basic expression like the following.

> The intellectualist's meaning of truth is so simple, so commonplace, so close at hand, that the pragmatist has quite overlooked it. By the truth of an idea the intellectualist means merely this simple thing, *that the object of which one is thinking is as one thinks it.*[34]

Well, it should be admitted that this somewhat Aristotelian expression is really not just that simple for most realists, especially transcendental realists. For example, these realists were always quick to add to this theory that the object's existence is independent of thought so that truth becomes quasi-independent of thought as well. Once this dualistic metaphysics is presumed, dualistic realists are forced to admit that (1) no one could ever verify the existence of any correspondence relation and hence never verify truths, (2) argue that facts can sometimes have a double life, simultaneously existing as both independent reality and subjective idea, or (3) argue that facts are but privileged ideas which carry their justification as knowledge. Those foundationalists who believe that we are capable of verified knowledge argue for perceptually known givens by adopting either the second or third option, depending on their tolerance for the positivistic empiricism implied by (3). We have already considered the hazards of the second and third options in the previous sections.

As for the first option, its skeptical attitude has often been taken by its adherents as the source of its philosophical *strength*. Some dualist realists, by emphasizing the isolation of truth from human experience, have defined the essence of realism as the assertion of truth's aloofness from any human effort to know truth. For example, Bertrand Russell defended such a realism by way of this version of correspondence, unimpeded by a concern for skepticism.

> The formal definition of truth by correspondence of a proposition with its objective seems the only one which is theoretically adequate. The further inquiry whether, if our definition of truth is correct, there is anything which can be known, is one that I cannot now undertake; but if the result of such an inquiry should prove adverse, I should not regard that as affording any theoretical objection to the proposed definition.[35]

Dewey completely agreed with this definition of truth as a correspondence, conceiving the objective of a proposition as a possible event in future human experience (*MW* 4: 98, *MW* 6: 6–8, *MW* 6: 33–34, *MW* 7: 359, *LW* 2: 11–12, *LW* 14: 178–179). Unfortunately Russell and other realists imposed metaphysical presuppositions by asserting the experience-independent existence of propositions (analytic realists) or essences (critical realists) or the ever-popular facts as truth objectives. This intellectualist appeal to transcendent entities evidently makes any verification problematic at best. As a bemused Dewey lamented,

> If there were anything in the so-called cognitive self-transcendency of ideas which concretely lighted upon their intended objects so that their truth or falsity was self- luminous, the appeal of the intellectualist to "agreement with reality" would have some bearing; but . . . such phosphorescence is notoriously lacking . . ." (*MW* 4: 77)

Many dualist realists, like Russell, are not dismayed by the skeptical fruits of this transcendental version of truth as correspondence. Among recent realists Peter van Inwagen forthrightly detects antirealism in the denial that a proposition's truth or falsity is independent of human mental states. Not surprisingly he is hardly impressed by antirealist defenses arguing that complete ignorance is impossible; he accepts the possibility of complete Cartesian ignorance with equanimity.[36] Of course, not just any realism, and certainly not naive realism, is so tightly linked with skepticism. For example, Michael Williams argues that only epistemological realism, as he defines it, carries skeptical implications.[37] Regardless of such labels, many self-proclaimed realists hold that epistemology must be isolated from the theoretical definition of truth. Dewey's critique of the ontological separation of fact and idea applies equally to any metaphysical separation of truth bearers from actual human experience and knowledge. Such a critique of course can have little impact on philosophers with an a priori commitment to transcendentalism.

Russell and other analytic realists also created a purely logical definition of realism. They merged their definition of truth as correspondence, a theory of the complete independence of propositions, and a metaphysical postulate that reality is always absolutely fixed and rigid in its characteristics, qualities, etc. Whatever reality is like, as a totality reality is like that *in only one way*. Therefore, for any proposition P, P is already determinately true or false. Put simply, if the truth of a proposition depends solely on its correspondence with reality and if that reality is *fixed*, the question of the correspondence is fixed. Many realists have defined realism by this principle of bivalence, even if they reject its metaphysical origins.

Realists actually do not deserve much credit for formulating these relationships between truth and reality since they follow the prominent absolute idealists such as T. H. Green and F. H. Bradley. These idealists had long before claimed that reality does not undergo change, and hence a logical principle like bivalence or noncontradiction must prevail over propositions about reality. Present-day discussion of realism, antirealism, and idealism has often forgotten this. That is why Dewey's philosophy cuts through the tangle by sharply distinguishing empiricist from transcendentalist metaphysics. Arguments between varieties of transcendentalism, because they must appeal to matters beyond human experience, inevitably make fallaciously rationalistic deductions concerning existences inferred from purely conceptual premises. The recent entanglement of metaphysics with linguistic philosophy, encouraging a fixation on one's own intuitions about the meanings of words, only worsens such rationalistic disputation.

However divided among themselves, transcendental philosophies unite to condemn the pragmatically empirical approach to truth. For example, it is easy to show that if an idea's truth lies in the process of verification, pragmatism will violate the principle of bivalence. This only requires a hypothetically constructed situation in which one inquirer can pragmatically verify proposition P while another can do the same for not-P.[38] Another way to phrase this objection is to point out that pragmatism cannot properly account for the discovery of error or falsity since a proposition about something at a specific point in time could be true in 1400 but not true in 1900. The proper pragmatic response starts from the view that bivalence serves only as a regulative ideal of fallible inquiry. Dewey does not connote by "verify" what transcendentalism means: the achievement of guaranteed infallible certainty. If two inquiries result in the verification of P and not-P, then for Dewey the ideal of bivalence simply exposes these inquiries as incomplete and fallible. The persistent efforts of transcendentalists to foist their own absolute notion of truth on Dewey led him to abandon the term altogether, replacing it with "warranted assertibility."[39]

Transcendentalists unite against pragmatism's personal or human version of truth, claiming that individuals, communities, or even the totality of all human beings are just too frail and untrustworthy to be relied on for a solid foundation and source of so precious and pure a thing as truth. They prefer a radically nonepistemic notion of truth, which can be explicitly tied to a correspondence theory of truth[40] or can be formulated simply by stating that for any sufficiently meaningful P, P is exclusively either true or false regardless of any human ability to discover that truth-value.[41] Many commentators therefore found Dewey's account of knowledge to be merely psychological in the subjective sense and refused to countenance the reduction of "purely" logical categories such as truth and correspondence down to that individualistic level. Pragmatism makes the notion of truth subservient to the notions of the good or the useful, and since these latter conceptions were widely regarded as hopelessly subjective as well, truth would be delivered into the clutches of relativism at best or, at worst, outright skepticism.[42] Dewey vociferously rejected the metaphysical absolutism and the correspondence theory of truth inherent in such criticisms, claiming that knowledge is an empirical matter. "Like knowledge itself, truth is an experienced relation of things, and it has no meaning outside of such relation" (*MW* 3: 118). Since Dewey will not license any talk of anything transcending (permanently beyond the range of) experience, present or potential, then "truth as correspondence" only can make sense if at minimum three conditions are satisfied. The things to be corresponded together must be related within experience, that relation must itself be experienced, and the subjectivist notion of experience must be relinquished.

Pragmatic Knowledge and Truth

Dewey's rejection of the transcendental theory of meaning asserts that meaningful experience does not reside in some ontologically distinct realm of mind and that objects of meaning do not exist in an experience-transcendent realm. This logically implies that knowledge, and hence truth, entirely resides within experience. If known objects are meaningful objects and if meaning consists of meaningful experiences, then the object of knowledge always consists of meaningful experiences.

To grasp fully Dewey's instrumentalist theory of the process of verification and the necessary relationship between his naive realism and his theories of meaning and knowledge, we must understand what he meant by the "object of knowledge." To do this we must apply Dewey's distinction between accomplished knowledge and the process of knowing. This distinction helps understand why knowledge always seems to lie in the future on his theory. Once knowledge is accomplished, Dewey's theory seems to say that it disappears from view. Accomplished knowledge is marked by the fact that the known object plays its proper role in habitual purposive activity.[43] This type of activity proceeds only because the meaningful knowledge experiences necessary for its unfolding are immediately present. As immediate, they are entirely taken for granted, and further notice can be taken of them only if they are deliberately placed in contrast with remembered experiences of the object prior to its becoming known. We can imaginatively suspend our easy-knowing familiarity with a pen, a bunch of grapes, a foreign language, or a friend if we recall how we first experienced these things or if we see such things anew through the eyes of a child. Dewey is not always careful to make clear when he uses "knowledge" to refer to the process of acquiring more knowledge. "Knowing" is the better term here since the verb form connotes both an activity and a process in time. The best term is probably "learning," but Dewey preferred to use that term in his writings aimed toward a popular or educational audience.

The "object of knowledge" is therefore better called the "object of knowing." If we recall that knowing is the process of increasing the meaning of our experiences and that meaning consists of a thing's ability to suggest another absent thing, then knowing is the process of increasing a thing's ability to suggest other absent things. Now, no notice has yet been taken of the fact that while meaning consists of suggestive power, there is never a guarantee that the absent thing suggested can actually be experienced if the suggestion is followed. Smoke suggests fire, but smoke may be present without any real fire to be discovered. Meanings do sometimes mislead us, and this fact must be taken into account in order to define knowing. We do not want deliberately to increase a thing's meaning if the additional meaning turns out to be misleading. Instead we want useful increases in meaning that consistently resolve doubtful situations, and for Dewey knowing is the process of finding them. To find such useful increases of meaning, we must test proposed new meanings by experimentally following up on the suggestions they provide. Successful new meanings of things, by bringing us to our goals, are thereby verified.

> If we exclude acting upon the idea, no conceivable amount or kind of intellectualistic procedure can confirm or refute an idea, or throw any light upon its validity. How does the nonpragmatic view consider that verification takes place? Does it suppose that we first look a long while at the facts and then a long time at the idea, until by some magical process the degree and kind of their agreement become visible? Unless there is some such conception as this, what conception of agreement is possible except the experimental or practical one? And if it be admitted that verification involves action, how can that action be relevant to the truth of an idea, unless the idea is itself is already relevant to action? (*MW* 4: 85)

Since knowing comes into existence when things are reconstructed by reflective thinking with new meaning and then verified as capable of directing us to our goals, the "object of knowing" is even better termed as the "objective of knowing." When a known object is generated by the process of knowing, "... the object thus determined is an object of *knowledge* only because of the thinking which has preceded it.... In short, the object of knowledge in the strict sense is its objective; and this objective is not constituted till it is reached" (*MW* 10: 329). The objective of knowledge then is the reconstructed meaning of experienced things which will permit the restoration of unproblematic activity. Vast confusion is generated if it is assumed that for Dewey the objective of knowing was only the real object. Instead the objective is the achievement of our goal: the experienced resolution of the problem which created the need for inquiry. "Knowing" then refers to the intellectual process of problem resolution. Strictly speaking, for Dewey no knowing occurs when a person is engaged in unproblematic activity, using the meaningful objects in one's environment to attain goals.

Notice that for Dewey the objective is no particular existent; to speak of an object of knowledge takes the risk of creating an assumption that knowledge always has but a single existent as its aim. His rejection of the spectator theory of knowledge requires the replacement of the notion that knowledge aims at preexisting and independent things. Using the example of the perceived star again, only after inference has done its work we are able to experience the seen star as an extremely distant, hot, and immense object which released its seen light a long time ago. Such an experience is the resolution of many problems; for example, why spectrographs of different stars reveal such disparate frequency patterns. Only if *both* stars and the seen light from them were altered from their basic meanings could spectrographs *both* be understood as providing information about the star's surface temperature and about the radiation energies comprising the seen light. Through the active manipulation of seen light using a prism, science has reconstructed both the star and the seen light since the meanings of both are dramatically altered by the process of theorizing. The general point is that "knowing" must denote *all* of the altered meanings of those things involved in the inquiry. Specifically it is not the star which is known better by science's investigations, but the entire system of natural things (from star to light to visible perception) that is involved. To select out arbitrarily one of the things involved for special status as "the object" of knowledge generates all the epistemological puzzles and mysteries explored in the previous section.

Critics might admit all this, yet still ask after the status of the theorizing. How can this too be part of the natural world? Dewey's reply declares that when knowing does occur, its processes are conducted in experience and hence in nature. Knowing is a natural event among any and all other natural events with its own distinctive natural traits. The epistemological problem of figuring out how one's internal mental information and inferences can be used to justify belief in a world "out there" completely disappears from view.[44] Epistemological problems remain, of course, for the empiricist, but they can at least be tackled by empirical methods instead of metaphysical systems. In Dewey's epistemology no lingering psychological dogmas, now parading as metaphysical a priori truths, can withstand fresh empirical examination or be immune from paradox and mystery.

Critics may also ask how Dewey can prove naive realism's truth using his theory of knowledge, but such a question only displays an ignorance of the proper roles for nature and knowledge. There is no Archimedean point, no Cartesian premise, from which to derive any of his philosophical theses. In the above example of stars and perceptions of them, knowledge is a matter of finding how both hang together, not how knowledge of one can be established by assuming knowledge of the other. So too does Dewey's naive realism and epistemology hang together. In Dewey's system epistemology and logic and psychology would accordingly overlap; philosophers doing logic would study and improve successful methods of practical thinking about natural existences across the natural and social sciences. Divisions of labor within this enterprise are efficient and expected, but philosophy has for too long been artificially chopped up into fields with proponents wrongly believing that their materials, methods, and purposes have nothing essential to do with the others. It is not regrettable that Dewey's empiricist epistemology is greeted with cries of "psychologism!" or "behaviorism!" or "scientism!" Such complaints are only signals that the lessons of Dewey's philosophy remain relevant and potentially useful. Transcendental realism, like transcendental idealism, could never help an engineer design a stable building, help a scientist design an experiment to test a theory, or help a philosopher design an explanation of the advantages of logical inference over faith in authority.

Instrumentalist Naturalism

As we have seen, some Dewey commentators claim that his metaphysics concerns existence and not merely (or not at all) experience. These efforts, as far as I can tell, receive inspiration from two considerations. First, it is possible to focus exclusively on Dewey's own descriptions of experience as organism-environment interactions (or, late in his career, transactions). Second, it is possible to see in a metaphysics only of experience a deleterious abdication of naturalistic philosophy to idealism. One can defend Dewey's metaphysics of experience by arguing for three theses: (1) Dewey's naturalistic metaphysics is a philosophical methodology, not an ontology; (2) Dewey's instrumentalism demands that experience be taken primarily as an absolute process enfolding all other terms as distinctions made within it; (3) Dewey's instrumentalism demands that experience be taken secondarily as an entity functionally situated in a wider context that gives its significance.

Empiricism

The first thesis is concerned with Dewey's notion of metaphysics as "the ground-map of criticism," where his critiques of other philosophies are based on metaphysical principles structuring his own philosophy. The second thesis is concerned with Dewey's philosophy of intelligence. Intelligence, as an aspect of active experience's growth, has two connotations: as intelligently active *experience* and as *intelligent* active experience. The complementary emphases flow from the two perspectives that philosophy must take upon intelligence. The first perspective considers intelligent experience as that which does all explaining while the second perspective considers intelligent experience as something to be explained. On the first perspective, philosophy sees that it is only a humanly intelligible philosophy and hence is modestly content with being just an aspect of intelligent experience, subject to the inherent limitations of any experience. On the second perspective, philosophy forgets its human limitations and temporarily transcends intelligence to survey its wider context and interactions with other things. Dewey's empiricism uses both perspectives without conflating them.

The basic connection among these three theses is that both thesis 2 and thesis 3 follow from thesis 1. Let us first consider the relationship between thesis 1 and 2. Experience in its primary sense must be the absolute because only this status as absolute squares with his methodological insistence on the first principle of philosophy: philosophy must only deal with experienced, and not transcendental, things. This declaration of "immediate empiricism" is a methodological principle, not an ontological principle, because Dewey's philosophy is designed to surmount the realist-idealist controversy over experience. The following quote exemplifies this design.

> Professor McGilvary inquires whether I am not, in any case, an idealist in the current sense of idealism—a sense which he states as follows: "the theory which regards all reality as embraced within experiences or within Experience".... What is meant by "embraced"? Is it to have an existential meaning?—that some thing called experience holds physically or metaphysically other things in its embrace? Then I do not accept the theory. Or is its meaning methodological? that philosophy, like science, proceeds intelligibly and fruitfully to verifiable results only by taking experienced, not transcendental, things, and by discussing them in the characters they empirically possess, not in the characters which, according to some a priori method, they ought to possess? In that case my answer might be affirmative, coupled with the admission that I know shamefully little about "all reality," since my empiricism is precisely that the only realities I do know anything about or ever shall know anything about are just experienced realities...." (*MW* 4: 154–155)

Dewey held that a consistent version of empiricism must obey thesis 1, whose loyalty to things as experienced is a methodological principle, not an ontological category. "The Concept of the Neutral in Recent Epistemology" (1917) reiterates this philosophical function of experience.

> [B]efore discussing whether a certain term, say "experience," has subjectivistic or objectivistic implications, we might have to consider whether, taken without specific qualifications, it was not rather a neutral term, a term to be used "without prejudice." Such neutral terms, understood to be aloof with reference to certain large antitheses which have had a great role in the history of thought, would certainly be a great aid in clearer discussion. . . . In contrast with this conceivable meaning of the term neutral, which might be called the logical, stands another which might be called the metaphysical or ontological, namely, that there is a certain sort of stuff which is, intrinsically, neutral. (MW 10: 49–50)

Dewey goes on to say that he cannot find any good, but only potential harm, in metaphysically neutral entities. Nothing should be permitted to stand ontologically aloof from the various ways that experienced things might be categorized as social, natural, individual, etc. A sound empiricism will take experience neutrally, without prejudice. This is Dewey's final verdict on James's neutral monism, but his radical empiricism as a broader thesis clearly impressed Dewey. In the introduction to the *Essays in Experimental Logic* the terms "experience" and "situation" are categorized as "infinity" words because by denoting everything they lack any determinate meaning themselves. The value of such terms, he notes, lies in their critical function, reminding one of greater context in which any reflective inquiry is always set (MW 10: 324). The ability of experience to serve this critical function, Dewey grew to understand, was impeded by modern philosophy's continued use of "experience" to denote only the individual perspective on things and not the things as they are. By 1951, when Dewey was ninety-one years old, his loyalty to the term "experience" had clearly waned but not his loyalty to what the term truly denotes.

> There was a period in modern philosophy when the appeal to "experience" was a thoroughly wholesome appeal to liberate philosophy from desiccated abstractions. But I failed to appreciate the fact that subsequent developments inside and outside of philosophy had corrupted and destroyed the wholesomeness of the appeal—that "experience" had become effectively identified with experiencing in the sense of the psychological, and the psychological had become established as that which is intrinsically psychical, mental, private. My insistence that "experience" also designates what is experienced was a mere ideological thundering in the Index for it ignored the ironical

twist which made this use of "experience" strange and incomprehensible. (*LW* 1: 362)

Dewey's efforts to revive an empiricism fully liberated from the metaphysically dualistic psychology of the eighteenth and nineteenth centuries had, in his own estimation, achieved but limited success. Without a grasp of his empiricism, his critics could hardly understand his naturalism, and least of all his instrumentalism. Instrumentalism requires a naturalistic context, which in turn requires an empiricist philosophy.

The need of instrumentalism for a naturalistic context can be discerned in the fact that thesis 3 also follows from thesis 1. The notion of experience as transaction cannot be primary because such primacy will not square with the first methodological principle. This is so because when we understand experience as a transaction between organism and environment, we are providing "experience" with a meaning only through the terms "organism" and "environment," both of which must already have sufficient meaning on their own. Could Dewey countenance the notion that these terms, noble as they are, could have sufficient meaning apart from experience? This route only erects "organism" and "environment" into things-in-themselves. The avoidance of this reduction replies that Dewey never supposed that we could have intelligible meanings of "organism" and "environment" except by way of the experiences of organisms and environments. Therefore the transactional understanding of experience must be offering a three-term organic relation in which "organism," "environment," and "experience" each has a meaning only through the others. Furthermore the fundamental origin of all their meanings must lie in experience and not in "organism" or "environment." This result raises a strange issue: how can experience serve as the source of the meaning of "organism" and "environment" and yet receive a fruitful increase in meaning by being set in this three-term relation? How could "experience" increase in meaning by mere give and take? Is Dewey offering a circular process of philosophical investigation in which we learn about experience by investigating its *relations* with other things that in turn can only receive *their* meaning from experience?

The relief from this conundrum comes by realizing that any informative study of experience as transaction comes from inquiry, in which no terms are assumed to have fixed and final meaning but must receive their meaning in the course of inquiry. Any understanding of transactional experience is the result of inquiry, and since inquiry is always set in a wider context to give it an origin and a conclusion, that wider context must be absolute experience. Absolute experience and transactional experience do not have the same meaning in Dewey's philosophy. Absolute experience is the placeholder for Dewey's ultimate methodological commitment to empiricism. Transactional experience stands for the study of life's intelligent activities as they take place in nature's wider context.

The study of life and conduct occurs within its proper setting, that of absolute empiricism, from which the terms "organism," "environment," and "transactional experience" receive meaning. In this second, naturalistic setting, the study of intelligent conduct can proceed—intelligent experience is thus a kind of experience which can be studied in its natural context. As reflective inquiry is an aspect of intelligent conduct, reflective experience can be studied in its wider context of intelligent conduct. Furthermore as logical inference and judgment is an aspect of reflective experience, logical experience can be studied in its wider context of reflective experience. Absolute experience, intelligent experience, reflective experience, logical experience—there are at least four notions of experience (and many more, such as aesthetic or moral experience) operating in Dewey's philosophy.

Let me make one last argument defending Dewey's metaphysics of experience over his metaphysics of existence. If, as the defenders of existence metaphysics hold, Dewey attempted an inquiry into traits of existence and not merely the traits of experience, then a dilemma arises. Either inquiry into existence is identical to inquiry into existence as experienced (in which case the alleged distinction evaporates), or inquiry into existence is not identical to inquiry into existence as experienced (in which case one would be attempting to inquire into things as they are, apart from how they are experienced). If the second horn of the dilemma is chosen, then defenders of existence metaphysics could never receive Dewey's approval, trapped as they are into chasing the elusive thing-in-itself.

Dewey does indeed offer a philosophical inquiry into the context of transactional experience, and there treats experience as a product of organism-environment transaction. But transactional experience is not the same as absolute experience. The defenders of existence metaphysics inverted their priority and wrongly elevated Dewey's naturalistic stance on experience to the highest status of philosophical methodology. To be a naturalist is not the same thing as being an empiricist. Although Dewey believed that the unbiased empirical study of experience would supply the justification for naturalism, only empiricism (the primary methodological principle) can supply naturalism its proper context. When Dewey describes experience as having a particular location in time and space and talks about stretches of geological time before any experience existed on the earth, he is using "experience" only in its transactional sense. To suppose that he is talking about absolute experience is to think falsely that Dewey is offering us a transcendental story about goings-on beyond the range of any possible human experience. No doubt I could be reminded that Dewey's principle of continuity forestalls any such thing-in-itself story since he held that experience and nature are continuous. This is a just and timely reminder; his principle of continuity does not describe a trait of absolute experience, but only a trait of transactional experience and thus is only designed to operate on the level of naturalism.

Despite appearances I am not eager to discover "two Deweys" or multiple Deweys who could not agree on the proper use of the term "experience." The four (or more) levels of experience operating in his philosophy account for his metaphysical principles and their interrelationships. We have already looked at his primary principle of empiricism, that philosophy can only deal with things as they are experienced. As Dewey says himself, no other principle can be deduced from this. However, as a methodological principle, the admonishment to go directly to experience can result in the establishment of additional philosophical principles and the discernment of the traits of existence/experience. Appropriate examples of a principle/trait belonging to the absolute experience level is that of growth and evolution, and of focus and fringe. On this hypothesis of four levels of experience, any careful approach to Dewey's metaphysics should appreciate that a principle or trait must be assigned to its proper level.

Empirical Naturalism

Dewey recognizes that there are levels of experience to be dealt with by philosophy; the assumption that only one can be discussed leads to foundationalism or reductionism. In "Nature and Experience" (1940) Dewey describes how philosophy should view the relationship between the philosophical conceptions of experience and nature.

> There is a circularity in the position taken regarding the connection of experience and nature. Upon one side, analysis and interpretation of nature is made dependent upon the conclusions of the natural sciences, especially upon biology, but upon a biology that is itself dependent upon physics and chemistry. But when I say "dependent" I mean that the intellectual instrumentalities, the organs, for understanding the new and distinctive material of experienced objects are provided by the natural sciences. I do not mean that the material of experienced things qua experienced must be translated into the terms of the material of the physical sciences; that view leads to a naturalism which denies distinctive significance to experience, thereby ending in the identification of naturalism with mechanistic materialism. The other aspect of the circle is found in the fact that it is held that experience itself, even ordinary gross macroscopic experience, contains the materials and the processes and operations which, when they are rightly laid hold of and used, lead to the methods and conclusions of the natural sciences; namely, to the very conclusions that provide the means for forming a theory of experience. That this circle exists is not so much admitted as claimed. It is also claimed that the circle is not vicious; for instead of being logical it is existential and historic. That is to say, if we look at human history

and especially at the historic development of the natural sciences, we
find progress made from a crude experience in which beliefs about
nature and natural events were very different from those now scientifically authorized. At the same time we find the latter now enable
us to frame a theory of experience by which we can tell how this development out of gross experience into the highly refined conclusions of science has taken place. (*LW* 14: 142–143)

"Ordinary, gross, macroscopic experience" is, on the interpretation offered here, the absolute experience, while the "theory of experience" is the naturalistic trans-actional experience. Since the results of every successful inquiry ultimately must enrich absolute experience, causing it to grow in width and depth, it should be expected that successful inquiry into transactional experience would have a tremendous bearing on absolute experience.[45] The issue of logical circularity does not apply to the relationship between absolute and transactional experience since this relationship is not a matter of deductive logic and there is no effort to make absolute experience the ultimate premise of a Cartesian hierarchy.

The most important principle operating on the naturalistic, transactional level of experience is the principle of continuity. This principle is just the de-mand for the organic perspective on reality that played such a crucial role in Dewey's early idealism. In his later works he came to rely on this principle quite heavily, as critic after critic took Dewey's use of "experience" to mean subjective mental states ontologically cut off from physical reality and only capable of try-ing to represent real things. Critics were thus prevented from understanding his philosophy of intelligent conduct since his theory demanded that conduct be treated as just a natural event standing in natural relations to other natural things. Without the principle of continuity, there could be no biological or be-havioral study of intelligence, knowing, and thought.[46] The continuity of experi-ence with nature is the foundation for understanding experience and all of its factors as natural events occurring together with other natural events.

If biological development be accepted, the subject of experience is at
least an animal, continuous with other organic forms in a process of
more complex organization. An animal in turn is at least continuous
with chemico-physical processes which, in living things, are so organized as really to constitute the activities of life with all their defining traits. And experience is not identical with brain action; it is the
entire organic agent-patient in all its interaction with the environment, natural and social. (*MW* 10: 26)

Experience is the result, the sign, and the reward of that interaction of
organism and environment which, when it is carried to the full, is a
transformation of interaction into participation and communication.

> ... [E]very experience is the result of interaction between a live creature and some aspect of the world in which he lives.(*LW* 10: 28, 50)

> An experience is always what it is because of a transaction taking place between an individual and what, at the time, constitutes his environment ... (*LW* 13: 25)

Dewey's empirical naturalism is the express repudiation of transcendentalism's attempts to reduce experience to the very limited realm of the mental or subjective, to be shunted aside as irrelevant whenever interest is taken in the real nature of the universe. Such interest can be satisfied, of course, only if one can form a more robust conception of that nature than the dubious notion of the bare thing-in-itself. If human experience by definition cannot supply that idea, the transcendentalist must claim that this idea has some nonexperiential origin, like reason. But what is reason, Dewey asked, but the inferential aspect of things in intelligent human experience? Transcendentalists will have nothing to do with a reason rendered subject to so frail and shabby a thing as experience, however, since experience is temporary, limited, subjective, partial, and fallible, just like the individual human beings which produce it. The vista of the whole is the aim of reason; the perspective of the fragmentary is the aim of experience. Dewey agrees that human experience suffers from much fragmentation and uncertainty. However, this experience is all we have, and only it, not some transcendently ideal existence, contains the resources of intelligence to reduce fragmentation and uncertainty.

In response to Santayana's accusation that Dewey's naturalism is halfhearted because it permits experience to pass judgment on the whole of nature,[47] Dewey replied that Santayana's naturalism is irrelevant and contradictory. To ask after a nature that lacks any perspective, any locality, any specificity, is to chase shadows.

> But there are an indefinite multitude of heres, nows, and perspectives. As many as there are existences. To swallow them up in one all-embracing substance is, moreover, to make the latter unknowable; it is the logical premise of a complete agnosticism. But such an embrace also makes substance inconceivable, for it leaves nothing for it to absorb or substantiate. (*LW* 3: 80)

An Empiricist Epistemology

Dewey's instrumentalism, like pragmatism in general, has historically been corrupted by other schools of philosophy. The imposition of their own notions of experience, thought, and mind not only obscured Dewey's own thought, but

The Reconstruction of Epistemology

substituted an imposter in its place. Circumstances in post-1940 Anglo-American philosophy, led largely by the rise of logical and positivistic empiricisms, have caused instrumentalism to be treated as just a kind of simplistic positivism or verificationism. The principles of Dewey's instrumentalism, listed below, serve to refute these prevalent interpretations. In brief, instrumentalism repudiates the nominalistic and subjectivistic view of experience presupposed by positivism. There are obvious common sympathies toward thought's subservience to experience and common antipathies against transcendentalism, but instrumentalism's functionalist and naturalist approach to intelligence parts company with positivism. With respect to verificationism, Dewey's instrumentalism also abjures transcendentalism but does not try to reduce reality to that which can be humanly verified. Instrumentalism's grounding in empiricism finds that experience always outruns human knowledge, and meaning accordingly extends further than just those logical meanings developed in reflective thought.[47] The principles of instrumentalism are as follows:

1. It is impossible to explain how meaning as a totality exists. By the nature of explanation, any explanation can only proceed from meaningful things to other meaningful things.

2. Explanations how experience increases in meaning must refer only to previously meaningful experience or future meaningful experience. No philosophical use can be made of anything which could exist beyond the reach of meaningful experience.

3. Intelligence is the ability to use meaningful things as means to further one's activities.

4. Reflective inquiry is that aspect of intelligence that increases the meanings in experience in order to resolve problematic situations.

5. Inquiry alters the meanings of things in experience, and since any notion of a thing apart from its meaning is impossible, inquiry really alters the existence of things in experience.

6. Inquiry uses ideals/rules/laws to select out present meanings and impose new meanings on things.

7. The data, those present meaningful things relevant to the inquiry, are created and altered in the course of inquiry to create the known object.

8. Inquiry only alters the problematic features of experience; those things which do not alter are called "facts" or the "real" while those things in the process of destruction/creation are called "ideas" or the "mental." This implies that the data are, for the purposes of inquiry, mental and not physically real.

9. The conclusion of the inference phase of inquiry is a practical judgment recommending that a particular action ought to be done. This judgment is a hypothetical proposal of new meaning(s) of thing(s), the new thing(s), to be followed out. The new thing(s) is (are) called the "object" of the knowing proposed by this inquiry.

10. Action on the practical judgment is a testing of the new meanings/things (the new object of knowing) hypothetically established by inquiry, to see if the inquiry's problem is solved. This testing is also an indirect test of the ideals/rules/laws used in the inquiry.

11. If the proposed action solves the inquiry's problem, the practical judgment is pronounced to be "verified." The new things are pronounced as "known" and are immediately/naively experienced as real, while the things destroyed in the inquiry are dismissed as false and unreal.

12. The term "truth" refers to the collection of truths. A "truth" denotes an object known through inquiry. Indirectly it can also be used to denote those ideals/rules/laws which have so far proven their usefulness in successful inquiries. In later works Dewey uses "warrantedly assertible" for "known," and his use of "truth" adjusts accordingly.

13. Inquiry always takes place in the wider context of settled, stable, experienced reality, which supplies the stimulus to inquiry and the testing of inquiry's results.

14. Inquiry results in the active alteration of things, and knowledge must require changes to reality. Specifically the object as known is created by the inquiry process. Knowledge does not alter the known object, but rather the materials used in inquiry to create the object.

15. Reality as such does not depend on thought/ideas/knowledge for its existence. Only known objects, while just as real as not-known objects, are created by thought. After their creation by thought and

The Reconstruction of Epistemology

verification by experience, their status as known objects drops away, and they are directly and immediately experienced as meaningful real things during habitual activity.

16. Known objects do not, and could never, exhaust the contents of reality. This implies that while all known objects are meaningful things, not all meaningful things are known objects.

17. The ability of relatively meaningful things to outnumber known objects is just another sign of experience's constant growth. Intelligence can only try to take advantage of the relative stabilities in experience to practically deal with the instabilities.

18. Intelligence and all of its aspects are just as naturally occurring as any natural event and can be reflectively and scientifically studied like any other natural event. "Epistemology" should stand for the study of knowings in their natural contexts, and "logic" should stand for the scientific inquiry into the improvement of inquiry's reasoning processes.

Appendix:
Chronology of Selected Dewey Writings

References are given by series, volume number and page to the *Works of John Dewey* where the series is indicated as follows.

EW   John Dewey, *The Early Works, 1882–1898*, in five volumes, 1969–1972
MW   John Dewey, *The Middle Works, 1899–1924*, in fifteen volumes, 1976–1983
LW   John Dewey, *The Later Works, 1925–1953*, in seventeen volumes, 1981–1990

Other abbreviations are as follows.

JH   *Johns Hopkins University Circulars*, by number
ID   *The Influence of Darwin on Philosophy and Other Essays*, 1910
EE   *Essays in Experimental Logic*, 1916
PC   *Philosophy and Civilization*, 1931

Apr 1882	EW 1:	3–8	"The Metaphysical Assumptions of Materialism"
Jul 1882		9–18	"The Pantheism of Spinoza"
Jan 1883		19–33	"Knowledge and the Relativity of Feeling"
Apr 1883	JH 22:	94	"Hegel and the Theory of Categories" (announcement)
Nov 1883	JH 28:	46	"The Psychology of Consciousness" (announcement)
Dec 1883		46	"Delboeuf on Living and Dead Matter" (announcement)
Apr 1884	EW 1:	34–47	"Kant and Philosophic Method"
Sep 1884		48–60	"The New Psychology"
Nov 1884		61–63	"The Obligation to Knowledge of God"
1885			*Selections from the Writings of George MacDonald, or, Helps for Weary Souls* (edited by Dewey)
Jan 1886		122–143	"The Psychological Standpoint"
Apr 1886		144–167	"Psychology as Philosophical Method"

Apr 1886		93–115	"Soul and Body"
Apr 1886		116–121	"Inventory of Philosophy Taught in American Colleges"
Nov 1886	EW 2:		*Psychology* (2d ed. 1889, 3rd ed. 1891)
Jan 1887	EW 1:	168–175	"'Illusory Psychology'"
Jun 1887		194–204	"Review of G. T. Ladd, *Elements of Physiological Psychology*"
Jun 1887		205–226	"Ethics and Physical Science"
Jul 1887		176–193	"Knowledge as Idealization"
1888		227–249	"The Ethics of Democracy"
May 1888		251–435	*Leibniz's New Essays Concerning the Human Understanding: A Critical Exposition*
1889	EW 3:	3–13	"The Late Professor Morris"
Jan 1889	EW 2		*Psychology* (2d edition)
Apr 1889	EW 3:	14–35	"The Philosophy of Thomas Hill Green"
Jan 1890		56–74	"On Some Current Conceptions of the Term 'Self'"
Jan 1890		75–82	"Is Logic a Dualistic Science?"
Mar 1890		180–184	"Review of E. Caird, *The Critical Philosophy of Immanuel Kant*"
Apr 1890		83–89	"The Logic of Verification"
Jan 1891		93–109	"Moral Theory and Practice"
Spr 1891		237–388	*Outlines of a Critical Theory of Ethics*
Aug 1891	EW 2:		*Psychology* (3rd edition)
Oct 1891	EW 3:	125–141	"The Present Position of Logical Theory"
Nov 1891		142–146	"How Do Concepts Arise from Percepts?"
Jan 1892		148–154	"The Scholastic and the Speculator"
Feb 1892		211–235	"Introduction to Philosophy: Syllabus"
Oct 1892	LW 17:	153–160	"Introduction to Philosophy"
Nov 1892	EW 3:	155–173	"Green's Theory of the Moral Motive"
1893	EW 4:	3–10	"Christianity and Democracy"
Jan 1893	EW 4:	189–197	"Review of B. Bosanquet, *A History of Aesthetic*"

Apr 1893	19–36	"The Superstition of Necessity"
Apr 1893	37–41	"Anthropology and Law"
Nov 1893	42–53	"Self-Realization as the Moral Ideal"
May 1894	91–95	"The Ego as Cause"
Jun 1894	96–105	"Reconstruction"
Dec 1894	219–362	*The Study of Ethics: A Syllabus.*
1895		*The Psychology of Number,* with J. A. McLellan
1895	EW 5: 111–150	"Interest as Related to Will" (rev. ed. 1899)
Mar 1896	25–33	"The Metaphysical Method in Ethics"
Mar 1896	350–354	"Review of J. Watson, *Hedonistic Theories from Aristippus to Spencer*"
Jul 1896	96–110	"The Reflex Arc Concept in Psychology" (*PC*)
1897	3–24	"The Significance of the Problem of Knowledge" (*ID*)
Jan 1897	84–95	"My Pedagogic Creed"
Jan 1897	151–163	"The Psychology of Effort"
Apr 1898	34–53	"Evolution and Ethics"
Jul 1898	385–399	"Review of J. M. Baldwin, *Social and Ethical Interpretations in Mental Development*"
Sep 1898	402–422	"Review of Baldwin, *Social and Ethical Interpretations in Mental Development*"
Nov 1898	399–401	"Rejoinder to Baldwin's Reply"
Aug 1899	MW 1: 113–130	"Psychology and Philosophic Method" (*ID*: "'Consciousness' and Experience")
May 1900	241–256	"Review of J. Royce, *The World and the Individual,* First Series"
Sep 1900	151–174	"Some Stages of Logical Thought" (*EE*)
1902	MW 2: 139–269	"Contributions to *Dictionary of Philosophy and Psychology*"
Mar 1902	3–20	"The Evolutionary Method as Applied to Morality I: Its Scientific Necessity"
May 1902	39–52	"The Interpretation of the Savage Mind" (*PC*)

Jul 1902	20–38	"The Evolutionary Method as Applied to Morality II: Its Significance for Conduct"
Jul 1902	120–137	"Review of J. Royce, *The World and the Individual*, Second Series"
1903	293–375	*Studies in Logical Theory*, Chapters 1–4 (*EE*)
1903	MW 3: 3–39	"Logical Conditions of a Scientific Treatment of Morality"
Feb 1904	62–68	"Notes upon Logical Topics I: A Classification of Contemporary Tendencies"
Mar 1904	68–72	"Notes upon Logical Topics II: The Meanings of the Term 'Idea'"
Jun 1905	153–157	"The Realism of Pragmatism"
Jul 1905	158–167	"The Postulate of Immediate Empiricism" (*ID*)
Oct 1905	168–170	"Immediate Empiricism"
Nov 1905	171–177	"The Knowledge Experience and Its Relationships"
Dec 1905	178–183	"The Knowledge Experience Again"
Jan 1906	79–82	"The Terms 'Conscious' and 'Consciousness'"
Mar 1906	83–100	"Beliefs and Realities" (*ID*: "Beliefs and Existences")
May 1906	101–106	"Reality as Experience"
Jul 1906	107–127	"The Experimental Theory of Knowledge" (*ID*)
Sep 1906	128–144	"Experience and Objective Idealism" (*ID*)
Apr 1907	MW 4: 78–82	"The Control of Ideas by Facts I" (*EE*)
May 1907	82–84	"The Control of Ideas by Facts II" (*EE*)
Jun 1907	84–90	"The Control of Ideas by Facts III, IV" (*EE*)
Jul 1907	50–75	"Reality and the Criterion for the Truth of Ideas" (*ID*: "The Intellectualist Criterion for Truth")
Jul 1907	120–124	"Pure Experience and Reality: A Disclaimer"
1908	31–49	"Ethics" (*ID*: "Intelligence and Morals")

1908		"Does Reality Possess Practical Character?" (*PC*)
1908	*MW* 5	*Ethics*, with James H. Tufts. (2d ed. 1932, *LW* 7)
Feb 1908	*MW* 4: 98–115	"What Does Pragmatism Means by Practical?" (*EE*: What Pragmatism Means by Practical")
Jul 1908	91–97	"The Logical Character of Ideas" (*EE*)
Dec 1908	178–191	"The Bearings of Pragmatism upon Education"
1909	*LW* 17: 361–373	"Knowledge and Existence"
1909	*MW* 4: 251–263	"The Pragmatic Movement of Contemporary Thought: A Syllabus"
Jan 1909	146–155	"Objects, Data, and Existences: A Reply to Professor McGilvary"
Mar 1909	116–117	"Discussion on Realism and Idealism"
Apr 1909	118–119	"Discussion on the 'Concept of a Sensation'"
Jul 1909	3–14	"Darwin's Influence upon Philosophy" (*ID:* "The Influence of Darwinism on Philosophy")
Jul 1909	15–30	"Is Nature Good? A Conversation" (*ID:* "Nature and Its Good: A Conversation")
Aug 1909	76–77	"The Dilemma of the Intellectualist Theory of Truth"
Jan 1910	*MW* 6: 69–79	"Science as Subject-Matter and as Method"
Mar 1910	177–356	*How We Think*. (2d ed. 1933, *LW* 8: 105–352)
Apr 1910		*The Influence of Darwin on Philosophy and Other Essays in Contemporary Thought.*
Apr 1910	*LW* 17: 39–41	"Preface" (*ID*)
Apr 1910	*MW* 6: 3–11	"A Short Catechism Concerning Truth" (*ID*)
Mar 1910	80–85	"Valid Knowledge and the 'Subjectivity of Experience'"
Sep 1910	86–90	"Some Implications of Anti-Intellectualism"
Sep 1910	138–142	"The Short-Cut to Realism Examined"

CHRONOLOGY OF SELECTED DEWEY WRITINGS

Feb 1911		143–145	"Rejoinder to Dr. Spaulding"
Feb 1911		12–68	"The Problem of Truth"
Jul 1911		103–111	"Brief Studies in Realism I: Naive Realism vs. Presentative Realism" (*EE*)
Sep 1911		111–122	"Brief Studies in Realism II: Epistemological Realism" (*EE*)
Oct 1911		146–152	"Joint Discussion with Articles of Agreement and Disagreement: Professor Dewey and Dr. Spaulding"
Jan 1912	*MW* 7:	64–78	"A Reply to Professor Royce's Critique of Instrumentalism"
Jan 1912	*MW* 4:	143–145	"A Reply to Professor McGilvary's Questions"
Jun 1912	*MW* 7:	142–148	"Review of W. James, *Essays in Radical Empiricism*"
Sep 1912		79–84	"In Response to Professor McGilvary"
Nov 1912		3–30	"Perception and Organic Action" (*PC*)
Nov 1912		31–43	"What Are States of Mind?"
ca. 1913	*LW* 17:	415–421	"Brief Studies in Realism III"
Sep 1914	*MW* 7:	47–55	"Psychological Doctrine and Philosophical Teaching"
Jun 1915	*MW* 8:	3–13	"The Subject-Matter of Metaphysical Inquiry"
Jul 1915		83–97	"The Existence of the World as a Problem" (*EE*: "The Existence of the World as a Logical Problem")
Sep 1915		14–82	"The Logic of Judgments of Practice" (*EE*)
1916	*MW* 9		*Democracy and Education*
Mar 1916	*MW* 10:	89–97	"Logical Objects"
Jun 1916		319–365	"Introduction" to *Essays in Experimental Logic*
Dec 1916		71–78	"The Pragmatism of Peirce"
1917		3–48	"The Need for a Recovery of Philosophy"
Apr 1917		98–108	"Concerning Novelties in Logic: A Reply to Mr. Robinson"
Mar 1917		49–52	"The Concept of the Neutral in Recent Epistemology"
Jul 1917		53–63	"The Need for Social Psychology"
Aug 1917		64–66	"Duality and Dualism"

CHRONOLOGY OF SELECTED DEWEY WRITINGS

Jan 1918	MW 11: 10–17	"Concerning Alleged Immediate Knowledge of Mind"
May 1918	3–9	"The Objects of Valuation"
1920	MW 12: 205–250	"Three Contemporary Philosophers: William James, Henri Bergson, and Bertrand Russell"
1920	77–204	*Reconstruction in Philosophy.*
Jan 1922	MW 13: 61–71	"An Analysis of Reflective Thought"
Feb 1922	MW 14:	*Human Nature and Conduct.*
Jun 1922	MW 13: 40–60	"Realism without Monism or Dualism"
Jul 1922	3–28	"Valuation and Experimental Knowledge"
Oct 1922	29–39	"Knowledge and Speech Reaction"
Mar 1923	MW 15: 14–19	"Tradition, Metaphysics, and Morals"
Nov 1923	20–26	"Values, Liking, and Thought"
Apr 1924	27–41	"Some Comments on Philosophical Discussion"
1925	LW 1: 3–326	*Experience and Nature* (2d ed., 1929)
1925	LW 2: 3–21	"The Development of American Pragmatism" (*PC*)
Feb 1925	69–77	"The Meaning of Value"
Oct 1925	44–54	"A Naturalistic Theory of Sense-Perception" (*PC*)
Jan 1926	141–157	"Substance, Power and Quality in Locke"
May 1926	62–68	"Events and the Future"
1927	235–372	*The Public and Its Problems*
Jan 1927	LW 3: 3–10	"The Role of Philosophy in the History of Civilization" (*PC:* "Philosophy and Civilization")
Feb 1927	73–81	"Half-Hearted Naturalism"
Aug 1927	55–72	"An Empirical Account of Experience" (*PC:* "Appearing and Appearance")
Apr 1928	41–54	"Social as a Category" (*PC:* "The Inclusive Philosophic Idea")
Jun 1928	82–91	"Meaning and Existence"
1929	LW 4	*The Quest For Certainty*

Dec 1929	LW 5: 197–202	"The Sphere of Application of the Excluded Middle"
1930	41–123	*Individualism, Old and New*
1930	147–160	"From Absolutism to Experimentalism"
1930	218–235	"Conduct and Experience" (*PC:* "Conduct and Experiences in Psychology")
Jan 1930	243–262	"Qualitative Thought"
May 1930	210–217	"In Reply to Some Criticisms"
1931	LW 6: 3–21	"Context and Thought"
1931		*Philosophy and Civilization*
1933	LW 8:	*How We Think*, 2d ed.
1934	LW 9: 1–58	*A Common Faith*
1934	LW 10	*Art as Experience*
1935	LW 11: 69–83	"An Empirical Survey of Empiricisms"
Dec 1935	86–94	"Peirce's Theory of Quality"
May 1936	95–104	"Characteristics and Characters: Kinds and Classes"
May 1936	105–114	"What Are Universals?"
1939	LW 12	*Logic: The Theory of Inquiry*
1939	LW 13: 189–253	"Theory of Valuation"
1939	LW 14: 3–90	"Experience, Knowledge and Value: A Rejoinder"
1940	98–114	"Time and Individuality"
Mar 1940	141–154	"Nature in Experience"
Mar 1941	168–188	"Propositions, Warranted Assertibility, and Truth"
Sept 1941	189–200	"The Objectivism-Subjectivism of Modern Philosophy"
1942	LW 15: 9–17	"William James as Empiricist"
Jan 1942	27–33	"How Is Mind to Be Known?"
Jan 1943	46–62	"Anti-Naturalism in Extremis"
June 1943	63–72	"Valuation Judgments and Immediate Quality"
Sept 1945	109–126	"Are Naturalists Materialists?"
Feb 1946	141–152	"Peirce's Theory of Linguistic Signs, Thought, and Meaning"
1949	LW 16: 1–294	*Knowing and the Known*, with Arthur F. Bentley

Notes

Introduction

1. Paul A. Schilpp, General Introduction, in *The Philosophy of John Dewey*, ed. Paul A. Schilpp (1939. 3d ed., La Salle, Ill.: Open Court, 1989), p. ix.
2. Sterling Lamprecht, "Review of *The Philosophy of John Dewey*," *Journal of Philosophy* 36 (December 1939): 691–695.
3. Dewey, "Experience, Knowledge, and Value: A Rejoinder," in *The Philosophy of John Dewey*, ed. Schilpp, pp. 565, 562 (*LW* 14: 49, 46).
4. Dewey, "From Absolutism to Experimentalism," in *Contemporary American Philosophy: Personal Statements,* ed. George P. Adams and William P. Montague (1930. Reprinted, New York: Russell and Russell, 1962), 2: 13–27 (*LW* 5: 147–160). Dewey's refusal is at *LW* 5: 155.

Chapter One: The Opportunity of Dewey's Early Philosophy

1. Arthur E. Murphy, "Dewey's Epistemology and Metaphysics" in *The Philosophy of John Dewey*, ed. Schilpp, p. 221.
2. Ibid., p. 223.
3. Sidney Hook, Introduction, in *Experience and Nature, LW* 1: vii–xxiii.
4. Ibid., p. xvii.
5. Ralph Sleeper, *The Necessity of Pragmatism: John Dewey's Conception of Philosophy* (New Haven: Yale University Press, 1986), p. 109. Sleeper is referring to George Santayana, "Dewey's Naturalistic Metaphysics," reprinted in *The Philosophy of John Dewey*, ed. Schilpp, pp. 243–261.
6. Hans Reichenbach, "Dewey's Theory of Science," in *The Philosophy of John Dewey,* ed. Schilpp, p. 173.
7. Stephen Pepper, "Some Questions on Dewey's Esthetics," in *The Philosophy of John Dewey*, ed. Schilpp, pp. 371–389.
8. Thomas Alexander, *John Dewey's Theory of Art, Experience, and Nature* (Albany: State University of New York Press, 1987), pp. 62–68.
9. John Herman Randall, Jr., "F. H. Bradley and the Working-out of Absolute Idealism" (1967), reprinted in *Philosophy after Darwin: Chapters for The Career of Philosophy, Volume 3, and Other Essays,* ed. Beth J. Singer (New York: Columbia University Press, 1977), p. 181.

10. Richard Bernstein, *John Dewey* (New York: Washington Square Press, 1966); John J. McDermott, Introduction, in *The Philosophy of John Dewey* (Chicago: University of Chicago Press, 1973), 1: xv–xxxiv.

11. John J. Stuhr, "Toward a Metaphysics of Experience" *Modern Schoolman* 57 (May 1980): 300–301. See also his "Reconstructing Metaphysics," *Metaphilosophy* 13 (July–October 1982): 290–300; "Dewey's Reconstruction of Metaphysics," *Transactions of the Charles S. Peirce Society* 28 (Spring 1992): 161–176; and *Genealogical Pragmatism: Philosophy, Experience, Community* (Albany: State University of New York Press, 1997), pp. 126–130.

12. Raymond D. Boisvert, *Dewey's Metaphysics* (New York: Fordham University Press, 1988), pp. 3–4. See also his "Dewey's Metaphysics: Ground-Map of the Prototypically Real" in *Reading Dewey: Interpretations for a Postmodern Generation*, ed. Larry Hickman (Bloomington: Indiana University Press, 1998), pp. 149–165; and *John Dewey: Rethinking Our Time* (Albany: State University of New York Press, 1998).

13. Alexander, *John Dewey's Theory of Art, Experience, and Nature*, p. 68.

14. Elizabeth Flower, "Dewey: Battling against Dualisms," chap. 14 of *A History of Philosophy in America* (New York: G. P. Putnam's Sons, 1977), pp. 811–887.

15. Ibid., p. 819.

16. Dewey, "What Does Pragmatism Mean by Practical?" *MW* 4: 404.

17. Richard Rorty, *Philosophy and the Mirror of Nature* (Princeton: Princeton University Press, 1979), p. 382. A recent critic of Rorty is John Stuhr, "Rorty as Elvis: Dewey's Reconstruction of Metaphysics," in *Genealogical Pragmatism: Philosophy, Experience, Community*, pp. 117–130.

18. See for example Michael Devitt, *Realism and Truth*, 2d ed. (Princeton: Princeton University Press, 1991), p. 128–131.

19. See Jennifer Welchman, *Dewey's Ethical Theory*. Ithaca, N.Y.: Cornell University Press, 1995.

20. "The Development of American Pragmatism" was first published as "Le Développement du pragmatisme américain," in *Revue Métaphysique* 29 (October–December 1922): 411–430. It was later published as "The Development of American Pragmatism" in *Studies in the History of Ideas*, by the Department of Philosophy of Columbia University (New York: Columbia University Press, 1925), 2: 353–377 (*LW* 2: 3–21). "From Absolutism to Experimentalism," supra note 5. "Biography of John Dewey," in *The Philosophy of John Dewey*, ed. Schilpp, pp. 3–45.

21. Dewey is likely referring to Thomas Huxley and W. J. Youmans, *Elements of Physiology and Hygiene*, rev. ed. (New York: American Book Company, 1873). This text is the American edition of Huxley's *Lessons in Elementary Physiology*, 6th ed. (London: Macmillan, 1872).

22. Morton White, *The Origin of Dewey's Instrumentalism* (New York: Columbia University Press, 1943). Joseph Ratner, Foreword in *Philosophy, Psychology and Social Practice*, ed. Joseph Ratner (New York: G. P. Putnam's Sons, 1963), pp. 9–15. Lewis Hahn, "Dewey's Philosophy and Philosophic Method," in *Guide To The Works of John Dewey*, ed. Jo Ann Boydston (Carbondale and Edwardsville: Southern Illinois University Press, 1970), pp. 15–60. Neil Coughlan, *Young John Dewey: An Essay in American Intellectual History* (Chicago: University of Chicago Press, 1975). Bruce Kuklick, "John Dewey's Instrumentalism," chap. 17 of *Churchmen and Philosophers: From Jonathan Edwards to John*

Dewey (New Haven: Yale University Press, 1985), pp. 241–253. H. O. Mounce, "Dewey: Background and Philosophical Psychology," chap. 8 of *The Two Pragmatisms: From Peirce to Rorty* (London and New York: Routledge, 1997), pp. 126–143.

23. Hahn, "Dewey's Philosophy and Philosophic Method," p. 26.

24. Kuklick, "John Dewey's Instrumentalism," p. 248.

Chapter Two: Absolute Idealism

1. Sterling Lamprecht, "An Idealistic Source of Instrumentalist Logic," *Mind* 33 (October 1924): 415–427. F. C. S. Schiller, "Instrumentalism and Idealism," *Mind* 34 (January 1925): 75–79.

2. An earlier commentator on Dewey's philosophical career, R. F. Alfred Hoernlé, focuses solely upon pragmatism's antipathy to the vision of the universe offered by idealism. See his "Review of Dewey, *Essays in Experimental Logic*." *Philosophical Review* 26 (July 1917): 421–430.

3. See George Dykhuizen, *The Life and Mind of John Dewey* (Carbondale: Southern Illinois University Press, 1973), pp. 30–31.

4. Close examinations of Trendelenburg's philosophy are provided by the following texts: G. S. Morris, "Friedrich Adolf Trendelenburg," *New Englander* 32 (April 1874): 287–336, reprinted in Marc Jones, *George Sylvester Morris: His Philosophical Career and Theistic Idealism* (Philadelphia: David McKay, 1948), pp. 335–384; Gershon G. Rosenstock, *F. A. Trendelenburg: Forerunner to John Dewey* (Carbondale: Southern Illinois University Press, 1964); and Klaus C. Kohnke, "Friedrich Adolf Trendelenburg as Mediator between Idealism and Neo-Kantianism," chap. 1 of *The Rise of Neo-Kantianism* (Cambridge: Cambridge University Press, 1991), pp. 11–35.

5. Robert Harper, "Tables of American Doctorates in Psychology," *American Journal of Psychology* 62 (October 1949): 579–587.

6. The April 1882 "The Metaphysical Assumptions of Materialism" and the July 1882 "The Pantheism of Spinoza" were published in the only American philosophy journal then existing, the *Journal of Speculative Philosophy*. See Osamu Kurita, "John Dewey's Philosophical Frame of Reference in His First Three Articles," *Educational Theory* 21 (Summer 1971): 338–346.

7. *EW* 1: 19–33. Abstracted in the *Johns Hopkins University Circulars* 2 (1883): 54.

8. Bertrand Russell, *Our Knowledge of the External World as a Field for Scientific Method in Philosophy* (London: George Allen and Unwin; Chicago: Open Court, 1914), p. 75.

9. G. S. Morris, *British Thought and Thinkers* (Chicago: S. C. Griggs, 1880), p. 295.

10. Edward Caird, *A Critical Account of the Philosophy of Kant* (Glasgow: Maclehose, 1877), p. 499.

11. G. S. Morris, "Friedrich Adolf Trendelenburg," p. 349.

12. Morris, *British Thought and Thinkers*, p. 296.

13. Ibid., p. 349.

14. Ibid., p. 364.

15. Ibid., p. 365.

16. Ibid., p. 370.
17. Ibid., p. 376.
18. Caird, *A Critical Account of the Philosophy of Kant*, p. 371.
19. G. S. Morris, *Kant's Critique of Pure Reason: A Critical Exposition* (Chicago: S. C. Griggs, 1882), pp. 120–121. Scholarship on Kant since the neo-idealists' time has progressed considerably, largely avoiding Hegelian lenses to view his transcendental deduction. See for example Paul Guyer, *Kant and the Claims of Knowledge* (Cambridge: Cambridge University Press, 1987).
20. Ibid., p. 121.
21. Caird's translation from Kant's *Prolegomena*, in his *A Critical Account of the Philosophy of Kant*, pp. 201–202.
22. See G. W. F. Hegel, *Hegel's Logic*, part 1 of the *Encyclopedia*, 3d ed., trans. William Wallace (Oxford: Clarendon Press, 1975), p. 97–101; Edward Caird, *Hegel* (Edinburgh: Blackwood, 1883), pp. 160–164; Caird, *A Critical Account of the Philosophy of Kant*, pp. 614–619.
23. G. S. Morris, *Philosophy and Christianity* (New York: Robert Carter and Brothers, 1883), p. 53.
24. Hegel, *Logic*, pp. 147–152. On Hegelian dialectic, logic, and epistemology, the reader may make use of the following books: Charles Taylor, *Hegel* (Cambridge: Cambridge University Press, 1975), especially pp. 225–349; Joseph C. Flay, *Hegel's Quest for Certainty* (Albany: State University of New York Press, 1984); and Tom Rockmore, *Hegel's Circular Epistemology* (Bloomington: Indiana University Press, 1986).
25. Rockmore, pp. 152–154.
26. See for example Morris, *Philosophy and Christianity*, p. 41.
27. Morris, *Kant's Critique of Pure Reason*, p. 143.
28. Ibid., p. 107.
29. Ibid., p. 196.
30. Caird, *A Critical Account of the Philosophy of Kant*, pp. 349–350.
31. Ibid., p. 372.
32. Hegel, *Logic*, pp. 364–366.
33. This debt to Caird is recorded in Jane Dewey's "Biography of Dewey," in *The Philosophy of John Dewey*, ed. Schilpp, p. 22.
34. Caird, *A Critical Account of the Philosophy of Kant*, pp. 372–373.
35. Dorothy Ross, *G. Stanley Hall: The Psychologist as Prophet* (Chicago: University of Chicago Press, 1972), p. 146.
36. Dewey to Torrey, 17 November 1883, Torrey Papers. I examined a transcript of this letter at the Center for Dewey Studies, Southern Illinois University.
37. A. H. Murray, *The Philosophy of James Ward* (Cambridge: Cambridge University Press, 1937), pp. 2–6.
38. Emmanual Leroux, "James Ward's Doctrine of Experience," *Monist* 36 (January 1926): 78–84; also Rudolf Metz, "James Ward," in his *A Hundred Years of British Philosophy* (London: Allen and Unwin, 1950), p. 400.
39. See Ralph B. Perry, *The Life and Character of William James* (Boston: Little, Brown, 1935), pp. 58–59; John Passmore, *A Hundred Years of Philosophy*, rev. ed. (New York: Basic Books, 1957), p. 107n.

40. Shadworth Hodgson, *The Philosophy of Reflection* (London: Longmans, Green, 1878), 1: 101.

41. James Ward, "Psychological Principles I: The Standpoint of Psychology," *Mind* o.s. 8 (April 1883): 163.

42. Ibid., p. 163.

43. Ibid., p. 167.

44. James, *The Principles of Psychology* (1890. Cambridge: Harvard University Press, 1981), 1: 195.

45. J. E. Tiles, *Dewey* (London and New York: Routledge, 1988), p. 29.

46. T. H. Green, *Prolegomena to Ethics* (Oxford: Clarendon Press, 1883), p. 119.

47. Ward, "Psychological Principles I: The Standpoint of Psychology," p. 158.

48. Ibid., pp. 158–159.

49. Ibid., p. 159, 160, 168.

50. Morris, *Kant's Critique of Pure Reason*, pp. 124–132.

51. Green, *Prolegomena to Ethics*, pp. 76, 77.

52. For others see Arthur Balfour, "Green's Metaphysics of Knowledge," *Mind* o.s. 9 (January 1884): 77–81; also H. Calderwood, "Another View of Green's Last Work," *Mind* o.s. 10 (January 1885): 75–78.

53. Edward Caird, "Professor Green's Last Work," *Mind* o.s. 8 (October 1883): 544–561.

54. Passmore, *A Hundred Years of Philosophy*, pp. 55–56; Rudolf Metz, *A Hundred Years of British Philosophy* (New York: Macmillan, 1950), pp. 272–273; Geoffrey Thomas, *The Moral Philosophy of T. H. Green* (Oxford: Clarendon Press, 1987), pp. 40–41.

55. Shadworth Hodgson, "The Metaphysical Method in Philosophy," *Mind* o.s. 9 (January 1884): 50–53.

56. Ibid., p. 55.

57. Benjamin Dumville, "The Standpoint of Psychology," *Proceedings of the Aristotelian Society* 11 (1911): 41–79; Hoernlé, "Review of Dewey, *Essays in Experimental Logic.*" Hoernlé relates that as a student he discovered these early articles revealing Dewey to be "the heaven-sent champion of absolute idealism."

58. As quoted in Perry, *The Life and Character of William James*, 1: 641.

59. Ibid., 2: 38.

60. On the Cairds see Meditatio Laici, "A School of Idealism," in *Philosophical Essays Presented to John Watson* (Kingston, Ont.: Queen's University Press, 1922. Reprinted, Freeport, N.Y.: Books for Libraries Press, 1971), pp. 1–36; and Hiralal Haldar, *Neo-Hegelianism* (London: Heath Cranton, 1927).

61. Caird, *Hegel*, p. 128, 129.

62. The distinct likelihood that Morris's own growth into the ranks of the idealists was materially aided by the Cairds is supported by Marc E. Jones, *George Sylvester Morris*, pp. 209–210.

63. John Caird, *Introduction to the Philosophy of Religion* (Glasgow: Maclehose, 1880). See Steven Rockefeller, *John Dewey: Religious Faith and Democratic Humanism* (New York: Columbia University Press, 1991), pp. 110–112.

64. See especially *Outlines of a Critical Theory of Ethics* (1891), *EW* 3: 237–388.

65. This also explains Dewey's initial lack of interest in Peirce's lectures at Johns Hopkins, which Dewey then could only see as excessively formal. See Dykhuizen, *The Life and Mind of John Dewey*, pp. 30–31.

66. Seth, later Andrew Seth Pringle-Pattison, infamously charged Hegelianism with wrongly extinguishing the individual self in *Hegelianism and Personality* (Edinburg: Blackwood, 1887). Dewey responded with "On Some Current Conceptions of the Term 'Self'" (1890), *EW* 3: 56–74.

67. See Dewey, "Review of John Watson, *Hedonistic Theories from Aristippus to Spencer*," *EW* 5: 350–354; also *The Study of Ethics* (1894), *EW* 4: 219–362. On Watson, see Leslie Armour and Elizabeth Trott, *The Faces of Reason: An Essay on Philosophy and Culture in English Canada, 1850–1950* (Waterloo, Ont.: Wilfred Laurier University Press, 1981), chapters 7 and 8.

Chapter Three: Wundtian Voluntarism

1. See Robert Westbrook, *John Dewey and American Democracy* (Ithaca, N.Y.: Cornell University Press, 1991), pp. 23–25; Steven Rockefeller, *John Dewey: Religious Faith and Democratic Humanism* (New York: Columbia University Press, 1991); Coughlan, *Young John Dewey*, p. 48; Robert Richards, "Materialism and Natural Events in Dewey's Developing Thought," *Journal of the History of Philosophy* 10 (January 1972): 56.

2. Morton G. White, *The Origin of Dewey's Instrumentalism* (New York: Columbia University Press, 1943), pp. 35–41; Hahn, "Dewey's Philosophy and Philosophic Method," pp. 19–20; Alexander, *John Dewey's Theory of Art, Experience, and Nature*, pp. 18, 25; James Collins, "How Dewey Became a Naturalist," in his *Three Paths in Philosophy* (Chicago: Henry Regnery, 1962), p. 190. The importance of organism and function in one of Dewey's articles prior to 1890 is noticed, without mentioning Wundt, by Andrew Reck, "The Influence of William James on John Dewey in Psychology," *Transactions of the Charles S. Peirce Society* 20 (Spring 1984): 87–118 (p. 89), and by William Sahakian, *History and Systems of Psychology* (New York: John Wiley and Sons, 1975), p. 359. On organicism in general, see D. C. Phillips, "Organicism in the Late Nineteenth and Early Twentieth Centuries," *Journal of the History of Ideas* 31 (July–September 1970): 413–432.

3. Alexander, *John Dewey's Theory of Art, Experience, and Nature*, pp. 41–42; Hahn, "Dewey's Philosophy and Philosophic Method," pp. 6–7; Sahakian, pp. 290, 357–358; Allen Smith, "Dewey's Transition Piece: the *Reflex Arc* Paper," *Tulane Studies in Philosophy* 22 (1973): 122–141; D.C. Phillips, "James, Dewey, and the Reflex Arc," *Journal of the History of Ideas* 32 (October–December 1971): 565–566; Claude Buxton, "American Functionalism," chapter 5 of *Points of View in the Modern History of Psychology*, ed. Claude Buxton (New York: Harcourt Brace Jovanovich, 1985), pp. 129–131; David Hothersall, *History of Psychology* (Philadelphia: Temple University Press, 1984), p. 275.

4. Phillips, "James, Dewey, and the Reflex Arc"; Reck, "The Influence of William James on John Dewey in Psychology"; J. E. Tiles, *Dewey*. Michael Buxton recognizes Dewey's early functionalism, Wundt's influence, and the need for de-emphasizing James's influence. See "The Influence of William James on John Dewey's Early Work," *Journal of the History of Ideas* 45 (July–September 1984): 451–463.

5. Kurt Danzinger, "Wundt and Two Traditions of Psychology," in *Wilhelm Wundt and the Making of a Scientific Psychology*, ed. R. W. Reiber (New York: Plenum Press, 1980), p. 85.

6. Theodore Mischel first raised this issue in "Wundt and the Conceptual Foundations of Psychology," *Philosophy and Phenomenological Research* 31 (September 1970): 1–26. Subsequent inquiries in this line include Arthur Blumenthal, "A Reappraisal of Wilhelm Wundt," *American Psychologist* 30 (November 1975): 1081–1088 and his "Wilhelm Wundt and Early American Psychology: A Clash of Cultures," in *Wilhelm Wundt and the Making of a Scientific Psychology*, ed. R. W. Reiber, pp. 117–135; Thomas Leahey, "The Mistaken Mirror: On Wundt's and Titchener's Psychologies," *Journal of the History of the Behavioral Sciences* 17 (April 1981): 273–282.

7. Edwin Boring, "Wilhelm Wundt," Chapter 16 of his *A History of Experimental Psychology*, 2d ed. (New York: Appleton-Century-Crofts, 1957), pp. 316–347. See also Edna Heidbreder, *Seven Psychologies* (New York: Century, 1933).

8. G. S. Morris, *Philosophy and Christianity*, p. 87.

9. Green, *Prolegomena to Ethics*, p. 158.

10. G. Stanley Hall, *Life and Confessions of a Psychologist* (New York: Appleton, 1927), p. 234.

11. Ross, *G. Stanley Hall*, pp. 150–157. See also R. W. Rieber, "Wundt and the Americans: From Flirtation to Abandonment," in, *Wilhelm Wundt and the Making of a Scientific Psychology*, ed. R. W. Reiber, p. 137n.

12. Dewey refers to Wundt's *Physiologischen Psychologie*, 2d ed. (1880), and *Untersuchungen zur Nerven und Nervecentren* (1876).

13. See David Leary, "Wundt and After," *Journal of the History of the Behavioral Sciences* 15 (July 1979): 234–235.

14. Hall makes the same point, using Dewey's analogy, in his identically named article "The New Psychology," *Andover Review* 3 (February 1885): 128. Dewey's article was published in September 1884; Hall's article was his inaugural lecture as professor of psychology, delivered in October 1884. This corrects Ross, *G. Stanley Hall*, pp. 139, 818.

15. "Selected Texts from Wundt," in *Wilhelm Wundt and the Making of a Scientific Psychology*, ed. R. W. Reiber, pp. 157–169.

16. See Kurt Danzinger, "The History of Introspection Reconsidered," *Journal of the History of the Behavioral Sciences* 16 (July 1980): 244–245.

17. See M. L. Zupan, "The Conceptual Development of Quantification in Experimental Psychology," *Journal of the History of the Behavioral Sciences* 12 (April 1976): 145–158; David Leary, "The Philosophical Development of the Conception of Psychology in Germany, 1780–1850," *Journal of the History of the Behavioral Sciences* 14 (April 1978): 113–121; Theodore Mischel, "Wundt and the Conceptual Foundations of Psychology," pp. 13–14; also Mischel, "Kant and the Possibility of a Science of Psychology," *Monist* 51 (October 1967): 599–622.

18. Edmund Hollands, "Wundt's Doctrine of Psychical Analysis and the Psychical Elements, and Some Recent Criticisms: I. The Criteria of the Elements and Attributes," *American Journal of Psychology* 16 (1905): 507–510; Kurt Danzinger, "The Positivist Repudiation of Wundt," *Journal of the History of the Behavioral Sciences* 15 (July 1979): 216; also Thomas Leahey, "Something Old, Something New: Attention in Wundt and

Modern Cognitive Psychology," *Journal of the History of the Behavioral Sciences* 15 (July 1979): 242–243.

19. Kurt Danzinger, "Wundt's Theory of Behavior and Volition," in *Wilhelm Wundt and the Making of a Scientific Psychology*, ed. R. W. Reiber, pp. 104–108.

20. Ibid., p. 96–98.

21. Blumenthal, "Wilhelm Wundt and Early American Psychology," pp. 125–126.

22. Mischel, "Wundt and the Conceptual Foundations of Psychology," p. 7; Hans Rappard, "Wundt's Voluntarism," in *Psychology as Self-Knowledge*, trans. Liane Faili (Assen, Netherlands: Van Gorcum, 1979), pp. 91–94. Recent psychology has rediscovered this very controversial question of attention's role in intellectual activities. One of Wundt's and Dewey's central theses, that attention is central to perception, is vigorously defended by the experimental investigations of Arien Mack and Irvin Rock, presented in *Inattentional Blindness* (Cambridge: Massachusetts Institute of Technology Press, 1998). Attentive, volitional perception is the cornerstone of Dewey's reconstruction of the reflex arc, discussed in section 3.

23. This writer's examination of Wundt's translated works and commentaries on the untranslated works has not revealed any use of the term "organic" by Wundt that goes beyond its original biological and physiological meaning.

24. Morris, *Philosophy and Christianity*, p. 73; see also p. 34.

25. See Mischel, "Wundt and the Conceptual Foundations of Psychology," pp. 6–7; also Danzinger's "The Positivist Repudiation of Wundt," pp. 207–208; also Willem van Hoorn and Thorn Verhave, "Wundt's Changing Conceptions of a General and Theoretical Psychology," in *Wundt Studies: A Centennial Collection*, eds. Wolfgang Bringmann and Ryan Tweeney (Toronto: C. J. Hogrefe, 1980), p. 72. It is Coughlan's theory that it was the obscure theologian Newman Smyth who revealed to Dewey that the new psychology was voluntaristic. While there are common views, Dewey's principal education clearly was owed to Wundt, to whom Dewey does refer in his writings. See Coughlan, *Young John Dewey*, pp. 42–53.

26. *Selections from the Writings of George MacDonald, or, Helps for Weary Souls*, ed. John Dewey (New York: Thomas R. Knox, 1885), pp. 37–38.

27. See Daniel Robinson, *Toward a Science of Human Nature: Essays on the Psychology of Mill, Hegel, Wundt, and James* (New York: Columbia University Press, 1982), pp. 135–137. Buxton's statement in "The Influence of William James on John Dewey's Early Work," p. 455, that "Wundt's separation of body and mind had no appeal for Dewey," is profoundly misleading.

28. Phillips, "James, Dewey and the Reflex Arc," p. 557. See also Robert Gault, "A Sketch of the History of Reflex Action in the Latter Half of the Nineteenth Century," *American Journal of Psychology* 15 (1904): 526–568.

29. Dewey was fully aware of the nature of this debate. His first publication (1882) was an attempt at idealistic reductionism, "The Metaphysical Assumptions of Materialism," *EW* 1: 3–8.

30. References are to the first (1886) edition, unless otherwise noted.

31. See Ernest Hilgard's "The Trilogy of Mind: Cognition, Affection, and Conation," *Journal of the History of the Behavioral Sciences* 16 (April 1980): 107–117.

32. Tiles, *Dewey*, pp. 28–32.

33. Gordon Allport, "Dewey's Individual and Social Psychology," in *The Philosophy of John Dewey*, ed. Schilpp, pp. 266–269.

34. Reck, "The Influence of William James on John Dewey in Psychology." See also Herbert Schneider's description of the third edition's changes in "Dewey's Psychology," chap. 1 of *Guide To The Works of John Dewey*, ed. Jo Ann Boydston (Carbondale and Edwardsville: Southern Illinois University Press, 1970), pp. 3–5.

35. James, *The Principles of Psychology*, 1: 436.

36. Dewey to John W. Cook, 16 January 1892. Archived at Northern Illinois University, Regional History Center, UA4 – Presidents' Papers, John Williston Cook, box 2, folder 27. My thanks go to Joan Metzger, assistant university archivist, who supplied a copy of this letter.

37. James, *The Principles of Psychology*, 1: 290–291.

38. Dewey to James, 6 May 1891, William James Papers bMS Am 1092.9 (28), Houghton Library, Harvard University. Quoted by permission of the Houghton Library, Harvard University.

39. James castigates German idealism, Green, and Caird in *The Principles of Psychology*, 1: 341–350.

40. Changes deleting reference to reproduction are at *EW* 2: 134–135, 137–139, 190, 299.

41. James, *The Principles of Psychology*, 1: 37.

42. James R. Angell and Addison W. Moore, "Reaction-Time: A Study in Attention and Habit," *Psychological Review* 3 (May 1896): 245–258.

43. James, *The Principles of Psychology*, 1: 36.

44. Geoffrey Thomas, *The Moral Philosophy of T. H. Green*, p. 41.

45. See Phillips, "Organicism in the Late Nineteenth and Twentieth Centuries," p. 413–432.

46. Jones, *George Sylvester Morris*, pp. 161–162. See R. M. Wenley, *The Life and Work of George Sylvester Morris* (New York: Macmillan, 1917).

47. Neil Coughlan did not ignore Trendelenburg's influence on Morris but could not discover Caird's or Wundt's influences on Dewey. As a result Coughlan places the burden of attracting Dewey to the relevence of the new psychology upon the shoulders of Newman Smyth. See *Young John Dewey*, pp. 42–53.

48. E. B. Titchener, "The Postulates of a Structural Psychology," *Philosophical Review* 7 (September 1898): 449–465.

49. On James and Wundt see Charles Judd, "Radical Empiricism and Wundt's Philosophy," *Journal of Philosophy* 2 (March 1905): 169–176; Charlene Seigfried, *William James's Radical Reconstruction of Philosophy* (Albany: State University of New York Press, 1990), p. 153; Daniel Bjork, *The Compromised Scientist: William James in the Development of American Psychology* (New York: Columbia University Press, 1983), pp. 40–43, 80–81.

50. Green, *Prolegomena to Ethics*, pp. 90–94, 123–127.

51. Ibid., p. 138–139.

52. Ibid., p. 158.

53. James, "The Sentiment of Rationality," reprinted in *The Will to Believe and Other Essays in Popular Philosophy* (1897. Cambridge: Harvard University Press, 1979), pp. 57–65.

54. Reck, "The Influence of William James on John Dewey in Psychology," 87–118. Michael Buxton, "The Influence of William James on John Dewey's Early Work," 451–463.

Chapter Four: The Absolute of Active Experience

1. George S. Morris, "Philosophy and Its Specific Problems," *Princeton Review* n.s. 9 (March 1882): 214.
2. Morris, *British Thought and Thinkers,* p. 384.
3. Morris, *Philosophy and Christianity,* p. 287.
4. For example, Ralph Sleeper's *The Necessity of Pragmatism* is more explicit than most in linking many aspects of Dewey's psychology, epistemology, and logic to Peirce, but it almost completely avoids the nature of truth. The term "truth" does not even appear in the index.
5. *CP* 5.405. *Writings,* 3: 273.
6. Steven Rockefeller offers panentheism as the best category for the religious standpoint of the *Psychology.* See *John Dewey: Religious Faith and Democratic Humanism,* p. 122.
7. Interestingly Seth reviewed Dewey's *Psychology* in 1887: "Mental Philosophy," *Contemporary Record* 52 (August 1887): 295. Seth praised the book's treatment of the stages of knowledge, which portrays the "inseparability and mutual dependence of the different forms of mental action." However, Seth says that "it may be doubted whether his philosophy of the universal Self is not too largely imported into the book. . . ."
8. Andrew Seth, *Hegelianism and Personality* (Edinburgh: William Blackwood and Sons, 1887), p. 217.
9. Ibid., p. 12–13, 19–20.
10. See Seth, later Andrew Seth Pringle-Pattison, *The Idea of God in the Light of Recent Philosophy* (Oxford: Clarendon Press, 1917).
11. Seth, *Hegelianism and Personality,* pp. 20–21.
12. I am indebted to Frank Ryan's exposition of Dewey's tactics, in "The Kantian Ground of Dewey's Functional Self," *Transactions of the Charles S. Peirce Society* 28 (Winter 1992): 127–144. Ryan and I agree that "On Some Current Conceptions of the Term 'Self'" is a path-breaking stride for Dewey away from all other neo-idealisms toward a thorough-going empiricism, and we agree that it was largely this effort that brought Dewey toward instrumentalism, not William James.
13. Bradley, *Ethical Studies,* 2d ed. (London: Oxford University Press, 1927), p. 319.
14. Green, *Prolegomena to Ethics,* pp. 200–202.
15. Ibid., pp. 197–198. An interesting discussion of Green's theological and ethical views is provided by Melvin Richter, *The Politics of Conscience: T. H. Green and His Age* (1964. Reprinted, Bristol, U.K.: Thoemmes Press, 1996).
16. Caird, *Hegel,* p. 213.
17. Morris, *Philosophy and Christianity,* p. 136.
18. Ibid., p. 153.

19. Martin Kusch, *Psychologism* (London and New York: Routledge, 1995), p. 130.

20. *Dialogue on John Dewey*, ed. Corliss Lamont (New York: Horizon Press, 1959), pp. 15–16.

21. Jane Dewey, "Biography of John Dewey," in *The Philosophy of John Dewey*, ed. Schilpp, pp. 17–18. She took this quotation from the original publication of "From Absolutism to Experimentalism" in *Contemporary American Philosophy: Personal Statements*, eds. George P. Adams and William P. Montague, vol. 2 (New York: Macmillan, 1930), p. 13–27. A subsequent reprinting of John Dewey's essay omitted this and other sections; *The Works of John Dewey* also omits them. Another influential factor contributing to Dewey's confidence in social psychology was the work of his colleague at Michigan and Chicago, George H. Mead. The precise nature of Mead's influence is uncertain, as Mead published very little during these years. See Gary Cook, *George Herbert Mead: The Making of a Social Pragmatist* (Chicago: University of Illinois Press, 1993), and Darnell Rucker, *The Chicago Pragmatists* (Minneapolis: University of Minnesota Press, 1969).

22. See Gregory Pappas, "Dewey's Moral Theory: Experience as Method," *Transactions of the Charles S. Peirce Society* 33 (Summer 1998): 520–556. See also his "Dewey's Ethics: Morality as Experience" in *Reading Dewey: Interpretations for a Postmodern Generation*, ed. Larry A. Hickman (Bloomington: Indiana University Press, 1998), pp. 100–123.

23. See Welchman, *Dewey's Ethical Thought*, pp. 75–83, for an explanation of Dewey's disagreements with Bradley's moral theory, to which my exposition is indebted.

24. On these issues of social ideals, intelligence, and democracy, two excellent recent books must be consulted: Michael Eldridge, *Transforming Experience: John Dewey's Cultural Instrumentalism* (Nashville: Vanderbilt University Press, 1998), and James Campbell, *Understanding John Dewey* (La Salle, Ill.: Open Court, 1995).

25. Green, *Prolegomena to Ethics*, p. 322–323.

26. Ibid., p. 336–337.

27. See Steven Fesmire, "Dramatic Rehearsal and the Moral Artist: A Deweyan Theory of Moral Understanding," *Transactions of the Charles S. Peirce Society* 31 (Summer 1995): 568–597.

28. For this reason I am unable to agree with Jennifer Welchman's judgment that *The Study of Ethics* "shows no sign of movement toward pragmatism." *Dewey's Ethical Thought*, p. 115.

Chapter Five: The Logic of Conduct

1. F. H. Bradley, *The Principles of Logic*, 2d ed. (London: Oxford University Press, 1922), pp. 2–9. On Bradley's theory of logic and knowledge, see Anthony Manser, *Bradley's Logic* (Oxford: Blackwell, 1983), and Phillip Ferreira, *Bradley and the Structure of Knowledge* (Albany: State University of New York Press, 1999).

2. Bradley, *Principles of Logic*, p. 44–45.

3. *CP* 7.624.

4. See Richard Bernstein, "Peirce's Theory of Perception," in *Studies in the Philosophy of Charles Sanders Peirce*, second series, ed. Edward C. Moore and Richard S. Robin (Amherst: University of Massachusetts Press, 1964), pp. 165–189.

5. Dewey's lectures during the 1890s reveal his continued work on this logic. See *Principles of Instrumental Logic: John Dewey's Lectures in Ethics and Politcal Ethics, 1895–1896*, ed. Donald F. Koch (Carbondale: Southern Illinois University Press, 1998). These lectures display his unification of the logic of morality and science.

6. The quotations of the *Studies* are from the revised version published in the 1916 *Essays in Experimental Logic*; their minor alterations do not signify any important change of views. For Dewey's lectures on logic, see Steven Nofsinger, ed., *John Dewey's "Lectures in the Theory of Logic": Delivered at the University of Chicago, Fall and Winter Quarters (1899–1900)*. Ph.D. dissertation, Michigan State University, 1989.

7. Dewey variously offers three to six or more phases in different analyses of inquiry across many writings. This list, found in "Some Stages of Logical Thought," is the typical organization. Compare the phases in the *Studies in Logical Theory* (MW 2: 307) and in *How We Think* (MW 6: 236–237).

8. In later years Dewey referred to successful harmonious activity as a consummatory experience, an essentially aesthetic experience. See Alexander, *John Dewey's Theory of Art, Experience and Nature*, pp. 198–213.

9. Jane Dewey, "Biography of John Dewey," in *The Philosophy of John Dewey*, ed. Schilpp, p. 18.

10. *Hegel's Philosophy of Spirit*. Typescript of lectures by John Dewey, taken by H. Heath Bawden. University of Chicago, 1897. I examined Ella Flagg Young's copy, on loan from the UCLA Research Library.

11. Ibid., p. 28. The question of the adequacy of Dewey's exposition is not germane here, but the extent of Dewey's debt to Hegel's teleology of active spirit deserves further examination. See Myriam Bienenstock, "Hegel's Conception of Teleology," in *Science, Mind, and Art*, Boston Studies in the Philosophy of Science, vol. 165 (Dordrecht: Kluwer, 1995), pp. 55–70.

12. Paul Kuntz recounts this story and provides many more examples of Lotze's high stature. He also lists the numerous philosophers and theologians indebted to Lotze, which reads like a who's who of Anglo-American philosophers and includes William James. See his introduction to George Santayana, *Lotze's System of Philosophy*, ed. Paul G. Kuntz (Bloomington: Indiana University Press, 1971), pp. 3–105.

13. See Peirce's review of the *Studies* (CP 8.188–190) and letters to Dewey (CP 8.239–244).

14. Sir Henry Jones, *A Critical Account of the Philosophy of Lotze* (London: Macmillan, 1895).

15. B. M. Humphries, "Dewey's *Studies in Logical Theory*." *Journal of the History of Philosophy* 9 (October 1971): 486.

16. CP 8.189.

17. Charles S. Peirce, "The Doctrine of Necessity Examined," *Monist* 2 (April 1892): 321–337 (CP 6.35–65).

18. The full list of Peirce's arguments is discussed by Victor Cosculluela, "Peirce on Tychism and Determinism," *Transactions of the Charles S. Peirce Society* 28 (Fall 1992): 741–755.

19. Ian Hacking, *The Taming of Chance* (Cambridge: Cambridge University Press, 1990), p. 9.

20. John T. Merz gives an excellent account of the rise of the statistical sciences in *A History of European Thought in the Nineteenth Century* (New York: Dover, 1965), 2: 548–626.

21. *CP* 6.44.

22. Peter Turley offers an overview of Peirce's changing views on chance in "Peirce on Chance," *Transactions of the Charles S. Peirce Society* 5 (Fall 1969): 243–254.

23. *John Dewey and Arthur F. Bentley: A Philosophical Correspondence, 1932–1951*, selected and edited by Sidney Ratner and Jules Altman (New Brunswick: Rutgers University Press, 1964), p. 523.

24. Ibid., p. 519.

25. James Clerk Maxwell, *Matter and Motion* (London: Society for Promoting Christian Knowledge, 1876), p. 84.

26. Jane Dewey, "Biography of John Dewey," in *The Philosophy of John Dewey*, ed. Schilpp, p. 23.

27. H. S. Thayer, "Dewey: Continuity–Hegel and Darwin." Appendix 1 of *Meaning and Action: A Critical History of Pragmatism* (Indianapolis: Bobbs-Merrill, 1968), pp. 460–487.

28. Jane Dewey, "Biography of John Dewey," in *The Philosophy of John Dewey*, ed. Schilpp, p. 10–11.

29. *CP* 2.330.

30. Dewey's theory of scientific principles has a large bearing on recent debates on whether it is impossible that water is not H_2O. Dewey, I think, would charge both sides with some degree of Aristotelian mind-set and an inadequate appreciation of the ability for scientific inquiry to reconstruct *all* the meanings of the things under study. Hilary Putnam's "Is Water Necessarily H_2O?" reprinted in *Realism with a Human Face*, ed. James Conant (Cambridge: Harvard University Press, 1990), pp. 54–79, is a good place to enter this debate.

Chapter Six: The Reconstruction of Epistemology

1. Dewey's philosophy has been typically held up as a paradigm for naturalism, scientism, and behaviorism, and the second half of the twentieth century has seen Dewey generally classified as a realist, not as an idealist. To make the same point, it can be noted that present-day idealists do not take inspiration from Dewey; they are far more likely to read Josiah Royce or Ernest Hocking. However, the philosophers refusing to grant that Dewey was a realist are legion. A few prominent examples are instructive. R. F. Alfred Hoernlé, commenting on a quotation from Dewey's *Experience and Nature* linking his philosophy with his view of experience, says that "what Dewey calls here his own empirical method is, in spirit and principle, if not in the actual details of its execution, identical with the idealistic method . . ." in "The Revival of Idealism in the United States" in

Contemporary Idealism in America, ed. Clifford Barrett (New York: Macmillan, 1932), p. 314. Hans Reichenbach argues that Dewey upholds nominalistic verificationism, thus denying "independent reality to scientific objects" in "Dewey's Theory of Science," in *The Philosophy of John Dewey*, ed. Schilpp, p. 173. Richard Rorty locates Dewey among those "edifying" philosophers who dismiss "truthfulness to reality in the sense postulated by philosophical realism" in *Philosophy and the Mirror of Nature* (Princeton: Princeton University Press, 1979), p. 382. Michael Devitt declares that instrumentalism rejects the existence of unobservables and classifies it as a quasi-realism, a positivism, and an antirealist doctrine in *Realism and Truth*, pp. 129, 130. Even a Peirce scholar, Christopher Hookway, labels Dewey's pragmatism as an "irrationalist doctrine" because it "denies that we desire to make our beliefs conform to a fixed external reality" in *Peirce* (London: Routledge and Kegan Paul, 1985), p. 51.

2. See Perry, *The Thought and Character of William James*, vol. 1, chapters 49–51.

3. Josiah Royce, *The World and the Individual*, first series: *The Four Historical Conceptions of Being* (1899. Reprinted, New York: Dover, 1959). On the origins of American neorealism see William H. Werkmeister, "Neo-Realism," in *A History of Philosophical Ideas in America* (New York: Ronald Press, 1949), p. 371; Herbert W. Schneider, "The Pragmatic Meeting of Minds," in *Sources of Contemporary Philosophical Realism in America* (Indianapolis: Bobbs-Merrill, 1964), pp. 14–16; and Victor Harlow, *A Bibliography and Genetic Study of American Realism* (1931. Reprinted, New York: Kraus Reprint, 1970), pp. 16–21. Realistic views prior to 1903 are outlined in Werkmeister, p. 371, and Harlow, pp. 24–28. William P. Montague's "Professor Royce's Refutation of Realism" appeared in *Philosophical Review* 11 (January 1902): 43–55; Ralph Barton Perry's "Prof. Royce's Refutation of Realism and Pluralism" appeared in *Monist* 12 (April 1902): 446–458.

4. Dykhuizen (*The Life and Mind of John Dewey*, p. 124) counts more than 30 such articles written between 1905 and 1914. Dewey later made several interesting observations on the effects of this drastic change of environment and academic focus. One stands out, in a letter written to Arthur Bentley in 1940. Dewey writes how he had recently come across a passage from A. W. Moore, a former student and colleague at Chicago. Dewey quotes Moore: "'My' consciousness is a function of a social process in which my body or brain or mind is only one factor. . . . 'My' thinking and feeling may be as truly a function of 'your' brain or mind as of my own. My thinking of sending for you as a physician to treat my headache is as truly a function of your medically trained brain as of my own aching one." Dewey then tells Bentley, "I don't know how I got so much switched off from following out this line. Partly lack of nerve, partly moving from Chicago to Columbia and getting into a new set of problems that interrupted, I guess. . . ." This letter is reprinted in Ratner and Altman, *John Dewey and Arthur F. Bentley: A Philosophical Correspondence, 1932–1951*, p. 78.

5. Other examples of Dewey's use of "naive realism" to qualify his philosophy are "The Experimental Theory of Knowledge" (1906, *MW* 3: 109), "Psychological Doctrine and Philosophical Teaching" (1913, *MW* 7: 48), introduction to the *Essays in Experimental Logic* (1916, *MW* 10: 345, 357), "The Need for a Recovery of Philosophy" (1917, *MW* 10: 39). Dewey does not use the term "naive realism" after 1917 but continues to praise the virtues of recognizing the primacy of "naive" experience.

NOTES TO CHAPTER SIX

6. Frederick J. E. Woodbridge, "Of What Sort Is Cognitive Experience?" *Journal of Philosophy* 2 (October 1905): 573–576 (*MW* 3: 393–397).

7. Charles M. Bakewell, "The Issue between Idealism and Immediate Empiricism," *Journal of Philosophy* 2 (December 1905): 687–691, and "An Open Letter to Professor Dewey Concerning Immediate Experience," *Journal of Philosophy*," 2 (September 1905): 520–522 (*MW* 3: 390–392). See also Boyd H. Bode, "Cognitive Experience and Its Object," *Journal of Philosophy* 2 (November 1905): 658–663 (*MW* 3: 398–404). Dewey's reply to Bakewell is "Immediate Experience" (*MW* 3: 168–170); his reply to Bode is "The Knowledge Experience Again" (*MW* 3: 178–183).

8. Hilary Putnam, *Reason, Truth and History* (Cambridge: Cambridge University Press, 1981), p. 51.

9. Bertrand Russell, "Dewey's New *Logic*," in *The Philosophy of John Dewey*, ed. Schilpp, p. 139.

10. See John H. Randall, Jr., "F. H. Bradley and the Working-out of Absolute Idealism." See also W. J. Mander, *An Introduction to Bradley's Metaphysics* (Oxford: Clarendon Press, 1994). A superb discussion of Dewey's and Bradley's similar projects but divergent methods is Paul Forster's "Unity, Theory, and Practice: F. H. Bradley and Pragmatism" in *Philosophy after F. H. Bradley*, ed. James Bradley (Bristol, U.K.: Thoemmes Press, 1996), pp. 169–191.

11. Christopher Kulp thoroughly explores Dewey's many confrontations with the spectator theory of knowledge in *The End of Epistemology: Dewey and His Current Allies on the Spectator Theory of Knowledge* (Westport, Conn.: Greenwood Press, 1992).

12. E. B. McGilvary, "The Chicago 'Idea' and Idealism," *Journal of Philosophy* 5 (October 1908): 589–597 (*MW* 4: 317–327).

13. Josiah Royce, *The World and the Individual*, first series: *The Four Historical Conceptions of Being*, p. 62.

14. Edwin B. Holt, et al. "The Program and First Platform of Six Realists." *Journal of Philosophy* 7 (July1910): 393–401 (*MW* 6: 472–482).

15. Tom Burke superbly defends Dewey against Russell's charge in *Dewey's New Logic: A Reply to Russell* (Chicago: University of Chicago, 1994), pp. 22–53.

16. Ralph B. Perry, *Present Philosophical Tendencies* (London: Longmans, Green, 1912), p. 244.

17. Edward G. Spaulding, "A Defense of Analysis," in *The New Realism*, by E. B. Holt et al. (New York: Macmillan, 1912), pp. 240–241.

18. Perry, *Present Philosophical Tendencies*, p. 308.

19. These matters are explained in greater detail by Alexander, *John Dewey's Theory of Art, Experience, and Nature*, pp. 94–96.

20. E. B. McGilvary, "Pure Experience and Reality," *Philosophical Review* 16 (May 1907): 266–284 (*MW* 4: 295–313).

21. Georges Dicker has given an excellent treatment of this distinction in Dewey's philosophy, in *Dewey's Theory of Knowing* (Philadelphia: University City Science Center, 1976). Also see H. S. Thayer, "Objects of Knowledge," in *Philosophy and the Reconstruction of Culture: Pragmatic Essays after Dewey*, ed. John J. Stuhr (Albany: State University of New York Press, 1993), pp. 187–201.

NOTES TO CHAPTER SIX

22. Montague, "Current Misconceptions of Realism," *Journal of Philosophy* 4 (February 1907): 101.

23. McGilvary, "The Chicago 'Idea' and Idealism," *Journal of Philosophy* 5 (October 1908): 589–597 (*MW* 4: 317–327). This quotation is found at *MW* 4: 323.

24. Durant Drake, Arthur O. Lovejoy, James B. Pratt, Arthur K. Rogers, George Santayana, Roy Wood Sellars, Charles A. Strong, *Essays in Critical Realism* (London: Macmillan, 1920). An example of Dewey's criticism is "Realism without Monism or Dualism" (*MW* 13: 40–60).

25. Russell, *Our Knowledge of the External World as a Field for Scientific Method in Philosophy*, p. 75.

26. Dewey, "The Existence of the World as a Logical Problem" (*MW* 8: 83–97). See Tom Burke's discussion of this exchange in *Dewey's New Logic: A Reply to Russell* (Chicago: University of Chicago Press, 1994).

27. Devitt, *Realism and Truth*, pp. 23–24.

28. This is one of the reasons why instrumentalist pragmatism must part company with Bas van Fraasen's constructive empiricism, which too narrowly restricts the sense of "observable." An excellent exposition of this problem is provided by Cheryl Misak, *Verificationism: Its History and Prospects* (London and New York: Routledge, 1995), pp. 163–171.

29. I am indebted to Mark Johnston's understanding of metaphysical realism in "Objectivity Refigured: Pragmatism without Verificationism" in *Reality, Representation, and Projection*, ed. John Haldane and Crispin Wright (Oxford: Oxford University Press, 1993), pp. 85–87. Johnston also uses the James quotation that follows.

30. William James, *The Meaning of Truth* (1909. Reprinted, Cambridge: Harvard University Press, 1975), p. 40.

31. The critics included most of the prominent idealists of the day. See James Seth, "The Utilitarian Estimate of Knowledge," *Philosophical Review* 10 (July 1901): 341–358; Josiah Royce, "The Eternal and the Practical," *Philosophical Review* 13 (March 1904): 113–142; Joseph A. Leighton, "Pragmatism," *Journal of Philosophy* 1 (March 1904): 148–156; James E. Creighton, "Purpose as a Logical Category," *Philosophical Review* 13 (May 1904): 284–297; F. H. Bradley, "On Truth and Practice," *Mind* n.s. 13 (July 1904): 309–335; A. E. Taylor, "Truth and Practice," *Philosophical Review* 14 (May 1905): 265–289. The best account of these early controversies between pragmatism and idealism is by R. F. Alfred Hoernlé, "Pragmatism V. Absolutism," *Mind* n.s. 14 (July/October 1905): 297–334, 441–478.

32. A. K. Rogers, "The Standpoint of Instrumental Logic," *Journal of Philosophy* 1 (April 1904): 208.

33. See for example W. B. Pitkin, "The Relation between the Act and the Object of Belief," *Journal of Philosophy* 3 (September 1906): 505–511.

34. James B. Pratt, "Truth and Its Verification," *Journal of Philosophy* 4 (June 1907): 322.

35. Bertrand Russell, "On Propositions: What They Are and How They Mean" (1919), p. 43. Reprinted in *Collected Papers of Bertrand Russell*, vol. 8, *The Philosophy of Logical Atomism and Other Essays, 1914–1919* (London: George Allen and Unwin, 1983), p. 306.

36. Peter van Inwagen, "On Always Being Wrong," in *Realism and Antirealism*, vol. 12 of Midwest Studies in Philosophy (Minneapolis: University of Minnesota Press, 1988), pp. 95–111.

37. See Michael Williams, "Realism and Scepticism" in *Reality, Representation, and Projection*, ed. John Haldane and Crispin Wright (Oxford: Oxford University Press, 1993), pp. 193–214. See also Williams, *Unnatural Doubts: Epistemological Realism and the Basis of Scepticism* (Princeton, N.J.: Princeton University Press, 1991). Williams, by renouncing epistemological realism's aim to provide some account of the relation between human knowledge as a totality and the world, similarly demonstrates how to undermine Cartesian skepticism. While Dewey was more concerned to avoid idealism, he too rejects such epistemological realism and, like Williams, accordingly disposes of modern skepticism.

38. Pratt does an exemplary job; see "Truth and Its Verification," pp. 322–324.

39. Dewey's *Logic: The Theory of Inquiry* gives his fullest exposition of warranted assertibility. For a comparison of the role of this concept in Dewey epistemology with the concept of truth, see Tom Burke, *Dewey's New Logic*, especially pp. 236–245.

40. For example, see Devitt, *Realism and Truth*. Interestingly Devitt claims that this notion of truth has no essential relation to metaphysical realism. Dewey would agree, since he was all too familiar with those absolute idealists who believed that humans could never rise to level of knowledge of the Absolute Mind, which contained all truths. Dewey would simply categorize Devitt and absolute idealists (and dualistic realists) together as transcendentalists.

41. Michael Dummett, among many others, has used a version of this notion of truth to define realism. For a discussion of Dummett's realism see Ian McFetridge, "Realism and Anti-Realism in a Historical Context," in Haldane and Wright, *Reality, Representation, and Projection*, pp. 39–61.

42. R. B. Perry is explicit, as are others, on this point. See "A Review of Pragmatism as a Theory of Knowledge," *Journal of Philosophy* 4 (July 1907): 365–374.

43. This all-important distinction between coming to know and having accomplished knowledge is carefully examined and defended by Frank Ryan, "Primary Experience as Settled Meaning: Dewey's Conception of Experience" *Philosophy Today* 38 (Spring 1994): 29–42.

44. Not surprisingly Dewey's epistemology disdains the current internalist/externalist debate. On Dewey's theory of knowledge, a person could not know P without experientially learning that P, which seems to imply that his theory is a variety of internalism. However, the intelligent process of learning requires this person's interaction with the environment, involving things external to the mental factors of intelligence. The transcendentalism of both parties is responsible for their false presupposition that the justification for knowing must primarily rest either in the mind or in physical reality. Richard Fumerton's *Metaepistemology and Skepticism* (Lanham, Md.: Rowman and Littlefield, 1995) sheds a great deal of light on the difficulties involved in the internalist/externalist debate, to which I am indebted.

45. See James Gouinlock, "Dewey: Creative Intelligence and Emergent Reality," in *Classical American Pragmatism: Its Contemporary Vitality*, eds. Sandra B. Rosenthal, Carl R. Hausman, and Douglas R. Anderson (Urbana: Univesity of Illinois Press, 1999), pp. 224–236.

46. This point has a tremendous bearing on the question of the possibility of a "naturalized epistemology." In recent philosophy, naturalized epistemology seems to be a matter of reducing epistemological and logical factors to purely physical entities and terms,

as part of a scientistic program in the tradition of Quine. See *Naturalizing Epistemology*, ed. Hilary Kornblith (Cambridge: Massachusetts Institute of Technology Press, 1985). Dewey's work could not be assimilated to this program; his theory of knowledge, like his moral philosophy, *uses* the results of empirical science without permitting science to *decide* epistemological questions. On this issue see Peter T. Manicas, "Naturalizing Epistemology: Reconstructing Philosophy," in *Philosophy and the Reconstruction of Culture: Pragmatic Essays after Dewey*, ed. Stuhr, pp. 151–174.

47. George Santayana, "Dewey's Naturalistic Metaphysics" (1925). Reprinted in *The Philosophy of John Dewey*, ed. Schilpp, pp. 243–261. John Stuhr discusses their exchange in "Experience and the Adoration of Matter: Santayana's Unnatural Naturalism," in his *Genealogical Pragmatism: Philosophy, Experience, Community*, pp. 131–146.

48. I fully agree with Mark Johnston, who similarly argues that pragmatism can and should be disentangled from verificationist notions. The four pragmatic theses he offers in "Objectivity Refigured," p. 117, are Deweyan to the core. Cheryl Misak also attempts to clarify the relationships between verificationism and pragmatism in "Peirce and the Pragmatic Maxim," in *Verificationism: Its History and Prospects* (London and New York: Routledge, 1995), pp. 97–127.

Bibliography

References for Dewey's writings reprinted in *The Works of John Dewey, 1883–1952*, are provided in the Appendix, Chronology of Selected Dewey Writings. This bibliography lists works consulted besides those mentioned in the notes to the chapters. Works of major thinkers significant to this book's topics are listed together here for the reader's convenience.

Works by or about Dewey

Axelson, John. "1884–1894, Decade of Ferment for Young Michigan Teacher John Dewey." *Michigan Education Journal* 43 (May 1966): 13–14.

Brodsky, Garry M. "Absolute Idealism and John Dewey's Instrumentalism." *Transactions of the Charles S. Peirce Society* 6 (Winter 1968): 44–62.

Burnett, Joe R. Introduction. 1976, *MW* 1: ix–xxiii.

Carleton, Lawrence R. "The Rise of Chicago Functionalism." *Erkenntnis* 18 (1982): 3–23.

Cohen, Morris R. "Some Difficulties in Dewey's Anthropocentric Naturalism." *Philosophical Review* 49 (March 1940): 196–228.

Crissman, Paul. "The Psychology of John Dewey." *Psychological Review* 49 (September 1942): 441–462.

Dewey, John. *Hegel's Philosophy of Spirit*. Typescript of lectures by John Dewey, taken by H. Heath Bawden. University of Chicago, 1897.

———. *The Collected Works of John Dewey, 1882–1953*, edited by Jo Ann Boydston. Carbondale: Southern Illinois University Press, 1969–1991. Published as *The Early Works: 1881–1898*, *The Middle Works, 1899–1924*, and *The Later Works, 1925–1953* (*EW*, *MW*, and *LW*).

———. *Lectures on Psychological and Political Ethics: 1898*. Edited and with an introduction by Donald F. Koch. New York: Macmillan, 1976.

———. *John Dewey's "Lectures in the Theory of Logic": Delivered at the University of Chicago, Fall and Winter Quarters (1899–1900)*. Edited and with an introduction by Steven Nofsinger. Ph.D. dissertation, Michigan State University, 1989.

———. *Lectures on Ethics: 1900–1901*. Edited and with an introduction by Donald F. Koch. Carbondale: Southern Illinois University Press, 1991.

———. *Principles of Instrumental Logic: John Dewey's Lectures in Ethics and Political Ethics, 1895–1896*. Edited by Donald F. Koch. Carbondale: Southern Illinois University Press, 1998.

———. *Ethics, 1895–1896*. Edited by Donald F. Koch. Carbondale: Southern Illinois University Press, 1998.

———, and Arthur F. Bentley. *John Dewey and Arthur F. Bentley: A Philosophical Correspondence, 1932–1951*, selected and edited by Sidney Ratner and Jules Altman. New Brunswick: Rutgers University Press, 1964.

———, and James A. McLellan. *The Psychology of Number and Its Applications to Methods of Teaching Arithmetic*. New York: D. Appleton, 1895.

———, ed. *Selections from the Writings of George MacDonald, or, Helps for Weary Souls*. New York: Thomas R. Knox, 1885.

Dewey, Robert E. *The Philosophy of John Dewey: A Critical Exposition of His Method, Metaphysics, and Theory of Knowledge*. The Hague: Martinus Nijhoff, 1977.

Eames, S. Morris. Introduction. 1969, *EW* 3: ix–xxvi.

Fay, Jay W. "John Dewey, James McCosh and B. P. Bowne." In *American Psychology before William James*. New Brunswick: Rutgers University Press, 1939, pp. 163–167.

Feffer, Andrew. *The Chicago Pragmatists and American Progressivism*. Ithaca: Cornell University Press, 1993.

Feibleman, James. "The Influence of Peirce on Dewey's Logic." *Education* 66 (September 1945): 18–24.

Fendrich, Roger. "The Problem of Anthropocentrism in Dewey's Metaphysics." *International Philosophical Quarterly* 15 (June 1975): 149–159.

———. "The Epistemological Status of Dewey's Metaphysics." *International Studies in Philosophy* 10 (1978): 101–120.

Feuer, Lewis. "H. A. P. Torrey and John Dewey: Teacher and Pupil." *American Quarterly* 10 (Spring 1958): 34–54.

———. "John Dewey's Reading at College." *Journal of the History of Philosophy* 19 (June 1958): 415–421.

———. "John Dewey and the Back to the People Movement in American Thought." *Journal of the History of Ideas* 20 (October–December 1959): 545–568.

Hahn, Lewis E. "Introduction: From Intuitionalism to Absolutism." 1969, *EW* 1: vii–xxi.

Haskins, Casey, and David I. Seiple, eds. *Dewey Reconfigured: Essays on Deweyan Pragmatism*. Albany, N.Y.: State University of New York Press, 1999.

Hickman, Larry. *John Dewey's Pragmatic Technology*. Bloomington: Indiana University Press, 1990.

———. "Dewey's Theory of Inquiry." In *Reading Dewey: Interpretations for a Postmodern Generation*, ed. Larry Hickman. Bloomington: Indiana University Press, 1998, pp. 166–186.
Hocking, William E. "Dewey's Concepts of Experience and Nature." *Philosophical Review* 49 (March 1940): 228–244.
Holder, John J. "An Epistemological Foundation for Thinking: A Deweyan Approach." *Studies in Philosophy and Education* 13:3–4 (1994–1995): 175–192. Reprinted in *The New Scholarship on Dewey*, ed. Jim Garrison. Dordrecht: Kluwer, 1995, pp. 7–24.
Holmes, Robert. "The Development of John Dewey's Ethical Thought." *Monist* 48 (July 1964): 392–407.
Hook, Sidney. Introduction to *Experience and Nature*. 1981, *LW* 1: vii–xxiii.
———. *The Metaphysics of Pragmatism*. Chicago: Open Court, 1927. Reprinted, Buffalo, N.Y.: Prometheus Press, 1995.
———. *John Dewey: An Intellectual Portrait*. New York: John Day, 1939. Reprinted, Buffalo, N.Y.: Prometheus Press, 1995.
Johns Hopkins University Circulars. Nos. 1–33, December 1879–September 1884. Baltimore: John Murphey, 1882–1884. Specifically relating to Dewey, see no. 16: 232–234; no. 19: 14, 17–19; no. 20: 36, 38, 39; no. 21: 54, 58, 59, 63, 64; no. 22: 81–82, 89, 93, 94; no. 23: 101; no. 24: 119, 120, 136; no. 25: 155, 156; no. 27: 12–13, 15, 18, 26, 27, 28; no. 28: 45, 46; no. 29: 68, 69, 70; no. 30: 95, 96; no. 31: 117, 118–119; no. 32: 138.
Kaufman, Felix. "John Dewey's Theory of Inquiry." In *John Dewey: Philosopher of Science and Freedom*, ed. Sidney Hook. New York: Barnes and Noble, 1960, pp. 217–230.
Kulp, Christopher. *The End of Epistemology: Dewey and His Current Allies on the Spectator Theory of Knowledge*. Westport, Conn.: Greenwood Press, 1992.
Leys, Wayne. Introduction. 1971, *EW* 4: ix–xx.
Long, Marcus. *The Morphology of Knowledge: A Study in the Logical Theories of Hermann Lotze, Bernard Bosanquet and John Dewey*. Ph.D. dissertation, University of Toronto, 1940.
Margolis, Joseph. "The Relevance of Dewey's Epistemology." In *New Studies in the Philosophy of John Dewey*, ed. Steven M. Cahn. Hanover, N.H.: University Press of New England, 1977, pp. 117–184.
Martland, T. R. *The Metaphysics of William James and John Dewey: Process and Structure in Philosophy and Religion*. New York: Greenwood Press, 1969.
McCaul, Robert. "Dewey's Chicago." *School Review* 67 (Summer 1959): 258–280.
———. "Dewey's School Days, 1867–75." *Elementary School Journal* 63 (October 1962): 15–21.
———. "Dewey in College, 1875–79." *School Review* 70 (Winter 1962): 437–456.
McDermott, John. "Dewey's Logic." *Transactions of the Charles S. Peirce Society* 6 (Winter 1970): 34–45.

McKenzie, William. "Introduction: Toward Unity of Thought and Action." 1972, *EW* 5: ix–xvi.
Morgan, Jack, and S. Samuel Shermis. "Origin, Theory and Practice: Dewey's Early Philosophy." *Midcontinent American Studies Journal* 11 (Spring 1970): 65–79.
Murphey, Gardner. "Some Reflections on John Dewey's Psychology." *University of Colorado Studies,* Series in Philosophy, no. 2 (1961): 26–34.
Nissen, Lowell. *John Dewey's Theory of Inquiry and Truth.* The Hague: Moulton, 1966.
Nofsinger, Steven. Introduction. In his edited work *John Dewey's "Lectures in the Theory of Logic": Delivered at the University of Chicago, Fall and Winter Quarters (1899–1900).* Ph.D. dissertation, Michigan State University, 1989.
Parodi, Dominique. "Knowledge and Action in Dewey's Philosophy." In *The Philosophy of John Dewey,* ed. Paul A. Schilpp. 1939. 3d ed., La Salle, Ill.: Open Court, 1989, pp. 229–242.
Pfunter, Carl. *An Examination of the Extent of Philosophical Dependence, Methodological and Metaphysical, of John Dewey on Charles Peirce.* Ph.D. dissertation, Georgetown University, 1967.
Piatt, Donald A. "Dewey's Logical Theory." In *The Philosophy of John Dewey,* ed. Paul A. Schilpp. 1939. 3d ed., La Salle, Ill.: Open Court, 1989, pp. 105–134.
Pronko, N. H., and D. T. Herman. "From Dewey's Reflex Arc Concept to Transactionalism and Beyond." *Behaviorism* 10 (Fall 1982): 229–254.
Raphelson, Alfred. "The Pre-Chicago Association of the Early Functionalists." *Journal of the History of the Behavioral Sciences* 9 (April 1973): 115–122.
Ratner, Joseph. "Introduction to John Dewey's Philosophy." In *Intelligence in the Modern World: John Dewey's Philosophy,* ed. Joseph Ratner. New York: Modern Library, 1939, pp. 3–241.
Ratner, Sidney. "The Development of Dewey's Evolutionary Naturalism." *Social Research* 20 (July 1953): 127–154.
———. "John Dewey's Critique of Leibniz and Locke." *Studia Leibnitiana* 19 (Issue 1 1987): 74–84.
Rucker, Darnell. "Dewey's Ethics: Part Two." In *Guide To The Works of John Dewey,* ed. Jo Ann Boydston. Carbondale: Southern Illinois University Press, 1970, pp. 112–130.
Savage, Willinda. *The Evolution of John Dewey's Philosophy of Experimentalism as Developed at the University of Michigan.* D.Ed. of Education dissertation, University of Michigan, 1950.
Schilpp, Paul A., ed. *The Philosophy of John Dewey.* 1939. 3d ed., La Salle, Ill.: Open Court, 1989.
Schneider, Herbert. "Introduction to Dewey's *Psychology.*" 1967, *EW* 2: vii–x.

———. "Dewey's Ethics: Part One." In *Guide To The Works of John Dewey*, ed. Jo Ann Boydston. Carbondale: Southern Illinois University Press, 1970, pp. 99–111.
Smith, Philip. "The Development and Formulation of John Dewey's Theory of Mind." *International Philosophy Quarterly* 14 (December 1976): 275–303.
Stuhr, John J., ed. *Philosophy and the Reconstruction of Culture: Pragmatic Essays after Dewey*. Albany: State University of New York Press, 1993.
Thayer, Horace S. *The Logic of Pragmatism: An Examination of John Dewey's Logic*. New York: Humanities Press, 1952.
Whittemore, Robert, ed. *Dewey and His Influence: Essays in Honor of George Estes Barton*. Vol. 22 of the Tulane Studies in Philosophy. New Orleans: Tulane University Press, 1973.
Wiggins, Forrest. "William James and John Dewey." *Personalist* 23 (April 1942): 182–198.
Wilkins, Burleigh. "James, Dewey, and Hegelian Idealism." *Journal of the History of Ideas* 17 (June 1956): 332–346.
Williams, Brian A. *Thought and Action: John Dewey at the University of Michigan* Ann Arbor: Bentley Historical Library, University of Michigan, 1998.
Wilson, R. Jackson. "Dewey's Hegelianism." *History of Education Quarterly* 15 (Spring 1975): 87–92.
Zelder, Beatrice. "Dewey's Theory of Knowledge." In *John Dewey: His Thought and Influence*, ed. John Blewitt. Westport, Conn.: Greenwood Press, 1973, pp. 59–84.

German Philosophy and Psychology

Anderson, Richard. "The Untranslated Content of Wundt's *Grundzuge der Physiologischen Psychologie*." *Journal of the History of the Behavioral Sciences* 11 (October 1975): 381–386.
Bringmann, Wolfgang, and Ryan Tweney, eds. *Wundt Studies: A Centennial Collection*. Toronto: C. J. Hogrefe, 1980.
Gouaux, Charles. "Kant's View on the Nature of Empirical Psychology." *Journal of the History of the Behavioral Sciences* 8 (April 1972): 237–242.
Harris, W. T. "Trendelenburg and Hegel." *Journal of Speculative Philosophy* 9 (1875): 70–80.
———. *Hegel's Logic*. Chicago: S. C. Griggs, 1890. Reprinted, New York: Kraus Reprint, 1970.
Hegel, G. W. F. *Hegel's Logic*. Translated from the *Encyclopedia* as *The Logic of Hegel*, with a prolegomena, by William Wallace. Oxford: Clarendon Press, 1874. 2d ed. (prolegomena omitted). Oxford: Clarendon Press, 1892. 3d ed., with a foreword by J. N. Findlay, 1975.

———. *Hegel's Philosophy of Mind*. Translated from the *Encyclopedia* with five introductory essays by William Wallace. Oxford: Clarendon Press, 1894. Reprinted, Oxford: Clarendon Press, 1971.

———. *Hegel's Science of Logic*. Translated by A. V. Miller. Atlantic Highlands, N.J.: Humanities Press, 1969.

———. *Hegel's Phenomenology of Spirit*. Translated by A. V. Miller with analysis of the text and a foreword by J. N. Findlay. Oxford: Oxford University Press, 1977.

———. *The Encyclopaedia Logic*. Translated by T. F. Geraets, W. A. Suchting, and H. S. Harris. Indianapolis: Hackett, 1991.

Judd, Charles. "Wundt's System of Philosophy." *Philosophical Review* 6 (July 1897): 371–385.

Kant, Immanuel. *Critique of Pure Reason*. Translated and ed. Paul Guyer and Allen W. Wood. Cambridge: Cambridge University Press, 1998.

Leary, David. "German Idealism and the Development of Psychology in the Nineteenth Century." *Journal of the History of Philosophy* 18 (July 1980): 299–317.

———. "Immanuel Kant and the Development of Modern Psychology." In *The Problematic Science: Psychology in Nineteenth-Century Thought*, ed. William Woodward and Mitchell Ash. New York: Praeger, 1982, pp. 17–42.

Lotze, R. Hermann. *Logic*, 2d ed. Translated by various, ed. Bernard Bosanquet. Oxford: Clarendon Press, 1888.

Solomon, Robert. *In the Spirit of Hegel*. Oxford: Oxford University Press, 1983.

Thomas, E. E. *Lotze's Theory of Reality*. London: Longmans Green, 1921.

Titchener, E. B. "The Leipsic School of Experimental Psychology." *Mind* n.s. 1 (April 1892): 206–234.

———. "The Postulates of a Structural Psychology." *Philosophical Review* 7 (September 1898): 449–465.

———. "Brentano and Wundt: Empirical and Experimental Psychology." *American Journal of Psychology* 32 (January 1921): 108–120.

———. "Wilhelm Wundt." *American Journal of Psychology* 32 (April 1921): 161–178.

———. "A Note on Wundt's Doctrine of Creative Synthesis." *American Journal of Psychology* 33 (July 1922): 351–360.

Trendelenburg, F. A. "The Logical Question in Hegel's System." 1843, translated by Thomas Davidson. *Journal of Speculative Philosophy* 5 (October 1871): 349–359, 6 (January, April, October 1872): 82–93, 163–175, 350–361.

Urban, Wilbur. "Professor Wundt's 'Über Naiven und Kritischen Realismus.'" *Psychological Review* 4 (November 1897): 643–646.

Woodward, William. "Hermann Lotze's Concept of Function: Its Kantian Origin and Its Impact on Evolutionism in the United States." In *Contributions to a History of Developmental Psychology*, ed. George Eckhardt,

Wolfgang Bringmann, and Lothar Sprung. New York: Mouton, 1982, pp. 147–156.

———. "Wundt's Program for the New Psychology." In *The Problematic Science: Psychology in Nineteenth-Century Thought*, ed. William Woodward and Mitchell Ash. New York: Praeger, 1982, pp. 167–197.

Wundt, Wilhelm. "Introduction: On the Methods of Psychology." Translation by Thorne Shipley of "Einleitung Ueber die Methoden in der Psychologie" from *Beitrage zur Theorie der Sinneswahrnehmung* (Leipzig: C. F. Winter, 1862). In *Classics in Psychology*, ed. Thorne Shipley. New York: Philosophical Library, 1961, pp. 51–78.

———. *Grundzuge der Physiologischen Psychologie*. Leipzig: Englemann, 1874. 2d ed., 1880. Reviewed by James Ward, *Mind* o.s. 6 (July 1881): 445–446. 3d ed., 1887. Reviewed by James McKeen Cattell, *Mind* o.s. 13 (1888): 435–439.

———. "The Task of Physiological Psychology." Translations of the introductory statements of each edition of *Grundzuge der Physiologischen Psychologie* (Leipzig: Englemann, 1874, 1880, 1887, 1893, 1902–1903, 1908–1911) by Solomon Diamond. In *Wilhelm Wundt and the Making of a Scientific Psychology*, ed. R. W. Rieber. New York: Plenum Press, 1980, pp. 155–172.

———. "Closing Remarks." Translation of "Schlussbemerkungen," *Grundzuge der Physiologischen Psychologie* (Leipzig: Englemann, 1874), pp. 858–863, by Solomon Diamond. In *Wilhelm Wundt and the Making of a Scientific Psychology*, ed. R. W. Rieber. New York: Plenum Press, 1980, pp. 172–177.

———. *Untersuchungen zur Mechanik der Nerven und Nervencentren*. Stuttgart: F. Enke, 1876.

———. "Central Innervation and Consciousness." *Mind* o.s. 1 (April 1876): 161–178.

———. "Philosophy in Germany." *Mind* o.s. 2 (October 1877): 493–518.

———. *Logik*. Stuttgart: Enke, 1880–1883. Vol. 1 reviewed by Alfred Sidgwick, *Mind* o.s. 5 (July 1880): 409–424; Vol. 2 reviewed by John Venn, *Mind* o.s. 9 (July 1884): 451–463.

———. "Ueber Psychologische Methoden." *Philosophische Studien* 1 (1883): 1–38.

———. *Essays*. Leipzig: Engleman, 1885.

———. *Ethik*. Stuttgart: Enke, 1886. 2d ed., 1893. Reviewed by Thomas Whittaker, *Mind* o.s. 12 (April 1887): 285–292.

———. *System der Philosophie*. Leipzig: Englemann, 1889. Reviewed by Thomas Whittaker, *Mind* o.s. 15 (January 1890): 103–120.

———. *Lectures on Human and Animal Psychology*. Translation of the 2d German edition, 1892, of *Vorlesungen uber die Menschen- und Tierseele* by J. E. Creighton and E. B. Titchener. New York: Macmillan, 1894.

———. *Outlines of Psychology.* Translation of the *Grundriss der Psychologie,* by C. H. Judd. Leipzig: Englemann, 1897. The final section, "The Principles and Laws of Psychical Development," is reprinted in *Wilhelm Wundt and the Making of a Scientific Psychology,* ed. R. W. Rieber. New York: Plenum Press, 1980, pp. 182–195.

———. *Principles of Physiological Psychology.* Translation of vol. 1 of the 5th German edition, 1902–1903, of *Grundzuge der Physiologischen Psychologie,* by E. B. Titchener. New York, Macmillan, 1904. Reprinted, New York: Kraus Reprint, 1969.

Zammito, John. *The Genesis of Kant's Critique of Judgment.* Chicago: University of Chicago Press, 1992.

British and American Philosophy and Psychology

Albrecht, Frank. *The New Psychology in America: 1880–1895.* Ph.D. dissertation, Johns Hopkins University, 1960.

Angell, James R. "The Relations of Structural and Functional Psychology to Philosophy." *Philosophical Review* 12 (May 1903): 243–271.

———. *Psychology.* New York: Henry Holt, 1904.

———. "The Province of Functional Psychology." *Psychological Review* 14 (March 1907): 61–91.

Boller, Paul. *American Thought in Transition: The Impact of Evolutionary Naturalism, 1865–1900.* Chicago: Rand McNally, 1969.

Bosanquet, Bernard. *Knowledge and Reality.* London: Swan Sonnenschein, 1885. Reprinted, New York: Kraus Reprint, 1968.

———. *Logic; or, the Morphology of Knowledge.* Oxford: Clarendon, 1888.

Bradley, F. H. *Ethical Studies.* London: H. S. King, 1876. 2d ed., London: Oxford University Press, 1927.

———. *The Principles of Logic.* London: K. Paul French, 1883. 2d ed., London: Oxford University Press, 1922.

———. *Appearance and Reality.* London: Swan Sonnenschein, 1893. 3d ed., Oxford: Clarendon Press, 1920.

———. *Essays on Truth and Reality.* Oxford, Clarendon Press, 1914.

Brett, George. *A History of Psychology.* New York: Macmillan, 1921. Revised edition, ed. R. S. Peters. Cambridge: MIT Press, 1965.

Buxton, Claude, ed. *Points of View in the Modern History of Psychology.* New York: Harcourt Brace Jovanovich, 1985.

Caird, Edward. *A Critical Account of the Philosophy of Kant.* Glasgow: Maclehose, 1877.

———. *Hegel.* Edinburgh: Blackwood, 1883.

———. "Metaphysic." Contribution to *The Encyclopaedia Britannica*, 9th ed., 16: 79–102. Philadelphia: J. M. Stoddart, 1883. Reprinted in *Essays on Literature and Philosophy*, 2: 384–539.

———. *The Critical Philosophy of Immanuel Kant*. Glasgow: Maclehose, 1889.

———. *Essays on Literature and Philosophy*. Glasgow: Maclehose and Sons, 1892.

Cunningham, G. Watts. *The Idealistic Argument in Recent British and American Philosophy*, 1933. Reprinted, Freeport, N.Y.: Books for Libraries Press, 1967.

Ewing, A. C. *Idealism: A Critical Survey*. New York: Humanities Press, 1933.

Green, T. H. General Introduction. In David Hume's *Treatise of Human Nature*, ed. Green and Grose, 1: 1–299. 1874. Reprinted, New York: Longmans Green, 1898. This introduction is reprinted in the *Works*, vol. 1.

———. "Review of E. Caird, A Critical Account of the Philosophy of Kant" *Academy* 12 (1877)" 297-300. Reprinted in *Works* vol. 3, pp. 126–137.

———. *Prolegomena to Ethics*. Ed. A. C. Bradley. Oxford: Clarendon Press, 1883.

———. *Works of Thomas Hill Green*, 3 vols., 2d ed. Ed. R. L. Nettleship. New York: Longmans Green, 1889–1890.

Hall, G. Stanley. "The New Psychology." *Andover Review* 3 (February, March 1885): 120–135, 239–248.

———. "Review of John Dewey, *Psychology*." *American Journal of Psychology* 1 (November 1887): 154–159.

———. "Wilhelm Wundt." Chapter 6 of *Founders of Modern Psychology* (New York: Appleton, 1912), pp. 311–458.

———. *Life and Confessions of a Psychologist*. New York: Appleton, 1927.

Hawkins, Hugh. *Pioneer: A History of the Johns Hopkins University, 1874–1889*. Ithaca: Cornell University Press, 1960.

Heidbreder, Edna. "Functionalism and the University of Chicago." In *Seven Psychologies* (New York: Century, 1933), pp. 201–233.

Hylton, Peter. "The Metaphysics of T. H. Green." *History of Philosophy Quarterly* 2 (January 1985): 91–110.

James, William. "The Sentiment of Rationality." *Mind* o.s. 4 (July 1879): 317–346. Reprinted in *The Works of William James, Essays in Psychology*. Cambridge: Harvard University Press, 1983, pp. 32–64.

———. "Reflex Action and Theism." *Unitarian Review* 16 (November 1881): 389–416. Reprinted in *The Works of William James, The Will to Believe*. Cambridge: Harvard University Press, 1979, pp. 90–113.

———. "Rationality, Activity and Faith." *Princeton Review* n.s. 10 (July 1882): 58–86. Absorbed into "The Sentiment of Rationality" in *The Works of William James, The Will to Believe*. Cambridge: Harvard University Press, 1979, pp. 57–89.

———. "On the Function of Cognition." *Mind* o.s. 10 (January 1885): 27–44. Reprinted in *The Works of William James, The Meaning of Truth*. Cambridge: Harvard University Press, 1975, pp. 13–32.

———. *The Principles of Psychology*. New York: Holt, 1890. Reprinted in *The Works of William James, The Principles of Psychology*. Cambridge: Harvard University Press, 1981.

———. "Philosophical Conceptions and Practical Results." *University of California Chronicle*, 1898. Reprinted in *The Works of William James, Pragmatism*, pp. 257–270. Cambridge: Harvard University Press, 1975.

———. "Does 'Consciousness' Exist?" *The Journal of Philosophy* 1 (September 1904): 477–501. Reprinted in *The Works of William James, Essays in Radical Empiricism*, pp. 3–19. Cambridge: Harvard University Press, 1976.

———. *The Works of William James, The Meaning of Truth*. Cambridge: Harvard University Press, 1975.

Lovejoy, Arthur O. *The Revolt against Dualism*, 2d ed. La Salle, Ill.: Open Court, 1960.

———. *The Thirteen Pragmatisms and Other Essays*. Baltimore: Johns Hopkins Press, 1963.

Mander, W. J. *An Introduction to Bradley's Metaphysics*. Oxford: Clarendon Press, 1994.

Morris, Charles. "Mind as Function." Chapter 6 of *Six Theories of Mind* (Chicago: University of Chicago, 1932), pp. 274–330.

Morris, George S. "The Final Cause as Principle of Cognition and Principle in Nature." *Journal of the Transactions of the Victoria Institute* 9 (1874): 176–204. Reprinted as a pamphlet. London: Robert Hardwicke, 1875.

———. "The Theory of Unconscious Intelligence, as Opposed to Theism." *Journal of the Transactions of the Victoria Institute* 11 (1876): 247–291. Reprinted as a pamphlet. London: Hardwicke and Bogue, [n.d.].

———. "The Immortality of the Human Soul." *Bibliotheca Sacra* 33 (October 1876): 695–715.

———. "The Philosophy of Art." *Journal of Speculative Philosophy* 10 (January 1876): 1–16.

———. "Spinoza—A Summary Account of His Life and Teaching." *Journal of Speculative Philosophy* 11 (July 1877): 278–299.

———. *British Thought and Thinkers*. Chicago: S. C. Griggs, 1880.

———. "A Report on Wundt's *Logik* (Bd. I. *Erkenntnisslehre*)." Abstract reported in the *Johns Hopkins University Circulars* 1 (January 1882): 84.

———. "Kant's Transcendental Deduction of the Categories." *Journal of Speculative Philosophy* 15 (July 1881): 253–274.

———. "English Deism and the Philosophy of Religion." Abstract reported in the *Johns Hopkins University Circulars* 1 (February 1882): 177.

———. *Kant's Critique of Pure Reason: A Critical Exposition*. Chicago: S. C. Griggs, 1882. Noticed in *Mind* o.s. 7 (October 1882): 604.

———. "Philosophy and Its Specific Problems." *Princeton Review* n.s. 9 (March 1882): 203–232. Pp. 221–230 are reprinted in *The American Hegelians*, ed. William Goetzman. New York: Alfred A. Knopf, 1973, pp. 141–148.

———. "The Fundamental Conceptions of University and Philosophy." Abstract reported in the *Johns Hopkins University Circulars* 2 (February 1883): 54.

———. *Philosophy and Christianity: A Series of Lectures*. New York: Robert Carter and Brothers, 1883.

———. "The Philosophical Conception of Life." Abstract reported in the *Johns Hopkins University Circulars* 3 (January 1883): 12–13.

———. *Hegel's Philosophy of State and of History: An Exposition*. Chicago: S. C. Griggs, 1887.

Myers, Gerald. *William James: His Life and Thought*. New Haven: Yale University Press, 1986.

Peirce, Charles S. *Collected Papers of Charles Sanders Peirce*, ed. C. Hartshorne, P. Weiss, and A. Burks, 8 vols. Cambridge: Harvard University Press, 1935–1958.

———. *Writings of Charles S. Peirce: A Chronological Edition*, ed. Edward C. Moore. Bloomington: Indiana University Press, 1982–1993.

Pringle-Pattison, Andrew Seth. "Hegel: An Exposition and Criticism." *Mind* o.s. 6 (October 1881): 513–530.

———. *The Development from Kant to Hegel*. London: Williams and Norgate, 1882.

———, and R. B. Haldane, eds. *Essays in Philosophical Criticism*. London: Longmans Green, 1883. Reprinted, New York: Burt Franklin, 1971.

———. *Scottish Philosophy: A Comparison of the Scottish and German Answers to Hume*. Edinburg: Blackwood, 1885. 2d ed., 1890. Reprinted, New York: Burt Franklin, 1971.

———. *Hegelianism and Personality*. Edinburg: Blackwood, 1887.

———. *The Philosophical Radicals and Other Essays*. London, Blackwood, 1907.

Randall, John H., Jr. "T. H. Green and Liberal Idealism." In *Philosophy after Darwin: Chapters for The Career of Philosophy, Volume 3, and Other Essays*, ed. Beth J. Singer. New York: Columbia University Press, 1977, pp. 65–96.

Ratner, Sidney. "Evolution and the Rise of the Scientific Spirit in America." *Philosophy of Science* 3 (January 1936): 104–122.

Sahakian, William. *History and Systems of Psychology*. New York: John Wiley and Sons, 1975.

Shook, John R. *Pragmatism: An Annotated Bibliography, 1898–1940*. With contributions by E. Paul Colella, Lesley Friedman, Frank X. Ryan, and Ignas K. Skrupskelis. Amsterdam: Editions Rodopi, 1998.

Sprigge, T. L. S. *James and Bradley: American Truth and British Reality*. Chicago: Open Court, 1993.
Thayer, Horace S. *Meaning and Action: A Critical History of Pragmatism*. Indianapolis: Hackett, 1981.
Wallace, William. "Prolegomena." In *The Logic of Hegel*, translated from the *Encyclopaedia* by William Wallace. Oxford: Clarendon Press, 1874, pp. xiii–clxxxiv
———. "Five Introductory Essays." In *Hegel's Philosophy of Mind*, translated from the *Encyclopedia* by William Wallace. Oxford: Clarendon Press, 1894. Reprinted, Oxford: Clarendon Press, 1971, pp. 9–159.
———. *Prolegomena to the Study of Hegel's Philosophy and Especially of His Logic*. 2d ed., revised and augmented. Oxford: Clarendon Press, 1894.
Watson, John. "Empiricism and Common Logic." *Journal of Speculative Philosophy* 9 (October 1875) pp. 17-36. "The Relativity of Knowledge." *Journal of Speculative Philosophy* 11 (January 1877): 19–48.
———. "The World as Force." *Journal of Speculative Philosophy* 12 (April 1878): 113–137.
———. "The Critical Philosophy in Its Relations to Realism and Sensationalism." *Journal of Speculative Philosophy* 15 (October 1881): 337–360.
———. *Kant and His English Critics*. New York: Macmillan, 1881. Reprinted, New York: Garland, 1976.
———. "The Critical Philosophy and Idealism." *Philosophical Review* 1 (January 1892): 9–23.
Wilson, Daniel. *Science, Community, and the Transformation of American Philosophy, 1860–1930*. Chicago: University of Chicago Press, 1990.

Index

absolute, 5, 15, 19, 22, 36, 51–62, 64, 66–70, 73–74, 203; as God, 43, 67, 73–74, 132–133, 148, 154, 229; and knowledge, 27–31, 113–115, 118, 120, 126, 187, 193, 208, 255; as reason, 40–43, 153–154; as unknowable, 27–28, 31–32, 126, 266; *see also* experience as absolute
abstraction, 41–42, 60–62, 68, 104, 125, 135, 151, 157–158, 164–174
activity, 73–74, 101, 120, 132–133, 160, 162; and experience, 18, 92–94, 100, 102, 107–108, 118, 121–123, 133–141, 143–149, 143, 155, 176–177, 198–199, 210–211; and knowledge, 2, 10, 72, 82–83, 98–102, 116–118, 155–158, 176–185, 190–192, 204, 207–212, 234, 256–261, 268; and meaning, 177–180, 185; and reflex-arc, 106, 109–113; and thought, 17, 20, 22, 25, 32, 43, 66, 69, 78–88, 92, 97–98, 136–138, 167–175; *also* will
adaptation, 86, 95, 101, 145, 175
Addams, Jane, 17
aesthetic, 9–10, 19, 34, 36, 72, 107, 123, 141–142, 146, 263
agnostic fallacy, 27–30, 54, 125
Alexander, Thomas, 9–10
Allport, Gordon, 100
analysis and synthesis, 34, 37–42, 48–50, 68–69, 92, 98, 112, 149–151, 159, 162–163, 169–175, 185–187, 194–195, 207–209, 227, 239–241
Angell, James R., 111

apperception, 90–98, 116, 123–124, 163; in Kant, 34–37, 60, 112; in Wundt, 78–79, 112
Archimedes, 259
Aristotelian Society, 63
Aristotle, 24, 63, 73, 81, 83, 87–88, 116, 187, 205–207, 253
attention, 71, 77, 93–96, 105, 110, 125, 159–160, 168–172, 179, 185

Bacon, Francis, 144
Bain, Alexander, 52–53, 55, 59, 63
Bakewell, Charles M., 225
behavior, 101, 122, 181–183, 265; as purposive, 86–87, 111, 167, 204; as social, 108, 145–150; *see also* habit
behaviorism, 5–6, 102, 224, 259
belief, 55, 144; and doubt, 98; and knowledge, 46, 103, 131, 214, 226–227, 248–253
Bentley, Arthur F., 200
Berkeley, George, 47, 53
Bernstein, Richard, 10
Bode, Boyd H., 225
Boisvert, Raymond, 10
Boring, Edwin G., 72
Bosanquet, Bernard, 15, 189
Bowne, Borden P., 154
Bradley, Francis Herbert, 12, 15, 66, 68, 153–154; on ethics, 148–149; on knowledge, 15, 90, 164–165, 189, 229, 237, 255; on religion, 133, 138–139
Brentano, Franz, 45
Bush, Wendell T., 217–218
Buxton, Michael, 119

INDEX

Caird, Edward, 21, 66, 69, 119–120; on absolute, 31, 58, 61–63, 67–68, 133; on knowledge, 33, 35, 38, 41–42, 68, 90, 105, 115; on religion, 138–139, 149

Caird, John, 12, 66, 68; on religion, 138–139

Cairdian school, 66–69

causation, 73, 82, 86, 180–181, 194–200, 206–207, 239

change, 25–26, 45, 49–50, 200, 234, 255, 268; and activity, 122–123

Clausius, Rudolf, 196

Coleridge, Samuel Taylor, 141

Comte, Auguste, 144

concept, 27, 38, 87, 101–103, 136–138, 163, 200, 204, 211–213; and knowledge, 42–43, 93, 98, 119, 164–176, 191, 207–210, 214–215, 238, 244, 246, 253, 257; and percept, 33, 65, 113, 189

Condorcet, Jean Antoine, 144

consciousness, 50–62, 123–143, 196, 240; as absolute, 28, 43–44, 51–61, 64, 118, 125–126, 132; and experience, 7, 67, 73, 100–101, 113–115, 164; as individual, 44, 51–59, 65, 124–128, 132–137, 141–146; and knowledge, 30–31, 42, 47–48, 208, 215, 221, 232, 237, 241–244; and solipsism, 28, 44, 135, 154; as self, 31–41, 58–62, 104–105, 132–143, 221; as stream, 45, 64–66, 102, 104–105; and the unconscious, 44, 77, 87, 95, 112, 171; as universal, 7, 19, 51–52, 55–60, 125–128

continuity, 101, 113, 131, 202; in experience, 45, 56, 90–91, 95, 102, 111–113, 121, 146–147; in nature, 19, 71, 76, 195–196, 231–235, 240–241, 263–265

Cook, John W., 104

Coughlan, Neil, 18–19

Darwin, Charles, 5, 16, 18–19, 86, 102, 117, 199–202, 238

deduction. *See* logic

democracy, 17, 148–149, 161, 184

Descartes, Réné, 34, 78, 83–84, 220, 241, 254, 259, 265; and dualism, 84, 109, 154, 189, 223, 232, 241

Devitt, Michael, 245–252

Dewey, Alice Chipman, 17

Dewey, John, at Chicago, 12, 17, 71, 81, 185, 189, 194, 201, 217; at Columbia, 217–218; and his development, 5–6, 11–12, 21, 154, 210–216; and early influences, 15–18, 23–26, 66–69, 72–75, 102–106, 113–120, 130, 138–140; at Johns Hopkins, 11, 15–16, 23, 26, 43, 71–72, 75, 92; at Michigan, 12, 15, 17–18, 23–24, 43, 116, 145–189, 200; at Vermont, 12, 15, 24, 141, 202

dualism, 12, 19, 25–26, 44, 67, 71, 74, 83–84, 87–89, 115, 125–126, 154, 180–184, 229, 262; and epistemology, 9, 52, 57, 61–62, 109, 129, 172–173, 189, 219–220, 224–226, 234–235, 239–244,. 252–254; and morality, 142; *see also* transcendentalism

education, 17, 155–156, 184

emotion, 77, 88–89, 141, 144, 153–158, 167; as subjective, 52, 55

empiricism, 6–7, 21–29, 33–34, 47–50, 69–70, 91, 121–123, 154, 183–184, 187, 191–193, 251, 255–267; in ethics, 158; as immediate, 49–50, 105, 130, 172, 218–230, 242, 260; as radical, 14, 19, 63, 215, 221, 224, 244, 261

309

epistemology, 3–6, 69–70, 103–104, 120, 128–132, 162, 170–176, 210–212, 229–240, 256–259, 267–269; and dualism, 26–32, 189–194, 232–233, 241–244; and idealism, 33–43, 114–115, 151–154, 162, 183–184, 191–193, 212, 219, 222, 233–235; and metaphysics, 6–11, 260–267; and morality, 157–160; and psychology, 45–50, 77–83; and transcendentalism, 223–226, 239–240, 252–256

ethics. *See* morality

evolution. *See* Darwin, Charles; psychology

experience, 7–11, 53–58, 89–92, 120, 184, 259–269; as absolute, 21, 32–33, 99–100, 113–115, 121–123, 127–128, 210–212, 259–266; as harmonized, 95–96, 100, 107, 128–131, 137–138, 142–143, 151–156, 163–166, 174–179, 185, 191, 194–195, 202, 209–211; as immediate, 49–50, 105, 130, 172, 218–230, 242, 260; as individual, 45–48, 59–61, 64–65, 132–138; and knowledge, 35–37, 49–50, 114–115, 143, 151–154, 162–180, 184, 190–194, 219–223, 226–246, 252–259; and meaning, 22, 69–70, 77–78, 163–175, 208–209, 223–227, 245; as moral, 147–151, 156–161; as religious, 138–142; as social, 143–148; and thought, 33–35, 49–51, 62–63, 92–98, 109–111, 155–156, 185–188; as transaction of organism and environment, 7–10, 16–20, 58, 80, 101, 123–124, 137, 184, 201–202, 234, 240, 244, 259–266

experiment. *See* problem solving

feeling, 26–32, 65, 72, 78, 88–91, 99–101, 107–109, 114, 117–120, 124–125, 141–144, 158, 210; *see also* sensation

Fichte, J. G., 79, 102
Flower, Elizabeth, 12–13, 18
freedom, 25, 156, 196, 198–199; *see also* necessity
functionalism, 1, 5–6, 12, 18–20, 32–34, 44, 54, 71–74, 77–79, 87–88, 97–103, 106–109, 113–120, 147–148, 151, 155–156, 162–163, 202, 215–217, 244, 267; and epistemology, 124–132, 164–169, 176–199, 208–213, 219, 234

Green, Thomas Hill, 21, 24, 44–45, 66–68, 255; on absolute, 57, 61–62, 64, 106, 113–115, 124–127, 129, 131, 133–134, 137–138, 151–152; and Dewey's early thought, 12, 19, 22, 26, 31, 33, 49, 58, 114, 118; on ethics, 114, 149–151; on experience, 34, 46–47, 51, 56, 61, 90; on religion, 138–139, 143; on voluntarism, 74–75, 105, 115–118

growth, 104–105, 196, 201–202, 204; of experience, 32, 56, 93–98, 121, 124–129, 150, 154–156, 162, 187, 210–211, 225, 260, 264–265; of knowledge, 25, 46, 49, 68, 79–81, 114–115, 143, 165–167; of reality, 26, 198

habit, 87, 94–95, 112, 155, 160–162, 177–202, 211–212, 219, 256, 269
Hacking, Ian, 195
Hahn, Lewis E., 18–19
Hall, G. Stanley, 16, 23, 26, 71–73, 75, 203
Hamilton, Sir William, 31
Hegel, G. W. F., 15, 21, 163

Hegelianism, 23, 45, 62, 116, 188–189; and absolute, 24, 73, 113–114, 133–135, 139, 198; and Dewey's early thought, 3, 15, 18–19, 26, 62–67, 71, 87, 103, 221; and dialectical logic, 1, 25, 31, 39–43, 49, 58, 60, 62, 68, 97, 136–138, 174–176, 185–186, 194, 202, 208; and experience, 33, 35, 107, 144, 175, 223, 225; and knowledge, 37–38; and psychology, 76, 81, 104–105, 186, 202

Herbart, J. F., 45, 188
Hodgson, Shadworth, 45, 63–66, 134
Holt, Edwin B., 236–237
Hook, Sidney, 8–10
Howison, George H., 154
Hume, David, 27, 34, 39, 46–48, 65, 82–83
Humphries, B. M., 189–190
Huxley, Thomas H., 15, 24, 85
hypothesis. *See* judgment, problem solving

idea. *See* concept
idealism, 10–15, 18–20, 47–49, 66–70, 90–91, 113–115, 210–211, 217–218, 225, 228–237, 242–244, 255, 259–260; and epistemology, 33–43, 114–115, 151–154, 162, 183–184, 191–193, 212, 219, 222, 233–235; as experimental, 113, 116, 155, 158–162, 204; and morality, 144–150, 156–162; as personal, 63, 68, 116; and pragmatism, 5, 10, 22–23, 71, 103–106, 118–120, 201–203, 210–211; and religion, 138–143, 148–149; as subjective, 28, 46, 49–57, 63, 100–102, 108, 113, 132–134, 154, 219, 225, 229, 253, 256, 261, 265–267; as voluntaristic, 73–81; *see also* absolute; Hegelianism

ideals. *See* problem solving
individual. *See* consciousness
induction. *See* logic
inquiry, 8–10, 17–18, 24, 87, 106, 121, 130–132, 147, 151, 155–162, 177–180, 222; as scientific, 68, 80, 89, 98–101, 116, 147, 160–161, 174–176, 185–187, 191–215, 219, 234–252, 258, 269; *see also* intelligence; problem solving
instrumentalism, 4–6, 15–17, 20, 22, 69–70, 130–132, 159–162, 201–202, 208–212, 215–216, 219, 246, 250–252, 267–269; and functionalism, 71, 87, 92, 99, 103, 107–108, 113, 120; and logic, 169–170, 176, 183–192; metaphysics, 11, 156, 259–269; *see also* pragmatism
intelligence, 25, 56–57, 72, 89, 100, 107, 126, 142, 155, 160–162, 175–182, 190–192, 210–212, 219, 234, 244, 260–269; and learning, 94–98, 109–118, 124–125, 155–156, 163, 174, 177–185, 257; *see also* problem solving; reason

James, William, 6, 11–19, 23, 26, 65–66, 69, 75, 100–105, 117–120, 194, 198, 199, 202, 204, 212–215, 218, 252; and psychologist's fallacy, 49; and radical empiricism, 63, 215, 221, 224–225, 237, 243–244, 261; and reflex arc, 72, 105–106, 109–112; and sensations, 90–92; and stream of consciousness, 45, 102
Jones, Henry, 189–190
Jones, Marc, 116
Joule, James P., 196

judgment, 77, 88, 98, 110, 113, 128–132, 164–165, 169–177, 187–196, 238, 263; as a posteriori, 45, 170–171, 175; as a priori, 33–34, 45, 113, 170–171, 175–176, 200–208; as categorical, 169–170, 205–208, 250; as hypothetical, 140, 157, 161, 169–170, 174, 183–185, 198, 204–211, 238, 250, 268; as moral, 143, 149–150, 159–161; as practical, 160–161, 208–212, 268; and proposition, 161, 170, 208–209, 238–239, 254–255; and subject/predicate, 27, 98, 169, 177

Kant, Immanuel, 15, 21, 26, 52, 58, 140–141; and thought, 33–41, 60–62, 68, 78, 82–83, 88, 94, 105, 123, 188–190, 194

Kantianism, 23–24, 26, 36, 45, 48–49, 52, 92, 112, 114, 118, 134–137, 153–155, 175, 186, 211; and categories, 33–40, 45, 49, 58, 61–62, 68–70, 113–115, 125, 135–142, 151–152, 175, 185; and the unknowable, 31, 66–67, 128, 150–152, 223–236

knowledge, 4, 16, 24, 38–42, 50–57, 69–70, 94–98, 120, 147, 163–180, 189, 194, 210–212, 217, 252–269; and activity, 2, 10, 72, 82–83, 98–102, 116–118, 155–158, 176–185, 190–192, 204, 207–212, 234, 256–261, 268; and desire, 74, 82, 88, 117–118, 125, 178–179, 185, 207–209; and experience, 35–37, 49–50, 114–115, 143, 151–154, 162–180, 184, 190–194, 219–223, 226–246, 252–259; as fallible, 130–131, 214, 220, 255, 266; as genetic, 2–3, 25, 52, 104, 189, 201, 204–207, 238; and genetic explanation, 2–4, 25, 52, 104, 189, 201, 204–207, 238; of individuals, 62, 98–99, 131, 163, 165–170, 177–178, 205, 213, 256–259; and inquiry, 2, 130–132, 147, 151, 155–162, 177–180, 222; and intuition, 41, 128, 132, 163–166, 174–177; and knowing, 2, 7, 70, 98–99, 151, 179, 187–188, 190–191, 211–212, 234, 238–239, 256–259, 268–269; and object known, 2, 7, 37, 70, 120, 136, 173–178, 191–192, 212, 214–220, 225–245, 253, 256–258; and representation, 52, 78, 219–220, 239; as reproduction, 57–60, 67, 106–107, 114–115, 124–128, 143, 190–193; as universal, 101, 106–107, 124–128, 158; *see also* concept; meaning; perception; problem solving; reality; relations; truth

Kuhn, Thomas, 251
Kuklick, Bruce, 18–19

Ladd, George T., 23
Lamprecht, Sterling P., 2–3, 22–23
learning. See education, intelligence
Leibniz, G. W., 36, 78–79, 84, 133–134, 188
Lloyd, Alfred H., 116
Locke, John, 34, 46–47, 52, 55, 59, 66, 80, 82–83, 232
logic, 15–17, 24, 58, 61–62, 113, 130–131, 156, 161–176, 185–194, 204–205, 208–209, 214, 227, 237–239, 252, 255, 259, 263; as abductive, 172, 252; as deductive, 68, 167, 171, 174–175, 187, 207–209, 220, 255, 265; as inductive, 68, 171, 174–176, 187, 209; as transcendental, 33, 68, 174–176, 185, 208–209, 223; *see also* analysis and synthesis; intelligence; judgment; reason

312

INDEX

Lotze, Rudolf Hermann, 15, 18, 45, 61, 225; on knowledge, 153, 188–189, 191–193, 226
Lovejoy, Arthur O., 8

MacDonald, George, 82
Maimon, Salomon, 63
Marsh, James, 141
Martineau, James, 199
Marvin, Walter T., 236–237
materialism, 59, 67, 73, 86–89, 104–105, 107, 154, 200, 203, 206–207, 264
Maxwell, James Clerk, 196, 200–201
McDermott, John J., 10
McGilvary, Evander B., 8, 228, 235, 242–243, 260
Mead, George Herbert, 17, 19, 81, 163, 184
meaning, 69–70, 96–99, 120, 211, 223–239, 267–269; and activity, 177–180, 185; and experience, 22, 69–70, 77–78, 163–175, 208–209, 223–227, 245; and knowledge, 66, 135–136, 151–152, 161, 173–175, 185, 191–193, 205–209, 212, 230, 238–239, 256–258; and perception, 22, 49, 123, 175, 181, 187, 233–235, 250; and relations, 90–92, 102, 173–177, 193; and reference, 96, 169, 193, 222, 227–228
memory, 32, 79–80, 112
metaphysics, 6–11, 89, 100–101, 113–115, 158, 221, 252–256; and epistemology, 6–11, 260–267; and ethics, 149; of existence, 8–9, 11, 259–264; of experience, 9–11, 121–123, 144–155, 202, 210, 240–241, 259–264; and psychology, 46–54, 87, 132–134
Mill, John Stuart, 52, 189

mind, 52–54, 72–80, 93–99, 162, 167–178, 213, 227, 235, 256; and body, 83–84; and nature, 25, 80, 115, 119, 219; *see also* consciousness; dualism; intelligence; reason
Montague, William P., 217, 236–237, 242–243
Moore, Addison W., 111
Moore, G. E., 220
morality, 5, 14, 73, 76, 82, 121, 139–151, 155–162, 184, 194; and ideals, 121, 139–141, 148, 154–162, 194–195; and religion, 138–144, 148–149; and science, 5, 17–18, 160–161, 201, 203–204
Morris, George S., 5, 12, 23–25, 43–45, 69, 144, 203; on experience, 62, 67–68, 80, 121–122; at Johns Hopkins University, 15, 23–24, 26; on knowledge, 30–34, 36, 38–41, 54, 56, 90; on religion, 133, 138–140, 149; on voluntarism, 72–75, 83, 94, 114–120
Mounce, H. O., 18–19
Muirhead, John H., 176
Murphy, Arthur, 2, 8–9

naive realism, 2, 7–10, 219–223, 230–235, 240, 244–246, 254, 256, 259, 268
naturalism and nature, 7–11, 24, 72, 103–104, 108, 121, 146, 159–160, 203, 232–233, 240, 259–267; and mind, 25, 80, 115, 119, 219
necessity, 205–207; and chance, 33, 61–62, 130, 194–199
new realism, 23, 92, 158, 166, 220, 236–240

organicism, 24–26, 32–33, 38–43, 54–56, 62, 66, 71–75, 80–82, 96, 109, 111–116, 140, 156, 165–166, 202

Pappas, Gregory Fernando, 147
Parmenides, 240
Peirce, Charles S., 6, 11, 13–14, 19, 23, 189, 194, 212–215, 252; on perception, 172; on science, 195–199, 205; on truth, 130–131, 212–213
Pepper, Stephen, 9
perception, 31, 60–61, 69, 78, 109–110, 119, 163, 220–221; as given, 29, 32, 34, 48, 50, 65, 92, 136, 165, 190, 230–235, 253; and knowledge, 4, 22, 26–32, 47–50, 98–99, 171–173, 189–190, 230–236, 244, 247–248, 259
Perry, Ralph B., 215, 236–240, 243–244
philosophy, 58–62, 160–161, 184, 200, 217, 259–262
Pitkin, Walter B., 236
Popper, Sir Karl, 251
positivism, 4, 6, 14, 19, 26, 92, 187–189, 217, 250, 253, 267
pragmatism, 12–14, 71, 119, 210–216; and idealism, 5, 10, 22–23, 71, 103–106, 118–120, 201–203, 210–211; and realism, 217–223, 237–240, 242–243, 253–256; *see also* instrumentalism
Pringle-Pattison, Andrew Seth, 66, 68, 116, 133–139, 154
problem solving, 96, 136, 159–160, 178–195, 204–212, 267–269; and activity, 151, 162, 179–180, 185, 191–192, 204, 268; and doubt, 98, 173–174, 197, 204, 212, 220, 222, 238, 257; and experiment, 98–100, 116, 121–122, 132, 148, 176, 200–201, 204–208, 219, 234, 257, 259; and harmony, 95–96, 100, 107, 128–131, 137–138, 142–143, 150–156, 162–164, 166, 174–179, 183–185, 191, 194–195, 200–202, 209–211; and hypothesis, 174, 183, 198, 204, 238; and ideals/rules, 156–162, 187, 205, 211, 267–268; and knowledge, 178–179, 183–184, 190–191, 204–205, 211–212, 223–224, 234, 258–259; and means and ends, 99, 108, 188, 195, 204–210, 234, 267; and morality, 159–160, 201, 204; and problematic situation, 8, 159, 178, 182, 195, 209–210; and reasoning, 143–144, 149, 155–156, 159, 162, 185, 204–205; and science, 147, 161–162, 201, 204–205, 209–212; *see also* inquiry
process, 7, 24, 221, 231–235, 241; and mind, 32, 45, 55–56, 72–81, 89, 94–98, 210, 213
proposition. *See* judgment
psychological standpoint, 21, 44–56, 58, 62–64, 106, 125–129
psychologist's fallacy, 46, 89, 105, 183, 199, 206, 225
psychology, 58–62, 71–88, 113–120; and biology, 16, 19, 55, 72, 78–81, 97, 101–103, 117, 123, 145, 178, 186, 202–203, 213, 219, 264–265; as experimental, 16, 26, 48, 75–77, 84, 118; and introspection, 16, 47–48, 77; and nervous system, 79–88, 103, 112, 167, 213, 265; and philosophy, 16, 58–62, 113–120; as physiological, 75–78, 83–86, 103–104, 109, 112; as social, 12, 15, 145, 149, 162; *see also* functionalism
Putnam, Hilary, 227

qualities, 92, 101, 110, 133, 147, 167–168, 174, 200, 222

Randall, John Herman, Jr., 10
rationalism, 16, 158, 184, 193, 214, 223, 225, 239
Ratner, Joseph, 18

realism, 6, 14, 49, 52, 92, 108, 154, 158–159, 166, 189, 193, 207, 215, 217–223, 237–240, 242–243, 253–256; as agnosticism, 26–30, 54, 125, 266; and nominalism, 9, 26, 109, 175, 187, 197, 267; *see also* naive realism; naturalism and nature; new realism; scientific realism; transcendentalism

reality, 7, 106–109, 113–115, 125–128, 138–143, 156, 175, 210–211, 221–223, 252, 265; and experience, 240–245, 251; as growing, 26, 198; and knowledge, 7, 47, 107–108, 115, 124, 192–199, 214–215, 221, 240–245; as transcendent, 35, 52, 135, 226–229; as unchanging, 115, 118, 217, 234, 253, 255; *see also* absolute; experience as absolute

reason, 16, 33, 36–37, 43, 98, 119, 153, 170–176, 202, 208–211, 266; and dialectical logic, 1, 25, 31, 39–43, 49, 58, 60, 62, 68, 97, 136–138, 174–176, 185–186, 194, 202, 208; and reality, 43, 153, 183–184, 188, 193, 234, 247–248, 266; *see also* analysis and synthesis; inquiry; intelligence; logic; problem solving

Reck, Andrew, 102, 119

reference. *See* meaning

reflex arc, 12, 19, 71–72, 77, 85–94, 103–113, 119, 167, 177, 180–185, 199

Reichenbach, Hans, 9

relations, 17, 56, 62, 172, 262, 265; as external, 33, 38, 115, 194, 215, 236–237, 239; as internal, 38, 42, 144, 236–237, 239; and knowledge, 30–32, 57, 66, 69–70, 90, 106, 114–115, 127, 165, 173, 225, 235–236, 240, 246; as mechanical, 32–34, 38, 45, 76–78, 81–84, 86–89, 99, 109–115, 174, 180–186, 194, 199–200; as organic, 38, 40, 42, 80–81, 111, 115, 119, 128, 158, 161, 165, 194–195, 199, 201, 214, 237, 262; *see also* meaning

relativism, 7, 132, 256

religion, 19, 67–68, 82–83, 132, 151; and Christianity, 74, 139, 148–149; and God, 43, 47, 67, 73–74, 79, 115–116, 126, 132–134, 139–143, 148, 154; and morality, 138–144, 148–149; and panentheism, 133; and pantheism, 126, 133; science, 26–27, 203; and theism, 19, 68, 140, 143

Robertson, G. Croom, 63

Rockefeller, Stephen, 68

Rogers, Arthur K., 253

Rorty, Richard, 10, 14

Rosenstock, Gershon George, 25

Royce, Josiah, 152, 188, 218, 236

rules. *See* problem solving

Russell, Bertrand, 8, 13, 30, 228, 237, 244, 254–255

Santayana, George, 8–9, 188, 266

Schelling, F. W. J., 24

Schiller, F. C. S., 22

Schneider, Herbert W., 141

Schopenhauer, Arthur, 79, 102, 188

science, 9, 14, 45, 58, 61, 77, 161–162, 187, 194–210, 221, 241, 245–252, 260, 264; and morality, 5, 17–18, 160–161, 201, 203–204; and natural laws, 147, 187, 195–196; and principles, 73, 84, 199–200; and probability, 196–197; *see also* inquiry; problem solving

scientific method, 16, 24, 68, 147, 161, 166, 174–176, 195–196, 200, 204–212, 234–239, 251, 258

scientific realism, 9, 189, 245–251

self. *See* consciousness

sensation, 22, 27–38, 47–51, 69–70, 77–80, 89–97, 101–102, 111–113, 122–124, 135–136, 163–164, 178–181, 186, 223, 226; *see also* feeling; perception; stimulus
Seth, Andrew. *See* Pringle-Pattison
Seth, James, 44–45
Sleeper, Ralph, 9
society, 16, 25, 76, 144–149, 161, 184, 203
sociology, 19, 161, 184, 186
Spaulding, Edward G., 236–237, 239
Spencer, Herbert, 26–27, 31–32, 59
Spinoza, Baruch, 40, 84
stimulus, 49–50, 84–86, 109–113, 176–185, 211, 268; *see also* sensation; feeling
Stuhr, John J., 10
synthesis. *See* analysis

teleology, 24–25, 69–73, 77, 81–89, 94, 97, 113, 116, 119–120, 136–140, 151–156, 180, 183, 186, 197–203, 211–216, 245
Thayer, H. Standish, 202
Thomas, Geoffrey, 113
Tiles, J. E., 49, 91–92
time, 25–26, 33–34, 52, 59, 126, 132, 137, 142, 165, 200–201, 207, 240–241, 263
Titchener, E. B., 72, 117
Torrey, H. A. P., 44
transcendentalism, 33, 44, 64, 157–159, 175, 192–194, 208, 215, 223–232, 242–247, 251–256, 260, 266–267; *see also* Hegelianism
Trendelenburg, Frederich Adolf, 24–25, 31, 62, 73, 81, 116, 121, 147, 202
truth, 33–35, 124–132, 188, 212–215, 252–259, 268; and bivalence, 255; and coherence, 35, 42, 127–130; and correspondence, 127, 173, 212, 227, 251–256; and knowledge, 16, 42–43, 82, 124–132, 190–192, 256–258, 268; and verification, 50, 132, 170–175, 190–191, 209–210, 253–258, 268; and warranted assertibility, 130, 209, 255, 268

universals, 37, 114, 135, 167, 252
value, 16, 18, 36, 120, 200, 204; and intelligence, 110–111, 123, 157–161, 165, 179, 190

Van Inwagen, Peter, 254
volition. *See* will
voluntarism, 5, 71–75, 79–83, 94, 102, 105, 113–120, 140, 176

Ward, James, 44–48, 53–55, 69, 71
Watson, John, 69, 119
Wenley, Robert Mark, 116–117
White, Morton G., 18–19, 116–117
will, 32, 74, 78–95, 99–111, 115–120; and activity, 99–100, 123–127, 142, 177–178, 237, 244; and religion, 132, 134, 138–143, 148–149; and volition, 20, 77–79, 82–83, 89, 93, 98–99, 114–120, 123–127, 133, 141, 177, 210, 215; *see also* activity; voluntarism
Williams, Michael, 254
Woodbridge, Frederick J. E., 8, 217–218, 222
Wundt, Wilhelm, 1, 5, 16, 26, 44, 45, 75, 80, 116–117; on philosophy, 71–73, 94; on psychology, 76–88, 103, 112, 115, 118, 120, 202, 204; on religion, 138, 140

Young, Ella Flagg, 17

JOHN SHOOK teaches philosophy at Corning Community College in New York. His previous publications include *Pragmatism: An Annotated Bibliography, 1898–1940.*